OPERATIONAL
FINANCIAL MANAGEMENT

robert e. pritchard

Chairman
Administrative Studies Department
and
Associate Professor of Finance
Glassboro State College

Adjunct Associate Professor of Finance
Graduate School of Business
Drexel University

PRENTICE-HALL, INC., Englewood Cliffs, New Jersey 07632

Library of Congress Cataloging in Publication Data

PRITCHARD, ROBERT E (date)
   Operational financial management.

   Bibliography: p.
   Includes index.
   1. Corporations—Finance. 2. Business enterprises—
Finance. I. Title.
HG4026.P74   658.1′5   76-25062
ISBN 0-13-637827-7

© 1977
by Prentice-Hall, Inc.
Englewood Cliffs, New Jersey 07632

Printed in the United States of America

10   9   8   7   6   5   4   3   2   1

Prentice-Hall International, Inc., *London*
Prentice-Hall of Australia Pty. Limited, *Sydney*
Prentice-Hall of Canada, Ltd., *Toronto*
Prentice-Hall of India Private Limited, *New Delhi*
Prentice-Hall of Japan, Inc., *Tokyo*
Prentice-Hall of Southeast Asia Pte. Ltd., *Singapore*
Whitehall Books Limited, *Wellington, New Zealand*

Contents

Preface

Operational Financial Management is written to provide students with a theoretical basis and a practical working knowledge of managerial finance. Although the primary focus is on corporate financial management, it is recognized that many businesses are sole proprietorships, partnerships, and Subchapter S Corporations. Hence, the text is not solely oriented to corporate finance. It is expected that the book will be utilized primarily by community and four-year college students as a first finance text. Many of these students will enter employment in small- and medium-sized businesses or public agencies and, as a consequence, require a strong background in the practical aspects of financial management as applied to firms of various sizes. Since the text includes material relating to financial operations of small businesses, it is also useful as a supplementary text for courses in small business operations and management.

In deciding upon the content of the text, the primary question addressed was, "What knowledge and basic skills in financial management does a student need when starting at an entry-level career position?" The basic content and structure was established using inputs from several of my colleagues who have had successful careers in both the public and private sectors. First, the text must provide the student with a realistic setting of financial operations. The goal of the firm is stressed heavily. While in some instances the goal may be to maximize the wealth of the owners, in other situations it may be to maintain a functioning organization which can be easily passed on by the owners to their heirs. Also, the firm may have as its main function the maintenance of a tax shield for its owners. As a consequence, depreciation and, especially, cash flow are emphasized heavily.

To understand and meet the owners' expectations it is necessary to have a working knowledge of personal and corporate tax laws. Hence chapters dealing with these topics have been included. In real life, tax rates are not 50% as assumed by many texts in finance. Further, capital gains and losses and recapture of depreciation are extremely important. In keeping with the theme of what a student should know, it was felt that there are several aspects of financial management which need not be covered in an introductory course. For example, topics such as bond refinancing and international finance were not included. While these topics are interesting, knowledge of them does not appear to be a requisite for students starting their careers in business. Also, these topics are included in advanced courses for students majoring in finance and accounting. To the financial manager of most firms cash flow is of utmost importance and profit ranks a close second, and to deal effectively with these, a good understanding of depreciation methods and taxation is very important.

To provide students with the working tools of financial management, the book has been organized in a somewhat nontraditional fashion. There are four sections: The Operating Environment, Financing the Firm, Capital Budgeting and Leasing, and Working Capital and Profitability Management. In the first section the student is provided with the setting in which the financial manager operates and the basic tools which he requires, namely, analysis of financial statements, cash flow (including sources and uses of funds), depreciation methods, and personal and corporate tax law. Applications are stressed throughout.

The second section on financing the firm commences with a detailed introduction to the economic, banking, and money and capital market structures as a basis for dealing with the processes of securing funds to finance the firm. These two introductory chapters provide the institutional characteristics of the financing process. Interest and annuity calculations are examined as a preface to the study of financial leverage and debt. The various types of short-, intermediate-, and long-term debt are described concisely to provide the student with a background as to types of debt financing available and how they may be advantageously used. However, the special characteristics of unique types of debt instruments such as railroad trust certificates are not included. The decision to omit this material was made on the premise that beginning-level students would not require such detailed information.

Within the context of financing, leasing has become extremely important during the last few years. Many firms are continuing to experience difficulty in raising needed capital. Therefore, a chapter has been devoted to leasing, but as the analysis of leasing requires the use of discounted cash flow processes, this chapter was deferred until the requisite material was covered in the section of the book dealing with capital budgeting.

Equity and dividend policy are combined in one chapter to indicate the relevance of the dividend decision to the financing decision. The characteristics of common and preferred stock are described in the context of providing an equity base to support the total financial structure. The use of convertible securities as a means of deferred equity financing demonstrates the flexibility of financial planning. The characteristics and uses of warrants and rights are described. The effects on earnings per share of the conversion of convertible securities and the exercising rights and warrants underscore the necessity of planning in financial decision making. The chapter concludes with a discussion of dividend policy and, in particular, its relevance to the process of financing the firm.

Additional background information relating to the operations of the money and capital markets is interspersed at appropriate points in the chapters dealing with equity and debt financing. The concluding chapter in the second section describes the theoretical basis and calculations involved in determining the cost of capital and, thus, provides a logical entry into the study of capital budgeting.

The chapters in the third section on capital budgeting and leasing are divided precisely to provide the instructor with added teaching flexibility. Rather than immediately jumping into the technical methods of evaluating capital budgeting projects, in the first chapter of this section we closely examine the entire capital budgeting process, including the assessment of the owner's needs, product line development, and the like. Following this somewhat comprehensive introduction to the topic, two chapters cover payback, present value, internal rate of return, and capital rationing. The instructor could stop at this juncture and proceed to leasing or directly to working capital and profitability management. However, three other important chapters are included. In the first techniques of capital budgeting under conditions of uncertainty are discussed. The second deals with the relationship of accelerated depreciation methods and investment tax credit to capital budgeting decisions. The increased use of accelerated depreciation and recent changes in the tax law increasing investment tax credit to 10% underscore the need for students to understand their relationship to capital budgeting decisions. In the third chapter we examine special applications of discounted cash flow, namely, capital budgeting for small business, annuity and pension fund applications (including deferred tax plans), and yield to maturity bond calculations.

In the final section we examine the important topics of working capital management, including cash, marketable securities, accounts receivable, inventories, and accounts payable. Then cash budgeting is introduced. In the chapter on profitability management we stress operating leverage and output analysis in relation to the needs of the owners, the tax environment, opportunities for raising funds in the money and capital markets, and proposed capital investments. The final chapter deals with expansion and contraction of business enterprises. Topics covered include business combinations, capital abandonment, and operations under conditions of insolvency.

For easy reference, the text includes four appendices. The first is a set of expanded compound interest, annuity, and present-value tables and tax rate tables. The second is the answers to the problems at the end of each chapter. The third is a summary of formulas commonly required in financial calculations. The last appendix is The Conference Board's "Sources of Economic and Financial Information." This is an especially useful tool for locating information required in financial management. Also a glossary of frequently used financial terms is included.

The book employs two effective pedagogical methods. First, numerous model problems are presented so that the student may learn by imitation in following their step-by-step solutions. Further information is presented concisely. Second, the Socratic method is used extensively. Information is first presented in the form of a question, and then the answer is presented, thus establishing the relevancy of the information and its relationship to the problem being treated. To reinforce the learning/study process, each chapter concludes with a list of pertinent questions for discussion, terms for the student to remember, and/or problems for solution.

The preparation of this text has included many inputs from students, faculty, members of the business and financial communities, trade associations, and other institutions. First, the author wishes to thank his students at Glassboro State College and Drexel University, who provided an uninhibited critique of the material as presented in three limited-edition paperback publications and a series of chapter handouts. Second, my most sincere appreciation goes to my many colleagues at Glassboro for their detailed examination and analysis of the organization and content:

Leo Beebe, formerly Executive Vice President, Philco-Ford;

Vincent Clemente, MBA, formerly Commander, USN and Naval Contract Administration at RCA;

Frank Kelemen, Chairman, Board of Managers, Cooper Hospital, Camden, and Professional Corporate Director;

Richard Knight, CPA, formerly accountant with Touche, Ross & Co.;

Sarah Lawton, CPA, practicing accountant and member of the American Institute of Certified Public Accountant's Advisory Grading Service;

Derrick Owles, LL.M., formerly International Operations Executive at IBM;

Charles J. Welsh, Ph.D., formerly Executive at General Motors, Overseas Operations.

My special appreciation and thanks go to R. Gene McCormick, CPA, former Vice President of Finance at Philco-Ford and Rollins International, and now a colleague at Glassboro State College, for his page-by-page critique of the manuscript and many suggestions and inputs to it.

Third, to the members of the business and financial community and colleagues at other colleges, I express my sincere appreciation:

Carl Biletta, Broker, Elkins, Stroud, Supplee and Company;

Harvey Cale, Cashier and Manager, National Bank of Mantua;

George Harris, Executive Vice President, National Bank of Mantua;

Lawrence N. Park, J.D., Professor Emeritus, Temple University School of Law.

Fourth, to the members of the academic community who reviewed *Operational Financial Management* during its production, I extend my gratitude:

Professor John DeYoung, Chairman, Business Division, Cumberland County College;

Professor Peter Goulet, Department of Business, University of Northern Iowa;

Professor Ernest Swift, Department of Finance, Georgia State University;

Dr. Sheldon Novack, Seton Hall University;

Professor Thomas J. McKenna, Department of Business Administration, Fresno City College;

Professor George Flanigan, Department of Business Administration, University of North Carolina;

Professor Morton Hirsch, Division of Behavioral and Social Sciences, Kingsborough Community College

Professor Mark Uchida, Department of Accounting and Finance, Marquette University.

Fifth, for their permission to use various materials, I extend appreciation to the Federal Reserve Bank of New York, The Conference Board, Technitrol Inc., and the Association of Consulting Managing Engineers, Inc.

Sixth, the author is very grateful to Marjorie Koch for editing the original manuscript, and expresses sincere appreciation to Eleanor Fillebrown for critiqueing and proofreading the text and preparing the index, to Mary Ann Frenzel for original layout design, and to Suzan D'Angelillio for proofreading, editing, and coordinating the preparation of the instructor's manual.

Finally, for their numerous hours of typing the many copies of manuscript, I thank Sandy Carnuccio, Betty Park, Marie Hunt, and Linda Todd.

ROBERT E. PRITCHARD
Glassboro, New Jersey

THE OPERATING ENVIRONMENT

section I

AN OVERVIEW

The basis for financial analysis and decision making is the understanding of the environment and constraints in which the financial manager operates. The environment and constraints may be both internal and external. Within the firm, the owners and management may set goals and objectives which determine the operating parameters. Or there may be a lack of a coherent set of objectives. Some firms and public agencies appear to lack any formal direction other than self-perpetuation. Of course, the lack of plans and goals makes the job of management at every level more difficult. Nonetheless, it is imperative for a manager to be able to assess the situation and work positively within it.

External constraints and environmental conditions are extremely important. The legal environment and, for the financial manager, the tax laws, in particular, are of special significance. The tax laws impact every financial decision. The financial manager must understand the implications of these laws in order to make the optimal decisions for financing and investment of funds.

Within the context of financial environment, the financial manager must be able to analyze and utilize information pertaining to cash flow, sources and uses of funds, and working capital. Several financial ratios may be utilized along with various financial statements to analyze current and historical data and to project future trends.

1

Once the financial manager has the tools of financial analysis in hand, along with a good knowledge of depreciation methods and tax laws, he is in the position to undertake the detailed study of methods which may be used to successfully operate the firm. The first section of *Operational Financial Management* provides the basic tools of financial analysis and the external environmental constraints which are fundamental to the firm's operation.

The Goal
of Financial Management

chapter 1

The field of finance is broad and varied. Its aspects range from the managing of one's own personal finances to the directing of financial operations of large manufacturing firms and government. Financial management embraces much more than manufacturing and distribution or government financial operations, however. It also includes the whole fields of banking, insurance, pension funding, and securities and commodities brokering. Although the particular roles of businesses, financial institutions and intermediaries (i.e., banks and insurance companies), and government differ, the basic, underlying principles of financial management which they utilize have fundamental similarities.

The financial manager in any organization is an important member of the management team. The management team includes representatives from areas such as marketing, personnel and labor relations, production, engineering design, and research and development. The financial manager must operate within the goal structure adopted by the owners or their elected representatives and other members of the management team. In some instances, especially in the case of smaller companies, the goals may be designed to meet special needs of the owners. In such cases, the financial manager must develop a complete understanding of the needs of the owners in order to satisfy them to the greatest possible extent. Some firms lack definite or explicit financial goals. Such circumstances require that the financial manager utilize perception, understanding, discretion, and judgment in devel-

FIGURE 1. Typical corporate financial structure.

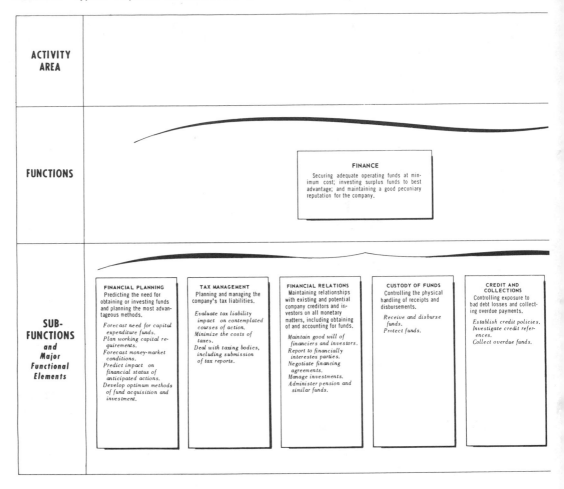

ACTIVITY AREA	
FUNCTIONS	**FINANCE** — Securing adequate operating funds at minimum cost; investing surplus funds to best advantage; and maintaining a good pecuniary reputation for the company.

SUB-FUNCTIONS and Major Functional Elements

FINANCIAL PLANNING
Predicting the need for obtaining or investing funds and planning the most advantageous methods.

Forecast need for capital expenditure funds.
Plan working capital requirements.
Forecast money-market conditions.
Predict impact on financial status of anticipated actions.
Develop optimum methods of fund acquisition and investment.

TAX MANAGEMENT
Planning and managing the company's tax liabilities.

Evaluate tax liability impact on contemplated courses of action.
Minimize the costs of taxes.
Deal with taxing bodies, including submission of tax reports.

FINANCIAL RELATIONS
Maintaining relationships with existing and potential company creditors and investors on all monetary matters, including obtaining of and accounting for funds.

Maintain good will of financiers and investors.
Report to financially interested parties.
Negotiate financing agreements.
Manage investments.
Administer pension and similar funds.

CUSTODY OF FUNDS
Controlling the physical handling of receipts and disbursements.

Receive and disburse funds.
Protect funds.

CREDIT AND COLLECTIONS
Controlling exposure to bad debt losses and collecting overdue payments.

Establish credit policies.
Investigate credit references.
Collect overdue funds.

From "Common Body of Knowledge Required by Professional Management Consultants." Reproduced by permission of Association of Consulting Management Engineers, Inc., 347 Madison Avenue, New York, N.Y.

oping financial policies and goals for the firm. Seldom may the financial manager establish goals without consultation with the other managers or owners of the firm.

The relationship of finance and accounting is shown in Fig. 1. Figure 1 shows a typical financial structure which would be used by a nonfinancial firm (i.e., a firm involved in manufacturing, distribution, or sales as opposed to a bank or insurance company).

To assure the satisfaction of the owners' requirements, it is necessary to adopt financial goals. The adoption of goals is necessary for personal financial management as well as for the financial management of small businesses, great corporate entities, and government operations. For most individuals, the establishment of financial objec-

CONTROL
Maintaining records and preparing reports to (1) meet corporate legal and tax requirements and (2) measure the results of the company operations; and providing accounting services structured for use by managers in planning and controlling the business.

INSURANCE
Securing and maintaining adequate financial protection against the hazards to which the company is exposed.

Appraise and evaluate.
Plan and negotiate coverage.

GENERAL ACCOUNTING
Maintaining formal records of what the company owns, owes, is owed, has earned, and is worth.

Maintain tax and related records.
Prepare periodic accounting reports and statements.
Maintain accounts receivable and issue bills.
Maintain accounts payable and initiate payments.

COST ACCOUNTING
Recording costs incurred in relation to work performed.

Record incurred costs.
Maintain supporting records for, compute, and initiate payment of employee earnings and deductions.
Develop cost standards.
Estimate costs.

PLANNING AND BUDGETING
Participating in the planning and control of operations by planning and measuring revenues, costs and profits; organizing financial and accounting information for use in making decisions, communicating decisions, and measuring results against plans.

Project profit results of alternative courses of action.
Develop planned costs for operations and for products and services.
State authorized plans in budgetary and planned cost formats.
Measure actual results against plans and standards and analyze variances.

INTERNAL AUDITING
Assuring the accuracy of accounting records and adherence to standard practices.

Audit financial records.
Audit adherence to standard procedures.

SYSTEMS AND PROCEDURES
Recommending effective methods of accomplishing the paperwork required to exercise control and facilitate action.

Control creation and use of forms and reports.
Establish clerical work flows.
Establish clerical work methods.
Measure clerical work.

tives is a relatively simple matter. From a purely financial point of view, a person generally attempts to achieve the goal of improving his or her standard of living to the greatest possible extent. As a rule, this goal is realized *by maximizing one's disposable income and ultimately increasing one's wealth.*

Although it is true that individuals may be said to "own" businesses, both large and small, and even the government, the establishment of financial goals for these institutions is not nearly so simple a matter. *It has been established that the goals of a business and its owners should coincide quite closely.* In addition to providing good-quality products and maintaining high standards as a community member, a business must also make a profit, or at least break even, to remain in existence. Many firms have set a goal of maximizing profits, while others attempt to achieve preestablished levels of sales, etc. However, to facilitate the study of financial management, we shall assume that *the primary purpose of the operation of a firm is the maximization of the owner's wealth as represented by the value of the business.*

The value of a small business is the price for which the business could be sold. Many individuals purchase small businesses, work hard to build them, and subsequently sell them for a profit, thereby increasing their personal wealth. The value of larger business firms, which are usually organized as corporations, is generally measured in terms of the market price of the firm's common stock. Each share of common stock represents a portion of the total ownership of the firm. There may be a large number of owners, i.e., shareholders, of a large firm. Some large firms may have as many as several thousand shareholders, some of whom may own only a few shares, with others owning many. When the price of the stock goes up, so does the shareholder's wealth.

The performance of the operating management of a firm, coupled with general economic conditions, is the primary determinant of the firm's value. The operational management is responsible for the production of the firm via the use of capital equipment such as machinery, production lines, and the like. The performance of the operating management is measured by the firm's profit; hence, it can be said that a firm's profitability greatly influences its value.

Judging the value of a business, whether it is large or small, is a difficult process. Consider the purchase of a small business. If this business were to be purchased outright, it would be necessary to place a value on such things as the physical plant, machinery, and goodwill as well as past, present, and future estimated profits. Further, if the existing management, technical experts, and skilled workers are expected to remain with the business after acquisition, their value would have to be considered as an important factor in establishing the business's value. If a price can be agreed upon by buyer and seller, then the sale will take place. Naturally, the seller attempts to make the business attractive to the buyer in order to obtain the highest possible price. The buyer, of course, wants to negotiate a low price in order to enhance the chances of increasing the return on his investment.

Unlike the buyer of a small business, who may also intend to act as the manager, shareholders in big businesses generally do not function as a part of management. They must, for the most part, accept the business as it is without being able to change it. Since nearly all big businesses are corporations, the owners hold common stock, which represents their partial ownership. As a stockholder, the owner has the right to participate in the election of the board of directors. The board of directors in turn makes management policy and appoints the firm's managers. Hence, in theory, the board members are responsible to the shareholders and should carry out the shareholders' desires. In reality, the election of directors is almost a perfunctory process, and if a shareholder does not like the way the firm is being operated, he has little choice but to sell his stock. In fact, many shareholders do not bother to vote in corporate elections. *For the most part, shareholders do not take any part in the corporate management and exhibit interest only in the financial aspects of the corporation and specifically in how much their own wealth will grow as a result of the firm's operations.* This fact is most significant to all financial managers.

Persons contemplating investment in large businesses examine several factors before purchasing stock in a firm. Evaluation implies objective appraisal—especially of the firm's management. The analysis requires accumulation of as much data as are available. Financial data are used, comparing the most recent with preceding years and with similar information for other firms. The comparison helps the investor to draw conclusions concerning the attitudes of the firm's management with respect to risk, their managerial ability, and overall ability. Investors continually reexamine the data to decide whether they should purchase additional shares or sell their shares and purchase another security. Four factors provide a critical base line against which the value of a firm may be judged. The first three represent a measure of managerial ability.

1. Earnings record: past, present, and expected future earnings per share of the common stock;
2. Dividends record: past, present and expected future dividends per share of the common stock;
3. Risk associated with future earnings of the firm;
4. The economic factors which may affect the firm.

The investment community of investors and shareholders gauges the value of a firm's stock as an investment by comparing the market price of the stock with the price of other stocks, keeping in mind the several factors of earnings, dividends, risk, and economic changes described above.

Profits or earnings provide periodic measurements in the life of a corporation. Generally, they are measured over the span of a year, although most large firms provide their shareholders with quarterly financial reports indicating earnings for each three-month period.

Earnings must be carefully measured in order to be meaningful.

Total profits, for example, tell very little in themselves. If the firm is a corporation, profits must be divided by the number of shares of common stock. If the business is organized as a partnership, it is necessary to know the number of partners and the proportionate ownership of each partner. For example, suppose a firm owned by two equal partners had a profit of $100,000. This would mean $50,000 for each partner—a substantial sum. If, however, there were ten equal partners, the profit for each would be substantially less—only $10,000.

The earnings per share (EPS) of a corporation are important because they indicate how much after-tax profit the firm has generated for each share of common stock outstanding. They are calculated by dividing the after-tax profits of the firm (less preferred stock dividends, if any) by the number of shares of common stock outstanding.

Example 1:   EARNINGS PER SHARE

Technitrol Inc. had after-tax profits of $466,393 in 1973. There were 1,360,750 shares of common stock outstanding. What were the earnings per share?

SOLUTION

Divide the total after-tax profits by the number of shares of common stock outstanding to determine the earnings per share:

$$\frac{\$466,393}{1,360,750} = \$.34 \text{ EPS}$$

The concept of earnings per share is extremely important to shareholders for two reasons. First, dividends come out of earnings, and investors are generally favorably disposed toward receiving dividends. Second, while the market price of most firms' stock tends to be highly correlated with the general stock market movements as a whole, there is also a relationship between the earnings per share and the market price per share. *Within the limits of the overall stock market movement, when a firm's earnings per share increase, there is often an upward movement in the price of the stock.* Sometimes, the price of a stock will be bid upward based on anticipated growth in earnings. Interestingly, in some instances, the price of the stock may go down after increases in earnings have been announced. This may result from the increase in earnings failing to meet investors' expectations. That is, the increase is not so large as anticipated by shareholders.

There is a correlation between a firm's earnings and its value as measured by the price of the common stock. However, sometimes increasing EPS in one year may actually result in a decrease in the market price of the common stock. For example, suppose the management of a firm decided to use up inventories at the end of the year and not replace the inventories until the following year. The result would be a lower cost of goods sold and a higher profit and EPS in the year when inventories were not replaced. For the firm to remain in business, the inventories would have to be replaced the following year. This would tend to increase cost of goods sold that year and hence decrease profits and EPS. Investors are critical analysts and examine inventory and other changes. If investors felt that management was attempting to manipulate profits through inventory contraction, they might become wary of the management and sell their stock. This would, of course, result in lowering the market price. Inventory contraction is but one example of how management may temporarily increase profits. Another action management may take to temporarily increase profits is to reduce regular and preventative maintenance of its plant and equipment. Initially, maintenance cost reductions will result in higher profits, but they generally lead to rapid deterioration and hence high replacement and repair or overhaul costs. The situation is analogous to not changing the crankcase oil in an automobile. It reduces operating costs temporarily but over a prolonged period will result in higher engine wear and increased repairs. *Investors are keenly aware of management practices and are favorably disposed to policies which will lead to continued growth in earnings rather than practices which result in temporary increases in earnings which cannot be sustained.*

Projecting the future EPS represents a rather difficult problem. Generally, the projection is made based on past performance. Thus, if the EPS have increased by 6% each year for the last five years, one might assume that they will increase by an additional 6% next year. It would be naive to stop here, however, for other factors such as plant expansion, change in product lines, and demand for the product must also be considered. When these factors are included, statistical techniques such as regression analysis are utilized to calculate the projected EPS.

The profits which a firm makes become a part of its assets. The firm may utilize the assets internally in the business or may distribute a portion of them as dividends, which are a form of return on the shareholders' investment. The portion of the assets resulting from profits which is retained by the firm is noted by an increase in the firm's retained earnings. The basis for a decision to retain earnings is that the use of the funds will either increase profits or, as a minimum, maintain profits at their present level. Investors normally expect management to retain a major portion of total earnings to increase assets or reduce liabilities.

The firm's board of directors has the legal authority to declare dividends. Generally, dividends are paid quarterly, and checks are mailed to the shareholders. If, for example, the EPS were $4.00, a dividend of $2.00 might be declared. An investor owning 100 shares of stock would then receive $200 per year. This dividend would help increase the shareholder's wealth.

Cash dividends are important to the owners of a firm for several reasons. First, as discussed above, *dividends represent a monetary return to the owners*. Many investors need a regular income to meet their living expenses, and the dividend is therefore very important to them. Second, *a cash dividend may resolve investor uncertainty*. In periods of business recession, the issuance of dividends informs investors that the management believes the future outlook is bright enough to continue cash distributions. If the business outlook is bleak, a business may discontinue dividends. For example, in mid-1974, a period of economic and investor uncertainty, Consolidated Edison skipped a regular dividend because very high fuel costs eroded profits and cash was needed to expand facilities. This action, combined with uncertain economic conditions and a generally bearish (downward-moving) stock market, caused the price of Consolidated Edison stock to drop substantially from a yearly high of $21.50 to a low of $6.00. Also, the price of many other electric utility stocks decreased as investors, fearing that they might not receive dividends, sold shares. For example, the price of Philadelphia Electric dropped from a yearly high of $19.50 to a low of $10.00. Further, *dividends may have an informational content to investors*. If, for example, a firm typically pays out 40% of its earnings in dividends, an increase in dividends without a proportional increase in earnings could indicate a change in dividend policy.

The risk factor is very important to investors in all types and sizes of businesses. There are two types of risks associated with a firm: business and financial. *Business risk refers to all those hazards inherent in the operation of the business itself*, such as the loss of valuable management talent to a competitor, fire, changing consumer preferences, nationalization of the firm's property in another country by the foreign government, obsolescence of equipment, and labor unrest. *Financial risk results from borrowing funds to finance a business and the concurrent possibility of not being able to meet interest and principal repayments if business conditions deteriorate.* In general, the use of debt increases financial risk by exposing the firm to a reduction of earnings resulting from interest payments. The greater the debt and accompanying interest payments, the greater the financial risk.

In addition to the earnings, dividends, and the risks associated with the operation of a business, there are numerous economic factors which are likely to affect its operation. These include such items as change in tax rates, imposition of strict environmental protection laws, impending recessions, and high interest rates. During early 1974, a major economic factor in operating business and government was an international oil shortage which resulted in rapidly increasing fuel prices. The shortage caused a great deal of investor uncertainty. Hence, the market price of common stock in many firms went down as investors sold their stock and bought more secure investments. *Another example of an economic factor which can affect the price of stock is a change in the general level of interest rates.* During mid-1974, interest rates soared, with the prime rate (the rate of interest which banks charge their best customers) exceeding 12%. Shareholders thus looked for investments which would provide them with higher returns. Subsequently, many sold their stock and purchased other securities. The result was a drastic decrease in the general price level of stock.

The ordinary shareholder in a large corporation is primarily, if not solely, interested in what return he will get on his investment. The return may take two parts: dividends and increased price of the stock. Investors, using the four-part criterion outlined above, attempt to estimate the amount of return they will receive from their investment and the degree of risk they will be exposed to as shareholders. *Most shareholders are risk-averters; that is, they want increasingly greater returns on their investment as the degree of risk increases.* Individual shareholders also have preferences as to the amount of dividends they want to receive as compared to the potential increase in the market price of their stock.

In many instances, there is a choice between the two methods of increasing shareholder wealth. For example, some firms pay little or no dividends and use the profits to invest in new capital equipment or for research and development. The result of such investment is generally greater growth than if profits were distributed as dividends. Consequently, the value of the firm should increase more rapidly. There are some shareholders who do not need dividends and are primarily interested in enjoying an increase in the price of the stock. On the other hand, some shareholders need dividends to meet living expenses and are not so interested in growth. Many shareholders desire a combination of dividends and appreciation in the price of the stock. It is very important that the financial manager know the preferences of the owners. Of course, the same is especially true for small firms. However, the information is much more readily available, since the owners are often the managers as well.

One could logically ask how a financial manager could know shareholder preferences with respect to retention or distribution of income or similar policies. In all but the smallest firms it is not possible to obtain this information except from, perhaps, the largest stockholders. However, if we assume that the present owners purchased and continue to hold their stock, it is because they approve of past and current policies. The financial manager can then assume that these policies are consistent with the owners' preferences.

While the process of examining and interpreting all these factors is somewhat complex, the procedure of determining the price of common stock in a large firm is generally quite simple. Stock is sold in several markets or exchanges, such as the New York Stock Exchange and the American Stock Exchange, where shareholders and prospective buyers, represented by their stockbrokers, buy and sell shares of stock. When the demand for a firm's stock exceeds supply, the price goes up; when supply exceeds demand, the price goes down. *The market price of a firm's stock, therefore, represents the collective judgment of all those persons participating in the buying and selling.*

The financial manager of a given firm is aware of the criteria which will be applied to determine the value of the firm and, in addition, the market price of the stock. The firm's financial manager works diligently to make the stock as attractive as possible to potential buyers and the present owners, thereby working to increase or at least to maintain the current level of demand for the stock. His goal is to increase the wealth of the owners by increasing the price of the common stock.

The primary goal of the financial manager of a business must—in the best interest of the business, the customers, and the community at large—be tempered by moral and social values. For any firm to operate successfully, it must produce a quality product. In the short run, sloppy workmanship and low quality may be covered cosmetically. Although this may lead to temporary high profits, in the long run both sales and profits will decrease. In addition, every firm and government agency must operate within the framework of high community standards. This, of course, makes the job of a financial manager increasingly difficult. Every major decision must be weighed not only on its financial merits but on its social and moral implications as well. This fact cannot be overemphasized. If each business and government agency does not operate circumspectly, laws will be passed which provide closer controls. Such laws often lead to greater costs and inefficiencies, as they fall upon both those who have been offenders and those who have not.

In government, unlike the private sector, there does not exist either profit or ownership by shareholders. Government operations are "owned" by a political body (a town, county, state, port authority, etc.). The lack of profit and owners does not change the basic financial operating principles. Government agencies must provide the highest-quality product or service at the minimum cost. To accomplish this goal, government financial managers use tools such as cost-benefit analysis to ascertain the benefits which accrue from a given operation in relation to the cost involved. They utilize financial management principles and attempt to maximize the benefits of an operation at the minimum cost. Maximizing the benefits increases the standards of living of the constituency and, hence, their well-being.

While business and government have somewhat differing financial goals, the question of social responsibility as a goal cannot be ignored. Social responsibility is difficult to define because it varies among industries and government agencies and falls much more heavily in some areas than others. Also, there are myriad dimensions to social responsibility. Those most readily apparent relate to our environment and physical surroundings. As a minimum, however, every individual, firm, and government must have a strong social conscience and awareness of actions as they affect others and the environment.

QUESTIONS
FOR
DISCUSSION

1. Define the following terms: disposable income, sole proprietorship, partnership, corporation shareholder, physical plant, goodwill, board of directors, earnings per share, dividends, management team, prime interest rate.
2. Explain why it is important to make good-quality products and maintain high standards as a community member.
3. Indicate how the implementation of strict environmental laws could affect the price of a firm's stock.
4. Explain and give examples of business risk and financial risk.
5. List and explain the primary factors investors examine in determining which securities to purchase.

6. Explain how government agencies use cost-benefit analysis as an aid in improving the efficiency of their operations.

7. Consider at least one major moral issue currently affecting business. Show that the laws regarding the issue fall much more heavily on some firms than others. Can you cite examples of firms which have been forced to go out of business because of such laws?

8. Describe the relationship between shareholders in a large business and the business's management.

9. Why are cash dividends important to investors?

10. Describe some of the economic factors which can affect the operation of a business.

CONCEPTS TO REMEMBER   This chapter presents foundation material for the study of financial management. The following terms and concepts are especially important:

Role of the Financial Manager
Nonfinancial Firm
Relationship of Finance to Accounting
Financial Intermediaries
Financial Goal of the Firm
Role of Shareholders in a Business
Earnings Per Share
Regression Analysis
Cash Dividends
Business Risk
Financial Risk
Return on Investment

Financial Analysis

chapter 2

The firm's management, its shareholders, and its creditors are all concerned with monitoring the firm's operations—and especially those related to its financial success. To facilitate the monitoring process a variety of tools and techniques which fall under the general heading of financial analysis has been developed. Continual evaluation of the firm's strengths and weaknesses is essential to assure its successful operation.

Financial analysis depends primarily on the evaluation of the firm's financial statements and, in particular, the balance sheet, and income statement. *The tools of financial analysis are financial ratios.* Numerous financial ratios have been developed. *Financial ratios provide a means for comparing the performance of firms within an industry and among industries.* Further, they are used to trace the operational and financial history of a single firm. A historical profile of a firm may be developed by comparing the firm's financial ratios over a period of years. A historical profile is useful in that it can be utilized to show trends in the operational and financial patterns of the firm. The development of these historical profiles is termed *trend analysis.* To proceed with financial analysis it is necessary to understand the various financial statements which are used to present the firm's operating condition. Following a review of financial statements, the use of financial ratio analysis will be discussed.

The financial statements are primary working tools of the financial manager. They reflect the position of the firm both in terms of financial worth and its operational successes. There are six parts to the financial statement "package":

Balance sheet
Statement of income
Statement of changes in owners' equity
Statement of sources and uses of funds
Notes to any and all statements
Auditor's opinion

The two basic financial statements are the balance sheet and income statement. The fundamental aspects of these statements are discussed in this chapter. The statements of changes in owners' equity and sources and uses of funds are developed from the balance sheet and income statement. Sources and uses of funds statements are examined in Chapter 3. Notes to financial statements are important since they provide additional information concerning the firm's financial position. They may include details of leasing arrangements, changes in amounts of stock outstanding, terms of new loans, and the like. Most firms, and all publicly held businesses, submit their records for a yearly audit. The auditor is an independent certified public accountant who compares the financial statement as prepared by management with the firm's accounting records. Then he renders an opinion as to the presentation of the financial statements in terms of maintenance and accuracy of records in accordance with generally accepted accounting procedures. The auditor's report is included with the financial statements in the annual report to shareholders.

BALANCE SHEET

The balance sheet is a financial statement showing the assets, liabilities, and owners' equity (or net worth) of a business. It is developed to show the cross section of a business at a point in time, usually the last day of the year. The balance sheet is based on the fundamental accounting equation:

$$\text{Assets} = \text{Liabilities} + \text{Owners' equity} \qquad (1)$$

The balance sheet shows the financial situation of a business by providing information as to the various asset, liability, and equity accounts. The balance sheet is a listing of the investments of the firm and a presentation of the sources of capital used to obtain and maintain these investments. As such, *the balance sheet is not a statement of the value of a firm*. The amounts listed in many of the accounts on the balance sheet reflect their accounting balances, which may differ significantly from their actual market value. This is especially true for older companies which purchased land and other fixed assets many years ago. However, *the real value of the assets to a firm is the amount which the firm can earn from the use of those assets*. The earnings, of course, depend on the management of the operation. Since the balance sheet does not list the value of management, which is the key asset of all firms, *the balance sheet does not reflect the value of a firm either in terms of earning ability or in terms of market value*.

Although the balance sheet does not reflect the true value of the firm directly, it is useful in many ways. First, it may be used to evaluate the solvency of the firm; *solvency reflects the firm's ability to meet its liabilities as they become due*. Second, the balance sheet exhibits profits which have been made in the past. Prepared at annual intervals, the balance sheet serves as a basis for showing the flow of income from period to period. Third, the balance sheet provides a basis for evaluation of the business from the viewpoint of its credit worthiness. Balance sheets, for example, are almost always used as a basis for commercial loans and mortgages. Further, they are required for submission to the Securities and Exchange Commission when a firm plans a public offering of securities such as stock or bonds. A firm's solvency, history of profits, and credit worthiness are all reflections of managerial ability.

Balance sheets are prepared in two main sections: assets in the left column and liabilities and owners' equity in the right column. The general form of a balance sheet is shown in Fig. 1. Each of the major categories within the balance sheet is examined briefly below, beginning with the asset structure.

The current assets are termed *current* because of the frequency with which they are converted into cash. Machinery, for example, is not often sold and converted into cash, whereas inventories are turned

FIGURE 1.   Typical balance sheet organization.

Assets	Liabilities
Current Assets	Current Liabilities
Long-Term Investments	
Fixed Assets	Long-Term Liabilities
Intangible Assets	Owner's Equity
Other Assets	Common Stock
	Paid in Capital
	Preferred Stock
	Retained Earnings

over frequently. Hence, while machinery is not included as a current asset, inventory is. Current assets are listed on a balance sheet in order of their liquidity. *Liquidity refers to the ease with which an asset can be converted into cash.* Hence, the listing is established as shown below:

Cash on hand or in banks, i.e., demand deposits (checking accounts)
Other bank deposits in passbook savings or time deposit accounts
Marketable securities
Notes receivable
Accounts receivable
Inventories
Prepaid expenses

Long-term investments include securities and other properties purchased for a variety of purposes, with the expectation of keeping them for a sustained period of time. Investments may be made to fulfill a variety of business needs. For example, a firm may seek to purchase a controlling interest in the stock of another firm. Other reasons for purchasing securities would be to enjoy income derived from them or to establish business relationships. For example, automobile manufacturers frequently invest funds in dealerships in order to aid them in growth. The manufacturers do not want to own the dealerships but rather to assure the dealership success so that more automobiles will be sold. However, long-term investments may include real or personal property in addition to securities. A firm might purchase land, precious metals, or commodities with the expectation of selling them at a profit at a future date.

Fixed assets are the land, machinery and plant equipment, buildings, and natural resources *used in the operation of the business.* The fixed assets are extremely important to the firm, for, in general, *nearly all of the firm's profit is derived from the use of the fixed assets.* Further, the liabilities and owners' equity are provided to support the asset accounts. *The whole operation of the firm revolves about the use of the fixed assets.*

Intangible assets include such items as copyrights, patents, leaseholds, trademarks, brand names, formulas, and the like. Their ownership has value as measured by their contribution to the earnings of the firm. Their valuation is, therefore, difficult to determine and depends on management's ability to fully and effectively use them.

The firm's liabilities may be divided into two categories: current and long-term. *Current liabilities are those which, in general, will require payment within a year.* Current liabilities are listed in a manner similar to the listing of current assets. That is, those which require most frequent payment are generally listed first, as shown:

Accounts payable
Notes payable
Dividends payable
Taxes payable
Accrued liabilities such as accrued wages and interest

Current liabilities represent, to a large extent, *permanent financing.* Accounts payable, for example, tends to "roll over," so that at any given time there may be an average number and dollar amount of accounts to be paid. While any given account must be paid within a period of time, it is replaced with another so that in total *the current liabilities tend to form a major portion of the permanent financing of the firm.* Of course, if a firm's sales change seasonally, accounts payable will vary in cycles following sales, and only a portion of the payables will be permanent.

Long-term liabilities are those which will normally not be paid within one year of the balance sheet date. Long-term liabilities include such items as mortgages, bonds, and notes. These forms of financing are incurred primarily to support the fixed asset structure of the firm.

The *owners' equity accounts represent the contributions made to the firm by the owners plus any earnings retained by the firm.* The two accounts, common stock and paid-in capital, represent the total amount which the owners paid for the outstanding stock at the time it was issued. It should be noted that the corporation's charter fixes the number of shares of common stock which it is authorized to issue. The firm may issue fewer but never more shares than are authorized. Also, from time to time the firm may repurchase issued stock. The repurchased stock is termed *treasury stock. The number of shares outstanding at any given time represents the ownership of the firm.* Determination of the number of shares outstanding is performed as follows:

$$\text{Shares issued} - \text{Shares repurchased} = \text{Shares outstanding} \quad (2)$$

The *common stock* account represents the number of shares outstanding multiplied by their stated or par value. The *paid-in capital is* the dollar amount equal to the number of shares outstanding multiplied by the dollar amount in *excess of par or stated value* at which the shares were originally sold. Thus, the sum of the two accounts represents the total amount originally paid by the owners when the stock was sold by the firm. For example, suppose that a firm originally sold stock to its shareholders for $25.00 per share and that the stock had a par value of $1.00 per share. In this case, for each share sold, $1.00 would go into the common stock account and $24.00 into the paid-in capital account. The amount paid originally by shareholders has little bearing on the current market price of the stock, and the two should not be confused.

The *preferred stock* account represents the total amount which was paid for the preferred stock when originally sold by the firm. It is the number of shares multiplied by the price paid per share. Like the market price of the common stock, the market price of preferred stock may be more or less than the original purchase price.

Retained earnings are the portion of the after-tax profits which have been retained in the business. Profits are either distributed in the form of dividends to the shareholders or retained as "retained earnings." The retained earnings belong to the corporation's shareholders and are kept by the firm to be used in order to maintain or increase the profits from operations. Retained earnings are usually used to purchase capital equipment or to increase inventories and the like. Generally only a small portion of retained earnings is held as cash, and much of the earnings is invested in the business. *Therefore, retained earnings should not be considered in terms of cash on hand.*

A change in retained earnings should be thought of in terms of the difference between the change in the book value of assets over the change in liabilities which takes place during the year. The total retained earnings is the cumulative effect of the changes in the values of the assets and liabilities over the period of operation of the firm, net of the reductions due to distributions of assets to shareholders in the forms of cash dividends. To repeat, retained earnings *should not* be thought of in terms of cash on hand.

Reproduced on pages 22 and 23 are the corporation's balance sheets of Technitrol, Inc. from their 1973 Annual Report. Technitrol is a medium-sized (sales of $10 million), diversified manufacturing firm. Their product line includes electronic components, electronic control systems, large electric motors, data processing systems, platform scales, and metallurgical electrical contacts.

The asset, liability, and owners' equity accounts grouped in the form shown in Fig. 1 may be rearranged in a manner more useful to the financial manager. Such a reorganized statement is shown schematically in Fig. 2.

The working capital is the difference between current assets and current liabilities:

$$\text{Working capital} = \text{Current assets} - \text{Current liabilities} \qquad (3)$$

The working capital accounts all support the operations of the fixed assets, and it is generally within the province of the financial manager to develop and recommend operating policies with regard to the maintenance of these accounts. Thus, policies are developed for cash management, maintenance of inventories, collections of accounts receiv-

FIGURE 2. Working capital balance sheet organization.

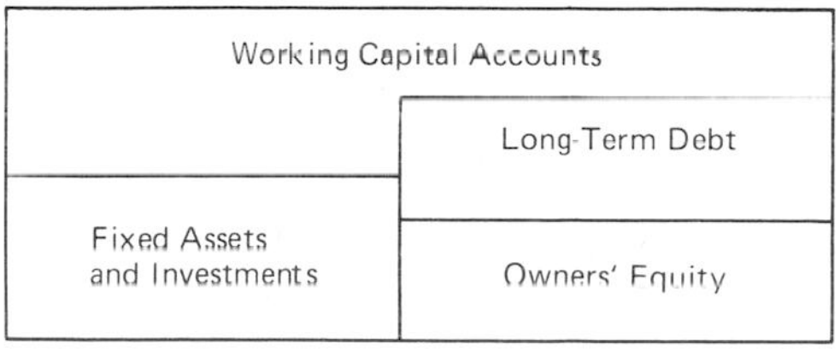

Assets	December 31, 1973	1972
Current Assets:		
Cash	$ 141,758	$ 314,902
Marketable securities (market value 1973, $828,733; 1972, $933,088)	964,155	975,630
Accounts and notes receivable		
Trade	1,294,989	920,993
Other	58,666	470,705
Affiliate	139,753	116,812
Income tax refund receivable		198,425
Inventories	2,164,487	1,707,411
Prepaid expenses	57,215	96,887
Total current assets	4,821,023	4,801,765
Property, plant, and equipment:		
Land	30,600	30,600
Buildings and improvements	342,077	320,465
Machinery and equipment	2,391,335	2,231,063
	2,764,012	2,582,128
Less accumulated depreciation	1,856,574	1,660,786
	907,438	921,342
Investment in affiliate	227,500	227,500
Other assets:		
Notes receivable, noncurrent	60,000	80,000
Cash value of officers' life insurance, net of policy loans; 1973, $177,575	23,048	182,706
Intangibles	116,822	144,405
Miscellaneous	3,137	1,975
	203,007	409,086
Total assets	$6,158,968	$6,359,693

able, payment of accounts payable, etc. All of these policies are developed so as to be consistent with the operational and financial goals of the firm. A discussion of the operation of these accounts and the development of policies pertaining to them is included under the general heading of *working capital management.*

Fixed assets are the primary and, in many firms, the only source for generating operating income. In general, the financial manager has little to do with operation of the fixed assets. However, the financial manager does provide input into the selection of the capital equipment

Liabilities and Shareholders' Equity

	1973	1972
Current liabilities:		
Current portion of long-term debt	$ 19,700	$ 19,700
Notes payable:		
Bank, demand, 5¾%		900,000
Other, 6% to 8%		25,847
Accounts payable, trade	366,483	447,387
Accrued wages and other expenses	309,755	220,638
Accrued payroll and other taxes	47,060	66,570
Income taxes	386,283	
Total current liabilities	1,129,281	1,680,142
Long-term debt, net of current portion	24,575	44,275
Deferred income taxes	16,300	
Commitments:		
Shareholders' equity		
Common stock, $.125 par; authorized		
3 million shares; issued 1,398,160 shares	174,770	174,770
Capital in excess of par	1,238,744	1,237,744
Retained earnings	3,679,255	3,222,762
	5,092,769	5,635,276
Less treasury stock, 37,410 shares	103,957	
	4,988,812	4,635,276
	$6,158,968	$6,359,693

to be purchased. The part of financial management which deals with the investment of funds in capital assets is *capital budgeting.*

Long-term debt and owners' equity are two primary sources of funds needed to operate the firm. These topics, along with the determination of dividend policy, are included under the heading of *financing the firm.*

INCOME STATEMENTS

The particular format of income statement used varies from company to company. The reason for the lack of uniformity in the preparation of income statements results from the difference in operations among firms by industry. Also, income statements may be prepared in varying degrees of detail according to their use. Thus, those prepared for shareholders and creditors are more general than those prepared for internal management use. The simplest is just a statement of revenues and expenses. The difference between revenues and expenses represents profits or losses.

From the viewpoint of a financial manager, the breakdown of costs is very important. Two plans for income statements which are useful to the financial manager are shown below:

Ajax Sales, Inc.

Income Statement December 31, 1974

		Amount	Percentage
Sales		$ 400,000	100%
Cost of goods sold (raw materials & labor)		− 240,000	− 60
Gross profit (gross margin)		$ 160,000	40%
Selling expenses			
Delivery	$ 12,000		
Commissions	8,000		
Allowances	8,000		
Warranties	20,000		
Advertising	32,000	− 80,000	− 20
Operating expenses			
Salaries	$ 32,000		
Rent	2,000		
Utilities	2,000		
Office supplies	400		
Travel	2,000		
Telephone	1,600		
Postage	800	− 40,800	− 10.2
Depreciation		− 12,000	− 3.0
Earnings before interest and taxes (EBIT)		$ 27,200	6.8%
Interest expense		− 4,000	− 1.0
Earnings before taxes (EBT)		$ 23,200	5.8%
Taxes (at 22% rate)		− 5,104	− 1.3%
After-tax profits (ATP)		$ 18,096	4.5%

The preceding form is useful to the financial manager in that it provides him with easy access to the following financial data:

1. *Gross profit or margin:* In this example the gross margin is important since it permits computation of the percentage of each dollar of sales which is taken by the cost of the product.
2. *Depreciation:* The depreciation is important since it represents a non-cash expense. Its significance will be further demonstrated in the chapter dealing with cash flow.
3. *Earnings before interest and taxes (EBIT):* EBIT are very important.

EBIT are the earnings utilized by the financial manager when evaluating the effects of varying the proportions of debt and equity used to finance the firm.

A second very useful form for presentation of an income statement is obtained by dividing costs into two areas: variable and fixed. *The variable costs are those which vary directly with output and can be controlled in the short run. Fixed costs include those which do not vary with output and cannot be changed readily within short time periods.* Examples of variable costs are labor, raw materials, and the like, while fixed costs include such items as rent, liability insurance, depreciation, and property taxes. The income statement shown below for Ajax Sales, Inc. represents a reorganization of the expenses into variable and fixed costs categories.

Ajax Sales, Inc.

Income Statement Dec. 31, 1974

		Amount	*Percentage*
Sales		$ 400,000	100%
Variable costs			
Product (raw materials and labor)	$240,000		
Delivery	12,000		
Commissions	8,000		
Allowances	8,000		
Warranties	20,000		
Advertising	32,000		
Total variable costs		− 320,000	− 80
Fixed costs			
Salaries	$ 32,000		
Rent	2,000		
Utilities	2,000		
Office supplies	400		
Travel	2,000		
Telephone	1,600		
Postage	800		
Interest	4,000		
Depreciation	12,000		
Total fixed costs		− 56,800	− 14.2
Earnings before taxes (EBT)		$ 23,200	5.8
Taxes (at 22% rate)		− 5,104	− 1.3
After-tax profits (ATP)		$ 18,096	4.5

The breakdown of costs into variable and fixed is very useful for the financial manager in the preparation of *break-even analysis* and profit projections for different levels of output. *A break-even analysis is used to determine the amount of output which must be produced and sold in order to just break even.* It is also useful in that it may be employed to project profit or loss at varying levels of output. Break-even analysis is described in detail under the heading of *profitability management.*

The income statement for Technitrol, Inc. is presented below. The

Technitrol, Inc.

Consolidated Statement of Income

	Years Ended December 31,	
	1973	*1972*
Net sales	$10,616,932	$4,721,417
Cost of sales	7,855,182	4,249,314
Gross profit	2,761,750	472,103
Selling, general, and administrative expenses	1,974,654	944,325
Income (loss) from operations	787,096	(472,222)
Other income (charges):		
Interest and dividend income	86,434	129,019
Interest expense	(38,797)	(7,394)
Royalty income, net of patent litigation costs	80,531	152,548
Idle plant expenses		(13,640)
Miscellaneous, net	308	9,155
	128,476	269,688
Income (loss) before income taxes	915,572	(202,534)
Income taxes (refund), net		
Current	432,879	(155,070)
Deferred	16,300	
	449,179	(155,070)
Income (loss) before extraordinary items	466,393	(47,464)
Extraordinary items		154,803
Net income	$ 466,393	$ 107,339
Earnings per common share and common equivalent share		
Income (loss) before royalty income, net of patent litigation costs and extraordinary items	$.31	($.08)
Royalty income, net of patent litigation costs and applicable income taxes	.03	.05
Extraordinary items, net of applicable income taxes		.11
Net income	$.34	$.08

financial manager can rearrange the figures given to the forms described above in order to perform needed analysis. Note, however, that the "Selling, general, and administrative expenses," some of which are variable and some fixed, are lumped together. This prevents the complete rearrangement of costs into fixed and variable categories.

The Technitrol income statement correctly separates extraordinary income from the income resulting from operations. Extraordinary items should always be shown separately so that the reader can see the results of the normal operations.

FINANCIAL RATIO ANALYSIS

There are various relationships between financial statement items which are important to the interpretation of both financial and operating data. These relationships may be expressed in terms of ratios. It is necessary to supplement the financial statement figures with ratios in order to indicate relationships between related items such as current assets and current liabilities. Taken alone, total current assets of $1 million might seem most impressive, but if current liabilities totaled $2 million, the current asset position would be very weak. Therefore, it is very important to compare related items in making a financial analysis.

Individual ratios are of little value without a bench mark for comparison. *For ratios to be useful they must be compared with standards for the industry involved.* Industry standards are developed by research agencies such as Robert Morris Associates and Dun and Bradstreet and industrial trade associations. Research agencies tend to provide general industrial ratios, while trade associations also focus on ratios which have special importance to a particular industry. Management uses the cross section of industrial data as a base line for comparison with their own operation. Such a *cross-sectional analysis* is very useful in pinpointing strengths and weaknesses which may exist in an individual firm.

Creditors, such as banks, are also concerned with cross-sectional comparison of financial and operating ratios. When a firm applies for a loan, the bank requires copies of up-to-date financial statements. The bank loan officers develop financial ratios from the statements and use them as one part of their loan analysis. The applicant's ratios are compared with industrial ratios in an attempt to determine the applicant's ability to repay the loan in a timely manner. It is helpful for the applicant to supply ratio data provided by its trade association to the bank since these data will usually have much more detail than the general industrial data available to the bank. Thus, trade association data are found to be useful both for internal financial management and for securing credit.

In addition to the cross-sectional analysis using financial ratios described above, *longitudinal or trend analysis* is very important to the firm's management, its creditors, and its shareholders. For a longitudinal analysis it is necessary to prepare financial ratios for a period of years. Then the changes from year to year can be noted. Such changes indicate the direction which a firm is taking. Even if year-to-year changes are only slight, they can indicate a trend and therefore act as a signal for managerial action.

Financial ratios have as their primary function the focusing of attention of a financial analyst on data which may require further investigation. The ratios do not substitute for the actual analysis which must be undertaken to determine why certain changes took place. Rather, financial ratios are the starting point for detailed financial analysis.

Financial ratios are generally divided into four categories based on their use. The various types of ratios are described below and examples provided. Many of the ratios are discussed in later sections of the book along with the particular subject matter to which they relate.

1. *Liquidity ratios:* These measure the firm's solvency and ability to meet short-term obligations.
2. *Leverage ratios:* There are two basic types of leverage ratios. The first measures the degree to which debt has been used to finance the firm (financial leverage). The second measures the change in pretax profits which can be expected from a given percentage change in output and sales (operating leverage).
3. *Profitability ratios:* These are used to measure profit as a function of sales and investment.
4. *Debt coverage ratios:* These measure the firm's ability to meet its debt obligations.

Liquidity Ratios

A firm's solvency, or its ability to meet its current obligations, is measured using two "financial ratios": the current ratio and the quick or acid test ratio. The first is the ratio of current assets to current liabilities:

$$\text{Current ratio} = \frac{\text{Current assets}}{\text{Current liabilities}} \qquad (4)$$

Since inventories are often not readily convertible to cash and hence cannot be used to pay bills, a second ratio, the acid test, is more frequently used as a measure of solvency:

$$\text{Quick or acid test ratio} = \frac{\text{Current assets—Inventories}}{\text{Current liabilities}} \qquad (5)$$

Values for financial ratios vary appreciably among industries, and hence there is no shortcut method to prescribing an exact ratio which should exist for all companies in general. Bankers generally refer to published statement studies such as those by Robert Morris Associates in order to determine the average for an industry when reviewing loan applications. For example, the average current ratio for manufacturers of men's working clothing is about 2.2. If a firm in this industry having a current ratio of only 1.4 applied for a loan, a banker would want to examine the reasons for the low ratio prior to granting the loan.

At some banks, the usefulness of the current and quick ratios is discounted in certain situations. These include firms which have sales which fluctuate substantially on a seasonal basis and firms with increasing sales. The first effect of increasing sales is usually a cash shortage since most sales are made on credit. Thus, a firm having increasing sales generally experiences a shortage of cash, which results in poor liquidity ratios. In such instances, bank officers are instructed to examine sales and cash forecasts rather than liquidity ratios in deciding if the bank should loan funds.

Example 1: CURRENT AND QUICK RATIOS

Refer to Technitrol's 1973 balance sheet, and determine the current and quick ratios. The balance sheet is on pp. 22 and 23.

SOLUTION

From the balance sheet, the amount of current assets, current liabilities, and inventories may be determined. They are listed below:

Current assets	$4,821,023
Current liabilities	1,129,281
Inventories	2,164,487

The value of current assets given on the balance sheet reflects the purchase price of marketable securities. The price of these securities has decreased since their purchase from $964,155 to $828,733. For purposes of developing financial ratios, the current assets should be reduced to $4,685,601 in order to reflect the decrease in value of the marketable securities:

$$\text{Current ratio} = \frac{\$4,685,601}{\$1,129,281} = 4.15$$

$$\text{Quick ratio} = \frac{\$4,685,601 - \$2,164,487}{\$1,129,281} = 2.23$$

It is interesting to note the substantial difference between the current and quick ratios in this example. The large amount of inventory carried by Technitrol substantially decreases its solvency. This does not mean that the inventory is unnecessary but rather that the quick ratio provides a much more accurate reflection of the firm's solvency (i.e., its ability to pay its bills as they come due) than the current ratio.

The liquidity of receivables is measured using the "average collection period ratio":

$$\text{Average collection period} = \frac{\text{Average receivables} \times 360}{\text{Annual credit sales}} \tag{6}$$

The liquidity of inventories is measured using the "inventory turnover ratio":

$$\text{Inventory turnover} = \frac{\text{Cost of goods sold}}{\text{Average inventory}} \tag{7}$$

Examples describing the application of the receivables and inventory ratios are included in Chapters 21 and 22, respectively.

Leverage Ratios

As indicated above, there are two types of leverage ratios. The first is used to measure the extent to which debt is used to finance the firm. The most commonly used measure of debt utilization is the "debt-to-net-worth" ratio:

$$\text{Debt-to-net-worth} = \frac{\text{Total debt}}{\text{Net worth}} \tag{8}$$

Example 2:   Debt-to-Net-Worth Ratio

Refer to Technitrol's 1973 balance sheet and determine the deb-to-net-worth ratio.

SOLUTION

From the balance sheet the total debts are calculated as follows:

Total current liabilities	$1,129,281
Long-term debt, net of current portion	24,575
Deferred income taxes	16,300
	$1,170,156

The net worth is shown as $4,988,812:

$$\text{Debt-to-net-worth} = \frac{\$1,170,156}{\$4,988,812} = 23\%$$

The second leverage ratio, the "degree of operating leverage" ratio, is used in measuring and projecting the change in pretax profits based on changes in sales. This ratio is discussed in depth in Chapter 23.

Profitability Ratios

The profitability of a business is very important to its owners, management, and creditors. Profitability is generally measured in terms of return on sales and return on assets. Two commonly used measures of profitability are the profit margin and the return on assets ratios. These are defined in equation form as follows:

$$\text{Profit margin} = \frac{\text{Earnings before taxes}}{\text{Sales}} \qquad (9)$$

$$\text{Return on assets} = \frac{\text{Earnings before taxes}}{\text{Average total assets}} \qquad (10)$$

These ratios provide a measure of a firm's profitability and can be compared with industry figures using a statement studies guide. Generally, profitability ratios are expressed as a percentage.

Example 3: PROFITABILITY RATIOS

Determine the profitability ratios of Technitrol for 1973. The statement of income is on page 26.

SOLUTION

Technitrol's earnings, sales, and total assets are indicated below as shown on their income statement and balance sheet:

Earnings before taxes	$ 915,572
Sales	$10,616,932
Total assets	$ 6,158,968

$$\text{Profit margin} = \frac{\text{Earnings before taxes}}{\text{Sales}} = \frac{\$915,572}{\$10,616,932} = 8.62\%$$

$$\text{Return on assets} = \frac{\text{Earnings before taxes}}{\text{Average total assets}} = \frac{\$915,572}{\$6,259,331} = 14.63\%$$

The $6,259,331 used for total assets was obtained by averaging the total assets at the beginning and end of 1973.

Debt Coverage Ratios

The firm's ability to meet its interest payments on oustanding debts and to repay principal in a timely manner is of extreme importance to creditors. The "interest coverage ratio" is used to indicate how much greater EBIT is than interest. This is important since interest is paid out of EBIT.

The interest coverage ratio is defined as follows:

$$\text{Interest coverage ratio} = \frac{\text{Earnings before interest \& taxes}}{\text{Interest for period}} \quad (11)$$

Example 4: INTEREST COVERAGE RATIO

Determine the interest coverage ratio for Ajax Sales, Inc.

SOLUTION

The interest is $4,000, while EBIT is $27,200.

$$\text{Interest coverage ratio} = \frac{\text{EBIT}}{\text{Interest}} = \frac{\$27,200}{\$4,000} = 6.8 \text{ times}$$

The EBIT cover interest payments 6.8 times. This high interest coverage would please creditors since earnings could fall substantially before interest payments would be jeopardized.

Financial analysis is important as a tool for comparison of various firms and for analysis of trends and changes in a firm. The financial manager, creditors, shareholders, suppliers, and customers are all concerned with the well-being of a business. Financial analysis and especially the use of financial ratios provide a measure of the firm's health.

1. Explain why the balance sheet does not provide a statement of the value of a company.
2. The value of the management is not shown on the balance sheet. How is the value of the management reflected?
3. Indicate at least three balance sheet accounts that often have significantly different book or accounting values and actual market values.
4. Indicate the primary uses for the balance sheet.
5. How does the balance sheet reflect the profits of the firm?
6. Explain the meaning of the following terms: liquidity, current assets, long-term investments, fixed assets, real property, personal property, current liabilities, paid-in capital, retained earnings.
7. Indicate why notes receivable are more liquid than accounts receivable. Why are prepaid expenses less liquid than inventories?
8. Notes payable are sometimes shown as current liabilities, while on other balance sheets they are listed as a part of long-term debt. Explain.
9. Differentiate authorized, issued, and outstanding shares and treasury stock.
10. Explain the meaning of par and stated value of stock. Do they have any significance to the financial manager?
11. Why is a reorganization of balance sheet accounts into working capital accounts, fixed assets and investments, long-term debt, and owners' equity especially useful to a financial manager?
12. Explain the significance of earnings before interest and taxes to the financial manager and to a firm's creditors.
13. Explain the usefulness of reorganizing an income statement in fixed and variable expenses.
14. Explain the reason for using the quick ratio as a measure of a firm's solvency rather than the current ratio.
15. Indicate why profitability is measured in two ways. Provide examples of types of businesses which would tend to have high profit margins and low returns on assets and vice versa.
16. Explain the meaning of trend analysis. Why is it used?

This chapter presents several important analytical concepts. Be sure you understand the following:

Balance Sheet
Statement of Income
Statement of Changes in Owners' Equity
Statement of Sources and Uses of Funds
Notes to Financial Statements
Auditor's Opinion
Owners' Equity

Current Assets
Current Liabilities
Fixed Assets
Long Term Liabilities
Intangible Assets
Accrued Liabilities
Permanent Financing
Shares of Common Stock Authorized, Issued, Repurchased, and Outstanding
Par Value
Paid-in Capital
Retained Earnings
Working Capital Balance Sheet Organization
Gross Profit
Depreciation
Earnings Before Interest and Taxes (EBIT)
Variable Costs
Fixed Costs
Break-Even Analysis
Liquidity Ratios—(Current Ratio, Quick Ratio, Average Collection Period and Inventory Turnover)
Leverage Ratios—(Debt-to-Net-Worth)
Profitability Ratios—(Profit Margin, Return on Assets)
Debt Coverage Ratios—(Interest Coverage)

PROBLEMS
1. Alexander Corporation had total after-tax profits of $5 million. If the EPS were $1.00 per share, how many shares of common stock were outstanding?
2. Balance sheet and income statements for Keyhole Express are given below. Determine the following financial ratios: current, quick, interest coverage, profit margin and return on assets.

Balance Sheet Dec. 31, 1976

Assets		*Liabilities and Owners' Equity*	
Cash	$ 3,000,000	Accounts payable	$ 6,000,000
Accounts receivable	6,000,000	Accrued wages	1,000,000
Investments at cost	3,000,000	Accrued taxes	500,000
(market value $2,600,000)		Notes payable (due 60 days)	500,000
Inventory	8,000,000	Long-term debt	20,000,000
Fixed assets, net	35,000,000	Common stock ($1 par)	3,000,000
Total	$55,000,000	Paid-in capital	10,000,000
		Retained earnings	14,000,000
		Total	$55,000,000

Income Statement Dec. 31, 1976

Sales		$ 16,600,000
Cost of goods sold		— 8,500,000
		$ 8,100,000
Operating expenses		
Salaries	$ 500,000	
Rent	1,000,000	
Utilities	300,000	
Other	400,000	
		— 2,200,000
Depreciation		— 1,000,000
EBIT		$ 4,900,000
Interest		— 2,000,000
EBT		$ 2,900,000
Taxes		— 1,400,000
After-tax profits		$ 1,500,000

3. Determine the profitability ratios for Ajax Sales, Inc. They have total assets of $1.5 million. (Refer to the income statement in the chapter.)
4. Determine the interest coverage ratios for Technitrol in 1972 and 1973. Discuss the change.
5. Reorganize the 1973 Technitrol Balance Sheet into the following accounts: working capital, fixed assets and investments, long-term debt, and owners' equity.
6. Reorganize the 1973 Technitrol Income Statement into variable and fixed costs. (Note, some costs listed under the same heading may be both fixed and variable.)

Cash Flow
and
Sources and Uses
of Funds

chapter 3

While the balance sheet and income statement are the primary financial statements used by most firms for purposes of obtaining credit and informing owners of their financial status, other kinds of statements are particularly important to the financial manager. One of them is the cash flow from operations; another is the sources and uses of funds statement.

Both of the statements deal with the flow of cash in the firm. *Cash flow* is a term used to describe a company's cash receipts and expenditures. An organization's cash flow may be poor, that is, the firm may have difficulty paying its obligations, even though it is operating at a profit and has many assets. For example, as sales increase, so will cost of goods sold. But, if collections of accounts receivable lag, an expanding operation may well result in a cash deficiency. Expansion and purchase of new fixed assets can also result in poor cash flow. The new assets may result in increasing profits but at the present time reduce the firm's cash balances. *Cash flow and maintaining sufficient cash balances to meet obligations are the most important ongoing concerns of the firm's management.*

CASH FLOW AND PROFITABILITY

The income statement indicates the extent to which the operation of a firm has been profitable over the period of a year. Further, the income statement indicates *the return on investment* (the profits) which the firm has realized during the year. However, it does not indicate the cash position of the firm and, in particular, the ability of the firm to meet its obligations. It is possible for a firm to have good earnings and concurrently be very short of cash or even become insolvent and unable to pay debts when they fall due. The cash flow of a firm and the firm's ability to meet its obligations are of extreme importance to the management and owners. In this section we shall deal with the question of generation of cash funds through profits and other "cash throwoffs" such as depreciation. In the next section we shall further treat the subject of cash flow, including all sources and uses of funds.

The cash flow which results from the operations of a firm may be determined by adding to the after-tax profits any cash throw-off or implicit expenses listed on the income statement. For example, depreciation, amortization of intangible assets, and depletion are all implicit expenses. Implicit expenses do not require the expenditure of cash, as opposed to explicit expenses such as wages, taxes, utilities, and the like which do require use of funds. Referring to the income statement for Ajax Sales, Inc., note that depreciation was $12,000 and after-tax profits $18,096. Thus, the funds generated through the operations of the firm were the sum of these, $30,096.

Example 1:   Finch Products has the income statement shown. Determine the cash inflow from its operations.

Income Statement

Sales		$	1,000,000
Cost of goods sold		−	600,000
Gross profit		$	400,000
Selling expenses	$200,000		
Operating expenses	100,000		
Depreciation	30,000		
Amortization of patent	10,000		
Total expense		−	340,000
EBIT		$	60,000
Interest		−	25,000
EBT		$	35,000
Tax		−	10,300
After-tax profits		$	24,700

SOLUTION

The cash inflows generated by the operation include the after-tax profits and depreciation and amortization cash throw-offs.

After-tax profit	$24,700
Depreciation	30,000
Amortization of patent	10,000
	$64,700

The firm generated a total of $64,700 through its operations during the year.

It should be noted that while profits represent returns *on* investment, the cash generated through implicit expenses such as depreciation and amortization represents returns *of* investment. *Depreciation is especially important since it is the vehicle by which the firm recovers its investments in capital equipment, buildings, vehicles, and the like.*

For purposes of financial planning it is important to be able to project changes in cash flow which are expected to result from a proposed management decision, such as the purchase of a new machine. The cash flow which will result from the use of new or replacement capital equipment, for example, is of extreme importance when deciding whether or not they should be purchased. Determination of the added income and cash flow is demonstrated below:

Example 2: PROFITABILITY AND CASH FLOW

A machine costs $15,000. It has a life of five years and will be depreciated straight-line to zero salvage value. The resulting depreciation will be $3,000 per year. Use of the machine is expected to result in an increase in income of $20,000 per year. Concurrently, operating expenses are expected to rise by $16,000 per year. Assume the firm considering the purchase of the machine has a 22% tax rate. Determine the profit and cash flow which can be expected from the machine.

SOLUTION

The profitability is calculated using the typical income statement method.

Income	$ 20,000
Less operating expenses	− 16,000
Less depreciation	− 3,000
Earnings before taxes	$ 1,000
Less tax	− 220
After-tax profit	$ 780

To determine the cash flow, it is necessary to add back the depreciation. The depreciation expenses did not result in any outflow of cash, so at the end of the year, management could expect to have an additional $780 + 3,000 = $3,780 from the use of the machine.

Example 3:   PROFITABILITY AND CASH FLOW

Consider the same machine as in Example 2 except that a loan is obtained to finance it. The loan requires that $2,000 be paid back each year and that interest payments be made in accordance with the schedule shown below. Assume a 22% tax rate, and determine the profitability and cash flow for the first year.

Year	Interest
1	$900
2	720
3	540
4	360
5	180

SOLUTION

The profitability is changed by the interest expense.

Income	$ 20,000
Less operating expenses	− 16,000
Less interest	− 900
Less depreciation	− 3,000
Earnings before taxes	$ 100
Less tax	− 22
After-tax profit	$ 78

The cash flow from operations includes the after-tax profit plus the depreciation as in Example 2 for a total of $3,078. However, the loan payment of $2,000 must be deducted.

After-tax profit	$ 78
Plus depreciation	3,000
Less loan principal payment	− 2,000
Net cash flow after loan repayment	$ 1,078

The examples relating to cash flow and profitability shown above demonstrated one method of determining cash flow: adding after-tax profit to depreciation and other implicit expense cash throw-offs. Another procedure which may be used to calculate cash flow is simply to subtract the cash outflows from the cash inflows:

$$\text{Net cash flow} = \text{Total cash inflows} - \text{Total cash outflows} \qquad (1)$$

When Eq. (1) is used to determine cash flow, only cash inflows are used in the calculations. That is, implicit expenses such as depreciation are not included. Use of Eq. (1) is demonstrated in Example 4.

Example 4: PROFITABILITY AND CASH FLOW

A small, older apartment house costing $32,000 has a yearly rental income of $5,460. Operating expenses are $2,720. The depreciation will be $1,400 per year. Financing will be by a $12,000 down payment and a 9%, 20-year mortgage. The first-year interest expense on the mortgage is $1,800, and principal repayment is $375. The owners are married, have a taxable income of $17,000, and are in the 28% marginal tax bracket. Determine the profit from the apartment house and the net cash flow to the owners for the first year.

SOLUTION

First, calculate the profit from the property.

Rentals	$ 5,460
Less operating expenses	− 2,720
Less interest	− 1,800
Less depreciation	− 1,400
Pretax profit	($ 460)

The owners are in the 28% marginal tax bracket. Hence, a loss of $460 on the property will result in a tax savings of .28 × $460 = $129.00. That is, their taxable income will be reduced by $460, and therefore they will have to pay $129 less in federal income tax. Next, calculate the cash flow.

Rentals	$5,460
Tax savings	129
Total cash inflows	$5,589
Operating expense	$2,720
Interest	1,800
Total cash outflows from operations	$4,520

$$\text{Net cash flow from operations} = \text{Total cash inflows} - \text{Total cash outflows}$$

$$= \$5,589 - \$4,520$$

$$= \$1,069$$

Thus, the first year the owners would receive an after-tax net cash inflow from operations of $1,069, based on an original investment of $12,000. However, they would have to repay $375 in principal, which would leave $694. *Note that principal repayments are not shown on the income statement, whereas interest payments do appear on the income statement.*

In terms of measuring the increase in wealth of the apartment owners in Example 4, the net cash flow is much more meaningful than the profit. In fact, it may be desirable to keep profits down if, by doing so, cash flows can be increased. The effort to increase cash flow is very important to both large and small firms. For example, during the 1974–1975 period of high inflation, many firms switched to LIFO accounting. LIFO, standing for last in, first out, is an inventory valuation method in which items used as inputs to production (raw materials) or purchased for resale are valued at the cost of the most recent acquisition. This tends to match current expenses with current revenues, thus providing a realistic portrait of profits. The change to LIFO has resulted in decreased profits for firms, but it has also reduced the federal income tax liability and thereby increased cash flow.

SOURCES AND ALLOCATIONS (USES) OF FUNDS AND CHANGES IN WORKING CAPITAL

In the last section the importance of cash flow was emphasized. The examples, however, were directed toward evaluation of individual investment projects rather than all of the operations of a firm. In this section we shall expand the study to include all inflows (sources) and outflows (uses) of funds (i.e., all cash flows).

The various *sources of funds* may be classified into several general groupings:

1. A net increase in any liability (such as borrowing money or increasing trade payables);
2. A net decrease in any asset other than cash (such as selling property or reducing inventories);

3. Proceeds derived from the sale of common or preferred stock;
4. After-tax profits.

Uses of funds may also be classified into several groupings:

1. A net decrease in any liability (such as paying off a debt);
2. A net increase in any asset other than cash (such as buying a new machine);
3. Retirement or repurchase of stock;
4. Cash dividends.

Sources and allocation of funds statements are extremely valuable to the financial manager, as they indicate the sources of funds and how they were used. Typically, a sources and uses of funds statement is constructed using the income statement and opening and closing balance sheets for a given year. Such sources and uses of funds statements based on the historical progress of a firm are especially useful to investors and creditors, as they indicate precisely how the firm obtained and used its funds. From an internal management perspective, however, such historical statements are not as important. Management knows at the end of the year what it did during the year. For internal management purposes, *pro-forma financial statements* are much more useful. Pro-forma statements are statements developed based on management expectations for the coming year. Typically, management will establish goals and develop pro-forma income statements and balance sheets based on the achievement of these goals. From these pro-forma statements a pro-forma sources and uses of funds statement may be developed. Management is concerned with the historical progress the firm has made, but much more concerned with anticipated progress. Hence, it develops pro-forma statements to anticipate its financial progress based on current expectations.

Financial planning is extremely important and involves decisions regarding expenditures for capital equipment, methods of financing, and the like. Once sales forecasts have been developed, costs projected, and a capital budgeting and financing program developed, management develops a cash operating budget for the year. A *cash operating budget* indicates the specific cash needs by day, week, or month (depending on its detail) for a year or longer period of time. Methods of financing a firm and capital budgeting procedures are included as separate sections in this book. The procedures for developing cash budgets are included as a part of the study of working capital management. Example 5 indicates the method for construction of a sources and uses of funds statement.

Example 5:   Sources and Uses of Funds

Arthur, Inc. has the following financial statements. Construct a sources and uses of funds statement.

Balance Sheet
(in millions)

Assets	Dec. 31, 1975	Dec. 31, 1976	Liability and Owners' Equity	Dec. 31, 1975	Dec. 31, 1976
Cash	$ 3	$ 1	Accounts payable	$ 3	$ 4
Accounts receivable	1.5	4	Long-term debt	4	9
Inventory	6	9	Common stock	8	8
Fixed assets, net*	35	40	Retained earnings	30.5	33
	$45.5	$54		$45.5	$54

Fixed assets less accumulated depreciation.

Income Statement
Dec. 31, 1976

Sales		$ 60,000,000
Expenses		
Cost of goods	$ 25,000,000	
Administration	14,000,000	
Depreciation	5,000,000	
Interest	1,000,000	
		− 45,000,000
Earnings before taxes		$ 15,000,000
Taxes		− 7,500,000
Net income after taxes		$ 7,500,000

Solution

Each change in a balance sheet account is evaluated to determine if it represents a source or use of funds.

a. *Accounts receivable* increased by $2.5 million. This represents an extension of credit to customers and is a use of funds.
b. *Inventory* increased by $3 million. This represents a use of funds.
c. *Net fixed assets* increased by $5 million. However, we note from the income statement that there was $5 million in depreciation. This means that $10 million in fixed assets must have been purchased during 1976, which is a use of funds. The calculation is shown below:

Fixed assets, Dec. 31, 1975	$ 35,000,000
Less depreciation for 1976	− 5,000,000
	$ 30,000,000
Purchases during 1976	10,000,000
Fixed assets, Dec. 31, 1976	$ 40,000,000

d. *Accounts payable* increased by $1 million. Arthur's suppliers extended additional trade credit to Arthur, Inc. This represents a source of funds.
e. *Long-term debt* increased by $5 million. This is a source of funds.
f. *Common stock* did not change.
g. *Retained earnings* changed. Retained earnings does not represent either a source or use of funds; rather, it indicates the results of a firm earning profits and paying cash dividends. Note that retained earnings increased by $2.5 million, while the firm had after-tax income of $7.5 million. Since after-tax profits can only go to pay dividends or into retained earnings, there must have been dividends paid.

After-tax profits	$ 7,500,000
Less increase in retained earnings	− 2,500,000
Dividends paid	$ 5,000,000

The *dividends* represent a use of funds. The *after-tax profit* represents a source of funds.

Upon completion of the balance sheet analysis, the income statement is reviewed. Part of this had already been completed with the classification of after-tax profits and dividends. There is one other item in the income statement: depreciation. The *depreciation* represents a source of funds of $5 million. For the sake of clarity, it must be noted that depreciation of itself *does not* generate any funds. The reason it is included with the sources is that in making the income statement it was deducted as an expense item, while actually it did *not result* in any payment of funds.

With the classification of changes complete, the various sources and funds are grouped.

Sources of Funds

Item	*Amount*
Increase in accounts payable	$ 1,000,000
Increase in long-term debt	5,000,000
After-tax profits	7,500,000
Depreciation	5,000,000
Total	$18,500,000
Decrease in cash	2,000,000
Total sources	$20,500,000

Uses of Funds

Item	Amount
Increase in accounts receivable	$ 2,500,000
Increase in inventory	3,000,000
Increase in fixed assets	10,000,000
Dividends	5,000,000
Total uses	$20,500,000

The uses are $2 million greater than the sources, indicating that cash should have decreased by that amount. A check of the balance sheet indicates that to be the case. In making a sources and uses of funds statement, it is customary to add the item "decrease in cash" to the sources so that it balances with uses. If the sources had been greater than the uses, the item "increase in cash" would be added to the uses of funds portion of the statement.

As indicated in Chapter 2, the management of working capital is very important to the successful operation of a firm. Working capital was defined as the difference between current assets and current liabilities. *Working capital management involves cash management, maintenance of inventories, collection of receivables, payment of accounts payable, and the like.* Working capital management is especially important since working capital reflects directly on the firm's liquidity, i.e., the firm's ability to pay its bills. Therefore, changes in the working capital statement, which shows changes in current asset and liability accounts, are developed. The changes in the working capital statement is similar in format to the sources and uses of funds statement but is used to show changes in the firm's liquidity position. Development of a changes of working capital statement requires an examination of just the working capital accounts, i.e., current assets and liabilities. Recall that working capital is defined as follows:

$$\text{Working capital} = \text{Current assets} - \text{Current liabilities} \qquad (2)$$

Example 6: CHANGES IN WORKING CAPITAL

Refer to Example 5 and prepare a changes in working capital statement.

SOLUTION

The decreases and increases are listed in columns to facilitate easy comparison.

Decreases in Working Capital		*Increases in Working Capital*	
Increase in accounts payable	$1.0	Increase in accounts receivable	$2.5
Decrease in cash	2.0	Increase in inventory	3.0
Total	$3.0	Total	$5.5

Working capital increased $2.5 million. While the firm is somewhat less liquid since its cash has decreased, its working capital has increased. The funds were derived from profits, depreciation, and additional long-term debt. They were used to increase working capital, fixed assets, and pay dividends.

A simple method to check the accuracy of a changes in working capital statement involves calculating the working capital for each year and subtracting to determine the difference.

Example 7: CHANGES IN WORKING CAPITAL—A CHECK

Refer to Example 6 and check the accuracy of the change in working capital.

SOLUTION

Working capital = Current assets − Current liabilities
Applying this formula to Example 6, the values for 1975 and 1976 are shown below:

	1975	1976
Current assets	$ 10.5	$ 14.0
Current liabilities	− 3.0	− 4.0
Working capital	$ 7.5	$ 10.0

Working capital did increase by $2.5 million from 1975 to 1976.

Example 8: SOURCES AND USES OF FUNDS (PRO-FORMA)

Hill Brothers, Inc. had the 1976 balance sheet shown below. They projected 1977 financial statements as shown. Construct a pro-forma sources and uses of funds statement for 1977.

Balance Sheet (pro-forma)
(in millions)

Assets	Dec. 31, 1976	1977	Liabilities and Owners' Equity	Dec. 31, 1976	1977
Cash	$ 3	$ 8	Accounts payable	$12	$13
Accounts receivable	10	8	Accrued wages	7	5
Inventory	12	16	Accrued taxes	6	5
Fixed assets (net)	30	20	Notes payable	6	8
	$55	$52	(long-term)		
			Long-term debt	10	8
			Common stock	8	6
			Retained earnings	6	7
				$55	$52

Income Statement (pro-forma) Dec. 31, 1977

Sales		$ 38
Materials	$10	
Rent	6	
Interest	2	
Salaries	7	
Depreciation	5	
Total expenses		− 30
Earnings before taxes		$ 8
Taxes		− 4
After-tax profit		$ 4

SOLUTION

The fixed assets account shows a net decrease of $10. This results from the decrease of fixed assets by $5 during the year. The solution is shown in tabular form.

Fixed assets, Dec. 31, 1976	$ 30
Less depreciation for 1977	− 5
	$ 25
Fixed assets, Dec. 31, 1977	− 20
Decrease in fixed assets	$ 5

Projected Sources and Uses of Funds Statement

Sources		*Uses*	
Decrease in account receivable	$ 2	Increase inventory	$ 4
Decrease in fixed assets	5	Decrease in accrued wages	2
Increase in accounts payable	1	Decrease in accrued taxes	1
Increase in notes payable	2	Decrease in long-term debt	2
After-tax profits	4	Decrease stock	2
Depreciation	5	Dividends	3
Total sources	$19		$14
		Increase cash	5
		Total uses	$19

The 1972 and 1973 sources and uses of funds statements for Technitrol, Inc. are shown below.

Technitrol, Inc.
Sources and Uses of Funds

| | Years Ended December 31, | |
	1973	1972
Source of funds:		
Income (loss) before extraordinary items	$466,393	($ 47,464)
Items not requiring outlay of working capital:		
Depreciation of property, plant and equipment	219,021	191,493
Amortization of intangibles and computer programs	10,181	18,613
Gain on sale of equipment	(2,944)	(5,623)
Working capital provided from operations, exclusive of extraordinary items	692,651	157,019
Extraordinary items		154,803
Deduct items not requiring outlay of working capital in the current year:		
Gain on sale of:		
Investment in subsidiary		(23,900)
Manufacturing facilities		(129,673)
Working capital provided from extraordinary items		1,230
Proceeds from sale of:		
Investment in subsidiary, net of working capital of $138,004 at date of disposition		25,394
Manufacturing facilities		829,200
Equipment	26,493	16,242
Increase in:		
Long-term debt		44,275
Deferred income taxes	16,300	
Loan on life insurance policy	177,575	
Decrease in:		
Noncurrent note receivable	20,000	
Intangibles	38,771	
Other assets	1,051	
Working capital		364,515
	280,190	1,279,626
	$972,841	$1,437,875
Application of funds:		
Purchase of:		
Property and equipment	$228,667	$ 551,146
Computer programs		27,550
Common stock for cancellation	8,900	29,584
Treasury stock	103,957	
Investment in affiliate		227,500
Increase in:		
Notes receivable, noncurrent		80,000
Cash value, officers' life insurance	17,916	17,610

(Cont.)   Technitrol, Inc.
                         Sources and Uses of Funds

| | Years Ended December 31, | |
	1973	1972
Excess cost of investment in subsidiary over underlying equity at acquisition		53,965
Other intangibles	21,632	247
Miscellaneous other assets	1,950	1,050
Reduction of:		
Loan on life insurance policy		148,029
Long-term debt	19,700	301,194
Increase in working capital	570,119	
	$972,841	$1,437,875

In both 1972 and 1973 a key source of funds was depreciation and amortization. Note that in each year they amounted to over $200,000.

The 1972 and 1973 changes in working capital statements for Technitrol, Inc. are provided below.

                              Technitrol, Inc.
                         Changes in Working Capital

| | Years Ended December 31, | |
	1973	1972
Summary of net changes in working capital:		
Increase (decrease) in current assets:		
Cash	($173,144)	$ 45,893
Short-term investment		(1,250,000)
Marketable securities	(11,475)	(29,370)
Accounts and notes receivable:		
Trade	373,996	208,556
Other	(412,039)	414,266
Affiliate	22,941	116,812
Federal income tax refund	(198,425)	198,425
Inventories	457,076	857,909
Prepaid expenses	(39,672)	78,826
	19,258	641,317
Decrease (increase) in current liabilities:		
Current portion of long-term debt		33,834
Notes payable	925,847	(925,847)
Accounts payable, trade	80,904	(264,691)
Accrued wages and other expenses	(89,117)	(45,643)
Accrued payroll and other taxes	19,510	(16,479)
Income taxes	(386,283)	212,994
	550,861	(1,005,832)
Increase (decrease) in working capital	$570,119	($ 364,515)

The working capital position improved dramatically from 1972 to 1973. However, even though the working capital increased by some $570,119 during 1973, the cash position deteriorated. $173,144 in cash was used, primarily to pay off the $925,847 in notes payable which had been accumulated during the prior year. It should also be noted that the company collected a large amount of receivables while concurrently expanding inventories.

Cash flow and profitability are closely interrelated. Profitability represents the return *on* investment which the firm has achieved through its operations. The cash throw-offs from depreciation, amortization, and other implicit expenses result in return *of* investment to the firm. *The total of after-tax profits plus implicit cash throw-offs is the cash flow from operations.* While the cash flow from operations is very important, to obtain the total picture of the flow of funds through a firm, it is necessary to construct a sources and uses of funds statement. The sources and uses of funds statement details all of the various sources of funds, including those from operations, and indicates how they were utilized by the firm.

QUESTIONS FOR DISCUSSION

1. Discuss the importance of cash flow versus profitability to the owners of a small and large business.
2. Explain the meaning and significance of cash flow.
3. Provide three examples of how a profitable firm could run short of cash.
4. How is the cash flow from the operations of the firm calculated?
5. Differentiate between implicit and explicit expenses.
6. Give six examples each of sources and uses of funds.
7. Differentiate between a sources and uses of funds statement and a changes in working capital statement.
8. Why are a change in cash balances and a change in retained earnings *not* considered to be either a source or use of funds?
9. Differentiate between return *on* investment and return *of* investment.

CONCEPTS TO REMEMBER

This chapter presents additional analytical tools which are a basis for financial management. Check to be sure you have them firmly in mind.

Cash Flow
Implicit Expenses
Explicit Expenses
Sources of Funds
Uses of Funds
Sources of Working Capital

Uses of Working Capital
Return on Investment
Return of Investment

PROBLEMS 1. The income statement from Peters Brothers is shown below. Determine the cash inflow from its operations.

Peters Brothers Income Statement

Sales		$ 500,000
Cost of goods sold	$200,000	
Gross profit		300,000
Selling expenses	$100,000	
Operating expenses	60,000	
Depreciation	30,000	
		− 190,000
EBIT		$ 110,000
Interest		− 25,000
EBT		$ 85,000
Tax		− 34,300
After-tax profits		$ 50,700

2. The operation of new equipment will result in added sales of $50,000 per year. Labor and materials will cost $35,000. The equipment will be depreciated at the rate of $7,000 per year. If the firm which owns the equipment has a 48% tax rate, determine the cash inflow which will result from using the equipment.

3. Suppose that a loan was made to buy the equipment in Problem 2. The loan requires yearly repayment of principal of $4,000, and the interest payment for the first year is $3,000. Determine the cash flow which will be generated during the first year the equipment is in use.

4. Smith and Kole had financial statements as shown. Construct a sources and uses funds statement for them.

Balance Sheet
(in millions)

Assets	Dec. 31, 1975	Dec. 31, 1976	Liabilities and Owners' Assets	Dec. 31, 1975	Dec. 31, 1976
Cash	$ 6	$ 2	Accounts payable	$ 6	$ 8
Accounts receivable	3	8	Long-term debt	8	18
Inventory	12	18	Common stock	16	16
Fixed assets (net)	70	80	Retained earnings	61	66
	$91	$108		$91	$108

Income Statement, Dec. 31, 1976

Sales		$ 120
Expenses		
Cost of goods	$50	
Administration	28	
Depreciation	10	
Interest	2	
		− 90
EBT		$ 30
Taxes		− 15
After-tax profits		$ 15

5. Construct a changes in working capital statement for Smith and Kole.
6. Construct a changes in working capital statement for Hill Brothers, Inc. using financial information provided in Example 8.
7. International Clothing had balance sheets and income statement as shown. Develop a sources and allocations of funds statement for 1976.

Balance Sheet
(in millions)

Assets	Dec. 31, 1975	1976	Liabilities and Owners' Assets	Dec. 31, 1975	1976
Cash	$ 1	$ 1.5	Accounts payable	$ 3	$ 4.5
Marketable securities	2	1	Notes payable	1	4.0
Inventory	5	6	Common stock	6	5.5
Accounts receivable	3	4.5	Retained earnings	4	4.5
Fixed assets, net	3	5.5			
	$14.0	$18.5		$14.0	$18.5

Income Statement, Dec. 31, 1976

Sales	$11,000,000
Cost of goods	− 5,000,000
Administrative expense	− 200,000
Depreciation	− 1,500,000
Interest	− 300,000
Earnings before taxes	$ 4,000,000
Taxes	− 2,000,000
After-tax profits	$ 2,000,000

Depreciation
and Amortization

chapter 4

In Chapter 3 we emphasized the importance of cash flow and the relation of depreciation and amortization to cash flow. In this chapter we shall discuss the methods which may be used to calculate depreciation and amortization.

DEPRECIATION

When an asset is purchased, it is necessary to match the expense with revenues during the years it is used. *Depreciation is a systematic recognition of such expenses in a historical framework so as to match the expense with revenues while the asset is being used.* Depreciation recognizes the eventual wasting of the asset through wear, obsolescence, or the like and provides for the recognition of the expense before or no later than its retirement.

The federal tax laws provide for the inclusion of depreciation as an income statement expense. The amount of depreciation represents a reasonable allowance for exhaustion, wear and tear, and obsolescence of depreciable assets used in a business. Inclusion of depreciation as a pre-tax (or tax-deductible) expense permits the recovery of the cost of an asset during its estimated useful life. The funds generated from depreciation (commonly termed depreciation cash throw-offs) may be used to replace the asset or, for other purposes. However, due to inflation, the funds generated through depreciation are seldom sufficient to replace the asset being depreciated.

To qualify for depreciation, an asset must have a useful life of one year or more and be used in a trade or business or held for production of income. Examples of depreciable assets include buildings (but not land), machinery, equipment, trucks, tools, and the like.

While depreciation is included on the income statement as an expense, it differs from other expenses in that it does not require any payment. Since depreciation does not require a cash outlay, it is categorized as an *implicit cost*. Other expenses which do require payment such as materials, labor, and electricity are called *explicit expenses*.

Depreciation is extremely important to accountants and financial managers for three reasons. First, it permits the appropriate allocation of costs for depreciable assets as they wear out in use or become obsolete. Second, it has extremely important effects on the amount of federal income taxes paid. Third, it is the primary vehicle through which the firm receives its return *of* investments.

To determine the depreciation for any asset, it is necessary to know three things:

1. The depreciable value of the item to be depreciated, that is, the amount of the cost of the item to be depreciated;
2. The useful life of the item to be depreciated;
3. The method of depreciation to be used in calculating the depreciation.

Depreciable Value

The depreciable value is merely the difference between the total cost of a depreciable asset and its estimated salvage value:

$$\text{Depreciable value} = \text{Total cost} - \text{Salvage value} \qquad (1)$$

The total cost of a depreciable asset includes its purchase price and all of the costs necessary to prepare it for use.

Example 1: TOTAL COST OF A DEPRECIABLE ASSET

Ridgeway Tool and Die is purchasing a turret lathe from Consolidated Suppliers. The purchase price is $12,000 FOB Madison, Wisconsin. Ridgeway is located in Newark, New Jersey. The shipping costs from Madison to Newark will be $750. Insurance will be $60 for the trip. Before Ridgeway can use the machine they must prepare a concrete foundation costing $750. The lathe will arrive on a railroad flatcar. Riggers with a crane will move the lathe from the car to the foundation for $250. Wiring and plumbing connecting costs will amount to $300. Determine the total cost of the lathe.

SOLUTION

All of the costs required to prepare the lathe for actual use are included in the total cost. It is this sum which would be listed on the balance sheet as the cost and which forms a basis for depreciation. The total cost is calculated as follows:

Purchase price	$12,000
Shipping	750
Insurance	60
Foundations	750
Rigging	250
Electrical & plumbing	300
Total cost	$14,110

Salvage value is the amount which management anticipates will be realized upon the sale of the asset when it is no longer useful in the business and retired from service. *The salvage value consists of an estimated sale price of the depreciated asset reduced by the cost of its removal and any selling costs involved:*

$$\text{Salvage value} = \text{Sale price} - (\text{Selling costs} + \text{Cost of removal}) \quad (2)$$

The sales price of many depreciable assets can be estimated with reasonable accuracy using industrial price guides or past experience. Similarly, the selling costs such as those incurred by holding an auction or removing machinery from its foundation to a railroad car can be estimated. Since selling and costs of removal often tend to be negligible, they are frequently ignored. Also, when the salvage value is expected to be quite low, it is set at zero. Then the depreciable value equals the total cost of the asset.

Example 2:   SALVAGE VALUE OF A DEPRECIABLE ASSET

Ace Finance provides automobiles for its collection agents. The cars are sold after three years. Using the National Auto Dealers Association (NADA) Wholesale Guide, Ace estimates the sales price to be $800 per car. On the average Ace has to spend about $100 to repair each car for sale. Determine the salvage value of a car.

SOLUTION

Sales price	$ 800
Less repairs	− 100
Salvage value	$ 700

The method of determining salvage value outlined above is used for all types of depreciable assets. Since most assets do decrease in value as they age, the salvage value is generally well below the purchase price. In some instances the value may actually increase with age. While it is unlikely that the value of a machine or other equipment would increase, except under conditions of rampant inflation, the value of buildings often does increase. If an asset such as a building should increase in value, any excessive depreciation is recaptured and taxed as ordinary income when it is sold.

Example 3:   DEPRECIABLE VALUE

The total cost of a new circular saw is $280. It is estimated to have a salvage value of $50. What is the depreciable value?

SOLUTION

$$\text{Depreciable value} = \text{Total cost} - \text{Salvage value}$$

Total cost	$ 280
Less salvage value	− 50
Depreciable value	$ 230

Useful Life of a Depreciable Asset

The useful life of an asset is the period over which that asset may reasonably be expected to function in a business. The useful life may be determined by the particular operating conditions and by experience gained in using similar assets *or* by adopting one of the useful life standards formulated by the Internal Revenue Service (IRS). One method provided by the IRS is the "Class Life Asset Depreciation Range System." To employ this system, the financial manager selects the useful life of an asset from a range of years designated for that particular class of assets. For example, the average useful life of a lightweight truck is four years. This is the period over which a business ordinarily would recover the cost of the truck by claiming annual depreciation deductions. Under the system, the depreciation period is selected from a range of years, the specified lower limit of which is three years and the specified upper limit, five years. A table providing the range of depreciable life for numerous classes of assets is included in IRS Publication 534, "Tax Information on Depreciation." Some excerpts from the table are provided below:

Asset Depreciation Range
(years)

Depreciable Asset	Lower Limit	Guideline Period	Upper Limit
Automobiles, taxis	2.5	3	3.5
Busses	7	9	11.0
Tugboats	14.5	18	21.5
Printing presses	9	11	13
Nuclear electric plants	16	20	24
Steam electric plants	22.5	28	33.5
Hotels	—	40	—

It should be noted that *the life periods specified above apply to new assets. For assets purchased used, the life is based on a reasonable estimate of the number of years remaining in the useful life of the asset.*

In some instances, it is desirable to depreciate assets rapidly over as short a period as possible in order to reduce taxable income as much as the law will permit. However, other circumstances may make it advantageous to depreciate over a longer period. Developing a strategy for depreciation will be examined in greater detail in Chapter 7.

Methods of Depreciation

Broadly speaking, there are two methods of depreciation: straight-line and accelerated. The latter includes sum-of-the-years'-digits and declining-balance. *Regardless of the method used, an asset may not be depreciated beyond its depreciable value.* Different methods provide for different rates of generating cash flow and profits. Nearly all corporations use both methods of depreciation. An accelerated method is used for calculation of taxable income since this reduces earnings before taxes and hence the firm's federal income tax liability. Straight-line is used to determine income for purposes of reporting to shareholders. The lower rate of depreciation obtained using straight-line results in higher EPS reported to shareholders. Reporting favorable earnings is desirable since dividends are derived from earnings, and earnings represent a measure of managerial ability. Both dividends and managerial ability are of key importance to investors. Since the federal income tax liability is established using an accelerated method, earnings before taxes reported to the IRS are minimized and, therefore, the tax is also minimized.

Examples of calculating depreciation by each of the commonly used methods are shown below. In applying each method, it is necessary to know the useful life and depreciable value of the asset.

1. *The straight-line method* is the simplest for computing depreciation. Under this method the cost or other basis of the property less its salvage value is deducted in equal annual amounts over the period of its estimated useful life.

Example 4:   STRAIGHT-LINE DEPRECIATION

A machine costs $11,000 and has a useful life of five years and a salvage value of $1,000. Find the yearly depreciation using the straight-line method.

SOLUTION

First determine the depreciable value.

Cost	$ 11,000
Less salvage value	− 1,000
Depreciable value	$ 10,000

Second, divide the depreciable value by the useful life of the machine. The result is the yearly depreciation.

$$\frac{\$10,000}{5 \text{ years}} = \$2,000/\text{year depreciation}$$

2. *Sum-of-the-years'-digits* depreciates greater portions of the depreciable value of an asset when the asset is newest or first put into use. Each year a fraction is multiplied by the depreciable value to obtain the amount of the yearly depreciation. The denominator of the fraction, which remains constant, is the total of the digits representing the years of estimated useful life of the property. For example, if the useful life is five years, the denominator is 15, that is, the sum of $1+2+3+4+5$.

The numerator of the fraction changes each year to represent the years of useful life remaining at the beginning of the year for which the computation is made. For the first year of a five-year estimated useful life, the numerator would be 5, for the second 4, etc.

Example 5:   SUM-OF-THE-YEARS'-DIGITS DEPRECIATION

A machine has an estimated useful life of four years. It cost $11,000 and has a salvage value of $1,000. Find the yearly depreciation.

SOLUTION

First add the digits of the life: $4+3+2+1=10$. Then multiply the fraction for each year by the depreciable value, $10,000.

Year	Fraction		Depreciable Value		Yearly Depreciation	Cumulative Depreciation
1	$\frac{4}{10}$	×	$10,000	=	$4,000	$ 4,000
2	$\frac{3}{10}$	×	10,000	=	3,000	7,000
3	$\frac{2}{10}$	×	10,000	=	2,000	9,000
4	$\frac{1}{10}$	×	10,000	=	1,000	10,000

3. *Declining-balance depreciation* subtracts the depreciation taken each year from the cost of the asset before computing the next year's depreciation, so that the same depreciation rate applies to a smaller or declining balance each year. Thus a larger depreciation deduction is taken in the first year and a gradually smaller deduction in succeeding years.

Within limits, the depreciation rate used is greater than the rate that would be applied in the straight-line method. Under some circumstances, twice the straight-line rate may be used; in other instances 1½ or 1¼ times the straight-line rate may be used.

The salvage value is not deducted from the cost of the asset in determining the annual depreciation allowance under the declining-balance method. That is, *the basis used to compute the depreciation is the total cost, not the depreciable value.* However, property may not be depreciated beyond its depreciable value.

Example 6:   DECLINING-BALANCE DEPRECIATION

A machine costs $15,000 and has a projected life of ten years and a salvage value of $3,000. Find the depreciation using 1½ declining balance.

SOLUTION

First determine the percentage depreciation which would be taken each year using the straight-line method. Since the life is ten years, 10% would be depreciated each year if straight-line were used.

Next, determine the percentage to be depreciated using 1½ times straight-line. 1½ × 10% = 15%.

Last, calculate the depreciation for each year. *Note that the depreciation is calculated using the total cost of $15,000, not the depreciable value of $12,000. However, the total depreciation may not exceed the $12,000.* The calculations are shown below:

Year			Yearly Depreciation	Cumulative Depreciation
1	.15 × $15,000	=	$2,250.00	$ 2,250.00
2	.15 × (15,000–2250)	=	1,912.50	4,162.50
3	.15 × (15,000–4162.50)	=	1,625.62	5,788.12
4	.15 × (15,000–5788.12)	=	1,381.78	7,169.90
5	.15 × (15,000–7169.90)	=	1,174.51	8,344.41
6	.15 × (15,000–8344.41)	=	998.33	9,342.74
7	.15 × (15,000–9342.74)	=	848.59	10,191.33
8	.15 × (15,000–10,191.33)	=	721.30	10,912.63
9	.15 × (15,000–10,912.63)	=	613.10	11,525.73
10	12,000–11,525.73	=	474.27	12,000.00

It should be noted that during the tenth year the amount of depreciation is obtained by subtracting the cumulative depreciation from the depreciable value. If the same method used for other years had been used in the tenth year, the depreciation would have been $521.14. If this had been used, the result would have been a cumulative or total depreciation of $12,046.87. Since property may not be depreciated beyond its depreciable value, depreciation is limited to $12,000 for this machine, and therefore the depreciation in the tenth year is limited to $474.27.

Selecting a Method of Depreciation

The process of selecting a method for depreciation consists of two steps:

1. Management decides whether there is a particular advantage in using an accelerated depreciation method rather than straight-line.
2. Then management determines which method of accelerated depreciation is permitted under tax law for the asset to be depreciated.

The first decision is the most difficult because it requires development of a financial strategy. As indicated previously, this subject will be dealt with in Chapter 7. However, for reference, the chart below shows the amount of depreciation which would be charged against an asset costing $10,000 and having no salvage value.

Year	Straight-Line Yearly Depn.	Cum. Depn.	Double-Declining Yearly Depn.	Cum. Depn.	Sum-of-the-Years'-Digits Yearly Depn.	Cum. Depn.
1	$1,000	$ 1,000	$2,000	$2,000	$1,820	$ 1,820
2	1,000	2,000	1,600	3,600	1,640	3,460
3	1,000	3,000	1,280	4,880	1,450	4,910
4	1,000	4,000	1,024	5,904	1,270	6,180
5	1,000	5,000	820	6,724	1,090	7,270
6	1,000	6,000	655	7,379	910	8,180
7	1,000	7,000	524	7,903	730	8,910
8	1,000	8,000	420	8,323	550	9,460
9	1,000	9,000	336	8,659	360	9,820
10	1,000	10,000	268	8,927	180	10,000

The substantial differences in the amounts of depreciation chargeable from year to year on the basis of the three methods in the illustration indicate that the selection of a method is a matter of considerable importance.

In this example the double-declining method results in total ten-year depreciation of only $8,927. To achieve the full $10,000 in depreciation, federal tax laws permit a firm to switch from declining-balance to straight-line at any time. This permits the firm to obtain the full depreciation of the asset. In the example the firm would switch from double-declining to straight-line in the seventh year. The total depreciation taken during the first six years is $7,379. Subtracting this figure from $10,000 leaves $2,621 to be depreciated over the remaining four years, or $655 per year. The switch is made in the seventh year because this provides the maximum acceleration under the double-declining method. If the switch were made in the sixth year, the straight-line depreciation would be less than that permitted under double-declining. *Usually the switch from double-declining-balance to straight-line is made after two-thirds of the estimated useful life of an asset has been exhausted.*

Determining which method of accelerated depreciation *may* be used is a relatively simple procedure of referring to the IRS Publication 534 mentioned earlier. Some examples of the types of assets which may be depreciated at accelerated rates are given below.

Straight-line: All new and used property.
Twice declining-balance (double-declining): New residential real estate

(such as apartment houses) and property other than real estate (such as machinery) acquired new and having a life of three or more years.

One and one-half declining-balance: New real estate other than residential and property other than real estate acquired used and having life of three or more years.

One and one-quarter declining-balance: Used residential real estate with a life of 20 years or more.

Sum-of-the-years'-digits: Same as twice declining-balance.

It should be noted that even though an asset may be depreciated at an accelerated rate, straight-line *may* always be used. In addition, if there is a slower accelerated rate, that also may be used. For example, new residential real estate may be depreciated using double-declining-balance. However, it may also be depreciated using one and one-half or one and one-quarter declining-balance or straight-line.

Depreciation—A Financial Viewpoint

The discussion of depreciation so far has dealt with its calculation as an expense item included in an income statement and reflected in the balance sheet. The balance sheet shows the book value of fixed assets equaling their original total cost less any accumulated depreciation:

$$\text{Book value} = \text{Total cost} - \text{Accumulated depreciation} \qquad (3)$$

While the book value is very important for accounting and record-keeping purposes, the actual market value of a particular asset may be either less than or greater than the book value. Knowledge of the actual fair market value of the asset is extremely important to the financial manager. This fact will be demonstrated in the examples below.

Example 7:   FAIR MARKET VALUE ABOVE BOOK VALUE

Colonial Investment purchased a new apartment house three years ago for $1 million. It had a 20-year life and was depreciated straight-line using a salvage value of $200,000. Recently it was appraised at $1.3 million. Find the difference between the book value and fair market value.

SOLUTION

First, determine the book value. The yearly depreciation is

$$.05\,(\$1,000,000 - \$200,000) = \$40,000.$$

Three years' depreciation would be $120,000.

Cost	$ 1,000,000
Less accumulated depreciation	− 120,000
Book value	$ 880,000
Fair market value	$ 1,300,000
Less book value	− 880,000
Difference	$ 420,000

As indicated in Chapter 2, the profitability of an investment is very important to the owners. One measure of profitability is the return on assets:

$$\text{Return on assets} = \frac{\text{Earnings before taxes}}{\text{Average total assets}} \qquad (4)$$

Example 8: RETURN ON ASSETS USING BOOK VALUE VERSUS FAIR MARKET VALUE

Continuing with Example 7, suppose the before-tax income from the apartment house is $100,000 per year. Calculate the return on assets using book value and fair market value.

a. Book value $\qquad \dfrac{\$\ 100,000}{\$\ 880,000} = 11.36\%$

b. Fair market value $\qquad \dfrac{\$\ 100,000}{\$1,300,000} = 7.69\%$

While continued ownership of the apartment may seem desirable based on book value, the financial manager should certainly consider the alternative of selling the property, paying the taxes involved, and investing the remainder in a project with a higher yield. Many owners of real estate, especially those using accelerated forms of depreciation, find it expedient to sell their investments after about seven years.

Example 9: BOOK VALUE ABOVE FAIR MARKET VALUE

Refer to Example 1. The total cost of the lathe to Ridgeway Tool and Die is $14,110. This included the purchase price and shipping and installation costs. Ridgeway decided to depreciate the machine over a ten-year life with an estimated salvage value of $4,110. After two years of use a new machine was introduced on the market which would be substantially less expensive to operate. How should the financial manager value the old machine?

SOLUTION

After two years the book value would be as shown:

Total cost	$ 14,110
Less accumulated depreciation	− 2,000
Book value	$ 12,110

This book value is not the market value of the machine. It is the value based on using the machine for another eight years and selling it as was originally planned. The actual current market value is the price a willing buyer will pay for the machine less any costs of preparation for sale. In this situation, where the machine is at least somewhat obsolete, the sale price might be less than half the original purchase price of $12,000. Further, cost of removal would probably range around $500. Thus, the realizable amount might be only about $5,500. This amount is significantly different from the book value of $12,110. In this case the book value is meaningless. The financial manager would need to have a realistic estimate as to the amount to be realized from the old machine. With this he could determine the additional investment required for the new machine and then decide if the savings in operating costs warranted the additional investment.

Usually if a machine, motor vehicle, or property other than real estate is sold in a relatively short period after purchase, the amount realized from the sale is significantly less than the book value. Normally, none of the costs of installing machinery or preparing it for use can ever be recovered. When the question of sale and replacement of a depreciable asset is under study, the actual amount which will be realized from the sale of the currently owned asset is of key importance. There is likely to be a *great* difference between the book value and the amount realizable to the firm.

AMORTIZATION

Amortization is very similar to depreciation. *Amortization is a procedure used to recover investment in intangible assets used in a business.* Examples of intangibles which may be amortized include secret formulas, patents, copyrights, and covenants not to compete. The process of amortization is quite similar to depreciation, but only the straight-line method may be used. Once the value of an intangible asset and its useful or legal life has been established, the amortization is calculated. *Only those intangibles which have a definite, specified useful or legal life may be amortized for purposes of determining federal income tax liability.* Thus, since goodwill and trade names do not have specific limited lives, they may not be amortized for tax purposes.

Patents, for example, may be amortized over their useful lives, which are 17 years. If an 8-year-old patent were purchased, it would be amortized over its remaining life of 9 years. Production processes are amortized over their expected useful lives. When intangibles are amortized, the salvage value is assumed to be zero, and the straight-line method is used.

A further restriction on amortization relates to the method used to acquire the asset. If a patented process is acquired for a given price, the amount is capitalized on the firm's books and amortized over the useful or legal life of the asset. If, however, a *process* is developed by a firm, the situation may differ substantially. Generally, firms which develop processes have research and development departments. Usually the cost of running these departments is charged as an ongoing expense of operating the business. Hence, if a process is developed and the cost of development is recorded as an operating expense, then the cost of developing the process is *not capitalized*. Consequently, the development costs may not be amortized.

Example 10:   AMORTIZATION OF A PATENTED PROCESS

Eastern Oil purchased a patented process used in the production of high-test gasoline in 1965. The patent cost $4 million and had a remaining life of 16 years. What was the yearly amortization of the patent?

SOLUTION

Using straight-line over 16 years: $\dfrac{\$4,000,000}{16} = \$250,000.$

The amortization is $250,000 per year.

Depreciation and amortization are very important to the financial management of a business. Both are used to recover the firm's investment whether it be in tangible or intangible property. It is necessary for the financial manager to understand the methods of depreciation allowable under law in order to select the method which will result in the most favorable profit picture from the viewpoint of the owners' needs.

QUESTIONS
FOR
DISCUSSION
1. Define depreciation, salvage value, depreciable value, total cost, useful life of an asset, book value, implicit cost, explicit cost, tangible and intangible asset.
2. Calculation of depreciation would be greatly simplified if straight-line were used exclusively. Why are other methods of depreciation used?
3. Explain how you would estimate the fair market value of an electric motor having an expected life of 15 years when it is 2 years old if it cost $75. Does this answer differ significantly from the book value? Why?
4. For purposes of depreciation, why is it necessary to use the total cost of an asset rather than just the purchase price?
5. Compare the yearly depreciation using sum-of-the-years'-digits versus double-declining-balance. What advantage would one have over the other?
6. Under what circumstances would the fair market value of an asset being depreciated be greater or less than the book value? Is it possible for the fair market value to be less than the book value at a given time and greater than book value at another time?
7. Differentiate between depreciation and amortization.
8. Why may patents be amortized while goodwill may not be amortized for purposes of calculating federal income tax liability?
9. Indicate all of the methods which may be used to depreciate the following assets: (a) a new machine having a life of 6 years, (b) an apartment house purchased used having a life of 20 years, (c) a machine purchased used having a life of 5 years.

CONCEPTS
TO
REMEMBER

This chapter has presented detailed procedures for determination of depreciation and amortization. While some of the following concepts have already been introduced, they are very important.

Implicit Costs
Explicit Costs
Depreciable Value
Salvage Value
Useful Life
Capital Good
Accelerated Depreciation
Amortization
Straight-Line
Declining Balance Depreciation
Sum-of-Years'-Digits Depreciation
Basis for Depreciation
Fair Market Value
Book Value
Return on Assets

PROBLEMS

1. A new machine costs $8,000 and has an estimated salvage value of $2,000 and a life of six years. Determine the following:

   (a) The depreciable value.
   (b) The yearly depreciation using straight-line depreciation.
   (c) The book value of the machine after three years.
   (d) The cumulative depreciation after four years.

2. A new machine costs $1,200 and has an estimated salvage value of $200. If it is depreciated over its four-year life using sum-of-the-years'-digits method, indicate the amount of depreciation per year and the cumulative depreciation.

Year	Depreciation	Cumulative Depreciation
1		
2		
3		
4		

3. Repeat Problem 2 using double-declining-balance depreciation. To depreciate the machine to its salvage value, how much would have to be depreciated in the fourth year?

4. A property has a projected life of 25 years. It cost $1 million including the land. However, land is not depreciable. The land has a value of $100,000, and the projected salvage value of the building is $200,000. Determine the difference between the straight-line and double-declining depreciation for the first 10 years of the life of the building.

5. A new piece of machinery has a purchase price of $10,000. Other costs required for installations, etc., are listed below:

Transportation	$500
Insurance during transit	35
Foundations	350
Electrical connection	250
Rigging costs	200

   If the salvage value is expected to be negligible, determine the depreciation for the first five years using sum-of-the-years'-digits. Assume a ten-year life.

6. Fortune, Inc. uses sum-of-the-years'-digits depreciation. It is depreciating a machine over five years. The original cost was $15,000, with expected salvage of $5,000. Determine the depreciation per year.

7. To achieve the maximum acceleration using a declining-balance

method of depreciation, it is often necessary to switch to straight-line during the latter part of the life of the asset. Consider an asset costing $10,000, with no salvage value and a ten-year life to be depreciated at double-declining-balance. To achieve the maximum degree of acceleration, determine the year the transition from double-declining to straight-line should be made.

8. Suppose you purchased a new apartment house having a life of 30 years and depreciated it using double-declining for 7 years. What proportion of the total depreciable value would remain? What does this imply about the profitability of the building in future years? Assume the apartment cost $50,000, not including the land.

9. Suppose you purchased a 25-year-old apartment house. Would the depreciation during the first 5 years be greater using straight-line with a 15-year life or one and one-quarter declining-balance with a 20-year life? Assume the building cost $30,000 exclusive of land and has an estimated salvage value of $5,000.

10. A patent was purchased for $1 million with an eight-year remaining life. Determine the amount by which it may be amortized per year.

Corporate Taxation

chapter 5

In Chapter 1, the basic goal of the operation of a business was stated as "maximizing the wealth of the owners." Increases in wealth of the owners generally come from after-tax profits. The purpose of studying taxation is to learn how taxes are calculated. With this knowledge, a strategy can be developed to minimize the amount of taxes paid. Minimizing the tax paid, of course, results in a greater sum of funds available for the owners, which may be distributed as dividends or retained by the firm for use in increasing profits or at least maintaining profits at their current level. In Chapter 5 we shall deal with fundamental principles of federal taxation of corporations. In Chapter 6 we shall explore some of the details of individual taxation. The two areas are further examined in Chapter 7, with special emphasis on selection of an organizational form for a business in order to minimize taxation.

TAXATION OF ORDINARY INCOME (Income derived from the usual operations of the firm)

The corporate taxable income (earnings before taxes) is that portion of the total income remaining after all of the operating and administrative expenses and interest are paid and depreciation is deducted. The calculation of tax payable is a simple matter once the taxable income has been determined. All corporations bear income tax on ordinary income at the same rate:

First $25,000 taxed at 20%
Next $25,000 taxed at 22%
Over $50,000 taxed at 48%

Note that prior to 1975, the first $25,000 of taxable income was taxed at 22%. Amounts over $25,000 were taxed at 48%. Congress and the president change tax rates periodically in keeping with fiscal economic policies.

Example 1: TAX ON OPERATING INCOME

Ridgeway Products, Inc. had taxable income of $100,000.
Determine their federal income tax liability for 1975.

SOLUTION

$$
\begin{array}{rl}
\$25,000 \times .20 = & \$\ 5,000 \\
25,000 \times .22 = & 5,500 \\
50,000 \times .48 = & 24,000 \\
\hline
\text{Total tax} & \$34,500 \\
\end{array}
$$

Example 2: CALCULATION OF TAXABLE INCOME

The Apex firm had yearly sales of $1 million.
Costs are listed below:

Cost of goods sold	$600,000
Administrative expense	100,000
Interest costs	40,000
Depreciation	50,000

Determine their federal income tax liability for 1975.

SOLUTION

Calculation of taxable income:

Sales	$ 1,000,000
Cost of goods sold	− 600,000
Administrative expense	− 100,000
Interest costs	− 40,000
Depreciation	− 50,000
Taxable income (EBT)	$ 210,000

Calculation of tax liability:

$$
\begin{array}{rl}
\$\ 25,000 \times .20 = & \$\ 5,000 \\
25,000 \times .22 = & 5,500 \\
160,000 \times .48 = & 76,800 \\
\hline
\text{Total tax} & \$87,300
\end{array}
$$

Taxable income (EBT)	$210,000
Total tax	− 87,300
After-tax profit	$122,700

Of course, a corporation may incur a loss in its operations. If a corporation has a net loss for any year (taking all its operations into account), the loss can be used to reopen the tax liability for previous years. Thus, if a firm has a net loss on all of its operations for any year (that is, losses exceed profits from various operations), the loss may be applied against taxable income from other years. *The process, known as loss carry back and carry forward, operates as follows: The loss must first be applied against taxable income made three years prior to the loss, then two years prior, working forward to the fifth year after the loss has occurred.* This permits the firm to apply a loss in one year against profits in *eight* years, starting three years before the loss and ending five years after the loss. Any unused loss remaining after the fifth year following the loss is no longer available to the corporation as a deduction. In practice, a corporation would file an application for refund with the Internal Revenue Service commencing with the third year prior to the loss and request a refund of tax.

Example 3:   TREATMENT OF A NET OPERATING LOSS

Taxable income and income tax paid are shown for Conway Corporation for the years 1972–1975:

	1972	1973	1974	1975
Taxable income (in $1,000s)	$500	$300	$200	($600)
Tax paid (actual amounts based on tax rates applicable for years shown)	233.5	137.5	89.5	0

Determine the amount of refund Conway would request.

SOLUTION

The loss for 1975 would first be offset against the profits for 1972; 1972 is three years before 1975.

Taxable income (1972)	$ 500
Less loss	− 600
Remaining loss carry back	$ 100

Since the 1975 loss exceeds the 1972 profit, an application for refund should be filed for 1972, requesting a refund of the entire $233,500 tax paid in 1972.

The balance of the 1975 loss would be offset against the 1973 profits:

Taxable income (1973)	$ 300
Less balance of loss	− 100
Remaining taxable income	$ 200
Original tax paid	$ 137.5
Less new tax (1973)	− 89.5
Refund due (1973)	$ 48.0

The new tax for 1973 is calculated as follows based on a taxable income of $200,000, using the pre-1975 tax rates:

$ 25 × .22 =	$ 5.5
175 × .48 =	84.0
Revised 1973 tax	$89.5

The total amount refunded would be

$$\$233.5 + \$48.0 = \$281.5 \quad \text{or} \quad \$281,500$$

If the loss in 1975 had exceeded $800,000, the process shown above would have been carried into 1974. Had the loss exceeded $1 million, then any remaining portion of the loss would be deducted from taxable income in the years following 1975, starting with 1976, until 1980.

TAX ON DIVIDENDS RECEIVED FROM DOMESTIC CORPORATIONS

If a corporation receives a dividend from another domestic corporation, only 15% of the dividend is subject to federal income tax. The 15% subject to tax is taxed as ordinary income.

Example 4: TAX ON DIVIDEND INCOME

Sterling Fabrics, Inc. had an operating income of $100,000 in 1976. The firm also received a dividend from another domestic firm of $45,000. What is the amount of the tax liability for 1976?

SOLUTION

Only 15% of the $45,000 dividend is subject to taxation. This amounts to $6,750. Thus, a total of $106,750 is taxed at ordinary income rates.

$$
\begin{array}{rcl}
\$25,000 \times .20 & = & \$\ 5,000 \\
25,000 \times .22 & = & 5,500 \\
56,750 \times .48 & = & 27,240 \\
\hline
\text{Total tax} & & \$37,740
\end{array}
$$

TAX ON PURCHASE AND SALE OF CAPITAL ASSETS, DEPRECIABLE AND REAL PROPERTY

Capital gains and losses take place when a firm buys and subsequently sells assets or securities which are not ordinarily purchased and sold in the business of the firm. For example, a fruit market is in the business of selling fruit. If this business purchased a piece of land for future expansion and subsequently sold the land, a capital gain or loss could be generated. However, the buying of fruit and subsequent resale at a higher price is *not* considered to be a capital gain for two reasons:

1. Fruit does *not* constitute a capital asset, depreciable, or real property;
2. The sale of fruit *is* the ordinary business of the store.

Some firms are in the business of buying and selling items which are generally categorized as capital goods. For example, a wholesale heavy machinery distributor purchases and sells heavy machinery. Even though this machinery is generally considered to be capital equipment by the final purchaser who uses the machinery, the profits or losses incurred in the sales *are not considered as capital gains or losses to the distributor.* Rather, the profits or losses are included as a part of the distributor's ordinary income. The reason for including them as ordinary income is that the sales are the ordinary business of the distributing firm.

There are two categories of capital gains and losses: short-term and long-term. Short-term refers to those gains or losses resulting from the sale of capital assets or securities *held six months or less*, while long-term refers to those purchased over six months prior to their sale.

Short-term capital gains and losses are added to obtain the net short-term capital gain (or loss). Any short-term gains are added to the firm's ordinary income. Thus, *short-term gains are taxed at the ordinary corporate tax rates as a part of ordinary income.*

Similarly, long-term capital gains and losses are added to obtain the net long-term capital gain (or loss). If the result is a net long-term capital gain (gains exceed losses), the gain is taxed as follows in accordance with the 1975 rates established by Congress.

1. Long-term capital gains are taxed as ordinary income at the 20% rate until the sum of the ordinary income plus the capital gain exceeds $25,000;
2. When the sum of ordinary income plus capital gains exceeds $25,000, any excess up to $50,000 is taxed at 22%;
3. When the sum of ordinary income plus capital gains exceeds $50,000, then capital gains are taxed at 30%.

If a firm has net long-term capital gains and short-term capital losses, the short-term losses are subtracted from the long-term gains. The difference is taxed as a long-term capital gain as described above.

Example 5:   TAX ON A LONG-TERM CAPITAL GAIN

The Langtree Corporation had ordinary income of $20,000 and a long-term capital gain of $15,000 in 1976. Determine the Langtree Corporation's tax liability for 1976.

SOLUTION

The first $5000 of the long-term capital gain is taxed at 20% along with the $20,000 ordinary income. The remaining $10,000 of the capital gain is taxed at 22%.

Ordinary income	$20,000 × .20 =	$4,000
Capital gain	5,000 × .20 =	1,000
Capital gain	10,000 × .22 =	2,200
Total tax		$7,200

Example 6:   TAX ON A LONG-TERM CAPITAL GAIN

Trying Corporation had a taxable income of $30,000 and a long-term capital gain of $30,000. Determine their federal income tax liability.

SOLUTION

The first $25,000 of the ordinary income is taxed at 20%; the remaining $5,000 is taxed at 22%. Since $5,000 of ordinary income is to be taxed at 22%, only $20,000 of the capital gain may be taxed at 22%. The remaining $10,000 is taxed at 30%. The tax is summarized below:

Ordinary income	$25,000 × .20 =	$ 5,000
Ordinary income	5,000 × .22 =	1,100
Capital gain	20,000 × .22 =	4,400
Capital gain	10,000 × .30 =	3,000
Total tax		$13,500

Recapture of Depreciation

Recapture of depreciation is a process which takes place when a *depreciated asset is sold for an amount in excess of its book value.* Since the sale price is in excess of the book value, we can conclude that it was depreciated too rapidly. The excessive depreciation is recaptured and taxed as ordinary income. *Recall that the amount and rate at which an asset is depreciated are set in order to approximate the actual reduction in value of the asset over its life. In many instances the actual rate at which an asset decreases in value does not equal the rate at which it is depreciated.* If the asset is depreciated too rapidly, a recapture of depreciation and, in some instances, a capital gain will be effected. If the asset is depreciated too slowly so that the book value is more than the actual salvage value, a capital loss is affected. *The amount of recapture of depreciation is added to ordinary income for tax purposes.* This is logical since depreciation was deducted as an expense to reduce income in the past.

Example 7:   DETERMINATION OF RECAPTURE OF DEPRECIATION AND
CAPITAL GAIN

Barbadose, Inc. purchased a property, including a building and land in 1965, for $1 million. It subsequently depreciated the building by $400,000, leaving the book value of the property at $600,000. In 1975, it sold the property for \$1.2 million. Barbadose had no other income in 1975. Determine the recapture of depreciation, the long-term capital gain, and the tax paid by Barbadose.

SOLUTION

The capital gain is the difference between the *sale* and *purchase* price.

Sale price	\$ 1,200,000
Less purchase price	− 1,000,000
Capital gain	\$ 200,000

The recapture of depreciation is the difference between the *purchase* price and the *book* value in this example.

Purchase price	\$ 1,000,000
Less book value	− 600,000
Recapture of depreciation	\$ 400,000

The tax is calculated as follows:

Recapture	\$ 25,000 × .20 =	\$ 5,000
Recapture	25,000 × .22 =	5,500
Recapture	350,000 × .48 =	168,000
Long-term capital gain	200,000 × .30 =	60,000
Total tax		\$238,500

Example 8: DETERMINATION OF RECAPTURE OF DEPRECIATION AND CAPITAL GAIN

Same as Example 7 except the sale price of the building is \$800,000.

SOLUTION

Since the sale price did not exceed the purchase price, there is no capital gain. However, there is a recapture of depreciation. The recapture of depreciation in this case is the difference between the *sale* price and the book value.

Sale price	\$ 800,000
Less book value	− 600,000
Recapture of depreciation	\$ 200,000

The recapture would be taxed as ordinary income as follows:

$$
\begin{array}{rl}
\$\ 25{,}000 \times .20 = & \$\ 5{,}000 \\
25{,}000 \times .22 = & 5{,}500 \\
150{,}000 \times .48 = & 72{,}000 \\
\hline
\text{Total tax} & \$82{,}500 \\
\end{array}
$$

Example 9:   TAX ON A CAPITAL GAIN AND RECAPTURE OF DEPRECIATION

A firm having ordinary income of $100,000 sold a machine for $70,000. It had purchased the machine several years ago for $50,000 and had depreciated it to a book value of $20,000. Determine the tax resulting from the sale.

SOLUTION

Sale price	$ 70,000
Less purchase price	− 50,000
Capital gain	$ 20,000
Purchase price	$ 50,000
Less book value	− 20,000
Recapture of depreciation	$ 30,000

Recapture is included as a part of ordinary income for tax calculations. The total income taxed at the ordinary rate is therefore $130,000.

$$
\begin{array}{rl}
\$25{,}000 \times .20 = & \$\ 5{,}000 \\
25{,}000 \times .22 = & 5{,}500 \\
80{,}000 \times .48 = & 38{,}400 \\
\hline
& \$48{,}900 \\
\end{array}
$$

Since the recapture and ordinary income exceed $50,000, the capital gain is taxed at 30%.

$$\$20{,}000 \times .30 = \$6{,}000$$

The total tax is therefore $48,900 + $6,000 = $54,900.

Long-Term Capital Losses

Section 1231 of the Internal Revenue Code provides that certain long-term capital losses may be deducted from ordinary income. The capital losses are limited to the following:

1. Losses incurred in the sale of real property used in the taxpayer's business;

2. Losses incurred in the sale of depreciable assets used in the taxpayer's business.

The treatment of Section 1231 applies only when the total capital losses exceed capital gains. Then the net losses which meet the requirements described above may be deducted from ordinary income. Real and depreciable assets are those which are used in the business, such as buildings, machinery, and the like. Land or precious metals purchased for speculative purposes and sold at a loss would not qualify for the liberal treatment offered under Section 1231.

Example 10:   CAPITAL LOSS (SECTION 1231)

The Finlay Floor Company purchased a piece of machinery in 1965 to install wall-to-wall carpeting for $30,000. It had depreciated the machine by $15,000 when it sold it in 1973 for $10,000. Determine the amount of capital loss.

SOLUTION

$$\text{Book value} - \text{Sale price} = \text{Capital loss}$$

Book value	$ 15,000
Less sale price	− 10,000
Capital loss	$ 5,000

The capital loss was incurred on a machine used in the business, and hence the loss may be deducted directly from Finlay's ordinary income for purposes of determining federal income tax liability.

The special treatment of long-term capital losses covered by Section 1231 is of particular importance to financial managers. The timing of sale of capital assets becomes very important. For example, suppose a firm could sell two assets. The sale of the first would result in a $10,000 long-term capital gain, while the second would result in a $10,000 loss covered by Section 1231. If the firm sold both in the same year, the gain and loss would just offset each other, and there would not be any change in tax paid. However, if the gain were taken one year and the loss the next, a substantial tax saving would be enjoyed. Assume the firm's tax rate is 48% on ordinary income and 30% on capital gains. The tax savings on the Section 1231 loss would be $4,800. However, the additional tax payable on the gain would be only $3,000 since the tax rate is 30%. A net tax savings of $1,800 would be obtained. Section 1231 makes the timing of disposal of capital assets extremely important.

If there is a net long-term capital loss in any year on the sale of assets not covered by Section 1231, it may not be deducted from ordinary income of the same or any other year. It must be applied against long-term capital gains from the other years. The loss must first be applied against long-term capital gains made three years *prior* to the loss, then two years prior, working forward to the fifth year *after* the loss has occurred. This permits the firm to apply a long-term capital loss in one year against gains in eight years, starting three years prior to the loss and ending five years after the loss. Any loss remaining after the fifth year following the loss is no longer available to the corporation as a deduction. In practice, the corporation should file an application for refund commencing with the third year prior to the loss and request a refund of tax.

Example 11:   TREATMENT OF A NET LONG-TERM CAPITAL LOSS

Richardson, Inc. had a record of earnings and long-term capital gains and losses through 1975 as shown (all figures in thousands):

	1971	1972	1973	1974	1975
Ordinary income	$300	$300	$250	$325	$350
Long-term capital gains (losses)	8	10	35	20	($ 47)*
Tax paid	139.9	140.5	124.0	155.5	

Losses not subject to Section 1231.

Determine Richardson's tax liability for 1975 and the amount of refunds it will request for prior years.

SOLUTION

Since capital losses may be applied only against gains, the ordinary income is irrelevant and need not be considered, other than in the calculation of the 1975 tax liability.

Calculation of 1975 Tax Liability

$$
\begin{array}{rcr}
\$\ 25{,}000 \times .20 & = \$ & 5{,}000 \\
25{,}000 \times .22 & = & 5{,}500 \\
300{,}000 \times .48 & = & 144{,}000 \\
\hline
\text{Total} & & \$154{,}500 \\
\end{array}
$$

Calculation of tax refund from prior years. The capital loss in 1975 is carried back three years to 1972 and applied to the capital gain in that year of $10,000. Since the capital loss of 1975 exceeds $10,000, a refund would be requested for all the tax paid on the 1972 capital gain. The tax rate is 30%, and the refund for 1972 is therefore

$$\$10,000 \times .30 = \$3,000$$

The remaining capital loss from 1975 is next applied against the capital gain of $35,000 in 1973. Since $37,000 of the 1975 loss still remains, a refund would be requested for all the tax paid on the 1973 capital gain. The refund requested for 1973 would be

$$\$35,000 \times .30 = \$10,500$$

The remaining portion of the capital loss is next applied against the capital gain of $20,000 in 1974. Since only $2,000 loss still remains, the refund for it is for the tax on $2,000 of capital gain:

$$\$2,000 \times .30 = \$600 \quad \text{refund requested for 1974}$$

Year	Refund Requested
1972	$ 3,000
1973	10,500
1974	600
Total refund	$14,100

MARGINAL AND AVERAGE TAX RATES

The marginal tax rate is the rate of tax applied to taxable income exceeding a given amount. For example, suppose a firm had taxable income of $30,000 in 1975. The marginal tax rate on taxable income in excess of $25,000 but not exceeding $50,000 is 22%. The marginal tax rate on taxable income exceeding $50,000 is 48%. Similarly, the marginal tax rate on capital gains if taxable income exceeded $50,000 would be 30%.

The average tax rate is obtained by dividing the total tax liability by the taxable income:

$$\text{Average tax rate} = \frac{\text{Tax liability}}{\text{Taxable income}} \tag{1}$$

Example 12: AVERAGE TAX RATE

Assume a firm had taxable income of $100,000. Calculate the average tax rate using the tax rates applying to 1974 and 1975.

SOLUTION

First, calculate the average rate for 1974. The tax is determined as shown:

$$
\begin{array}{rl}
\$25,000 \times .22 = & \$\ 5,500 \\
\$75,000 \times .48 = & 36,000 \\
\text{Total} \quad = & \$41,500
\end{array}
$$

The average rate is determined using Eq. (1):

$$
\text{Average tax rate} = \frac{\$41,500}{\$100,000} = 41.5\%
$$

Next, calculate the average rate for 1975. The tax is determined as shown:

$$
\begin{array}{rl}
\$25,000 \times .20 = & \$\ 5,000 \\
\$25,000 \times .22 = & 5,500 \\
\$50,000 \times .48 = & 24,000 \\
\text{Total} & \$34,500
\end{array}
$$

The average rate is determined using Eq. (1):

$$
\text{Average tax rate} = \frac{\$34,500}{\$100,000} = 34.5\%
$$

Note that with the reduced tax rates applying to 1975 the average tax rate decreased from 41.5% to 34.5% in this example. The reduction in tax rate has been especially important to small businesses since many of them have low taxable incomes.

SUBCHAPTER S CORPORATIONS

The tax laws included as Subchapter S of the Internal Revenue Code provide that the owners of small corporations may elect to be taxed as though the firm were a sole proprietorship or partnership. Subchapter S is limited to corporations with ten or fewer shareholders. The owners declare any corporate profits as a part of their personal income and pay the appropriate tax. The advantage to this procedure is that the shareholders may avail themselves of the legal advantages of a corporation while avoiding corporate income taxes. This may be financially advantageous and will be discussed further in Chapter 7.

1. Define the following terms: tax shelter, ordinary income, taxable income, capital gain, recapture of depreciation, domestic corporation, Subchapter S Corporation.
2. Explain how a net operating loss is treated for purposes of federal income taxation.
3. Explain how the corporate income tax is calculated on dividends received from other domestic corporations.
4. Distinguish the sale of a capital asset from the sale of other assets such as inventory in a business operation.
5. In some instances, recapture of depreciation equals the purchase price of a depreciable asset less the book value. In other instances, the recapture equals the sale price less the book value. Explain.
6. Explain how a net capital loss is treated for purposes of federal income taxation. Include a discussion of the treatment afforded under Section 1231.
7. When Section 1231 is involved, why is the timing of the sale of assets very important?

CONCEPTS
TO
REMEMBER

   This chapter introduces the processes of corporate taxation. Several very important new procedures and concepts are introduced. Be sure you understand them.

Ordinary Income
Taxable Income
Operating Loss
Capital Gain (Short- and Long-Term)
Capital Loss
Subchapter S Corporation
Capital Goods
Recapture of Depreciation
Section 1231 Capital Losses
Loss Carry Forward and Back
Marginal Tax Rate
Average Tax Rate

PROBLEMS
1. The Robert's Shoe Store, Inc. had taxable income in 1975 of $125,000. Calculate the amount of tax it had to pay.
2. Referring to Problem 1, what was the *average* rate of tax paid by Robert's in 1975? What would the average rate have been if the taxes were based on the pre-1975 rates?
3. Zenith, Inc. has had the taxable income shown in the table below. In 1975 it had a loss of $450,000. If the firm files applications for refunds for the appropriate years, indicate the amount of refund it will request. The firm derived all of its income from its operations.

	1971	1972	1973	1974	1975
Taxable income	$300,000	$200,000	$200,000	$100,000	($450,000)

4. Referring to Problem 3, suppose that the loss in 1975 were $600,000 and that the taxable income resulting from profits in 1976 were $250,000. How much tax would Zenith, Inc. have to pay in 1976?

5. The ABC Company purchased a building for $500,000 ten years ago. It has depreciated the building by $300,000, giving a book value of $200,000. If it sells the building for $600,000, how much *additional* tax will it have to pay? Assume the firm has a taxable income from ordinary operations of $100,000.

6. The Andus Corporation has received a dividend of $50,000 from another domestic corporation. Andus already has $100,000 in taxable ordinary income. Calculate the total tax Andus will have to pay.

7. A machine is purchased for $90,000 and depreciated by $35,000 so that the book value is $55,000. At the time the book value is $55,000, the machine is sold for $125,000. If the corporation has no other taxable income, how much tax will it have to pay on the sale?

8. The ABC Company has a marginal tax rate of 48%, with 30% for capital gains. It purchased a piece of machinery ten years ago for $50,000, having depreciated it straight-line, based on a 20-year life and $10,000 salvage value. The company is considering selling the machine for $60,000. Calculate the additional tax it will have to pay if it sells the machine.

9. Referring to Problem 8, suppose the firm sold the machine for $25,000. What would be the effect on ABC's tax liability?

10. Delano, Inc. has a 48% marginal tax rate, with 30% for capital gains. It has two assets which they may sell. The former will result in a $50,000 long-term capital gain and the latter a $60,000 capital loss under Section 1231. Determine the additional tax savings if the assets are sold in two different years rather than during the same year.

11. The following information is known concerning Concord, Inc. for 1975:

Sales	$2,000,000
Cost of goods	1,300,000
Interest expense	200,000
Administrative expense	75,000
Depreciation	50,000

In 1974 Concord had incurred a major loss. The loss was carried back for all of the three previous years, and $100,000 still remains of the 1974 loss. In 1965, a machine was purchased for $55,000. It had a projected life of 20 years and a salvage value of $5,000 and had been depreciated using the straight-line method. The company sold the machine in 1975 when it was 10 years old for $40,000. Determine the tax liability for Concord in 1975.

12. Garnet Company had a record of earnings and long-term capital gains and losses through 1975 as shown (all figures in thousands):

	1971	1972	1973	1974	1975
Ordinary income	$200	$180	$200	$250	$300
Long-term capital gain (losses)	10	.15	20	($ 5)*	($ 20)*

*Losses are not subject to Section 1231.

Determine Garnet's tax liability for each of the years shown based on the information for that year; then compute the amount of refund Garnet would request for those years when they incurred long-term capital losses.

13. Capital equipment was purchased with a total cost of $80,000. The projected life was ten years, and the salvage value was $20,000. It was depreciated using sum-of-the-years'-digits for five years at which time it was sold for $100,000. The corporation which owned the asset had other income from operations of $15,000. Calculate the firm's federal income tax liability.

14. Altier, Inc. had income from operations as shown. If they suffered a loss of $300,000 in 1975, determine the amount of refund they would request.

	1972	1973	1974	1975
Pretax income	$200,000	$500,000	$100,000	($300,000)

15. Suppose Altier had an income statement for 1975 as shown below. Determine Altier's cash flow for 1975. Be sure to consider the tax refund from prior years.

Sales	$ 1,000,000
Cost of goods	— 600,000
Administrative costs	— 200,000
Interest	— 200,000
Depreciation	— 300,000
EBT	($ 300,000)

Personal Taxation

chapter 6

The primary function of operating a business has been indicated to be the maximization of the wealth of the owners. If the business is a large corporation, then the owners may enjoy increases in wealth via cash dividends or capital gains if the market price of the common stock increases. If the firm is a small corporation, the owners may participate in the operations, and in addition to dividends and stock price increases they may receive wages or salaries. Further, if the firm is a sole proprietorship or partnership, the owners receive remuneration as wages or salaries. All forms of remuneration, whether they be salaries, wages, dividends, or capital gains, are subject to federal taxation. It is important to the individual, both as an investor and employee, and the firm's management to know how taxation affects management decisions and investors' and employees' income. With the knowledge of taxation the investor may decide his individual preference for dividends versus capital gains as a method for wealth maximization. In addition, it is important for all persons who are employed to understand the basics of federal taxation.

The purpose of this chapter is to provide a brief overview of the federal tax laws relating to taxation of individuals and married couples. The material is presented to introduce the basic procedures used to compute federal tax liability.

The procedures used to calculate tax for individuals and couples differ substantially from the corporate tax laws. In particular, individuals are taxed at varying rates depending on their income and marital status. Also, whereas the tax rate applied to corporations is a simple 20%, 22%, or 48% for ordinary income and 30% maximum for capital gains, the rates for individuals and couples increase in gradual steps to a maximum 70% (with 50% maximum on earned income).

CALCULATION OF FEDERAL TAX LIABILITY

There are four different tax rate tables for persons depending on their marital status. The most important are the tables for single taxpayers and for married taxpayers filing joint returns. The rates given may change from year to year, but for purposes of problem solving, the rates applicable to 1976 are included as Tables V and VI in Appendix A at the end of the book. The IRS also provides other very detailed tax schedules. These are useful for persons with gross incomes up to $15,000 and indicate the exact amount of tax payable depending on the number of dependents the taxpayer has.

Example 1: Tax Liability for a Married Couple

John and Mary Cline have a taxable income of $16,350. Determine their federal income tax liability.

Solution

Refer to Table VI in Appendix A. The Clines' taxable income is over $16,000 but less than $20,000. Hence, their tax is $3,260 plus 28% of the amount *exceeding* $16,000.

$$.28 \times \$350 = \$ \quad 98$$
$$\underline{3,260}$$
$$\text{Total tax} = \overline{\underline{\$3,358}}$$

Example 2: Tax Liability for a Single Person

Barbara Dunlap, an executive secretary, has a taxable income of $10,300. Determine her federal income tax liability.

Solution

Refer to Table V in Appendix A. Barbara's taxable income is over

$10,000 but less than $12,000. Hence, her tax is $2,090 plus 27% of the amount exceeding $10,000.

$$.27 \times \$300 = \$\ \ \ 81$$
$$2,090$$
$$\text{Total tax} = \overline{\$2,171}$$

CALCULATION OF "ADJUSTED GROSS INCOME"

To calculate taxable income, the amount of total income which an individual or married couple has received over the year must be known. While income from almost all sources is subject to taxation, there are two common exceptions which should be noted. Under most circumstances the following types of income are not subject to federal income tax:

1. The first $100 of dividend income received by a single person or the first $200 of dividend income received by a married couple.
2. Interest received from municipal bonds. The term *municipal bond* includes most state, county, and local bond issues and some bonds issued by government authorities such as turnpike authorities.

The most important types of income which are subject to federal taxation are wages, salaries, tips, and other forms of employee compensation (earned income) as well as dividends and interest (except as noted above), capital gains, and income from the operation of a proprietorship or partnership (business income). For a given year, the various types of income are added to form *the adjusted gross income*. One exception should be noted: Only one-half of long-term capital gains is subject to taxation, while all short-term capital gains are taxed.

Example 3:   ADJUSTED GROSS INCOME

Richard and Clara Smith are both employed. Richard works in a steel mill. Last year his base salary was $11,232. In addition, he made $2,315 in overtime. Clara is a waitress. She received a salary of $3,500 and received $4,300 in tips. The Smiths have bank accounts and a savings certificate. They receive interest from these amounting to $1,650. Calculate their adjusted gross income.

SOLUTION

All of the income listed above is subject to tax.

Richard's salary	$11,232
Richard's overtime	2,315
Clara's salary	3,500
Clara's tips	4,300
Interest	1,650
Adjusted gross income	$22,997

Example 4:   ADJUSTED GROSS INCOME

Donald Smith, who is not married, has a salary of $8,700. In addition, he operates a small business as a sole proprietorship. The business had a profit of $2,600. Donald owns stock and received $300 in dividends. His interest income from bank accounts amounted to $275. Determine his adjusted gross income.

SOLUTION

All of the income items listed above form a part of the adjusted gross income. However, the first $100 of dividends is not taxed.

Salary	$ 8,700
Business income	2,600
Dividend: ($300 less $100 exclusion)	200
Interest	275
Adjusted gross income	$11,775

Example 5:   ADJUSTED GROSS INCOME

Michael and Donna Jones have income as shown below:

Michael's salary	$ 8,700
Donna's salary	13,000
Interest	400
Dividends	1,200
Long-term capital gain	850
Short-term capital gain	600
Total sources of income	$24,750

Michael also operates a small apartment house. The income statement for the apartment house is shown below:

Income Statement

Rents		$ 6,000
Expenses		
Taxes	$1,200	
Interest on mortgage	2,300	
Repairs	400	
Heat	500	
Electricity	200	
Other	250	
Depreciation	1,500	
		− 6,350
Pretax profit (loss)		($ 350)

Determine the Jones' adjusted gross income.

SOLUTION

All of the items listed are subject to taxation. However, $200 of the dividends is excluded, and only one-half of the long-term capital gains is taxed.

Michael's salary	$	8,700
Donna's salary		13,000
Interest		400
Dividends. ($1,200 less $200 exclusion)		1,000
Long-term capital gain		425
Short-term capital gain		600
	$	24,125
Less business loss	−	350
Adjusted gross income	$	23,775

CALCULATION OF DEDUCTIONS

Various deductions may be subtracted from the adjusted gross income in order to determine the taxable income.

$$\text{Taxable income} = \text{Adjusted gross income} - \text{Deductions} \qquad (1)$$

Deductions fall into two basic categories: deductions for dependents and either standard or itemized deductions.

Deduction for Dependents

For each dependent, including yourself, your spouse, and your children, $750 may be deducted as an exemption. Further, if you or your spouse is over 65 years of age or blind, an additional $750 may be deducted for each (i.e., if a person were blind *and* over 65, then he or she would be allowed an added $1,500 deduction, for a total of $2,250).

Example 6:   DEDUCTION FOR DEPENDENTS

Harry and Mildred White have four children. Two of the children are married and not supported by the Whites. The other two children are living at home and depend on the Whites for support. Mr. White is 67 years old. Mrs. White is 62. Determine the total deductions for dependents.

SOLUTION

The calculation of dependents is shown below:

	Dependent Exemptions
Mr. White (over 65)	2
Mrs. White	1
Two children	2
Total	5

5 dependent exemptions × $750 per exemption = $3,750

Standard and Itemized Deductions

1. *Standard deduction:* For persons who do not itemize their deductions as described in paragraph 2 below, a standard deduction is available. The amount of the standard deduction depends on the marital status of the taxpayers. The minimum standard deduction is $1,600 for an individual and $1,900 for a married couple. This minimum is also referred to as a low-income allowance. The maximum increases to 16% of adjusted gross income up to $2,300 for a single person and $2,600 for a married couple. Prior to 1975 the deduction was limited to 15% of adjusted gross income up to a maximum of $2,000 for both single persons and married couples.

Example 7:   STANDARD DEDUCTION

The Smiths are married and have an adjusted gross income of $21,000. Determine their standard deduction.

SOLUTION

16% of $21,000 is $3,360. Since $2,600 is the maximum standard deduction, they are limited to $2,600.

Example 8:   STANDARD DEDUCTION

Ellen Watson is single and has an adjusted gross income of $7,500. Determine her standard deduction.

SOLUTION

16% of $7,500 is $1,200. Since the minimum standard deduction for an individual is $1,600, Ellen would have a standard deduction of $1,600.

2. *Itemized deductions:* Rather than using a standard deduction, some taxpayers find it advantageous to itemize their deductions. The types of expenses which may be included as itemized deductions are listed below:

a. Medical and dental expenses not covered by insurance. The amount deductible is limited to that *in excess of* 3% of the adjusted gross income (with some exceptions).

b. Taxes such as state and local income, real estate (local property), state and local sales, state gasoline, and personal property.

c. Interest expense such as that incurred on a home mortgage, car purchase, installment loan, charge accounts, and the like; but *not* repayment of any loan principal.

d. Charitable contributions such as those to religious organizations or educational institutions.

e. Certain casualty and theft losses.

f. Miscellaneous items such as alimony payments, union dues, etc.

Normally, in preparing an income tax return, a taxpayer would add the items included in the itemized category. If the sum exceeds the standard deduction, then the itemized deduction would be used. If not, the standard deduction would be used.

In addition to the aspects of federal tax regulations described below, the 1975 tax law includes an additional $30 deduction from tax liability for each personal exemption. This exemption is limited to $30 per person regardless of age or whether the person is blind. This one-year special exemption was designed to stimulate economic growth and might not be extended. Therefore, it is not included as a part of the calculation of tax in this book.

CALCULATION OF TAXABLE INCOME

The calculation of taxable income as indicated above is simply a matter of subtracting the deductions from the adjusted gross income:

$$\text{Taxable income} = \text{Adjusted gross income} - \text{Deductions}$$

Example 9:   TAXABLE INCOME

Peter and Laura Dugan are married and have one child. Their income is listed below:

Peter's salary	$10,300
Laura's salary	12,600
Dividends	450
Interest	300
Total	$23,650

They have various expenses, some of which may be used as itemized deductions as follows:

Local property taxes	$1,050
State income tax	300
State sales tax	500
Total medical expenses not covered by insurance	650
Charitable contributions	400
Interest on mortgage	1,500
Interest on car payment	200
Interest on charge accounts	40

Determine Peter and Laura's federal income tax liability.

SOLUTION

First, determine the adjusted gross income. Note that all of the income items listed are subject to tax. However, the first $200 of dividend income is excluded.

Peter's salary	$10,300
Laura's salary	12,600
Dividend income	250
Interest	300
Adjusted gross income	$23,450

Second, determine the deductions for dependents which the Dugans are allowed. There are three persons in the family, and since the Dugans are not blind or over 65, they are entitled to three deductions:

3 dependents × $750 per dependent = $2,250 deduction for dependents

Third, determine the Dugans' itemized and standard deductions. One or the other may be used, whichever is greater. The standard deduction is 16% of the adjusted gross income, limited to $2,600.00 maximum.

$$\$23,450 \times .16 = \$3,752.00$$

Since $3,752.00 exceeds the $2,600.00 maximum, the Dugans' standard deduction is limited to $2,600. If their itemized deduction exceeds $2,600, they will use it rather than the standard deduction.

All of the expense items listed may be included as itemized deductions. However, only the medical expenses exceeding 3% of the adjusted gross income may be included as an itemized deduction. This amount is calculated below:

$$\$23,450 \times .03 = \$703.50$$

Since the medical expenses are less than $703.50, none may be deducted. The other expenses total as shown:

Local property taxes	$1,050
State income tax	300
Sales tax	500
Charitable contributions	400
Interest on mortgage	1,500
Interest on car payment	200
Interest on charge account	40
Itemized deductions	$3,990

Fourth, determine the taxable income.

$$\text{Taxable income} = \text{Adjusted gross income} - \text{Deductions}$$

$$\text{Taxable income} = \$23,450 - (\$2,250 + \$3,990)$$

$$\text{Taxable income} = \$17,210$$

Last, determine the Dugans' federal income tax liability. Refer to Table VI in Appendix A. The Dugans' taxable income falls between $16,000 and $20,000. Therefore, their tax is $3,260 + 28% of the amount exceeding the $16,000.

$.28 \times \$1,210 =$	$ 338.80
	3,260.00
Tax liability =	$3,598.80

The Dugans' total federal income tax liability is $3,598.80.

Example 10:   TAXABLE INCOME

Repeat Example 9, but assume the Dugans rented an apartment for $300 per month instead of owning a home.

SOLUTION

The Dugans' adjusted gross income and deductions for dependents remain the same. However, not owning a home, they would not have deductions for mortgage interest or house taxes as itemized deductions.

First, determine the Dugans' itemized deductions.

State income tax	$ 300
Sales tax	500
Charitable contributions	400
Interest on car payment	200
Interest on charge account	40
Itemized deductions	$1,440

Since the total itemized deductions *are less* than the permitted standard deduction of $2,600, the Dugans would use the standard deduction.

Second, determine taxable income.

$$\text{Taxable income} = \text{Adjusted gross income} - \text{Deductions}$$

$$= \$23,450 - (\$2,250 + \$2,600)$$

$$\text{Taxable income} = \$18,600$$

Last, determine the Dugans' federal income tax liability. Refer to Table VI in Appendix A. The Dugans' taxable income falls between $16,000 and $20,000. Therefore, their tax is $3,260 + 28\%$ of the amount exceeding $16,000.

.28 × $2,600	=	$ 728
		3,260
Tax liability	=	$3,988

The Dugans' tax liability is $389.20 greater if they rent rather than own a property with property taxes and mortagage interest as indicated in Example 9. Even though a family may pay more for rent than they would on property taxes and mortgage interest, none of the rent is deductible. This fact has resulted in many people claiming that the federal tax laws favor homeowners rather than renters. Also, it has led to increased popularity of condominiums. Condominium owners enjoy apartment style living while paying property taxes, service fees, and mortgage interest (if a mortgage is used). The property taxes and interest may be included as itemized deductions.

SOCIAL SECURITY TAXES

In addition to federal income taxes, Social Security (FICA) taxes are imposed on all persons having earned income. Earned income includes salaries, wages, tips, etc., but does not include income from dividends, interest, capital gains, etc. Social Security tax is imposed on nearly all working people, with the major exception being employees of the federal government.

Both persons who are subject to Social Security and their employers pay 5.85% of the employees' salaries up to a base amount established by Congress. During 1974, the base amount was $13,200, and so both employer and employee paid a maximum of $772.20 per year for a total of $1,544.40. The base amount increased during 1975 to $14,000, raising the maximum contribution to $824.85 each. The base was again increased in 1976 to $15,300, for a maximum contribution of $895.05 and is projected to increase to $16,500 in 1977. Persons who are self-employed also pay the Social Security tax, but at a rate of 7.9%. Thus, in 1976, the *total* contribution for a self-employed person would be $1,208.70. The Social Security tax has increased significantly in recent years as the number of persons receiving benefits and the amount of benefits have been increased.

The amount of Social Security tax paid does not depend on marital status. Thus, if both husband and wife work at jobs covered by Social Security, each must pay the tax.

Example 11:   SOCIAL SECURITY TAX

Referring to Example 9, Peter and Laura Dugan's incomes are listed below:

Peter's salary	$10,300
Laura's salary	12,600
Dividends	450
Interest	300
Total	$23,650

Determine the amount of Social Security tax they will pay.

SOLUTION

Note first that only the earned income is subject to Social Security tax. The tax is calculated separately for each person.

Peter:	$10,300 × .0585	$ 602.55
Laura:	$12,600 × .0585	737.10
	Total Social Security tax	$1,339.65

TOTAL PERSONAL TAXES

As a conclusion to this chapter, it is valuable to determine the total taxes which a family pays during a year. The total is the sum of the following taxes: federal income tax, Social Security tax, state income tax, state sales tax, local income tax, local sales tax, property and all other taxes (gasoline, etc.).

Example 12: TOTAL TAXATION

Referring to Example 9, calculate the total taxes the Dugans will pay, assuming they own their home.

SOLUTION

The taxes are listed below. They were obtained using the list of itemized deductions in Example 9 and the answers to Examples 9 and 11.

Local property taxes	$1,050.00
State income tax	300.00
Sales tax	500.00
Federal income tax	3,598.80
Social Security tax	1,339.65
Total	$6,788.45

Actually, the Dugans pay many other taxes, such as gasoline and numerous hidden taxes. However, this example shows that they pay nearly $7,000 in just the major taxes. Starting with an income of $23,650, only $16,861.55 remains.

QUESTIONS
FOR
DISCUSSION

1. Some people claim that the tax laws favor single people over married couples. Examine the tax tables (Tables V and VI in Appendix A) and see if you agree.
2. A $750 deduction is allowed for each dependent. For a family with

a taxable income of $14,000, how much of a savings in tax dollars will result from one additional dependent? Is this amount sufficient to support a child? Do the federal income tax laws encourage or discourage having families?

3. Do you feel that the federal income tax laws discriminate against those who rent rather than own their homes? Why?

CONCEPTS TO REMEMBER   This chapter details the procedures used in determining personal tax liability. Several new terms and concepts are introduced which are of special interest to the reader.

Adjusted Gross Income
Municipal Bond
Taxable Income
Deductions for Dependents
Standard Deduction
Itemized Deduction
Social Security Taxes

PROBLEMS

1. For a single person and married couple, determine the federal income tax liability given the following taxable incomes: $8,300, $14,500, $43,000.

2. Richard and Clara Dunlap are married and have no children. Their adjusted gross income is $15,600. They have the expenses listed below:

House property taxes	$ 850
Total interest	1,300
Sales tax	200
State income tax	150
Gasoline tax	200
Charity	600

Determine their total federal income tax liability if they file a joint income tax return.

3. Donald White, who is single, works for an insurance company and also operates a small apartment house. His salary is $15,000. In addition, he received commissions of $2,300. The apartment house operated at a loss of $1,400. Determine Donald's adjusted gross income. If he had one dependent in addition to himself, and standard deductions, determine his federal income tax liability.

4. The Browns have an adjusted gross income of $22,000 for 1975. They have incurred expenses listed below during the year:

Local property taxes	$1,400
Mortgage interest	1,500
Auto loan interest	200
Installment loan interest	175
Sales taxes	275
Charitable contributions	1,100
Medical expenses*	1,200
Gasoline taxes	300

Of this, $400 was covered by insurance.

(a) If the Browns have two children, determine their federal tax liability.

(b) A portion of the Browns' income resulted from salaries and wages as follows: Mr. Brown, $14,000; Mrs. Brown, $6,000. Determine the Social Security tax each of the Browns paid and their total yearly tax bill. Use the 1976 Social Security rates.

5. Peter and Thelma Seymour have income for 1975 as follows:

Peter's salary	$17,500
Thelma's salary	15,000
Interest	2,200
Dividends	500
Long-term capital gains	1,400
Short-term capital gains	600

The Seymours have three children and the expenses listed below:

Property taxes	$2,400
Mortgage interest	2,000
Other interest	600
Medical expenses	300
Sales tax	400
State income tax	600

(a) Determine the Seymours' federal income tax liability.

(b) Determine the amount of Social Security tax the Seymours will have to pay using the 1976 rates.

(c) Recalculate the Seymours' federal income tax liability based on their renting a home rather than purchasing one.

6. The Social Security tax has been growing substantially in recent years. At present, many individuals and married couples pay more in Social Security tax than in federal income tax. Consider a family of four with one working person, a standard deduction, and no unearned income.

Determine how much the wc
fore the amount of federal in
Security tax paid.

7. Bill and Sally live together.
standard deduction. If they g
pay more or less total federa
instance. (*Note*: This proble
rather unusual impacts of the

8. Richard and Donna had incoi
They are married and have
come tax liability.

Sour

Richard's sal
Donna's salai
Donna's com
Interest
Dividends
Long-term ca
Short-term ca

Property taxes
Mortgage interest
Mortgage princip
Installment loan i
Sales tax
Medical expenses
State income tax

9. Referring to Problem 8, if D
Security taxes, determine the
which Richard and Donna will
rates.

Summary of Taxation and Its Relationship To Business Operations

chapter 7

For the complex of knowledge concerning depreciation methods and tax laws introduced earlier to be of value to the financial manager, he must be able to apply the procedures to practical situations. Specifically, these topics must be considered by the financial manager as he pursues his goals within a business firm or government agency or in his own personal life. In this chapter we shall indicate some ways in which the information may be utilized. Specifically, two important topics are examined, with particular emphasis on their tax implications:

1. Organization of a small business: corporation versus sole proprietorship;
2. Selection of a method of depreciation.

ORGANIZATION OF A SMALL BUSINESS

In the study of business law, the relative benefits of various forms of business organizations are discussed. One attractive feature of the corporate form is that the shareholders generally cannot be held liable for any debts or claims against the corporation. For example, if the corporation should incur large debts and find itself unable to pay them, the shareholders may not be called upon to assume the payment of the debt. The most the shareholders can lose is their investment, that is, the amount they paid for the stock. The concept of *limited shareholder liability* was clearly evident with the bankruptcy of the Penn Central Railroad. While the firm owes millions of dollars to numerous creditors, the shareholders, as such, are not liable for any of the debt.

The situation tends to be different for small businesses. Major creditors such as banks will usually not lend funds to small corporations unless the owners are willing to pledge their personal assets as collateral for the loans. Then, if the corporation is unable to repay the debts, the owners may be forced to do so.

There is a second aspect to the concept of limited liability of the corporation. Assume, for example, that a business owned property and that through some negligence on the part of the business someone were severely injured. The business, of course, would be liable for a just award to the injured party. The award might be very large. If the business were a sole proprietorship or partnership, the owners would have to pay the award, assuming the business did not have sufficient insurance or other funds to pay. Under the corporate form of organization, the owners would not be liable. The owners would be protected by the corporate shield. Their loss would be limited to the value of the business, but their personal assets would be left intact.

To avoid the potentially severe consequences of such a financial loss, sole proprietors and members of partnerships usually purchase large liability insurance policies. One type of policy is called an "umbrella policy." This policy extends the coverage of other insurance policies such as automobile liability and property liability. Automobile liability, for example, is often $50,000/$100,000. This means that if one person is injured, the maximum liability payment from the insurance company will be $50,000, while if more than one person is involved, the maximum is $100,000. An "umbrella policy," for example, could pick up any additional liability exceeding the $50,000 or $100,000 and extend it up to $1 million.

Since the owner of a small business organized as a proprietorship can insure himself against liability for accidents, and since he generally must cosign and assume personal responsibility for repayment of business loans, the choice between the proprietorship and corporate form of ownership must be decided on another basis.

One important consideration in the organization of a small business is transferability of ownership. For example, an older person may want to facilitate the transfer of ownership of his business to the heirs upon death, or an owner may want to sell a portion of the business. Each of these transfers is greatly facilitated if the business is a corporation as opposed to a sole proprietorship or partnership.

A most important criterion in the selection of an organizational form is usually the amount of federal income tax which must be paid. If the corporate form is used, then both corporate and individual income taxes must be paid. If the organization is a sole proprietorship or Subchapter S Corporation, then only individual tax must be paid since the Subchapter S corporate income is included as a part of individual income. In some instances the total tax liability is less using the corporate form, while in other instances the sole proprietorship or Subchapter S Corporation organizational form results in lower tax. If a firm is organized as a partnership, each partner is taxed individually based on his share of the total profit.

Example 1:   PROPRIETORSHIP VERSUS CORPORATION ORGANIZATION

Donald and Ellen Eaton are contemplating the purchase of a business. They expect the earnings to amount to $40,000 before payment of salaries (to themselves), dividends, or taxes. The Eatons have two children and will have itemized deductions of $3,500. If the corporate form of organization is used, Donald will be paid $18,000 in salary, and Ellen $12,000. Determine whether a sole proprietorship or corporate form of organization would result in lower taxes.

SOLUTION

First consider the corporate form of organization. The corporation tax is calculated as follows:

Earnings	$ 40,000
Less salaries	− 30,000
Earnings before taxes	$ 10,000
Less taxes	− 2,000
After-tax profit	$ 8,000

In addition, the Eatons would have to pay personal taxes as follows:

Ronald's salary	$ 18,000
Ellen's salary	12,000
Adjusted gross income	$ 30,000
Less deductions for dependents	− 3,000
Less itemized deductions	− 3,500
Taxable income	$ 23,500
Less tax (Table VI[1])	− 5,500
Remainder	$ 18,000

[1] *Appendix A.*

Using the corporate form of ownership, the Eatons will have to pay $2,000 + $5,500 = $7,500 in federal income taxes.

Second, consider the sole proprietorship form of organization. The tax is calculated as follows:

Total earnings	$ 40,000
Less deductions for dependents	− 3,000
Less itemized deductions	− 3,500
Taxable income	$ 33,500
Less tax (Table VI)	− 9,290
Remainder	$ 24,210

Using the sole proprietorship form of ownership, the Eatons would have to pay $9,290 in federal income taxes. The Eatons would save $1,790 in federal income tax using the corporate form of organization. This results primarily from the lower corporate tax on income up to $25,000. The rate is only 20%, whereas the marginal tax rate for married couples with taxable income of $25,000 is 36%.

Example 1 points out that a real tax advantage may exist for persons who use the corporate form of organization for small businesses. The example did not, however, deal with the question of how much a corporation may pay its owners for their services. The IRS rulings limit the salaries paid to the owners to approximately the amount they would receive if employed doing the same work in a business owned by someone else. The IRS considers any payments in excess of legitimate salaries to be dividends. This results in "double taxation," as demonstrated in the following examples.

Example 2: PROPRIETORSHIP VERSUS CORPORATE ORGANIZATION

The Gordons own a business with sales of $2 million. Mr. Gordon is the president and operating manager and pays himself $65,000 per year. Mrs. Gordon is the vice president and is paid $50,000 per year. In reality, Mrs. Gordon functions only to a very limited extent in the business. The Gordons have four children and itemized deductions of $28,000. The business has earnings of $145,000 before deducting the Gordons' salaries and taxes. Determine the total tax paid.

SOLUTION

First, calculate the corporate tax.

Earnings	$ 145,000
Less Gordons' salaries	− 115,000
Taxable income	$ 30,000
Less tax	− 6,100
After-tax profit	$ 23,900

Then calculate the Gordons' personal taxes.

Salaries	$ 115,000
Less deductions for dependents	− 4,500
Less itemized deductions	− 28,000
Taxable income	$ 82,500
Less tax (Table VI)	− 34,790
Remainder	$ 47,710

The total tax bill would be $6,100 + $34,790 = $40,890.

Example 3:   LIMITATION OF SALARIES

The IRS investigated the Gordons and their business and determined that Mrs. Gordon's salary was excessive. The Gordons agreed that only $10,000 was legitimate and that the remaining $40,000 was really a dividend. Determine the additional tax which will be paid.

SOLUTION

First, calculate the corporate tax.

Earnings	$ 145,000
Less salaries	− 75,000
Taxable income	$ 70,000
Less Tax	− 20,100
After-tax profit	$ 49,900
Less dividends	− 40,000
Increase in retained earnings	$ 9,900

Then calculate the Gordons' personal taxes.

Salaries	$ 75,000
Dividends (less $200)	39,800
Adjusted gross income	$ 114,800
Less deductions for dependents	− 4,500
Less itemized deductions	− 28,000
Taxable income	$ 82,300
Less tax (Table VI)	− 34,584
Remainder	$ 47,716

The total tax bill would be $20,100 + $34,584 = $54,684. Thus, the Gordons and their business would pay an additional $13,794 in tax.

Example 3 demonstrates the concept of double taxation of dividends under the corporate form of organization. The dividends are taken from the *after-tax profit* of the corporation and are then subject to tax as a part of individual income. Two logical questions arise at this point:

1. Since the Gordons own the firm, would they be better off in the future to keep the earnings in the corporation rather than distributing them as dividends?
2. Would the Gordons be better off to operate under the guidelines for a Subchapter S Corporation?

The answer to the first question depends primarily upon whether or not the Gordons need the dividends to meet their living expenses. Assuming they do not need the dividend income, then they probably would be wiser to retain the earnings in the firm. However, the IRS *limits the amount of earnings which may be retained as cash or securities.* Generally, even a small corporation may keep up to $150,000. However, beyond that amount, unless the firm has a specific reason for building cash reserves, the reserves must be paid as dividends. The IRS may tax excess reserves at the rate of 27½% on the first $100,-000 of excess and 38½% on amounts over $100,000 of excess. This tax is called an *accumulated profits* tax. There may, however, be legitimate reasons for holding funds in excess of $150,000. For example, a firm might want to buy out another firm or purchase buildings or equipment, etc. Although some companies employ large amounts of debt in the purchase of their assets, other firms grow entirely from funds generated within the company and, hence, need large reserves from time to time. For example, the large multinational DuPont Corporation utilizes little debt. Rather, it generates funds internally to finance most of its expansion.

To determine the benefits of operating as a Subchapter S Corporation, it is necessary to calculate the tax involved.

Example 4:   SUBCHAPTER S CORPORATION

Subchapter S of the tax laws provides that the income from a small corporation may be included as a part of individual income. Referring to Example 2, the corporation had pretax earnings of $145,000. Also, the Gordons had four children and itemized deductions of $28,000. Determine the tax as a Subchapter S Corporation.

SOLUTION

The tax would be calculated in the same manner as if the $145,000 were salaries to the Gordons.

Earnings	$ 145,000
Less deductions for dependents	− 4,500
Less itemized deductions	− 28,000
Taxable income	$ 112,500
Less tax (Table VI)	− 52,930
Remainder	$ 59,570

The tax of $52,930 is less than the $54,684 calculated in Example 3. Thus, if the Gordons could not leave a major portion of earnings in the firm or pay Mrs. Gordon a large salary, they would be better off to operate as a Subchapter S Corporation.

As demonstrated above, the selection of an organizational form is extremely important for a small business. However, as a business grows, it almost always becomes necessary to utilize the corporate form, primarily because it is generally much easier to raise funds for expansion using the corporate form. As small firms grow, they often "go public." That is, they offer to sell stock to the public at large in order to raise needed funds. Normally, when the stock is sold to the public at large, the sale is accomplished through a securities broker, also called an investment banker. *The initial sale of stock to the new shareholders is called a primary sale.* The new owners may sell the stock or purchase more from other owners. These sales are called *secondary sales* and are generally accomplished through a stock exchange. Usually, when a firm first goes public, its stock is traded on the over-the-counter market. If the firm continues to grow, the stock may be traded on the American Stock Exchange (AMEX) or, ultimately, on the New York Stock Exchange (NYSE).

When a firm first goes public, the original owners usually retain a major portion of the ownership. That is, they remain major stockholders. Once an active *secondary market* for the stock has been established, the original owners often sell some of their shares of stock. They can put the funds into other investments and thereby build a diversified portfolio. *Utilization of a diversified portfolio serves to reduce the risk of their incurring severe economic loss.* If a person has all his funds tied up in one business and the business suffers losses, he is likely to also suffer substantial losses. However, if an investor spreads his funds among several businesses and one investment goes bad, he will lose only a small portion of his total investment. As indicated in Chapter 1, investors tend to be risk-averters.

If the owner of a business had as a primary goal only the building of a diversified portfolio, rather than going public, it would be logical to consider either selling the business outright or bringing in a partner. *It should be noted that the owner can usually realize a much higher price by selling his stock once the firm has gone public than he could have if he sold the firm or a portion thereof to an individual buyer.* The realization of a higher price results from the difference in the criteria applied by the purchasers. When an individual purchases a business he tends to weigh the value of the physical plant very heavily, especially if he will assume the managerial role after the purchase. In such instances an offer to purchase may be based almost exclusively on the value of the physical assets rather than the record of earnings under existing management. On the other hand, when shareholders contemplate the purchase of stock in a company, they weigh earnings, dividends, risk, economic factors affecting the business, and managerial ability more heavily than the value of the physical assets. The result is that the value of a firm's outstanding stock (number of shares multiplied by the market price per share) may often be *several times greater* than the value of the physical assets.

SELECTION OF A METHOD OF DEPRECIATION

In Chapter 4, the IRS guidelines for maximum allowable rates of depreciation were presented. They are reproduced again below for easy reference.

Straight-line: All new and used property.
Double-declining-balance: New residential real estate (such as an apartment house) and property other than real estate acquired new and having life of three or more years.
One and one-half declining-balance: New real estate other than residential (such as a manufacturing plant) and property other than real estate acquired used and having life of three or more years.
One and one-quarter declining-balance: Used residential real estate with a life of 20 years or more.
Sum-of-the-years'-digits: Same as double-declining-balance.

As indicated above, there may be no choice but to use straight-line for some types of properties. Further, straight-line *may* be used for *all* types of depreciable properties if the owners so desire. The other methods shown give the *maximum* rate at which an asset may be depreciated. For example, new residential property may be depreciated using double-declining-balance. However, it may also be depreciated at a slower rate such as one and one-half declining-balance or straight-line.

A strong argument in favor of accelerated depreciation is that heavy charges for depreciation should be concentrated in the early years of useful life because expenses for repairs and maintenance are likely to be relatively small in those years. In this way the overall cost of using the assets tends to be roughly equalized annually over the course of their lives. Another reason to seek a speedy write-off is obsolescence. New equipment may be developed which is superior to the equipment purchased only a few years ago. Obsolescence may reduce the market value of an asset very quickly. A third reason to accelerate depreciation is that during inflationary periods, prices of replacement equipment and facilities rise rapidly. Hence, it is desirable to generate cash through depreciation cash throw-offs as early in the life of an asset as possible.

The primary consideration in selecting an accelerated method versus straight-line is that it tends to *reduce* profits and income taxes while *increasing* cash flow.

Example 5: STRAIGHT-LINE VERSUS ACCELERATED DEPRECIATION

A small, older apartment house costing $32,000 has yearly rentals of $5,460. Operating expenses are $2,720. It will be depreciated over 20 years. Assume the building is worth $28,000 and has zero salvage value. Financing will be by a $12,000 down payment and a 9%, 20-year mortgage. The first-year interest expense on the mortgage is $1,800, and the principal repayment is $375. The owners are married and have a taxable income of $17,000. Determine the profit from the apartment house and the net cash flow to the owners the first year, based on straight-line and one and one-quarter declining-balance depreciation.

SOLUTION (Straight-line depreciation)

First, calculate the profit from the property.

Rentals	$ 5,460
Less operating expenses	−2,720
Less interest	−1,800
Less depreciation	−1,400
Pretax profit (loss)	($ 460)

The owners have a taxable income of $17,000 and, therefore, are in the 28% marginal tax bracket. Hence, a loss of $460 on the property will result in a reduction of their tax by .28 × $460 = $129.00. Next, calculate the cash flow.

Rental	$5,460
Tax savings	129
Total inflows	$5,589
Operating expense	2,720
Interest	1,800
Principal repayment	375
Total outflows	$4,895

Net cash flow = Total inflows − Total outflows

Total inflows	$5,589
Less outflows	−4,895
Net cash flow	$ 694

Thus, the first year the owners would receive an after-tax net cash inflow of $694, based on an original investment of $12,000.

SOLUTION (One and one-quarter declining-balance)

First, calculate the profit from the property.

Rentals	$ 5,460
Less operating expenses	−2,720
Less interest	−1,800
Less depreciation	−1,750
Pretax profit (loss)	($ 810)

The owners have a taxable income of $17,000 and are in the 28% marginal tax bracket. Hence, a loss of $810 in the property will result in a tax savings of .28 × $810 = $227.

Next, calculate the cash flow.

Rentals	$5,460
Tax savings	227
Total inflows	$5,687
Operating expenses	$2,720
Interest	1,800
Principal repayment	375
Total outflows	$4,895

Net cash flow = Cash inflows − Cash outflows

Total inflows	$ 5,687
Less total outflows	− 4,895
Net cash flow	$ 792

Thus, the owners would have $792 if they used the allowable form of accelerated depreciation rather than $694 if they had used straight-line. Of course, the advantage of using an accelerated form would decrease each year. But, initially, the cash flow would be greater. This example also shows that the loss using the accelerated form of depreciation is increased by $350.

When an investment such as an apartment house is operated at a loss but generates a positive cash flow, the investment is said to be a *tax shelter*. If the owner's tax rate had been greater, the advantages would have grown proportionately. In Example 5, the owners had only a 28% tax rate and were shielded from $227 in tax. If they had a marginal tax rate of 50%, corresponding to a taxable income between $44,000 and $52,000, their tax shield would have been $405. The resulting net cash flow would have been $970.

A primary drawback of using accelerated depreciation methods is that profits are lowered substantially. From the viewpoint of a shareholder or prospective shareholder in a large corporation, profits are very important. As pointed out in Chapter 1, the price of a stock is related to profits. Also, dividends are paid out of profits. If a firm is operating at a loss, even though it may have good cash flow, it cannot pay dividends for long, if at all. This argument *does not* hold for small, closely held corporations. For these firms, the owners generally try to avoid paying dividends since they result in double taxation. Rather, as pointed out earlier in this chapter, the owners may elect to operate as a Subchapter S Corporation and thereby avoid the problem of dividends.

Large corporations are faced with a problem concerning the choice of a method for depreciation. If they use accelerated depreciation, the profits will be lower while cash flows will be higher. If they use straight-line, profits will be higher but cash flows lower. It is desirable to maintain profits as high as possible to keep shareholders' interest. On the other hand, the firm needs cash flow to meet expenses, purchase new equipment, and expand. To overcome this problem, firms usually use two sets of records, one for the calculation of income taxes and another for shareholders. For purposes of taxes they use accelerated depreciation and thereby minimize tax payments. For reporting to shareholders, they usually use straight-line to maximize profits.

Although in most instances it is desirable to depreciate assets as rapidly as possible so as to maximize cash flow, in certain circumstances this may not be the case. If the owners in Example 5 had little other income, the tax shelter would have been of little value. In that case, they should depreciate the property slowly since a greater tax shelter will be available in future years when, hopefully, their income from other sources will be greater.

1. Discuss the advantages and disadvantages of the corporate form of ownership for a small business.
2. Discuss the concept of limited shareholder liability as applied to a small business.
3. Explain the idea of double taxation of dividends.
4. Discuss the importance of cash flow versus profitability to the owners of a small and large business.
5. Explain the advantages and disadvantages of using an accelerated form of depreciation as opposed to straight-line.
6. Explain why a tax shield is of greater significance to persons having higher adjusted gross income than lower.
7. Explain why the IRS limits the amount of salaries the owners of corporations may receive.
8. Why do many small businesses ultimately become corporations?

This chapter summarizes the study of taxation and its relationship to business operations. Along with the study concepts and terms listed below, review those from Chapters 4 through 6.

Sole Proprietorship
Partnership
Corporation
Limited Shareholder Liability
Corporate Shield
Umbrella Policy
Portfolio
Diversified Portfolio
Subchapter S Corporation
Double Taxation of Dividends
Accumulated Profits Tax
Go Public
Investment Banker

Stock Market
Risk-Averter
Tax Shelter

PROBLEMS
1. The Ridgeways are planning to purchase a business. They anticipate earnings of $30,000 prior to payment of salaries to themselves, dividends, or taxes. The Ridgeways have three children and will have itemized deductions of $2,700. If the corporate form of organization is used, the Ridgeways will pay themselves $26,000 in salaries and pay themselves $2,000 in dividends. Determine the total federal income tax liability they will have under the following organizational plans:

(a) Corporate.
(b) Corporate—Subchapter S.
(c) Sole proprietorship.

2. The Cardinals own a small firm. Earnings before taxes, dividends, or salaries paid to themselves are $130,000. They have no children but $18,000 in itemized deductions. Currently they are organized as a sole proprietorship. If they can pay themselves up to $90,000 per year in salaries, would their tax liability be greater or lower if the corporate form of Subchapter S Corporate form were used?

3. Referring to Problem 2, if the IRS ruled that the Cardinals could pay themselves only $70,000 in salaries and that they must distribute at least $20,000 in dividends, would the corporate or corporate Subchapter S form of organization reduce tax liability?

4. The following information refers to a four-unit apartment house costing $47,000:

Rentals			$7,560.00
Expenses:	Property taxes	$1,147	
	Insurance	200	
	Heat	900	
	Water	84	
	Sewer	120	
	Electric	60	
	Maintenance	500	
	Contingency	300	

The value of the building is $40,000. It is about 35 years old and could be depreciated based on a 20-year life to salvage value of $10,-000. Financing is available at 9% for up to 80% of the purchase price. The terms of the financing are 20 years with *equal repayment of principal each year*. If the maximum financing is used, determine the profitability and cash flow for the first year of operation if purchased by a family with taxable income of $15,000 per year.

5. Paul and Sandra Smith operate a small business. Part of the income statement is shown below:

Sales	$200,000
Cost of goods	130,000
Rent	10,000
Depreciation	8,000
Utilities	4,000
Miscellaneous expenses	5,000

The Smiths are trying to determine which method of business organization will result in the minimum tax liability. They have two children and itemized deductions of $6,300. The IRS has indicated that they may take salaries up to a total of $35,000 for the work they do but that any remuneration beyond that would be considered a dividend if they elect the corporate form. If they did use the corporate form, they would take a $2,000 dividend. Your job is to evaluate the tax situation and advise the Smiths as to which method of organization will result in the lowest tax. As a part of your work you are to list the various organizational forms and their tax liability for each.

FINANCING THE FIRM

section II

One of the primary functions of a financial manager is the acquiring of funds necessary for the firm's growth and continued operation. Further, there are frequent periods in a firm's life when it has excess funds which should be invested rather than lying idle. Therefore, it is necessary that management be knowledgeable of the financial institutions and procedures necessary to both secure and lend funds. Study of the *financial institutions*, which include *the money and capital markets* and the associated operations of the *commercial banking* and *Federal Reserve System*, requires a general understanding of the economy. Thus, this section commences with a chapter dealing with the economic environment.

With the basics of the economic system and the money and capital markets completed, study is directed toward determination of interest rates and annuity values for a wide variety of loans and investments. Then attention is directed to the development of policies for use of debt financing in a business. Debt is categorized by term—short, intermediate, and long—and each source is evaluated in terms of its usefulness to the firm.

With the study of debt financing completed, equity financing and dividend policy are addressed. Equity includes both common and preferred stock. Each is examined in terms of its usefulness as sources of funds to finance the firm.

The section is completed with a study of the firm's cost of capital.

The cost of capital is the average of the costs of debt, equity, and retained earnings. This average has special significance as it represents the minimum return which the firm must receive on its investments. The cost of capital forms the basis for capital budgeting decisions, which are discussed in Section III of the book.

The Economic Functions
of Finance

chapter 8

Financing of business has to do with raising funds necessary for continued operations and possible expansion. Most of the funds are generated through profits. However, when a new business is started and when expansion of business is undertaken, funds usually must be obtained from external sources. There are numerous sources from which funds may be obtained. For a small business the owners may use their own funds or borrow from a bank. Larger businesses may sell stock or bonds or borrow from banks or life insurance companies. To develop a full appreciation for the operations involved in financing business it is necessary to have a basic understanding of the economic environment, the banking system, including the functions of the Federal Reserve Banks, and the money and capital markets. In this and the following chapter we shall deal with these topics.

THE REQUISITES OF AN ECONOMIC SYSTEM

The study of financial management presupposes the existence of a sophisticated economic system—a system which includes three primary features:

1. A unit of account;
2. A mechanism for creation of capital goods and equipment (capital formation); and
3. A mechanism for exchange of claims to wealth.

The unit of account is simply the unit used to measure prices. It is an index of value, commonly known as currency. In the United States the unit of account is the dollar. In other countries it is the pound sterling, mark, franc, etc. The existence of a unit of account permits valuation of all goods, services, land, precious objects, etc., in terms of a common denominator. For example, in the United States, workers receive wages in dollars for their work, goods are sold in stores for dollars, etc. Without a unit of account, an economy would be limited to a barter system of trade, and wealth could be accumulated only by maintaining stores of goods, precious metals, and the like. In general, each country has its own unit of account. To facilitate international trade, international currency markets operate to exchange the unit of account used in one country for that used in other countries. The ratios used in exchanging units of account are established by a process involving the supply and demand of the currencies involved. For example, the British pound sterling may be worth 2 U.S. dollars today and perhaps more or less in the future. The actual exchange rates existing at any time are easily obtainable in financial publications such as the *Wall Street Journal,* under the heading of "Foreign Exchange."

Capital goods are those assets used in the manufacture, production, distribution, or sale of other goods or services. Examples include machinery, buildings, or other similar properties. Electric generators, railroads, and highways are also capital goods. The *creation of capital goods within an economy requires a twofold process of savings and investment to take place. Saving in the economic sense means giving up consumption of something at one point in time so that it may either be consumed by someone else or at a later date.* In a simple sense it means not spending all of one's income and making the unspent portion available for expenditure by someone else. The latter could be accomplished, for example, by depositing any unspent income in a bank. *Typically, individuals and households tend to save, while businesses and governments borrow (dissave). In addition to saving, the creation of capital goods requires investment.*

Investment is the process of utilizing the savings to purchase capital equipment. Consider a simple example of a carpenter working in a woodshop with hand tools. If the carpenter saves some of his profits (or salary) rather than purchasing additional consumer goods, he will be able to buy some electric-powered tools. The purchase of power tools is an investment. *As defined in an economic sense investment is, in our society, carried out primarily by business and government.* Business invests in new plants, machinery, and the like. Government invests in such things as roads, sewage disposal plants, and schools. The term *investment* is also used in another context. It may be applied to describe the purchase of stocks, bonds, or real estate. However, *in the economic sense* investment takes place only when resources are allocated (money spent) to purchase capital goods. *The mechanism for capital formation, then, consists of two parts: saving and investment.*

In a simple economy the carpenter both saves and invests. He completes the entire act of capital formation. However, in a sophisticated economy, the act of capital formation is much more complex and involves individuals, business, and often government, using the services of financial intermediaries such as banks, savings and loan associations, and insurance companies. Rather than saving goods and services, a currency is saved. Surpluses in the form of currency, which exist in some sectors of the economy, primarily households, are saved and deposited with the *financial intermediaries*. The act of saving in a sophisticated economy still includes giving up consumption, that is, not spending all of one's income. The saving results in the accumulation of dollars. For capital formation to take place, the savings must be made available for investment. Placing one's saved money under a mattress, therefore, is not sufficient for capital formation to take place since the dollars accumulated are not made available for investment.

The process of saving often takes place by individuals giving up a portion of their income and putting the money in a bank, pension fund, or life insurance. The bank collects the savings of many individuals and makes them available in the form of loans to fulfill various purposes such as the construction of roads, the purchasing of manufacturing equipment, and the purchasing of property. A similar process takes place when individuals save for their retirement by putting funds into a pension fund. They give a portion of their income to the manager of the pension fund, often an insurance company. The insurance company makes the funds available for investment by business and government. In general, businesses and government are the primary investors in capital goods. Governments, as mentioned earlier, build roads, colleges, solid waste disposal plants, etc. Governments borrow much of the money needed for such construction. Also, a portion of the taxes paid by individuals and businesses goes for such capital formation. Taxes used for such purposes represent *forced savings*.

The existence of financial intermediaries, such as banks and insurance companies, greatly facilitates the collection of savings and makes them available for investment. The financial intermediaries provide the mechanism for *exchanging claims to wealth*. One claim to wealth, *money, includes paper and metal currency as well as checking accounts (demand deposits)*. Money may be readily exchanged for goods and services. Banks serve as a mechanism for saving, lending, and exchanging money. Banks also issue claims to wealth such as bank books and savings certificates. Other claims to wealth include deeds and mortgages to properties as well as stocks and bonds. A sophisticated economy requires the existence of procedures and facilities for *The primary goal of an economic system is to allocate resources (goods and services) within a society in order to provide for the optimal satisfaction of economic needs*. The "optimal" satisfaction of economic

GOALS AND OBJECTIVES OF THE ECONOMIC SYSTEM

The primary goal of an economic system is to allocate resources (goods and services) within a society in order to provide for the optimal satisfaction of economic needs. The "optimal" satisfaction of economic wants is, of course, interpreted in a variety of ways by different persons. Further, the approaches to achieving economic goals vary among countries. In the United States, the economic system has been based on the concepts of free enterprise and capitalism. *Free enterprise is an economic system whereby private industry operates with little government control within freely competitive market conditions. Capitalism refers to an economic system whereby most of the product and distribution systems are privately owned and operated for profit*. However, with government regulation and ownership of some businesses, the economic system might now be better described as modified capitalism. Two other economic systems are also well known: socialism and communism. Both of these systems incorporate a much greater degree of government control and ownership of business. Regardless of the economic system in use, the basic requirement is to allocate goods and services.

All resources are scarce. There is not enough food, clothing, housing, automobiles, and the like to satisfy everyone. Many people would like to own a large home, two new cars, a new wardrobe, and other consumer goods. At the current level of economic output, however, there are just not enough goods and services available to satisfy everyone's demands. At present, about 10 million automobiles are produced each year in the United States. With a population of some 220 million people, this provides one new car for about every 22 people. Of course, there are many people, children, for example, who do not need or want an automobile. From a practical viewpoint, about one new car is produced for every 10 to 12 people who would actually desire it. From this discussion, it could be concluded that an economy has two objectives:

1. To increase production of those goods and services which are in strong demand (provide for economic growth);
2. To distribute the existing goods and services in an equitable manner.

Beyond these objectives, it is also most desirable to achieve a stable economy. Three requisites of stability are listed below:

1. A high and stable rate of employment (low unemployment).
2. A reasonable stable level of prices or low inflation. (Inflation is an economic condition during which price increases are not accompanied by increases in production of goods and services. The net result is a decrease in the purchasing power of money.)
3. An equilibrium in the balance of payments (payments made among countries for the sale of goods and sources and the like).

To achieve the various objectives, *two general categories of economic tools are available: monetary and fiscal. The monetary tools handled by the Federal Reserve Banking System (FED) deal primarily with the expansion and contraction of the money supply. The fiscal tools used by the federal government deal primarily with taxation and spending the revenues generated from taxes.*

THE FEDERAL RESERVE BANKING SYSTEM

Most countries have a national bank which acts as the bank for the country. The United States tried this approach and over time had two national banks, neither of which proved to be completely satisfactory. Thus, in 1913, the Federal Reserve Act was passed and the Federal Reserve System was initiated.

The FED has as its primary functions handling the banking transactions for the U.S. government, issuing currency, regulating the banking system, and regulating the money supply. These functions are described in more detail below. The Federal Reserve System is divided into 12 geographical districts, each having a Federal Reserve Bank. Each FED bank issues currency and engraves its official designation on each bill printed. Examine the face of a Federal Reserve Note (paper currency). Note on the left side a circle with a large letter such as A, B, etc. This letter identifies the FED bank which issued the currency. B stands for New York, F for Atlanta, D for Cleveland, L for San Francisco, etc.

All nationally chartered banks are members of the Federal Reserve System. Also, many state-chartered banks and trust companies are members. Member banks hold over 80% of all deposits in commercial banks.

Each of the 12 FED banks has nine directors appointed for three-year terms. The directors must be residents of the district in which the bank is located. They are selected to represent the banking, commercial, industrial, and agricultural interests in the district. In addition to the 12 FED banks, there are 24 branch banks located primarily in the western states. These were established to serve large geographical districts.

The FED system is managed by a seven-member Board of Governors who serve 14-year terms. The long length of term was designed to minimize political pressures. Appointments to the Board of Governors are made by the president with the consent of the Senate. The Board of Governors is charged with the responsibility of overseeing the operation of the entire FED system.

The FED has functions which relate both to the management and operation of the banking system and also to the monetary management of the economy. The banking functions are described briefly below:

1. *Establish bank reserve requirements:* All banks are required by the FED to maintain reserves, which must be held as vault cash and deposits in a FED bank. All members of the FED must have an account in the regional FED bank. Congress establishes the range of reserve requirements (percentage of total deposits which must be held as reserves), and the FED sets the exact requirements within the range.
2. *Issuance of currency:* The FED issues Federal Reserve Notes, which are the paper currency used in the United States. These notes are backed by both the FED and the U.S. government. The backing consists primarily of government notes and bonds. The currency is not backed by gold or silver. The FED controls the issuance of currency to meet the needs of economic and population growth.
3. *Clearance and collection of checks:* Within each FED district, each district bank acts as a clearing house for all checks processed. Further, the FED in Washington has an interdistrict settlement function so that the FED system clears all of the billions of checks issued yearly throughout

the country. The bulk of the actual operations is handled using high-speed computers, and daily tallies are established to permit the transfer of funds among district FED banks within each district. To facilitate the check clearing function, each check is presented with a series of magnetic ink symbols which are read by a computer reader.

4. *Provision of loans and discounts to banks:* The FED may loan money to both member and nonmember banks. The loans are secured by bank promissory notes, U.S. Government Securities, and the like. The FED, in essence, is a banker's bank.

5. *Regulation and supervision of banks:* Due to the extremely important role of the banking system within the operation of the economy, bank regulation and supervision is extremely important. Banks are regulated by different agencies. For example, all national banks are regulated by

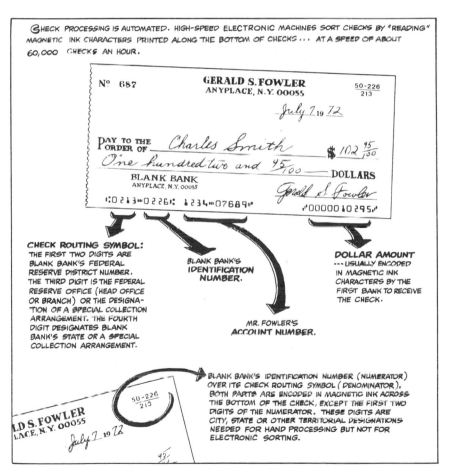

From The Story of Checks, *5th ed., published by the Public Information Department, Federal Reserve Bank of New York, 1972.*

the Comptroller of the Currency. All must be members of the Federal Deposit Insurance Corporation (FDIC) and operate under the rules of the FDIC. Members of the FED system are further subject to regulation by the FED. Actually, the FED does little itself by the way of examination of national banks but rather relies upon reports from the Comptroller of the Currency. Most of the FED's examination activities are limited to state banks, which are not examined by the Comptroller of the Currency.

The FED acts as the fiscal agent for the U.S. government. In this role it holds the primary checking accounts of the U.S. Treasury. Also, it assists in tax collections, sells and redeems U.S. Government Securities, and pays coupon interest on Federal Securities. Federal Securities include U.S. Savings Bonds, Treasury Bills, Treasury Notes, and other obligations. The FED performs these duties without charge to the government.

In addition to its role in banking operations and as fiscal agent for the government, the FED has a very significant function in the control of the economy. *The FED's primary operating tool used in controlling the economy is its open market operations.* The FED buys and sells Treasury Securities in the "open market" to individuals, banks, businesses, and some governmental agencies. If the FED purchases securities, the result is an *increase* in the money supply since the FED pays money to the sellers. Conversely, if the FED sells securities, the result is a *decrease* in the money supply since the FED collects money from the buyers. The sale and purchase of securities by the FED also affect the general level of interest rates. If, for example, the FED reduces the money supply, then the interest paid for the use of the available money will be bid upward by those needing the funds. As the interest rate is bid upward some potential borrowers will be eliminated because they cannot afford the higher rates. An equilibrium position will ultimately be reached where the supply and demand for funds is approximately equal. *The FED attempts to control economic growth, interest rates, inflation, and the like by using its monetary tools.* Increasing interest rates and tightening the money supply tend to reduce demand for goods and services on the part of individuals, businesses, and government. A reduction in demand usually results in a decrease in the level of prices or at least a slowing of the rate at which prices increase, and, hence, a reduction in the rate of inflation.

Raising the interest rate may reduce inflation because high interest rates tend to decrease the demand for many goods. The reason for the change is twofold. First, higher interest rates result in greater manufacturing cost since most firms borrow funds to help finance their operations. Second, many individuals and businesses borrow funds to make purchases. The amount paid in interest adds to the purchase price. For example, the interest rate on home mortgages has increased in recent years from about 6 percent to 9 percent. This has greatly increased the cost of purchasing homes and, hence, in part, reduced the demand for houses.

In addition to the open market operations, the FED has several other tools which it may use to affect monetary availability and interest rates. Adjusting bank reserve requirements within the prescribed limits affects the availability of money. For example, increasing the reserve requirements reduces the amounts which banks may loan. Similarly, reducing reserve requirements increases the amounts which banks may loan. However, it should be noted that if the FED decreases reserve requirements, it does not mean that banks will actually loan more money. They may, but whether they will or not depends on the bank management.

Other FED tools include consumer credit controls, real estate credit controls, and establishing margin requirements. The FED has not used its power to control consumer credit frequently. It was asked during World War II to reduce the purchase of consumer durables such as automobiles, refrigerators, and the like. The Truth-in-Lending Act passed in 1968 requires the FED to provide regulations which will assure full disclosure of credit terms for consumer comparison. Regulation X, issued in 1950 by the FED, regulated real estate credit in terms of amounts which could be borrowed, length of loan, etc. This restriction was removed in 1952 and has not been used since.

Stock, bonds, and other securities may be purchased on *margin*. That is, the purchaser may borrow a portion of the funds from the stockbroker and pay only the "margin." The FED establishes limits on the amounts which stockbrokers and bankers may loan against securities when the loan is used to purchase securities. The restrictions are not applied if, for example, a business wants to use securities as collateral to borrow funds for use in the business.

The FED, to a great extent, controls the supply of money. In periods of inflation it tends to decrease the money supply in order to reduce demand, as described above. In periods of recession it usually increases the money supply and concurrently lowers interest rates so as to stimulate investment and employment. The FED, which is basically a nonpolitical body, is faced with the very difficult task of regulating the monetary aspects of the economy.

FISCAL ECONOMIC CONTROLS

Fiscal tools are used by the federal government. Basically, they consist of taxation and spending the tax revenues, plus any additional funds which the government may borrow. To reduce demand in the household and business sectors, the government can increase taxes. Increasing income taxes, for example, results in decreasing individual and business income. As a result, they have less to spend. Decreasing demand should result in lowering the rate of inflation. If the government wants to increase demand in periods of recession and high unemployment, it may reduce taxes. Also, it may borrow funds and spend the money to create demand and thereby stimulate economic growth.

Another method the federal government can use to reduce inflation is the reduction of its own demand. That is, it can reduce some of its own expenditures by cutting back on programs such as defense, welfare, education, etc. Both of the alternatives open to the federal government are hazardous from a political point of view. Individuals and businesses are seldom favorably disposed to added taxes. Further, cutting back on programs results in reduction in federal payrolls and decreases in purchases by the federal government. Reductions of this sort have adverse effects upon workers and businesses.

The federal government may take action in other ways beyond its fiscal powers. One method commonly used is called "jawboning." This occurs when political leaders such as the president and key members of Congress place verbal pressure on unions to refrain from demanding large increases in wages or on business to refrain from increasing prices. Such action is often used because it indicates an interest in the problem on the part of politicians while it does not place them in political jeopardy.

Another tool available to the federal government is wage and price controls. Such controls were used at different times in the United States but were later phased out. It is very difficult to evaluate the effectiveness of wage and price controls, especially if they are employed for only a short period of time. Usually, however, inflation increases dramatically after controls are removed, since both labor and business try to make up for lost time with increasing prices the result.

The federal government is controlled by elected officials and, therefore, tends to move very slowly to control problems in the economy. Further, the federal government lacks any coherent economic planning system. As a consequence, much of the economic control exercised by the federal government is of a "firefighting" nature and frequently is carried out too slowly to be effective.

In addition to the economic consequences of any action government officials may undertake, the political consequences are always a primary consideration. This frequently leaves the FED with a rather awesome responsibility of attempting to control inflation, recession, and unemployment with the limited tools of monetary policy.

SOURCES OF ECONOMIC INFORMATION

The financial manager as an individual, or as an executive in business and government, can do very little to control any aspect of the economy. Therefore, it is essential that he understand the workings of monetary and fiscal controls so that he can anticipate changes in the economy as the various controls are implemented.

Several sources of up-to-date economic information are readily available to the financial manager. A primary source is the *Wall Street Journal*. *Business Week* magazine, which includes weekly figures on production output, trade, prices, and finance, is a fine barometer of economic activity. Many of the Federal Reserve Banks publish monthly reports which provide insight into important economic issues. These are frequently keyed to special problems of regional importance. Trade journals also provide economic information, which is especially important to specific industries. A good source of annual and historical economic information is included in the yearly *Economic Report of the President*. This report, which averages over 350 pages in length, is released around February of each year and is available from the Superintendent of Documents in Washington. The financial manager must keep abreast of changing economic activities. Other sources of economic information are contained in Appendix D.

QUESTIONS
FOR
DISCUSSION

1. Discuss the three primary features of an economic system.
2. Describe the interaction of saving and investment as a part of the capital formation process.
3. How do financial intermediaries function in the process of capital formation?
4. Explain how taxation represents forced savings.
5. Describe the three types of money. Why are credit cards *not* considered to be money?

6. Describe the concepts of free enterprise and capitalism.
7. Describe the conditions of economic stability. Why is it important to have a stable economy?
8. Detail the primary functions of the FED.
9. The FED acts as the fiscal agent for the U.S. government. Explain.
10. Describe the FED's "open market operations." How do these affect the money supply?
11. How do changes in interest rates affect economic growth and inflation?
12. What is the meaning of purchasing securities "on margin"?
13. Differentiate between fiscal and monetary economic controls.

CONCEPTS TO REMEMBER

This chapter introduces many important concepts which relate economic factors to financial management. Be sure to be familiar with the following:

Unit of Account
Capital Formation
Barter System
Saving and Investment
Money
Federal Reserve System (FED)
Monetary Tools
Economic Needs
Inflation
Balance of Payments
Federal Reserve Note
Bank Reserve Requirements
Open Market
Fiscal Tools
Security Purchase on "Margin"

Banking
and
the Money and Capital Markets

chapter 9

The banking system and the money and capital markets provide the mechanisms for transferring savings and claims to wealth. These financial intermediaries are of key importance to the orderly operation of the economy and perform many roles which are essential to all business operations.

BANKS AND BANK FUNCTIONS

Banks are institutions which provide a wide variety of services to the public. *Their basic function is to act as a depository for savers and as a source of funds for borrowers.* Thus, banks act as a primary financial intermediary between savers and borrowers. *Commercial banks* have the unique distinction of providing three types of deposit accounts:

1. Checking (demand deposits).
2. Passbook Savings (no limitations on deposits or withdrawals).
3. Time Deposits (time certificates and limited withdrawal passbook accounts).

The *commercial banking system* includes the nationally chartered banks, state chartered banks and trust companies, trust companies, and private and industrial banks. Trust companies are organized to accept and carry out trusts. They act as trustees for wills, administer estates, register bonds and stocks, and may also engage in general banking business. There are other types of savings institutions such as mutual savings banks, credit unions, and savings and loan associations. These are limited in the scope of activities which they may perform to acting as depositories for funds and lending money for specific purposes. For example, savings and loan institutions may not provide checking accounts, and their scope of lending is essentially limited to home mortgage loans.

Some of the many functions provided by commerical banks are described briefly below. It should be noted that many commerical banks do not perform all of the functions listed and that some specialize in certain areas such as equipment leasing or trust functions.

1. Accept deposits in checking accounts, and pay checks drawn against those accounts.
2. Accept deposits in time and savings deposit accounts, pay interest on those accounts, and permit withdrawals from them.
3. Supply loans to individuals and businesses.
4. Transfer money between banks within the United States and foreign banks.
5. Issue money orders, cashier's checks, and certified checks. A *cashier's check* is a check issued to a borrower when a loan is made to him. It is the bank's own check and therefore a direct obligation of the bank as opposed to someone's personal check, which is *not* a direct obligation of the bank. A *certified check* is certified as genuine and there are ample funds on account to cover its payment. The amount of funds needed to cover the check is set aside to pay the check so that the check cannot be refused for insufficient funds. A certified check then becomes an obligation of the bank. This is *significantly different* from a noncertified check. An ordinary check is *an order* for the bank to pay funds. However, if sufficient funds are not available in the checking account to cover the amount of the check, the bank is *not* under any obligation to pay the check.
6. Provide safe deposit boxes.
7. Provide credit card services such as BankAmericards.
8. Establish and execute trusts.
9. Lease equipment through wholly owned subsidiary corporations.
10. Act as stock transfer agents, register stock, and pay dividends for corporations. When stock is bought and sold through the various stock exchanges, records must be maintained as to the ownership. Corporations frequently designate a bank to provide this record-keeping service.

11. Purchase government securities such as city bonds.
12. Issue travelers checks and provide Christmas Club accounts.

Beyond the specific functions described above, banks provide very important advisory services for their customers. Banks offer a variety of savings accounts and advise customers as to which account will best meet their needs. Also, banks provide many services to borrowers. They discuss customer loan requirements and develop loans designed to be most beneficial to the borrowers. In examining loan applications, banks are careful to advise potential borrowers of any hazards. For example, when a mortgage loan application is received, banks have the property appraised in order to assure that its value is consistent with the proposed sale price. This protects both the potential borrower and the bank from possible future loss.

THE MONEY AND CAPITAL MARKETS

The Money Markets are the markets where short-term funds are traded. Money Markets are open markets as opposed to a banking relationship where the bank accepts deposits or lends funds to *specific customers.* Short-term funds are defined as those which mature in a year or less. The Money Markets consist of borrowers and lenders. The borrowers are generally the federal government, securities dealers (stock brokers), state and local governments, and businesses. The lenders include commercial banks and other financial institutions, foreign lenders, business firms, individuals and the FED. The FED only loans indirectly through commercial banks. It does not loan directly to businesses.

The primary function of the Money Markets is to provide a mechanism which permits the various borrowers and lenders to adjust their liquidity positions on a day-to-day basis. Thus, a firm could go to the Money Market to secure funds needed to purchase extra inventories but would not seek long-term funds for construction of a new plant.

The Capital Markets are contrasted to the Money Markets in that they have to do with longer-term obligations. Intermediate-term funds, such as loans with maturity up to five years, and long-term funds, such as stocks and bonds, are sold and traded in the Capital Markets. The lenders and borrowers in the Capital Markets are basically the same groups as involved in Money Market transactions but also include, to a greater extent, insurance and pension institutions, mutual funds, trust operations, and individual investors. Many insurance companies and state, local, and private pension funds provide large sums of money for investment in the Capital Markets.

The Money Markets include several well-organized short-term markets. The most important deal with U.S. Government obligations, commercial paper, bank acceptances, and Federal Funds. The Government obligations consist primarily of Treasury Bills, which are traded in two market segments: the sale of new issues and trading in outstanding bills. Treasury Bills are sold weekly and mature in three to six months. The bills do not pay interest but rather are sold at a discount. The Treasury does not set the selling price. Individuals and financial institutions submit sealed bids for new issues, and the bills are sold to the highest bidders. There is also a large market for outstanding bills. These are sold by a small number of specialists. *Commercial paper* consists of short-term unsecured promissory notes issued by large corporations. *Bankers' acceptances* come about when a bank's customer agrees to buy goods and the bank agrees to pay any bills submitted by the seller. The buyer in turn promises to pay the bank before the bank pays the seller. The bank, in effect, guarantees the payment and substitutes its high credit standing for that of the buyer. Bankers' acceptances are used extensively in international trade when a seller may not know the credit standing of the buyer. When a seller receives a banker's acceptance, he may wish to collect the amount owed immediately rather than waiting until the payment date, which could be 90 days in the future. The market for bankers' acceptances permits the holders of acceptances to sell them at a discount and thus collect the funds owed to them (less the discount) immediately.

Federal Funds are those funds which banks have on deposit at the FED. Federal Funds may be borrowed for short periods (one day) from banks having excess reserves on deposit. The borrowers are banks which need the funds. When a bank submits checks to the local FED bank for credit, the checks are not credited immediately. The delay may come about as a result of the distance to the bank on which the check is drawn. Collection may take one or more days. Banks cannot afford to wait this long for the checks to clear so they may write checks on their accounts at the FED if they have excess funds on deposit. If a bank which does not have excess funds on deposit with the FED needs money, it may borrow from another bank having excess funds through the accounts at the FED.

The Capital Markets consist of a group of markets which deal in claims or titles to capital. Claims or titles include stock, bonds, and the like. The Capital Markets include institutions and mechanisms for the sale of both new (primary) and outstanding (secondary) securities. The transactions involving secondary issues vastly outnumber the transactions in new issues. Within the context of the Capital Markets, the terms stock market and bond market are frequently used. These terms are used to refer to the *secondary* markets for stocks and bonds.

INVESTMENT BANKING

Investment bankers are financial intermediaries. They act as middle-men between the issuers of securities (businesses, government, etc.) and the individuals and institutions which purchase the securities. They are involved primarily with the issuance of new long-term securities such as stocks and bonds. Investment bankers have three primary functions: recommendation and advisement, underwriting the sale of securities, and selling the securities.

Investment bankers maintain a continual pulse on the money and capital markets. They are fully cognizant of current and expected interest rates, demand for new issues of securities, and the like. As such, they are of extreme value to the financial manager who may be contemplating acquisition of funds. The investment banker works very closely with the firm's financial manager and advises as to the exact type of security to issue, the time to issue it, and the expected cost in terms of interest or dividends. The investment banker's recommendation and management acceptance at the time is the primary determinant in making decisions regarding financing a firm.

Once a decision has been reached regarding the issuance of new securities, the investment banker's role continues. The investment banker may actually purchase the entire security issue for subsequent resale to investors. The price at which the securities are sold is usually slightly higher than the price paid by the investment banker, and substantially higher in high-risk issues. The difference in price covers the costs involved in selling the security and the risks involved. Unlike secondary sales of securities, when investors purchase securities in a primary sale, they *do not* pay any brokerage commission. Another method used to sell primary issues of securities involves an *under-writing agreement* between the investment banker and the issuing firm. Such agreements obligate the investment banker to purchase any of the securities which are not bought by investors. Under such an agreement, the investment banker tries to assure price stability of the new security. At a later date the investment banker may sell the securities which it has purchased and thereby maintain equilibrium in the market place. A third method used in issuing securities via an investment banker involves "best-effort selling." The investment banker does his best to sell the issue but makes no guarantee to sell all of the securities involved. Under this arrangement the investment banker is paid on a fee basis for the securities which it sells.

Investment bankers are more commonly known as *security brokers* or *stockbrokers*. This results from the fact that the bulk of all security transactions are in secondary markets. Investment bankers use their local retail security dealers to market new issues of securities. When an investment banker accepts the assignment of selling a new security, it may assign a given number of shares to each of its offices. The security broker in each office then contacts potential purchasers and attempts to sell the new securities. Frequently a new security issue will be so large that a single investment banker (brokerage house) lacks the financial resources and marketing staff to sell the entire issue. In such instances, which are very frequent, a syndicate is formed. The *syndicate* consists of a group of brokerage houses (perhaps 10 to 50) which work together in selling the new security.

While most large issues of securities are sold to the public at large, some securities are sold through *direct placement*. Direct sales are made primarily to large insurance companies and pension funds. The advantage of direct placement as opposed to sale to the public at large is that *direct placement eliminates the expense and time required to prepare information required by the Securities and Exchange Commission*. Also, *public disclosure* of the firm's financial condition is eliminated. While some stock is sold via direct placement, most direct placement is limited to bonds.

SECURITY EXCHANGES AND DEALERS

As indicated, the most important aspect of security transactions in terms of numbers of sales is for outstanding issues. Stocks, bonds, and other forms of securities are bought and sold (traded) primarily through the security exchanges. There are several exchanges of which the New York Stock Exchange (NYSE) is the best known in the United States. The NYSE has 1,366 members who meet to transact sales. In addition to the NYSE, there is the American Stock Exchange (AMEX), several regional exchanges, and the over-the-counter market. While the members do own and trade their stock, the bulk of all transactions is made for the members' customers. When the owner of a security desires to sell it, he contacts a local stockbroker. The broker places a sell order, which is transmitted to the exchange. If a buy order has been placed at the same price, a sale is made. Sometimes it is necessary to wait several days before a sale can be executed if a buyer or seller wants to make a trade at a price which differs from the market price. In fact, most brokers review such open orders to buy or sell for 90 days. However, sales can be completed rapidly if the buyer or seller is willing to trade at the going market price.

There are six types of stock exchange members: commission brokers, floor brokers, floor traders, odd-lot dealers, specialists, and bond brokers. The *commission brokers* are commonly called stockbrokers or security dealers. They maintain customer offices in local regions and solicit business to buy and sell securities for their customers. One of the functions of many commission brokers is to act as investment bankers. Thus, commission brokers play a dual role of selling primary issues and trading outstanding issues. *Floor brokers* own a seat on the exchange but usually do not belong to a firm which is a member of the exchange. Floor brokers trade stock for other brokers. There are about 200 floor brokers on the NYSE. Floor traders are primarily involved with the trading of their own securities. They buy and sell securities for their own accounts. They usually maintain large portfolios and deal very actively even to make only small profits. Stock is exchanged in round lots, that is, in 100-share lots; when a customer wants to buy or sell a smaller number of shares (called an odd lot), an odd-lot dealer is involved. *Odd-lot dealers* buy and sell odd lots and accumulate these into round lots, which are traded on the exchange. Thus, the odd-lot dealer "makes" a market for small orders. *Specialists* deal primarily in their own accounts but limit their portfolios to a few "specialized" stocks. They may also serve in the role as floor traders. *Bond brokers* specialize in trading bonds. There are about 1,400 bond issues traded on the NYSE by about 12 bond brokers.

The banking community and the institutions of the Money and Capital Markets provide a most important function in the exchange of claims to wealth and in the process of savings and investment. Corporations, the government, and individuals depend on these institutions to facilitate the needs for capital formation and economic growth.

1. Differentiate among the three types of deposit accounts held by commercial banks.
2. Differentiate among money orders, cashier's checks, and certified checks.
3. Describe the advisory service which banks provide for their customers.
4. Differentiate between the Money and Capital Markets.
5. What is the primary function of the Money Markets?
6. Describe bankers' acceptances and how they are used.
7. What are Federal Funds?
8. Describe the primary functions of investment bankers.
9. Describe the purpose of an underwriting agreement.
10. What is a syndicate?
11. Indicate the advantages of "direct placement."
12. Describe the process which takes place when an individual purchases or sells stock. How is the process affected if an odd lot is involved?
13. There are six types of stock exchange members. Describe the function of each.

Be sure to have a firm grip on the new analytical concepts introduced in this chapter.

Check (Demand Deposit)
Passbook Savings
Time Deposits
Commercial Banking System
Trust Companies
Primary Market for Securities
Secondary Market for Securities
Underwriting
"Best-Effort Selling"
Certified Check
Cashier's Check
Money Markets
Capital Markets
Treasury Bills
Federal Funds
Investment Banker
Investment Syndicate
Public Disclosure
Commission Broker
Specialist
Odd Lot Broker
Bond Broker

Interest and Annuity Calculations

chapter 10

While funds realized from the sale of stock, profits, and other internally generated funds provide a primary part of a firm's financial requirements, a large portion of all financing is accomplished through the use of borrowed funds. Therefore, it is very important to be able to determine the exact dollar amount and rate of interest paid on all debts. The accurate calculation of interest payments and rates is important for both borrower and lender.

In addition to borrowing and lending money, individuals, businesses, and government agencies often place funds with financial intermediaries, such as banks and pension associations. Funds may be placed in bank savings accounts or pension annuities which provide for regular growth through compounding of interest. To know how money placed at interest will grow, it is necessary to calculate both compound interest and annuities. In the first section of the chapter we shall deal with the payment of interest on borrowed funds, while in the second we shall examine the collection of interest on funds lent or placed at interest in financial institutions.

THE COST OF CREDIT

There are many different types of loans available to individuals, businesses, and government. Without examining the features of specific loans, in this section we shall detail the methods which may be used to calculate interest rates and costs.

Collect Interest Loans

Collect interest loans are the simplest with respect to calculation of interest. Interest is paid at the time the loan is repaid or on the unpaid balance if the loan is repaid in installments. Many demand loans, installment loans, and mortgages are collect interest loans.

Example 1:   COLLECT INTEREST LOANS

Weisz Brothers borrowed $3,000 from the National Bank. The loan is to be repaid at the rate of $1,000 per year. Interest is computed on the annual outstanding balance, at a rate of 14%. Determine the annual interest payment.

SOLUTION

The amount of interest owed at the end of each year is 14% of the principal outstanding during the year. The costs are tabulated below:

Time	Principal Outstanding During Year	Principal Paid at Year's End	Interest Owed at Year's End
First Year	$3,000	$1,000	.14 × $3,000 = $420
Second Year	2,000	1,000	.14 × 2,000 = 280
Third Year	1,000	1,000	.14 × 1,000 = 140
			Total interest $840

The total interest paid over the duration of the loan is $840. The interest payments are deductible as expenses in the calculation of federal income tax liability.

Mortgages are generally paid by the month. The total payment consists of interest and principal. The monthly interest is calculated using one-twelfth of the annual rate applied to the outstanding balance of the loan. A small portion of the principal is also repaid each month. Usually, when individuals purchase property using mortgages, the lending institution pays the property taxes every three months. The lending institution then adds one-third of the quarterly tax payment to the monthly mortgage payment. Hence, the total monthly payment usually consists of interest and principal, which is the mortgage payment, plus one-twelfth of the yearly taxes.

Constant payment mortgages are very popular. They provide for equal monthly payments over the life of the loan. Initially, the monthly interest payment is large and the repayment of principal (amortization) is quite small. As the loan is repaid, the principal owed is reduced, and hence less interest and more principal is paid each month. It takes roughly two-thirds of the total period of a constant payment mortgage to repay half of the principal. Thus, after 20 years of a 30-year mortgage, about half of the amount of the original loan is repaid. Table 1 shows a 15-year, 9% equal monthly payment mortgage schedule for a $20,000 mortgage. Such schedules are available for mortgages of varying amounts, lengths, and interest rates. The schedules are not easy to develop because many calculations are required. Hence, computer programs have been developed to produce this type of mortgage schedule.

TABLE 1

$20,000, 15-Year, 9% Equal Payment Mortgage; Payments Are $203.00 Per Month

Year	Interest	Repayment of Principal	Balance of Principal
1	$ 1,773.20	$ 662.80	$19,337.20
2	1,711.00	725.00	18,612.20
3	1,642.80	793.20	17,819.00
4	1,568.60	867.40	16,951.60
5	1,486.80	949.20	16,002.40
6	1,398.40	1,037.60	14,964.80
7	1,300.60	1,135.40	13,839.40
8	1,194.40	1,241.60	12,587.80
9	1,078.00	1,358.00	11,229.80
10	950.60	1,485.40	9,744.40
11	811.40	1,624.60	8,119.80
12	658.40	1,777.60	6,342.20
13	491.80	1,944.20	4,398.00
14	186.00	2,126.00	2,272.00
15	110.20	2,272.00	0.00
Total Interest	$16,362.20		

The other commonly used mortgage is the *direct reduction*. The principal payments are constant each month, but the interest payments decrease as the amount of the loan decreases. The interest payment is calculated on the unpaid balance of the loan. Thus, the total mortgage payment decreases as each payment is made. Since the same amount of principal is repaid with each payment, it takes only one-half of the period of the loan to repay half of it. After 20 years of a 30-year direct reduction mortgage, two-thirds of the principal would be repaid.

Bonds are another type of collect loan. In this case, the corporation or government agency selling the bond is the borrower; the purchaser of the bond is the lender. Bond interest is usually paid twice a year. Each semiannual payment represents half of the total yearly payment. Bonds are generally sold in $1,000 denominations and pay a certain dollar amount of interest each year. The dollar amount divided by the $1,000 price is called the *stated yield*.

Example 2:   STATED YIELD

A bond is sold for $1,000 and pays yearly interest of $80.00. Determine its stated yield.

SOLUTION

Divide the dollar interest by the price:

$$\frac{\$80}{\$1,000} = .08 = 8\%$$

The stated yield is 8%

Bond prices fluctuate as the general rate of prevailing interest changes. *As the general level of interest rates increases, the prices of outstanding bonds (bonds which have been issued sometime in the past) tend to decrease, and vice versa.* This is to be expected, since investors want the highest return possible on their investments consistent with the risk to which they are exposed. Consider, for example, a bond sold in 1963 which paid $60 per year interest, or a stated yield of 6%. If similar-quality bonds were issued at a later date which yielded $90, the owners of the older bonds would want to sell the older bonds and buy the new higher-yield bonds. The sale of the older bonds would naturally force their price down until the point that they yielded approximately the same amount as the newly issued bonds. The market price of the older bonds would fall from the issue price of $1000 to a lower amount. The rate of return which a bond yields, based on its current market price, is called the *current or market yield:*

$$\text{Current yield} = \frac{\text{Yearly interest payment in dollars}}{\text{Market price of the bond}} \qquad (1)$$

It should be noted that the current yield on all bonds listed on the New York Bond Market is provided on a daily basis in the *Wall Street Journal*.

Example 3:   CURRENT OR MARKET YIELD OF BONDS

Suppose a bond originally issued in 1965 paid $65 per year interest and that the general level of interest increased so that newly issued bonds of the same quality paid $93 per year. How far would the price of the bonds issued in 1965 have to fall in order to have the same current yield as the new bonds?

SOLUTION

First, determine the current yield of the new bonds using Eq. (1):

$$\text{Current yield} = \frac{\$93}{\$1,000} = .093 = 9.3\%$$

Next, determine the price of the old bonds which will result in a current yield of 9.3%. Keep in mind that the dollar yield of the old bonds stays fixed at $65. Use Eq. (1).

$$.093 = \frac{\$65}{\text{New price}}$$

$$\text{New price} = \frac{\$65}{.093}$$

$$= \$700$$

The price of the bonds issued in 1965 would have to fall to $700 in order for these bonds to have a current yield of 9.3%. However, bond investors are generally more interested in the *yield to maturity* than the current yield. The yield to maturity takes into consideration both the current yearly dollar interest payment plus any capital gain which would be received when the bond matures. In Example 3, an investor paying $700 for the bond would receive $65 per year until maturity and then $300 in capital gains when the bond was redeemed for $1,000. Since issued bonds, which are traded on the various bond exchanges, almost never sell for their redemption price of $1,000, investors compare yield to maturity as a part of their analysis to determine the optimum bond investment for them. Determination of the yield to maturity requires the use of discounted cash flow calculations, which are included under the heading of capital budgeting. Calculation of the yield to maturity is considered in Chapter 19.

Mortgage interest rates also follow the prevailing interest rate levels. During the mid-1970s interest rates on newly granted mortgages on residential property have been ranging from about 9% to 10½%. However, during the 1960s, mortgage interest rates were about 6%. Many of these 6% mortgages are still outstanding, with a large portion of the principal still unpaid. In many instances, banks and other savings institutions which hold the mortgages are paying interest rates to

their depositors in excess of 6%. Thus, in some cases, the savings institutions are losing money on older mortgages. As a result, some savings
institutions have offered to buy back mortgages. For example, suppose
that a person owed $10,000 on a 6% mortgage granted in the early
1960s, with final payment due in 1992. A savings institution might
offer the person the option of paying $9,000 now rather than paying
back the $10,000 (plus interest) over the next 18 years. If the person
owing the mortgage were able to pay the $9,000 now, he would save
$1,000 of principal repayment. The savings institution would also
benefit because it could lend the $9,000 at a higher rate, say 9%. It
would then collect $810 interest on the new $9,000 loan, whereas it
was collecting only $600 per year interest on the existing $10,000 loan.

Discount Loans

Interest may be subtracted or discounted from the amount of the
principal given to the borrower when a loan is granted. For example,
suppose a loan of $1,000 is granted for a year at the annual interest
rate of 6%. The interest would be $60. However, if the loan is of the
discount type, the interest is deducted from the principal so that the
borrower would receive only $940. The effective rate of interest may
be calculated as follows:

$$\text{Effective interest rate} = \frac{\text{Yearly interest payment}}{\text{Amount of principal received}} \qquad (2)$$

If $1,000 were borrowed for a year at 6% and the principal dis-
counted, then the effective rate of interest would be calculated using
Eq. 2:

$$\text{Effective rate} = \frac{\$60}{\$940} = .0638 = 6.38\%$$

Example 4:   DISCOUNT LOANS

Suppose $3,000 were borrowed at a stated rate of 8% for a period of
two years and that the interest was discounted when the loan was made.
Determine the effective rate of interest.

SOLUTION

The yearly interest would be .08 × $3,000 = $240. For two years, this
amounts to $480. Thus the borrower would receive $3,000 − $480 =
$2,520. Hence, the borrower would actually be paying $240 per year for

the use of $2,520. Using Eq. (2), the effective rate of interest may be determined:

$$\text{Effective rate} = \frac{\$240}{\$2,520} = .095 = 9.5\%$$

It should be noted that if the borrower actually needed the use of the full $3,000, then a substantially larger sum would have to be borrowed.

Example 5:   DISCOUNT LOANS

Donalson Mfg. needs $80,000 for a three-year period. A local bank will provide a three-year discount loan at a stated rate of 10%. Determine how much Donalson must borrow in order to have use of the $80,000. Also calculate the effective rate of interest on the loan.

SOLUTION

Let X equal the amount of the loan. Then $.10X$ is the annual interest payment. Since interest for three years will be subtracted from the total loan, the interest will be $.3X$.

$$X - .3X = \$80,000$$

$$.7X = \$80,000$$

$$X = \frac{\$80,000}{.7}$$

$$X = \$114,286$$

The total loan would be $114,286. Yearly interest at 10% would be $11,428.60. The effective rate of interest is therefore

$$\frac{\$11,428.60}{\$80,000} = .143 = 14.3\%$$

Prior to the passage of the Truth-in-Lending Act, many automobile dealers and finance companies advertised 6% automobile loans which were of the discount type and had an effective rate of interest of about 12%. This practice is now illegal, and the effective rate of interest on the loan must be stated.

Installment Loans

Many installment loans call for equal monthly payments. A purchase of a $200 television might require 12 payments of $18. The total amount repaid is thus $12 \times \$18 = \$216$. It would appear that $16 is the interest and that the annual rate is therefore 8%. It must be remembered, however, that the original $200 is not owed over the entire duration of the loan, but rather a portion of the principal is repaid each month. Hence, the effective interest rate is more than 8%. The *approximate effective rate* may be determined using a *constant ratio formula* of the type shown in Eq. (3). The exact rate may be determined using "Recovery of Investment Tables", which are not included in this text.

$$R = \frac{2mD}{P(n+1)} \tag{3}$$

where R = approximate effective rate of interest
$\quad m$ = number of payments per year
$\quad D$ = dollar cost of credit
$\quad P$ = principal sum
$\quad n$ = actual number of payments

Example 6: INSTALLMENT LOANS

An automobile is purchased for $4,000. A down payment of $1,000 is credited toward the purchase price, leaving $3,000 as the amount of the loan. The monthly payments are $98.33 for 36 months. Determine the approximate effective rate of interest.

SOLUTION

Using Eq. (3),

m is the number of payments per year, 12.
D is the dollar cost of the credit.
This is determined by subtracting the $3,000 loan from the total amount to be repaid ($36 \times \$98.33 = \$3,539.88$). The dollar cost of the credit is $3,539.88 - \$3,000 = \$539.88$.
P is the principal sum, $3,000.
n is the number of actual payments, 36.

$$R = \frac{2(12)(\$539.88)}{\$3,000(36+1)} = \frac{12,957.12}{111,000} = .1167$$

The approximate effective interest rate is 11.67%.

Consumer Charge Account Loans

Two methods of computing charge account interest are used. The older method, known as the *adjusted balance system,* provides for determination of interest based on the outstanding balance at the end of the billing period. The newer *average daily balance* method also provides for interest based on the outstanding balance, but the earlier one pays, the lower the average balance and the lower the interest. With both systems if the entire bill is paid within the first billing period, there is no interest charge, but there may be a service charge. The interest rates charged under both systems are the same: usually 1½ % per month (18% per year) on balances up to $700 and 1% per month (12% per year) on amounts exceeding $700. Often there is a minimum monthly interest charge.

Example 7: ADJUSTED BALANCE CHARGE ACCOUNT

Robert Petterson made a $300 charge account purchase on January 25. The billing date for his account is February 5 and he has 25 days to pay before any interest is charged. On February 23 he paid $200, leaving a balance of $100. If Robert does not make any further purchases, determine the March billing interest charge.

SOLUTION

Robert would be charged interest on the $100 at the rate of 1½ % per month so that the March interest billing would be $1.50.

Example 8: AVERAGE DAILY BALANCE CHARGE ACCOUNT

Using the information provided in Example 7, determine the March interest charge using the average daily balance method.

SOLUTION

From the February 5 billing date until the February 23 payment date $300 was owed. From February 23 until start of the next billing period on March 5, $100 was owed. This amounts to 18 days at $300 and 10 days at $100. To find the average daily balance, multiply the balance by the number of days involved and divide by the total number of days, as shown:

$$\$300 \times 18 = 5,400$$
$$\$100 \times 10 = 1,000$$
$$\text{Total} = 6,400 \text{ dollar days}$$

$$\frac{6,400 \text{ dollar days}}{28 \text{ days}} = \$228.57 \text{ average daily balance}$$

Next, multiply the average daily balance by the interest rate per day, and multiply that product by the number of days involved. The daily interest rate is $\frac{1}{360}$ of the annual rate.

$$\frac{1}{360} \times .18 = .0005 \text{ (daily interest rate)}$$

$$\$228.57 \times .0005 \times 28 = \$3.20$$

The interest on the March bill would be \$3.20.

COMPOUND INTEREST AND ANNUITIES

An understanding of the calculation of compound interest and annuities is very important to all investors, firms, and lending institutions.

Simple Compounding

Banks, savings and loan associations, and other savings institutions offer a wide variety of methods for saving. One savings and loan association recently offered eight optional methods utilizing passbook and savings certificates. Each had a different yield and requirements for minimum deposit and time during which the funds had to be left on deposit. Examples are listed below:

Passbook Savings

5 %	Regular passbook, deposit or withdraw anytime; no minimum deposit
5½%	Golden passbook, 90 days notice for withdrawal; \$500 minimum balance

Certificates

5¾%	3-month holding period; \$1,000 minimum balance
6 %	1-year holding period; \$1,000 minimum balance
6½%	2-year holding period; \$1,000 minimum balance
6¾%	30-month holding period; \$1,000 minimum balance
7 %	4-year holding period; \$1,000 minimum balance
7½%	4-year holding period; \$2,500 minimum balance

In many instances, deposits are compounded quarterly (four times a year) or even daily. When compounded daily, 7½% savings certificates have an effective yield of 7.9%. With such a wide variety of savings plans available, it is necessary to be able to perform simple compounding calculations. Such calculations indicate how much interest will be received on a deposit held for a specified period of time.

When funds are deposited in a savings account, interest is received on the deposit. If interest is received only once per year (annual compounding), the total amount on deposit after the year (compound sum) may be determined using

$$S = P(1 + i) \qquad (4)$$

where S = compound sum
$\quad P$ = principal (original deposit)
$\quad i$ = interest rate

Example 9:   SIMPLE INTEREST

John Smith deposited $500 in a savings account. If interest is compounded annually at 6%, how much will John have at the end of one year?

SOLUTION

Using Eq. (4), the compound sum is determined:

$$S = \$500(1 + .06) = \$530$$

John will have $530 at the end of the year. The interest payment is $30 and is subject to federal income tax.

In many instances, a sum may be left on deposit with interest accruing for several years. To determine the compound sum after a number of years, Eq. (4) is modified to become

$$S = P(1 + i)^n \qquad (5)$$

where n is the number of periods.

Example 10:   COMPOUND SUM

Suppose John Smith leaves his funds on deposit with interest accruing at 6% for six years. How much will he have at the end of that period?

SOLUTION

Using Eq. (5) and noting that there are six periods involved, the compound sum is determined:

$$S = \$500(1 + .06)^6$$
$$= 500(1.06)^6$$
$$= 500(1.4185)$$
$$= \$709.25$$

At the end of six years, John would have $709.25

To solve Example 10, it was necessary to raise 1.06 to the sixth power. This is a tedious calculation. To facilitate calculations such as this, tables have been prepared which give compound sums for various interest rates and periods. Table I in Appendix A at the end of this book provides the compound sums of $1. Utilization of the table is demonstrated in Example 11.

Example 11:   COMPOUND SUM

If $1,250 is invested at 8% with interest compounded annually, how much will have accrued at the end of ten years?

SOLUTION

Utilize Eq. (5), but in place of the term $(1 + i)^n$, use the appropriate compounding factor from Table I. The compounding factor is found by referring to the 8% column and the ten-year row. The factor is 2.159.

$$S = \$1,250(2.159)$$
$$= \$2,698.75$$

The $1,250 would grow to $2,698.75 in ten years.

In many instances, interest is compounded semiannually or quarterly. Table I may be used to determine the compound sum in a manner quite similar to Example 11. *When interest is compounded semiannually, the compounding factor is found by doubling the number of years and halving the interest rate.* Similarly, if the interest is compounded quarterly, the compound factor is found by multiplying the number of years by 4 and dividing the interest rate by 4.

Example 12:   COMPOUND SUM

$1,500 is placed in a savings account at 6% compounded semianually for two years. What will the compound sum be at the end of two years?

SOLUTION

Use the 3% column and the four-year row of Table I.

$$S = \$1,500(1.1255)$$
$$= \$1,688.25$$

The $1,500 would have grown to $1,688.25 at the end of two years.

If the interest had been compounded on an annual basis, the $1,500 in Example 12 would have grown to $1,685.40. The difference is quite small in this example. However, if the interest is compounded more frequently and for a longer period of years, the difference is quite appreciable.

Compound Sum of an Annuity

An annuity is a series of equal payments made at given periods, usually at the end of the fiscal or calendar year. Many people save at regular intervals. For example, they may save $200 each year. Pension funds often require regular payments of a stipulated amount in order to achieve a goal of having a certain amount of money sometime in the future.

Example 13: COMPOUND SUM OF AN ANNUITY

Bill Jones makes annual payments of $200 per year into a trust. How much will he have at the end of four years if the interest rate is 6%?

SOLUTION

Normally, annuity payments are made at the *end* of the year. Therefore, the series of payments would receive interest as follows:

Year 1:	$200 at 6% for 3 years, $200 (1.1910) = $238.20
Year 2:	$200 at 6% for 2 years, $200 (1.1236) = 224.72
Year 3:	$200 at 6% for 1 year, $200 (1.0600) = 212.00
Year 4:	$200 without interest = 200.00
	Total = $874.92

Bill would have $874.92 at the end of four years, assuming his payments were made at the end of each year.

To assist in making annuity calculations, Table II in Appendix A has been provided. Table II gives the factors for future values of an annuity. The factors are used in conjunction with Eq. (6).

$$\text{Compound sum} = \text{Annuity} \times \text{Interest factor} \qquad (6)$$

Examples demonstrating the calculation of compound sums of an annuity are provided below.

Example 14:   COMPOUND SUM OF AN ANNUITY

Solve Example 13 using the appropriate factor in Table II.

SOLUTION

The annuity is four years at 6%. Refer to the 6% column and four-year row for the factor, 4.3746. Utilize Eq. (6). Compound sum = $200(4.3746) = $874.92.

Example 15:   COMPOUND SUM OF AN ANNUITY

If $500 is put in a 7% savings account at the end of each year and compounded annually, how much will accrue in ten years?

SOLUTION

Use Eq. (6) in conjunction with Table II, 7% column and ten-year row. Compound sum = $500(13.8164) = $6,908.20.

Example 16:   COMPOUND SUM OF AN ANNUITY

How much will a 20-year-old student have to save each year to have $200,000 at age 50? Assume annual compounding at 6%.
Equation (6) is employed as follows:

$$\$200,000 = \text{Annuity} \times \text{Interest factor}$$

The interest factor from Table II, 6% column and 30-year row, is 79.0582.

$$\$200,000 = \text{Annuity} \times 79.0852$$

$$\text{Annuity} = \frac{\$200,000}{79.0582} = \$2,529.78$$

The student would have to save $2,529.78 each year.

Example 17:   SINKING FUND

Borax Company is establishing a sinking fund to retire a $1 million bond issue which matures in 15 years. How much do they have to put into the fund at the end of each year to accumulate the $1 million assuming the funds are compounded at 7% annually?

SOLUTION

The sinking fund is a typical application of a compound annuity. Equation (6) may be employed:

$$\$1,000,000 = \text{Annuity} \times \text{Interest factor}$$

From Table II, 7% column and 15-year row, the interest factor is 25.1290.

$$\$1,000,000 = \text{Annuity} \times 25.1290$$

$$\text{Annuity} = \frac{\$1,000,000}{25.1290} = \$39,794.65$$

Borax will have to put \$39,794.65 into the sinking fund each year.

Some problems involve the combination of compound sum and compound sum of an annuity. An example is provided.

Example 18:   COMPOUND SUM AND COMPOUND SUM OF AN ANNUITY

If \$3,000 is put in a savings account yielding 6% compounded annually and another \$1,000 is added each year, how much will have accrued in ten years?

SOLUTION

This problem may be solved in two parts. First, calculate how much the original \$3000 will have increased in ten years. Use Table I.

$$S = \$3,000(1.7908) = \$5,372.40$$

Next, determine how much the additional \$1,000 will amount to in ten years. Use Table II.

$$S = \$1,000(13.1808) = \$13,180.80$$

The total of the two figures is \$18,553.20.

QUESTIONS
FOR
DISCUSSION

1. Differentiate collect and discount interest loans, constant payment and direct reduction mortgages, stated and current yield of bonds, stated and effective interest rates on loans.
2. Why do many people prefer a constant payment mortgage to a direct reduction mortgage, especially in inflationary periods?
3. Explain the importance of simple compounding calculations for persons having savings accounts.
4. Differentiate simple compounding from compounding of an annuity.
5. Indicate various ways in which compounding of an annuity calculation may be used in making business decisions.

CONCEPTS
TO
REMEMBER

This chapter deals with the procedures used to calculate interest and annuities. Several new concepts are introduced.

Collect Interest Loan
Constant Payment Mortgage

Direct Reduction Mortgage
Compound Interest
Sinking Fund
Current Yield (Bond)
Constant Ratio Formula
Annuity

1. Paul Sanders borrowed $5,000 for three years. He is to pay back $2,000 of the principal at the end of the first and second years and the remainder at the end of the third year. If the annual interest rate is 10%, determine the total yearly payments.

2. Peter Richardson borrowed $6,000 from the National Bank. The annual rate of interest is 8%, and the loan is to be paid back in 12 monthly installments. Each installment is to include equal payments of principal in addition to interest on the outstanding monthly balance. Determine the amount of each of the payments.

3. Pamela Jones has three charge accounts. Interest on all three accounts is charged as follows: 1½% per month on balances of $700 or less; 1% per month on balances over $700. If the interest calculated using the rates given is less than 50 cents, 50 cents is charged as the interest. For the last three months her balances have been as follows:

	January	February	March
Charge A	$ 45.00	$ 35.00	$ 7.50
Charge B	182.00	230.00	175.00
Charge C	800.00	403.00	372.00

Determine the total amount of interest which Pamela paid on the three accounts over the last three months using the adjusted balance system.

4. Several bonds were priced and had stated yields as shown below. Compute the current yield of each bond.

Bond	Market Price	Stated Yield
ATT, due 2003	$770	7⅛ %
Chrysler, due 1998	705	8 %
Philadelphia Electric, due 2004	770	8½ %
Sears, Roebuck, due 1995	950	9 %

5. Denise Colbroth borrowed $4,500 for three years on a discount loan. The $4,500 is to be paid back at the end of the three years. The

stated rate was 8%. How much of the principal did she actually have use of? What was the effective rate of interest?

6. Ace Corporation plans to purchase a new machine for $10,000. Monthly payments will be $217.50 for 60 months. Find the approximate effective rate of interest.

7. Peter Simmons is considering the purchase of a new car. It costs $5,600, but his present car will bring $1,600 on a trade-in. The auto dealer is willing to finance the $4,000 loan over three years for monthly payments of $133. Peter has also inquired about a loan at the local bank. They will lend him the $4,000 with monthly payments of $195 for two years. Is the auto dealer or the bank charging the lower rate of interest?

8. Jackson, Inc. is borrowing $80,000 from a bank. It is a discount loan at 8% for three years. Determine the effective interest rate on the loan.

9. Hamilton Jones borrowed $4,000 from a friend. The friend calculated the interest using the discount method, and gave Hamilton $3,200. If Hamilton had to pay back the $4,000 in two years, determine the effective rate of interest for the loan.

10. Richard Smothers has a 6% passbook account at a local savings and loan association. If the interest is compounded semiannually, how much will he have at the end of one year if he has $100 on deposit at the start of the year?

11. Sandy Weber has an 8% growth certificate purchased from a bank. Interest is compounded quarterly. If she lets the interest accumulate, it will also be compounded at the same rate. The certificate cost $5,000 and has a life of four years. How much will she receive from the bank when the certificate matures?

12. The Jones' are planning for their retirement. If they have $10,000 now and will add $1,500 at the end of each year, how much will they have in ten years if the funds are invested at 8%?

13. Paul and Sandy want to build up an estate for their children. If they save $1,000 per year for 30 years and the money is compounded annually at 6%, how much will they have? Assume they save the $1,000 at the end of each year.

14. Edna Jones needs $30,000 in ten years to buy a piece of property. How much will she need to save each year if her savings will grow at a rate of 7% compounded annually?

15. John and Lillian Small have a savings account of $8,500. John is to retire in ten years. If they save $2,000 per year for the next ten years and their original savings plus the yearly savings is compounded annually at 6%, how much will they have when John retires?

16. Crothers, Inc. must have $300,000 in 15 years to pay off a bond issue. How much must they put into a sinking fund at the end of each

year to accumulate the $300,000 if funds are compounded at an annual rate of 8%?

17. Kline Industries needs to put a certain amount in a sinking fund at the end of each year for 15 years to pay off a $4.5 million bond issue. If the funds receive interest at the rate of 6%, determine the yearly sinking fund payment.

18. National Bank and Trust advertises passbook accounts paying 5% with a higher effective interest rate. If they compound interest quarterly, what is the effective interest rate?

19. Samuel Drucker put $1,000 in the bank three years ago. During the first year he received 5% interest compounded semiannually. During the last two years the rate was 6% compounded quarterly. How much did Drucker have at the end of the three years?

Financial Leverage
and
Debt Financing

chapter 11

Debt is a major source of funds for financing the needs of business, government, and households. There are two primary reasons for using debt. First, the borrower may not be able to secure the required funds in any other manner. This is especially true for individuals and government. Second, using debt as opposed to equity, profits, or other internally generated funds may substantially increase the profitability of a business. The amount of existing debt is shown below.

Debt in the United States*

Borrower	Amount (billions)
Corporations	$1,254
Mortgages	$ 755
U.S. government	$ 620
State and local government	$ 206
Consumer	$ 164

*Sources: Federal Reserve and Treasury Department.

This indicates the great importance of debt as a source of funds for financing expenditures for every level of government, business, and personal needs.

FINANCIAL LEVERAGE

It is possible to increase profits through the use of debt if the cost of the debt (interest) is less than the return generated through the use of the debt. Thus, if funds can be borrowed at 10% and invested so as to return 12%, an increase in profits will result. The concept of borrowing funds to reinvest for increased profits is called *financial leverage*. While financial leverage is used to increase profits, it may also result in *reduction of profits*. If, for example, sales decline, heavy debt burdens may severely erode profits.

Example 1: FINANCIAL LEVERAGE

Suppose a firm requires a total of $10,000 in funds and may select between two financing mixes: all common stock *or* half common stock and half debt at 8% effective interest rate. Suppose further that the firm can sell common stock for $25 per share, has a tax rate of 20%, and expects EBIT of $1,000. Determine the earnings per share (EPS) using each of the possible financial mixes.

SOLUTION

	Plan A All Equity	Plan B Half Equity and Debt
EBIT	$ 1,000	$ 1,000
Less interest	0	− 400
EBT	$ 1,000	$ 600
Less taxes	− 200	− 120
After-tax profit	$ 800	$ 480
Shares of stock	400	200
EPS	$ 2.00	$ 2.40

The interest of $400 was obtained by multiplying $5,000 by 8%. The number of shares was determined by dividing the amount to be financed using equity (common stock) by $25 per share. Thus, when half equity or $5,000 was used, the number of shares is $5,000 ÷ $25 = 200 shares.

By way of analysis, it is often useful to examine the relationship between EPS and EBIT using graphical methods. An EPS-EBIT line can be developed for each financing plan available to the firm.

Example 2:   GRAPHING EPS-EBIT

Graph the EPS-EBIT line for plan B in Example 1.

SOLUTION

To draw a line, two points are required. For plan B one point has already been determined: EBIT = \$1,000 and EPS = \$2.40. To obtain the second point necessary for the construction of the EPS-EBIT line, it is convenient to choose a value of EBIT which exactly equals the interest. Selection of a value for EBIT which just equals the interest cost will result in zero EPS. Thus, a second point is EBIT = \$400 and EPS = 0. The EPS-EBIT line for Plan B is shown in Fig. 1.

FIGURE 1.

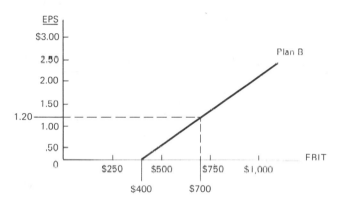

Once an EPS-EBIT line has been constructed, it is possible to determine the EPS for various values of EBIT. For example, when EBIT are \$700, EPS are \$1.20, as shown in Fig. 1.

While it is useful to be able to rapidly ascertain values of EPS corresponding to different values of EBIT, this is not the primary use of an EPS-EBIT line. The primary purpose is to determine the points of intersection between EPS-EBIT lines corresponding to the available financing plans. The EPS-EBIT lines for financing plans A and B are shown in Fig. 2.

From Fig. 2 it can be seen that the two lines intersect when EBIT = \$800 and EPS = \$1.60. Note that the line corresponding to plan A shows *higher* EPS for values of EBIT *less* than \$800, while plan B shows *higher* EPS for values of EBIT *exceeding* \$800. Thus, if EBIT were expected to be less than \$800, plan A would be preferred, while B would be selected for values of EBIT exceeding \$800.

Example 1 indicates that EPS may be increased by using debt, provided the cost of debt is sufficiently low. If the cost of debt is

FIGURE 2.

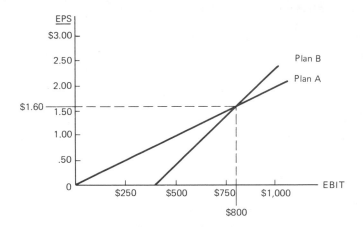

increased, the advantage will decrease and ultimately EPS will actually decrease if more debt is employed. This is demonstrated in Example 3.

Example 3: FINANCIAL LEVERAGE

Solve Example 1, given the cost of debt as 12% and note the change in EPS.

SOLUTION

	All Equity	Half Equity and Debt
EBIT	$ 1,000	$ 1,000
Less interest	0	— ·600
EBT	$ 1,000	$ 400
Less taxes	— 200	— 80
After-tax profit	$ 800	$ 320
Shares of stock	400	200
EPS	$ 2.00	$ 1.60

In general, *as a firm uses increasing amounts of debt to finance its operations, with the amount of equity held constant, the financial risk increases.* That is, the risk of the firm's defaulting on its payment of interest and repayment of principal increases. Thus, it is not uncommon for lenders to increase interest rates as they lend increasingly larger amounts to a given borrower. For example, the interest rate on the first $100,000 of a loan to a firm might be 10%, while the rate on the next $50,000 borrowed might be 12%, and so on. *The interest rate charged on the last increment of debt borrowed is called the marginal interest rate.* Thus the marginal cost of debt to the firm borrowing $150,000 would be 12%. If the firm borrowed more than $150,000, then the marginal cost of debt would likely increase to 14% or beyond. Ultimately, unless a borrower increases the amount of equity (their own investment), they will be unable to secure any additional loans. In general, the marginal cost of debt increases as more debt is used to finance a firm unless the equity base is increased proportionately. Further, if the firm is a corporation, the shareholders may be hesitant concerning borrowing large sums if such borrowing increases financial risk. If a firm borrows excessively, shareholders may either sell the stock with a resulting decrease in its market price or look to greater dividends to compensate for the added financial risk.

It should be noted that an EBIT-EPS analysis may be used to evaluate the impact of financing individual projects. Suppose, for example, that a firm had EPS of $2.00 and was considering an investment. The management would want to be sure that the return from the investment would be sufficient to produce at least a $2.00 earnings per share on any stock that was issued to cover the cost of the investment. Management would avoid selecting any financial plan which would tend to reduce EPS in the long run.

Example 4:   FINANCIAL LEVERAGE

Three financing plans are available to Casone Products, which needs $1 million for construction of a new plant. Casone wants to maximize EPS. Currently, the stock is selling for $30 per share. The EBIT resulting from the plant operation are expected to run about $150,000 per year. Casone's marginal tax rate is 48%. Money can be borrowed at the rates indicated:

Up to $100,000, at 10%
Over $100,000 to $500,000, at 14%
Over $500,000, at 18%

If funds in excess of $500,000 are borrowed, Casone anticipates a drop in the price of the stock to $25 per share. The three financing plans are as follows:

Plan A: Use $100,000 debt.
Plan B: Use $300,000 debt.
Plan C: Use $600,000 debt.

Determine the EPS for these three plans and indicate the financing plan which will result in the highest EPS.

SOLUTION

	Plan A	Plan B	Plan C
EBIT	$ 150,000	$ 150,000	$ 150,000
Less interest	− 10,000	− 38,000	− 84,000
EBT	$ 140,000	$ 112,000	$ 66,000
Less taxes	− 67,200	− 53,760	− 31,680
After-tax profit	$ 72,800	$ 58,240	$ 34,320
Shares of stock	30,000	23,333	16,000
EPS	$ 2.43	$ 2.50	$ 2.15

Plan B results in the highest EPS.

The calculation of the interest in each of the plans is critical to obtaining the correct profit. The interest for plan C is determined as follows:

	Interest
$100,000 at 10%	$10,000
400,000 at 14%	56,000
100,000 at 18%	18,000
Total	$84,000

Example 4 demonstrates how, in some instances, using greater amounts of debt may result in decreased EPS and negative leverage.

The three financing plans for Casone Products are shown in graphical form in Fig. 3. Plan A is preferable for values of EBIT up to x_1. For values of EBIT between x_1 and x_2, plan B is preferable. Above x_2, plan C is preferable. In each instance the preference is based on the desire to maximize EPS.

It should be noted that both the graphs for Examples 1 and 4 assumed a constant rate of taxation; 20% in Example 1 and 48% in Example 4. If a problem had been selected in which the tax rate included 20, 22, and 48%, the lines depicting the relationship between EPS and EBIT would have been kinked. Initially, with the lower 20% and 22% tax rates, EPS would have increased rapidly as EBIT increased. When the taxable income had increased so that the 48% rate was imposed, EPS would increase at a slower rate.

The use of EBIT-EPS analysis indicates to management the projected EPS for different financial plans. *Generally, management wants to maximize EPS if doing so also satisfies the primary goal of financial management—maximization of the owner's wealth as represented by*

FIGURE 3

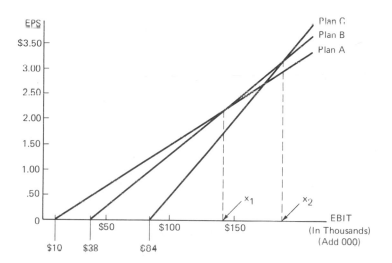

the value of the business, i.e., the value of the firm's common stock.
As noted in the examples above, if a firm attempts to use excessive
amounts of debt, shareholders (who are risk-averters) may sell their
stock, and thus its price will fall. While the use of large amounts of
debt may result in higher EPS, it may also result in a reduction in the
price of the firm's stock. *The optimum financial structure for a firm
(that is, the use of debt in relationship to equity and retained earnings
as sources of financing) should be the one which maximizes the price
of the common stock.*

There are theoretical models available which management can use
to project the optimal structure. The owner of a small business using
such a model might conclude that the "optimal" financial structure for
his firm is 20% equity and 80% debt. In reality, the financial structure will be established by the money and capital markets. In particular, for a small business, the bank will decide how much it will loan to
the business. The amount of debt will be determined by forces outside
of the firm, and the firm will have to accept the decision of the lenders.
The same situation holds for larger businesses which finance using the
services of investment bankers. The investment bankers assess the
market and advise the firm as to the most practical form of financing
given the mood of capital markets. A firm may desire to finance with
bonds, but if the investment banker indicates that the market for purchase of bonds is weak, the firm may be forced to issue additional
stock regardless of its "optimum" financial structure.

SHORT-TERM DEBT

Short-term debt is generally categorized as debt which will be repaid in a period of one year or less. Various types of short-term debt may be available to a firm. The primary forms are *trade credit, unsecured bank loans, inventory loans, receivable loans, and commercial paper.*

Trade Credit

Trade credit is a source of funds to the purchaser of goods or services when the seller need not be paid at the time of the sale. The purchase generates an account payable for the buyer and an account receivable for the seller. As long as the account is open (unpaid), the buyer is, in essence, borrowing from the seller. In many instances the conditions of sale permit a small discount if the bill is paid within a stated period of time. This is called a *cash discount*. One commonly used is 2/10, net 30. This means that the buyer may deduct 2% from the bill if he pays within 10 days. Otherwise the entire bill is due in 30 days.

There are two costs involved in trade credit. The first is the cost of not taking any available discount. Thus, the cost of not paying within 10 days if the terms are 2/10 would be 2% of the bill. The second cost is incurred when the bill is not paid when due. The cost incurred may be a loss of credit rating with subsequent difficulty in securing credit. It is difficult to place a dollar value on the latter, but the dollar cost and effective interest rate of not taking cash discounts may be easily determined as demonstrated in Example 5.

Example 5:   Trade Credit

Peters International purchased $30,000 of goods on terms 2/10, net 30. If they wait until the thirtieth day before paying, determine the dollar cost and effective rate of interest.

Solution

The 2% discount on $30,000 amounts to $600. By waiting until the thirtieth day, the firm is, in effect, borrowing $30,000 − $600 = $29,400 for 20 days at a cost of $600. The effective rate of interest is calculated as shown:

$$\frac{\$600}{\$29,400} \times \frac{360}{20} = .367 = 36.7\%$$

In the calculation, 360 represents the number of days in the year, and 20 the number of days of credit extension. The resulting 36.7% is a very high rate of interest. Hence, cash discounts are generally taken.

Commercial Paper

Commercial paper consists of negotiable promissory notes issued by a company which mature in less than one year, usually four to six months. Commercial paper denominations range upward from about $5,000 to $1 million. Commercial paper is a means of borrowing open to only the most credit-worthy companies, since the borrower does not give any security (collateral) to the lender as a pledge of payment for the loan.

Commercial paper is sold by the borrower to a lender, which is generally a bank, insurance company, pension fund, or another firm. *Sometimes the paper is sold directly; that is, a firm borrows directly from a lender. In other instances the sale is handled through a broker.* About two-thirds of the commercial paper is placed directly. Commercial paper is a very important source of short-term financing. As of June 1976, over $49 billion of commerical paper were outstanding.

Commercial paper normally does not provide for payment of interest. Rather, the notes are sold at a discount and repaid at the face amount. The difference between the face amount and the amount received by the issuing firm from the lender is the interest.

Example 6: COMMERCIAL PAPER

Gerald Mfg. Co. plans to issue six-month notes with a face value of $100,000. If they sell the notes for $95,000, determine the effective rate of interest.

SOLUTION

The notes are sold for $95,000. This is the actual amount Gerald is borrowing. The interest paid is the difference between the face value and the sale price, or $5,000. Thus, Gerald is paying $5,000 for the use of $95,000 for six months. The calculation of the effective interest rate is carried out in the same manner as for trade credit.

$$\frac{\$5,000}{\$95,000} \times \frac{360}{180} = .105 = 10\frac{1}{2}\%$$

Unsecured Bank Loans

Unsecured loans include various types such as a line of credit, revolving credit, and transaction loans. The word *unsecured* means that the bank does not hold any security as *collateral* for the loan.

A line of credit is an informal agreement between a bank and a customer for the bank to lend up to a stated maximum amount to the customer. The actual amount of the loan may vary appreciably over the year. The bank normally requires that the loan be paid off in its entirety at some time during the year, usually for a period of 30 to 45 days. Often a line of credit may be extended from year to year.

Revolving credit is similar to a line of credit. The difference is that *a revolving credit agreement represents a formal agreement between the bank and its customer.* Thus, the customer may request and receive any amount up to the maximum amount specified in the agreement upon short notice. As a result, the bank must maintain greater reserves than would otherwise be required. To compensate for maintaining greater reserves, a bank will often charge a *commitment fee* on the unused portion of the loan. Thus, if maximum credit extension under a revolving credit agreement were $10,000 and the customer borrowed only $4,000, the bank would charge a fee of about ½ of 1% on the unused $6,000.

Transaction loans, as the name implies, are short-term loans used to finance a transaction. For example, an importer may purchase a large shipment of goods and require a loan for a short period until they are sold and payment received.

Usually the interest on short-term unsecured loans is calculated on the unpaid monthly balance or on a collect basis at the time the loan is repaid. Sometimes a bank may require a "compensating balance" when it lends money. For example, a bank might require that a firm maintain a minimum checking account balance in the bank amounting to 10% of the loan.

Example 7:   COMPENSATING BALANCES

Bankers Trust Company will lend Royal Cleaners $20,000 at 9% to be paid on a collect basis at the time the loan is repaid in one year. A 15% compensating balance is required. Determine the actual amount of the loan which Royal will have use of, and the effective rate of interest.

SOLUTION

A 15% compensating balance is 15% of the $20,000 loan, or $3,000. This means that Royal will have use of only $17,000. However, the interest is calculated based on the $20,000 loan. The interest is 9% of the $20,000 or $1,800. The effective rate of interest is calculated below:

$$\frac{\$1,800}{\$17,000} = .106 = 10.6\%$$

Example 8:   COMPENSATING BALANCES

Nicol Corporation needs the use of $25,000. They may borrow from First National Bank at an annual interest rate of 10% and a 12% compensating balance. Determine how much Nicol must borrow to *have use* of the $25,000 and the effective rate of interest.

SOLUTION

First National requires a 12% compensating balance of the loan. Let x be the amount of the loan. Then, $.12x$ is the compensating balance.

$$x - .12x = \$25,000$$
$$.88x = \$25,000$$
$$x = \frac{\$25,000}{.88}$$
$$x = \$28,410$$

Nicol will have to borrow $28,410. The interest will be 10% of the $28,410 or $2,841. The effective rate of interest is calculated below:

$$\frac{\$2,841}{\$25,000} = .1136 = 11.36\%$$

Inventory Loans

Inventory provides a basis for collateral to support loans. *Collateral is the security given by the borrower to a lender as a pledge for the repayment of a loan.* Many types of inventory may be used as collateral: physical inventories of merchandise, goods in process, and finished goods. The amount which a lender will lend against a firm's inventory depends primarily on four factors, in addition to the lender's assessment of the borrower's ability to repay the loan. The four factors considered are the *price stability of the inventory, its marketability, its perishability, and the difficulty and expense involved in selling it.* If the inventory has a ready market, such as grains, the firm may be able to borrow up to 90% of its market value. If the inventory is highly sophisticated electronic equipment having limited applications, then the inventory may not be suitable as collateral to any lender.

Inventory loans are generally handled through one of three methods: *blanket inventory liens, trust receipts, or warehouse financing. Blanket inventory liens involve general liens against all of the borrower's inventory which the borrower is free to sell.* Naturally, as the inventory is sold the borrower is expected to pay back the loan in accordance with the loan agreement. *Trust receipts involve identifying specific goods owned by the borrower which form the collateral for the loan.* The identified goods are segregated from the other inventory and labeled appropriately, usually with identifying serial numbers which facilitate inspection and audit by the lender. When the goods are sold the proceeds are forwarded to the lender.

Warehouse financing involves the most stringent segregation and identification of that inventory which forms collateral for a loan. Frequently the inventory is stored in a public warehouse or a field warehouse operated by a third party and constructed (often by fencing off an appropriate area) on the borrower's property. In either case, the inventory is monitored by a third party—a public warehouseman. The public warehouseman acts as a supervisory agent for the lender, notifying the lender of any inventory added or removed. If necessary the lender can then take steps to ensure prompt repayment of the loan or a portion thereof.

Inventory provides a solid basis for collateral to support loans. Usually the lender determines a percentage of the value of the inventory upon which to base the loan. Inventory loans may be set up to meet the needs of firms that have widely varying inventory levels. Many firms have seasonal product lines; inventory levels are very low during periods of high sales and build up as sales fall off. Inventories may be financed using short-term bank loans, with the inventory acting as collateral. Another approach is to borrow funds long-term and reinvest funds which may not be needed during periods when inventory levels are low. Determination of the costs involved in the alternative modes of financing is demonstrated in Example 9.

Example 9:   INVENTORY FINANCING

Duncan Industries has a seasonal fluctuating inventory and must borrow funds to cover the cost of its inventory. Projected inventories for the upcoming months are shown below:

Month	Amount of Inventory
January	$800,000
February	800,000
March	400,000
April	400,000
May	200,000
June	100,000
July	100,000
August	100,000
September	200,000
October	400,000
November	400,000
December	800,000

Duncan can secure long-term funds (permanent financing) at the rate of 10% and reinvest these funds on a short-term basis at 6% when they are not needed. *Or* Duncan can secure short-term funds at 12% and pay interest only on the amount it actually needs during any given month. All interest rates indicated are effective annual rates. Determine the cost of each type of financing.

SOLUTION

Consider the short-term borrowing first. The monthly interest cost is one-twelfth of the annual rate, or 1%. Hence, the cost per month is 1% of the amount needed, that is, the amount of the inventory.

Month	Inventory	Monthly Interest Cost
January	$800,000	$ 8,000
February	800,000	8,000
March	400,000	4,000
April	400,000	4,000
May	200,000	2,000
June	100,000	1,000
July	100,000	1,000
August	100,000	1,000
September	200,000	2,000
October	400,000	4,000
November	400,000	4,000
December	800,000	8,000
	Total	$47,000

The total yearly interest using short-term financing is $47,000.

Next, consider long-term borrowing. $800,000 will have to be borrowed in order to cover the maximum amount of inventory on hand during the year. At 10% this will cost $80,000. However, when the funds are not needed, they may be invested at 6% annually, or ½% per month. The amount realized from the short-term investments is calculated using the table below:

Month	Excess Funds	Monthly Investment Interest
January	$ 0	$ 0
February	0	0
March	400,000	2,000
April	400,000	2,000
May	600,000	3,000
June	700,000	3,500
July	700,000	3,500
August	700,000	3,500
September	600,000	3,000
October	400,000	2,000
November	400,000	2,000
December	0	0
	Total	$24,500

Thus, if Duncan uses long-term financing, the net cost is $80,000 − $24,500 = $55,500. Since this exceeds the $47,000 cost of short-term financing, short-term should be used.

Receivable Loans

Another type of collateral used to support short-term loans is a firm's accounts receivable. These accounts represent debts owed to the firm and as such provide a sound basis for borrowing. When accounts receivable are used as collateral for a bank loan, the bank may take physical possession of the receivables. As the firm collects the receivables, it notifies the bank. Similarly, when sales are made and receivables generated, the firm gives them to the bank. Hence, there is a continual turnover of receivables and a good deal of record keeping required, on the part of both the firm and the bank. Naturally, the bank must receive compensation for the work, and the cost may be built into the interest rate on the loan or added on as an extra charge. Sometimes banks will provide *blanket loans* on receivables and thereby eliminate the detailed bookkeeping described above. Banks normally will lend an amount up to about 80% of the face value of the accounts receivable. This provides the bank with a measure of protection in case the firm has difficulty in collecting the receivables and repaying the bank.

Example 10: ACCOUNTS RECEIVABLE LOANS

Quinn Electronics has an average of $100,000 in credit sales per month. They are collected in 60 days. First National Bank will provide Quinn with a loan for 80% of the face amount of the receivables at an annual rate of 10%. First National will also charge a service fee of 1% of the accounts receivable processed. Determine the annual dollar cost of the loan and service fee and the effective interest rate.

SOLUTION

The face amount of the receivables will average $200,000 since monthly sales average $100,000 and collections take 60 days. The loan is 80% of $200,000, or $160,000. The interest at 10% is $16,000 per year. The service fee is charged on accounts receivable processed. On the average, $100,000 of accounts receivable will be processed every 30 days. The cost is $100,000 × .01 = $1,000 every 30 days, or 12 times per year. The total service charge is 12 × $1,000 = $12,000. The total cost is $16,000 + $12,000 = $28,000. The effective interest rate is therefore:

$$\frac{\$28,000}{\$160,000} = .175 = 17.5\%$$

Factoring Receivables

In addition to borrowing and using accounts receivable as collateral, *the accounts may actually be sold (factored) to a factor which collects the receivables*. Factoring receivables may have advantages to small firms since it may eliminate the need for a collection department within the firm. The factor pays the firm as the receivables are collected. In some instances the factor may pay for the receivables when provided by the firm, in effect lending the firm funds, with the receivables being used as collateral. Frequently when a firm factors its receivables it is short of cash and may be close to insolvency. Therefore the firm's customers may lose confidence in a firm which factors its receivables. Hence, the sales force must be ready to explain the reason for this action to all customers in order to maintain confidence in the firm. Such a goal is usually difficult to achieve. Therefore, factoring of receivables is generally the last source of funds which a firm would tap. However, it should be noted that while factoring is not generally regarded as a prime source of funds, it is used extensively in certain industries. In New York, in the garment industry, factoring is common. Factors frequently specialize in an industry. They know the buyers in that industry and can, therefore, consolidate the receivables from several sellers and thereby reduce the required bookkeeping.

Example 11:   FACTORING RECEIVABLES

A factor will buy a firm's receivables ($100,000 per month), which have a collection period of 60 days. The factor will lend up to 75% of the face value of the receivables for an annual charge of 8%. The factor will also charge a 2% fee on all receivables purchased. It has been estimated that the factor's services will save the company a credit department expense and bad debts expense of $1,500 per month. Determine the dollar cost and effective interest rate based on borrowing the maximum possible from the factor.

SOLUTION

Since the receivables take 60 days to collect, the factor will have approximately 2 months ($200,000) of receivables on hand at any given time. Since the most they will loan is 75%, the maximum loan is $150,000. At 8%, the annual interest on the loan is $12,000. The factor will purchase $100,000 per month of receivables, or $1.2 million per year. The factoring fee charged is 2% of the $1.2 million or $24,000. Thus, the total charges amount to $36,000. A savings of $1,500 a month will be enjoyed by the borrower. This amounts to $18,000 per year. Thus the actual cost to the firm is

Interest plus factoring fee	$ 36,000
Less savings	− 18,000
Actual cost	$ 18,000

The effective interest rate is calculated as follows:

$$\frac{\$18,000}{\$150,000} = .12 = 12\%$$

INTERMEDIATE-TERM DEBT

Intermediate-term financing ranges from roughly one to five years. Unlike short-term financing, intermediate-term financing is used for fixed asset requirements, extensive building of inventories, receivables, and the like. Many assets, such as trucks and light machinery, are financed in periods of five years or less.

Banks provide intermediate-term financing through term loans, lines of credit, and revolving credit agreements. Insurance companies also provide a source of intermediate-term loans. The Small Business Administration makes loans directly or participates with banks in lending funds to small businesses.

A great number of intermediate-term loans are used for purchase of equipment. Usually term loans calling for regular installment payments are involved in equipment financing. Leases are becoming increasingly important as a source of funds for financing equipment. Leasing is discussed in detail as a part of the study of capital budgeting.

Example 12:   INTERMEDIATE-TERM FINANCING

The Garard Company plans to purchase a new piece of machinery which will cost $100,000. They have no excess cash, but the bank will lend them the amount for 10% interest provided they maintain a 10% compensating balance. Garard will have to borrow the money for the compensating balance from the bank, thus increasing their loan to a greater amount.

a. Calculate the amount of the initial loan.
b. If the loan is to be paid back over five years with equal annual payments on the *principal*, calculate the yearly payments of interest and principal.

c. Calculate the effective rate of interest of the loan for the $100,000 actually needed by the firm.

SOLUTION

Part a. The bank requires a 10% compensating balance. Let y be the amount of the loan. Then $.10y$ is the compensating balance:

$$y - .10y = \$100,000$$
$$.90y = \$100,000$$
$$y = \$111,111$$

The original loan will be for $111,111.

Part b. The principal is to be paid back in equal annual installments. Thus, each year one-fifth of the $111,111 or $22,222 will be paid back. The interest for the year is determined by multiplying the amount of the loan which was outstanding for the year by the 10% interest rate. The calculations are shown in tabular form below:

Year	Amount of Loan Outstanding During Year	Interest Payment at Year's End	Principal Payment at Year's End
1	$111,111	$11,111	$22,222
2	88,889	8,889	22,222
3	66,667	6,667	22,222
4	44,445	4,445	22,222
5	22,223	2,222	22,223

Part c. The effective rate of interest is determined as follows:

$$\frac{\$11,111}{\$100,000} = .111 = 11.1\%$$

Some intermediate-term loans provide for a *balloon repayment* feature. *The balloon feature establishes a repayment schedule whereby the major portion of the loan remains unpaid at the completion of the loan period. The unpaid amount is called the balloon.* Such a loan for $100,000 might require principal repayment of only $5,000 per year for five years at which time $75,000 would still be outstanding. Assuming the borrower operated within the loan agreement, the loan would be renewed for another five years. Balloon intermediate-term loans are very important for small businesses, which often are unable to secure extensive long-term financing.

Almost all intermediate-term loans are with banks, although occasionally insurance companies will provide loans for periods of five years or less. For a bank to protect itself from default of a loan, there are provisions written into the loan agreement which permit the bank to take appropriate action as necessary. These provisions are called *protective covenants* and fall into three general categories: *general provisions, routine provisions,* and *specific provisions.*

General provisions usually cover such things as requirements for maintenance of a specified level of working capital, limitations of dividends and repurchase of stock, limitations on capital expenditures, and limitations on acquiring other indebtedness. The purpose of these provisions is to assure that the firm will be able to pay the interest and repay the principal in a timely manner. The details of the provisions are arranged so as to meet the needs of the firm and also protect the bank against possible default.

Routine provisions require the borrower to provide the bank with financial statements, to maintain insurance, not to sell a major portion of its assets, to pay its taxes, and the like. Further, a negative pledge clause is generally included as a routine provision. A *negative pledge clause* precludes the firm from mortgaging its assets. Other routine provisions preclude entry into leasing or rental agreements beyond a preestablished level, selling receivables, etc.

Special provisions deal with such things as the uses of the borrowed funds. The use of the funds may be specified and limited to particular expenditures. Similarly, the investments which a firm is permitted to make may be limited. Total salaries and bonuses to executives may be limited, and if any employees are key to the functioning of the firm, the firm may have to take out insurance policies on them payable to the firm or the bank.

The provisions described above are designed to protect the bank from default and permit the bank to take appropriate action to prevent default. While the provisions may permit a bank to call the loan if any of the provisions are broken, usually the bank will not call the loan. Rather, the bank will provide managerial expertise and control to bring the borrowing firm back into line with the restrictions. Thus, the restrictions are beneficial to both the bank and the borrowing firm.

LONG-TERM DEBT

Bonds are the major form of long-term debt used by large firms and government. Smaller businesses use bonds only to a limited extent due to the high cost involved in their sale combined with a limited number of purchasers willing to invest in firms that are not well known. Thus, small businesses requiring long-term financing are usually limited to mortgages or intermediate-term loans with a balloon repayment feature.

There are several types of bonds. The most common is the *debenture*. Debentures are secured by the general property of the firm, but not by any property in particular. Only companies with high credit ratings are able to issue debentures since investors in these securities must look to the earning power of the firm to meet principal and interest payments.

Other types of bonds include *subordinated debentures,* mortgage bonds, and income bonds. Subordinated debentures are bonds which rank behind general debentures on claim to a firm's assets. This "subordination" becomes important if the firm is to be liquidated, and especially if the liquidation is an outgrowth of bankruptcy. *Mortgage bonds* are secured by specific corporate assets such as a building or land. *Income bonds* are unique in that interest need be paid only when it is earned. With all types of bonds, creditors are primarily interested in the earning power of the firm as the determinate of its credit worthiness.

Most bonds are issued to the public, although some are sold to insurance companies and pension funds. The latter process is known as *direct placement. When bonds are sold publicly, a trustee is appointed and designated to represent the interests of the bondholders.* The trustee's primary obligations have to do with making sure that the borrowing firm keeps all of the contractual agreements in the bond indenture. *The indenture is the legal agreement between the issuing firm and the bondholders.* The indenture indicates the terms of the bonds (rate of interest payable, payment dates, time of retirement, etc.) and protective covenants. The protective covenants are similar to those discussed in the section on intermediate-term financing.

Several methods are used in the retirement of bonds. *Retirement refers to repayment of investors and redemption of the bonds.* Most corporate bonds and federal government bonds are paid off on the date of maturity. All of the owners are repaid at one time. In many instances, the firm may issue another series of bonds just prior to paying off the maturing issue. The proceeds from the new issue are used to pay off the old issue. This process is called "rolling over" debt. Some bonds require that a *sinking fund* be established by a firm. Periodic payments are made by the firm to the sinking fund to provide sufficient funds to retire the bonds. Sinking funds are managed by the bond trustee, who can retire the bonds. Most bonds issued by government agencies and state and local governments are retired serially. That is, bonds with certain serial numbers are paid off each year so that all of the bonds are redeemed by the time the issue matures. Using serial retirement, usually about the same number of bonds are redeemed each year. Thus, if the bond series had a maturity of 20 years, 5% of the bonds would be redeemed each year.

Most corporate bonds contain a *call feature. This permits the corporation to buy back the bonds at a stated price and time before the bonds mature.* The call date, in effect, represents an early maturity date. The stated call price is usually $10 to $80 above the $1,000 maturity value of the bond. The premium usually decreases over time. Thus, the *call premium* might be $80 during the first year after the bond has been issued, $70 after the second, and so on. The reason that corporations desire a call feature is that it permits them to retire bond issues before maturity. This is extremely important if the prevailing rate of interest goes down. Companies can call existing bonds and refinance at lower interest rates. The call premium is required by investors since if the bond is called the investor will have to reinvest the funds. Reinvestment of funds may require the expense of brokerage fees. Further, if the general level of interest rates declines, the investor may have to settle for a lower return. For the exposure to such risk, investors require a premium.

Some bonds are *convertible* to common stock. This permits the bondholder to enjoy a secure income from the bond interest and also participate in the growth of the firm. If the value of the common stock increases, the bondholder may find it advantageous to convert the bond to stock. Convertible securities are discussed in more detail in Chapter 12.

QUESTIONS
FOR
DISCUSSION

1. Explain the significance of the points of intersection of the EBIT versus EPS graphs.
2. Explain how use of financial leverage may result in increasing financial risk.
3. Why, in some instances, may the price of a firm's common stock decrease as it borrows more funds?
4. List the various types of short-term debt available to business firms.
5. Differentiate between a line of credit and revolving credit.
6. Explain the operations of a factor.
7. Indicate the types of purchases that are generally financed using intermediate-term debt.
8. Differentiate between a debenture and a mortgage bond.
9. Explain serial retirement.
10. What is the purpose of a call feature of a bond?
11. Why is the call feature important to investors?

PROBLEMS

1. Suppose a firm requires $150,000 in financing. It may use all common stock or half common stock and half debt financing. The common stock can be sold for $25.00 per share, while the effective cost of the debt is 10%. The firm anticipates EBIT of $20,000. The tax rate is 20%. Determine which method of financing will result in the higher EPS.

2. A firm requires $2 million in financing for a new program which will result in EBIT of $250,000 per year. It has two choices for financial structure: 70% stock and 30% debt or 50% stock and 50% debt. Under the first plan the stock can be sold for $25 per share, and the interest rate on the debt will be 10%. Under the second plan the stock will sell for $22 per share, and the interest rate on the debt will be 11%. Determine the EPS for each plan. The firm has a 48% marginal tax rate.

3. Three financing plans are available to Acorn Products: all equity, 70% equity and 30% debt, or 40% equity and 60% debt. EBIT are $150,000. Total financing required is $1 million. Stock can be sold for $50 per share. Funds can be borrowed as follows: up to and including $200,000 at 14%, $200,000 through $500,000 at 16%, over $500,000 at 20%. Determine the EPS for each plan assuming a 48% marginal tax rate.

4. Three financing plans are available to Dwyer Products, which needs $500,000 for construction of a new plant. Dwyer wants to maximize EPS. Currently, the stock is selling for $40 per share. The EBIT resulting from the plant operation are expected to run about $100,000 per year. Dwyer's marginal tax rate is 48%. Money can be borrowed at the rates indicated:

Up to $50,000, at 10%
Over $50,000 to $200,000, at 16%
Over $200,000, at 18%

If funds in excess of $250,000 are borrowed, Dwyer anticipates a drop in the price of the stock to $35 per share. The three financing plans are as follows:

a. Use all equity;
b. Use $100,000 debt;
c. Use $300,000 debt.

Calculate the EPS for each plan, and construct an EPS versus EBIT graph. From the graph, determine the transition points and indicate the specific range of EBIT which result in the highest EPS under each of the three plans.

5. Winters Corporation purchased $50,000 of merchandise on terms of 3/20, net 90. If they wait until the ninetieth day before paying, determine the dollar cost and effective rate of interest.

6. Abbott Corporation purchased $50,000 of merchandise on terms 3/15, net 120. If they do not take the discount, indicate the effective rate of interest.

7. Dilworth Industries plans to sell 270-day commercial notes having a face value of $5 million. If they sell the notes for $4.6 million, determine the effective rate of interest.

8. South Steel is planning to sell 300-day commercial paper having a face value of $4 million. If they sell them for $3.7 million, determine the effective rate of interest.

9. The Fortune Company plans to purchase a new piece of machinery which will cost $200,000. They have no excess cash, but the bank will loan them the amount for 12% interest provided they maintain a 15% compensating balance. Fortune will have to borrow the money for the compensating balance from the bank, thus increasing their loan to a greater amount.

a. Calculate the amount of the initial loan.
b. If the loan is to be paid back over five years with equal annual payments on the *principal*, calculate the yearly payments of interest and principal.
c. Calculate the effective rate of interest of the loan for the $200,000 actually needed by the firm.

10. Zeron Electronics can borrow $1 million on a two-year loan from the bank. Interest is 10% on the outstanding balance. The principal is to be paid back in equal amounts semiannually over a two-year period.

   a. If the bank charges a 10% compensating balance on funds borrowed, determine how much Zeron will have to borrow initially in order to have the use of $1 million.

   b. Complete the table shown below, indicating the payments:

	Principal	Interest	Total
First payment			
Second payment			
Third payment			
Fourth payment			
Totals			

11. ABC has a seasonal fluctuating inventory and borrows funds to cover the cost of its inventory. Projected inventories for the upcoming months are shown below:

Month	Amount or Inventory
January	$1,000,000
February	800,000
March	600,000
April	400,000
May	200,000
June	100,000
July	50,000
August	50,000
September	200,000
October	400,000
November	600,000
December	800,000

   ABC can secure long-term funds (permanent financing) at the rate of 8% and reinvest these funds on a short-term basis at 6%. *Or* ABC can secure short-term funds at 10% and pay interest only on the amount it actually needs during any given month. Determine the cost using each method of financing.

12. The Canoe Company needs $100,000 in the near future. It could raise the funds utilizing the methods discussed below. Calculate the effective interest rate of each.

   a. Trade credit: Canoe buys about $50,000 of materials per month at terms of 2/30, net 90. It pays its bills in 30 days but could extend the period to 90 days.

   b. Bank loan: The bank will lend money at 11%. Also, a 25% compensating balance is required.

c. A factor will buy Canoe's receivables ($150,000 per month), which have a collection period of 90 days. The factor will advance the $100,000 for an annual charge of 10%. The factor also charges 3% fee on all receivables purchased. However, using the factor will save Canoe $2,500 per month in credit department and bad debt expenses.

13. Martin Company has an average $50,000 in receivables per month. They are collected, on the average, in 90 days. The National Bank will provide Martin with a loan for an amount up to 60% of their outstanding receivables at an annual rate of 12%. The bank also charges a processing fee of 1½% of all receivables processed. Determine the maximum amount which the bank will lend to Martin, the annual dollar cost of the loan, the service fee, and the effective interest rate.

Equity Financing and

Dividend Policy

chapter 12

Equity financing represents the owners' investment in a business. It includes the down payment which a sole proprietor invests in a property, such as an apartment house, as well as stock sold by corporations. Equity financing is extremely important as it forms the basis for debt financing and the acquisition of funds required for purchase of the firm's assets. Once an equity base is established in a business, funds may be borrowed and a credit base established. If the firm is profitable, *any profits which are not distributed to the owners and are kept by the firm increase the firm's equity.* As the equity increases, the firm will be able to support additional debt and, having sufficient funds, will be able to expand. Thus, equity financing is the initial requirement for the financing of all business.

COMMON STOCK

Common stock is the most important form of financing used by business firms. It is the basis for financing all corporations. *The holders of the common stock are the owners of a corporation.* If the firm is profitable, it is their wealth which will increase. On the other hand, if the firm faces hard times and ultimately is liquidated, the common shareholders receive only the residue after all creditors and preferred shareholders are paid in full. Hence, shareholders of common stock are sometimes referred to as the residual owners of a firm.

Value of Common Stock

Common stock value is measured in four ways: par, book, liquidating, and market. The par value of common stock is a stated value which has no significance. Historically, the *par value* was the amount received for the stock when it was initially sold to shareholders. When states imposed taxes on the issue of stock, based on its par value, companies reduced the par value of new issues, and thus the par value is now meaningless.

The amount of owners' equity attached to each share of common stock is called the *book value* of common stock. The book value of common stock is defined as follows:

Book value =

$$\frac{\text{Owners' Equity} - \text{Par value of preferred stock outstanding}}{\text{Number of shares of common stock outstanding}} \quad (1)$$

where

$$\text{Owners' equity} = \text{Assets} - \text{Liabilities} \quad (2)$$

Generally accepted accounting principles provide for the recording of assets and costs at historical dollar amounts. The theory is that this is the most objective criterion, and although financial statements are subject to personal judgments, the valuations subject to management's discretion are minimized by this basic concept. Accordingly, *balance sheets prepared as of points in time in the life of a business do not purport to show (1) the amount of cash that would be realized if the business were terminated or (2) the amount that a buyer would pay for the business as a going concern.* Thus, accounting procedures often cause the value of a firm's land, investments, and fixed assets to be understated on the balance sheet. As a consequence, the owners' equity and concurrently the book value are often understated.

The value a share of stock would have if the assets were sold or liquidated is called the liquidating value. It may be calculated as follows:

Liquidating value =

$$\frac{\text{Sale price of assets} - (\text{Creditors' claims} + \text{Par value pfd. stock})}{\text{Number of shares of common stock outstanding}} \quad (3)$$

The book and liquidating values of stocks consider only the value of those accounts listed on the balance sheet. The most important asset, management, is not included. It is management which organizes labor and the use of the firm's capital equipment to produce output and ultimately profits. It is the application of this managerial talent which investors examine as a part of their evaluation process in the buying and selling of stock, for it is management which affects earnings, dividends, and much of the risk to which a firm is exposed. It is through the free market process, as carried out in one of the stock exchanges, that the *market price* of a firm's stock is established. As indicated in Chapter 1, *the market price is a measure of the collective judgment of all the participants in the exchange process.* The market price is of great importance to the financial manager as it is a determinant of the wealth of the shareholders.

Example 1:   BOOK VALUE OF COMMON STOCK

Lightening Limited has the balance sheet shown. Determine the book value of the common stock.

Balance Sheet, Dec. 31 (in millions)

Assets		*Liabilities and Owners' Equity*	
Cash	$ 3.0	Accounts payable	$ 4.0
Accounts receivable	4.0	Notes payable	1.0
Inventory	6.0	Long-term debt	8.0
Land	3.0	Preferred stock (10,000 shares par	
Fixed assets, net	7.0	value $100)	1.0
Other	1.0	Common stock (500,000 shares	
Total	$24.0	outstanding, par $.30)	.15
		Paid-in capital	2.85
		Retained earnings	7.0
			$24.0

SOLUTION

$$\text{Owners' equity} = \text{Assets} - \text{Liabilities} = \$24 \text{ million} - \$13 \text{ million} = \$11 \text{ million}$$

Using Eq. (2), the owners' equity is determined to be $11 million. The par value of the preferred is $1 million.

$$\text{Book value} = \frac{\$11,000,000 - \$1,000,000}{500,000} = \$20 \text{ per share}$$

Rights of Shareholders

Shareholders may have several rights including voting power, right to income, preemptive right, and right to examine the firm's books. In small firms these rights are important. However, shareholders in a large firm must, essentially, accept a firm as it is or sell their shares. As a consequence *most shareholders are not interested in the operation of a firm except insofar as the operations affect their wealth.*

Voting power constitutes the right to elect the board of directors. Normally each shareholder has one vote for each opening on the board of directors for each share owned. Thus, if three vacancies existed and a shareholder owned 100 shares of stock, he could cast 100 votes in *each* of the three elections for candidates to fill the three board vacancies. A disadvantage of this method of voting is that it virtually assures control of every seat on the board by majority shareholders. For this reason, *cumulative voting* is required for boards of directors in 22 states and is permissible in 18 others. *Under the cumulative voting system, a shareholder may "cumulate" all of his votes and vote them for one board member or however he wishes.* Thus, in the example above, the shareholder owning 100 shares of stock in a situation where three vacancies exist could cast *all 300 votes* for one candidate for one seat on the board. The method of cumulative voting helps to assure representation of minority shareholders on the board of directors.

To facilitate voting, large corporations use *proxy statements, which permit a designated person to vote in place of shareholders who are unable or unwilling to attend the corporate meeting.* Management advises the shareholders as to any questions before the board of directors and to the qualifications of those persons placed in nomination for election to the board. Management suggests how shareholders should vote on any questions and that shareholders elect as board members those persons nominated by management. Since shareholders are generally a disorganized group, they usually go along with management and instruct the proxy to vote as management suggests. As a consequence, *voting power is virtually meaningless in large firms, and therefore large firms can be controlled by ownership of only a small portion of the outstanding stock.*

Probably the most significant shareholder right is to a portion of the firm's profits, if dividends are declared. *Generally, the major portion of profits is retained in order to provide for growth and to replace capital equipment as it wears out or becomes obsolete.* If profits are sufficient, the board of directors may declare dividends, which are paid to shareholders usually either quarterly or semiannually. If a shareholder is dissatisfied with the dividend, he has little recourse but to sell the stock, although under special circumstances shareholders may sue the board of directors and force the declaration of dividends. Such suits are expensive, time-consuming, and not within the realistic province of small shareholders.

While the charters of most firms do not provide for *preemptive rights,* if such rights are included, they guarantee current shareholders the right to purchase enough shares of any new issue to maintain their existing portion of the ownership of the firm. Thus, if there were 10,000 shares of stock outstanding and a certain shareholder owned 1,000 shares, his ownership would represent one-tenth of the total. If a new issue of 1,000 shares were to be sold by the firm, this owner would have the right to buy 100 shares in order to maintain the one-tenth ownership. Preemptive rights are important in small, closely held firms but generally have little importance to shareholders of large firms.

The need to examine books may arise when a shareholder feels the firm is not operating in the best interest of the shareholders. Shareholders in large firms seldom desire to see the books. If they do, usually management will not permit them to see the books unless the shareholders bring suit. The shareholders must satisfy the court that the reason they want to see the books is in the best interest of the firm. Management usually assumes that shareholders who want to see the books do not have the best interest of the firm in mind. Instead management assumes that such a shareholder may give proprietary information to a competitor. Hence, the decision rests in the hands of the courts.

PREFERRED STOCK

Preferred stock derives its name from the fact that it has preference over common stock in the event of liquidation. While creditors must be satisfied first, preferred shareholders' claims to assets come ahead of those of the common shareholders. Preferred shareholders' claims are usually limited to the par value of the preferred stock. *The par value of preferred stock is usually the price at which the preferred stock was originally sold* (i.e., the price which is reflected on the firm's balance sheet). Therefore, the par value of preferred stock is significant in the event of liquidation.

In addition to the preference in liquidation, most preferred stock has a *cumulative feature.* This feature provides that any unpaid preferred stock dividends must be paid in full before common stock dividends may be paid.

Some preferred stock also enjoys a *participation feature.* The participation feature establishes a sharing of residual earnings of the firm according to a formula. For example, a formula might specify that preferred shareholders will share equally with common shareholders all dividends declared above a preestablished level such as $3.00 per share.

Unlike common shareholders, preferred shareholders do not enjoy the right to vote at corporate meetings or to elect directors. However, the terms of issuance of the preferred stock may set forth certain circumstances under which the preferred shareholders may elect directors. Such circumstances often include a failure on the part of the firm to pay preferred dividends for a stated period, failure to maintain specified financial ratios, or the like.

Preferred stock, like common stock, does not have a stated maturity. *To provide management with the flexibility to retire preferred stock, most issues have a call feature.* The call feature permits management to repurchase the preferred at a stated price, usually several dollars above the price at which the preferred was issued. Some preferred issues require the establishment of a sinking fund, which is used to retire the stock. The trustee of the preferred stock uses the money in the sinking fund to either repurchase the preferred stock on the open market or to call it.

Some preferred issues are *convertible* into common stock. That is, each share of preferred stock may be exchanged for a stated number of shares of common stock. Convertible issues almost always have a call feature so that management can force the conversion. When preferred stock is converted, the owners, as indicated above, receive common stock in its place.

CONVERTIBLE SECURITIES

Convertible securities include issues of both preferred stock and bonds which may be converted into common stock. Convertible securities are commonly called *deferred equity financing.* Since the securities are convertible into common stock, the issuing firm is actually selling today's common stock at tomorrow's price. For example, suppose a firm's common stock is currently selling at $25 per share and management believes the price will go up but needs money now. The firm might issue a bond convertible to 20 shares of common stock. Corporate bonds are sold for $1,000. As the price of the stock increased to $50, the 20 shares would be worth $1,000, the same amount as was paid for the bond. When the conversion takes place, management has, in effect, succeeded in obtaining the $50 per share of common stock. They obtained the $1,000 when the stock was selling for $25 per share and were able to obtain "tomorrow's price" ($50) for the 20 shares.

If the price of the common stock increased beyond $50 per share, then the market price of the bonds would usually increase proportionately. Generally, convertible securities have a call feature. This permits management to call the security and thereby *force conversion into common stock*. The call price is generally significantly above the maturity price. Thus, in this example, the call price might be $1,100.

Convertible securities are advantageous for both the issuing firm and the purchasing investor. The investor, whether purchasing a convertible bond or convertible preferred stock, will enjoy a stated income (either bond interest or preferred stock dividend) which is likely to vary very little. Seldom do firms omit bond interest payments or preferred stock dividends. However, if the firm grows and is successful and the market price of common stock increases, then the owner of the convertible issue participates in the success in that he may convert his fixed income security into common stock and thereby enjoy appreciation of his capital. Because of the significant advantage of the conversion feature, convertible securities usually have slightly lower yields than comparable-quality securities which lack the conversion feature.

Example 2:   CONVERTIBLE SECURITIES

Ace Products is offering convertible preferred stock at $50 per share. It yields $3.50 and is convertible into 1.4 shares of common stock. The preferred is callable at $62. Suppose the common stock started to increase in price. Determine the price of the common stock at which the preferred shareholders would exercise their conversion privilege.

SOLUTION

Since the call price of the preferred is $62, preferred shareholders would want to convert to common stock when the value of 1.4 shares of common equaled $62.

$$1.4 \text{ shares common} = \$62$$

Therefore,

$$1 \text{ share common} = \$44.29$$

Thus, when the common stock reached $44.29 per share, the preferred shareholders would convert. The owners of the preferred would enjoy a gain of $12 per share, thereby participating in the growth and profitability of the firm.

WARRANTS

A warrant is an option to purchase common stock. The option period is generally several years and may even be perpetual. Warrants may be sold by a firm but are frequently attached to bonds or preferred stock as "sweeteners," designed to make the bonds or preferred stock more attractive as potential investments. *The warrants permit the owners to purchase a stated number of shares of common stock at a specified price within a given period of time, referred to as the exercise period.* When the warrant is issued, the option price is generally above the current price of the common stock. For example, warrants might be issued permitting the purchase of one share of common stock at $50 for each warrant held. If the price of the common were $40, the warrant would be worthless except for speculative value. However, if the price of the common stock were to approach $50, the warrants would become more interesting to investors. Theoretically, when the price of the common reaches $50, the warrants should be worth exactly nothing. As the price of the common increases above $50, the warrants should increase in value in exact dollar amounts. Thus, if the stock sold for $58, the warrant is worth $8 if exercised. *Investors speculate in warrants so that their market price often greatly exceeds their value if exercised.* As the exercise period draws to an end, the market price of the warrants will equal their exercise value.

Warrants are very attractive to speculative investors since they offer the opportunity to make substantial profits. However, they also expose investors to the possibility of substantial losses.

Example 3: WARRANTS

The Carbide Corporation issued warrants entitling the owner to purchase one share of Carbide common stock at $30 for each warrant held. John Robertson is considering the purchase of either Carbide common stock, which is selling at $35, or warrants, which are selling at $8. He believes the common stock is likely to increase in price to $40 within the exercise period, and the warrants to $12. If he has $1,050 to invest, determine his return if he buys the common stock or the warrants.

SOLUTION

Without considering stockbroker fees, John could buy 30 shares of common stock for $1,050. If the stock appreciated in value to $40, he could sell it for $40 × 30 = $1,200 and thus realize a profit of $150. If John purchased warrants at $8, he would obtain 131 of them. If they increased in value to $12, he could sell them for $12 × 131 = $1,572, thus realizing a profit of $522. Hence, the opportunity for profit in purchasing warrants is much greater than in purchasing the related common stock. However, the risk of loss is also equally great.

Example 4: WARRANTS

Continuing with Example 3, suppose the price of Carbide common did not increase as rapidly as anticipated and reached $40 at the end of the exercise period. How much profit would Mr. Robertson realize from his 131 warrants?

SOLUTION

At the end of the exercise period, the warrants would be worth exactly the difference between the market price of the common stock and the option price.

Market price	$40
Option price	− 30
Value of warrant	$10

Mr. Robertson's warrants would be worth $10 each, or $1,310. He would, thus, profit $260.

Example 5: WARRANTS

Continue with Example 3, and assume the price of Carbide fell to $32 at the end of the exercise period. Determine the loss which Mr. Robertson would incur.

SOLUTION

If Mr. Robertson had purchased the common stock at $35 per share, his loss would be $3 per share or $3 × 30 = $90. If he had purchased the warrants at $8 and they subsequently decreased to $2, his loss would be $6 per warrant or $6 × 131 = $786. The $2 warrant price was obtained by subtracting the option price of the stock from the market price: $32 − $30 = $2.

RIGHTS

Most externally obtained long-term funds are secured through the services of underwriters who sell new issues of stock and bonds to the investment community at large, or through direct placement of debt in the form of bonds or mortgages. However, *sometimes it is advantageous to sell common stock directly to the firm's present shareholders. The mechanism of such a sale is called a "rights offering."* The primary advantage of selling to current shareholders is that it is generally less expensive than selling shares through an underwriter.

When a firm decides to sell stock to its shareholders, it mails them rights. *The rights permit the purchase of a stipulated number of shares of common stock at a stated price for a given period of time, known as the exercise period.* The price is, of course, less than the market price of the common stock when the rights are issued. For example, a rights offering might permit the holder of five rights to purchase one share of common stock from the firm for $32 at any time for a period up to three years after the rights are issued. Suppose within the exercise period the market price of the stock increases to $40; the shareholder could exercise rights and purchase shares at $32 or sell the rights to someone else. Either way, the use of the rights would result in a profit. Usually the sale of stock through the use of rights, which is termed *privileged subscription,* is quite successful.

IMPLICATIONS OF CONVERTIBLE SECURITIES, RIGHTS AND WARRANTS ON EARNINGS PER SHARE

When a convertible security is converted to common stock the number of shares of common stock outstanding increases. *Since earnings per share are computed by dividing the total after-tax profits (less preferred stock dividends, if any) by the number of shares of common stock outstanding, an increase in the number of shares outstanding will decrease EPS unless total profits increase.* When bonds are converted to stock, the interest on bonds ceases to be an expense to the firm. This decrease in expense will increase profits. Whether the increase in profits resulting from decreasing interest will be sufficient to maintain EPS at the preconversion level is problematical. This question requires serious attention at the time a convertible securities offering is being considered. The same argument holds for convertible preferred stock since preferred stock dividends are subtracted from a firm's after-tax profits before computing EPS. *Thus, eliminating preferred stock and their dividends would increase EPS if there were not any shares of common stock added. Of course, when preferred stock is converted the number of shares of common stock is increased.* The question as to whether the EPS will be altered as a result of preferred stock conversion depends on the amount of the preferred stock dividend and the number of shares of common each share of preferred will convert to. Again, this matter requires managerial attention at the time the convertible offer is being made. Further, if management can force conversion of bonds or preferred stock through a call feature, use of the call feature necessitates close examination as to its effects on EPS.

Warrants and rights differ from convertible securities in two significant ways. *First, neither warrants nor rights cost the firm anything before they are exercised. Second, when the option of a warrant or right is exercised, the firm sells the holder of the option common stock at a preestablished price.* Thus, the firm *does* receive a cash inflow from the result of the sale of the common stock via the medium of warrants and rights. Accordingly, the number of shares of common stock will increase and affect the EPS. This differs significantly from the conversion of a convertible security, which has to do only with the exchange of one type of security for another—cash is not received by the firm when the conversion is made.

The question of the effect of exercising warrant or right options on EPS lies in the ability of management to efficiently use the funds received from the sale of the common stock. The funds will be used to increase assets or decrease liabilities, hopefully so as to increase after-tax profits. How much after-tax profits will increase is difficult to predict. Naturally, management will attempt to maintain EPS at their existing level even though more shares of common stock are outstanding.

DIVIDEND POLICY

The scope of dividend policy includes three aspects: cash dividends, stock dividends, and stock splits. Each of these topics is discussed below. The topic of cash dividend policy is generally limited to decisions regarding common stock since preferred stock dividends are almost always fixed at the time the preferred stock is issued.

Cash Dividends

Cash dividends are generally regarded to be quite important to shareholders for a variety of reasons. As a result, *most firms attempt to establish and maintain a cash dividend policy which provides for constant or slowly increasing cash dividends.* Such a stable dividend policy which does not fluctuate appreciably, as a firm's earnings often do, is generally preferred by shareholders.

Fundamental to the establishment of a dividend policy is the question of choice between current or future shareholder income. Cash dividends naturally provide for current income. However, if funds are kept within the firm rather than distributed as dividends, the firm's rate of growth and profitability is likely to increase. The increase in growth and profitability is often accompanied by appreciation in the market price of the common stock. If the price of the stock goes up, a shareholder may sell the stock and enjoy a capital gain. If the shareholder has owned the stock for more than six months prior to selling it, the capital gain will be long-term and taxed at a lower rate than dividend income. Hence, an argument could be developed for reinvesting earnings in the firm and not paying any cash dividends. The choice, of course, must rest on meeting shareholder needs to the greatest extent possible.

There are several arguments *for* utilization of cash dividends. First, *many investors desire current income as opposed to income in the future.* Of course, if a firm did not issue cash dividends and the market price of the stock appreciated in value, a shareholder could sell a few shares periodically to provide current income. The problem with this approach is that stockbrokers have minimum fee schedules. Thus, the sale of a few shares might be extremely expensive and, in fact, wipe out any potential capital gain. Second, *cash dividends tend to help maintain shareholder confidence in the firm.* For example, if economic conditions change, the maintenance of a stable dividend tells shareholders that management feels earnings are likely to remain at or close to their present levels in the future. Third, *many investors depend on their cash dividends for a major portion of their income.* This is especially true for older persons. Such shareholders look forward to receiving dividend checks in order to meet their expenses. As a consequence of the reasons described above, most firms adopt policies which call for stable cash dividends.

Stock Dividends

A stock dividend represents a distribution of stock to current shareholders. The stock is distributed on a percentage basis so that each shareholder retains his proportionate ownership of the firm. Actually, *a stock dividend represents nothing more than a recapitalization of the owners' equity portion of the firm's balance sheet.* The recapitalization may be illustrated by showing the capital structure of a firm before and after a stock dividend.

Example 6:   STOCK DIVIDEND

Wellington International had capitalization as shown:

Common stock ($2 par, 100,000 shares)	$ 200,000
Paid-in capital	3,000,000
Retained earnings	4,000,000
Total owners' equity	$7,200,000

Wellington paid a 10% stock dividend. At the time of the stock dividend, the stock was selling for $50 per share. Show the new capitalization.

SOLUTION

A 10% stock dividend would represent 10,000 new shares (10% of 100,000 shares outstanding). At $50 per share, the total amount would be $500,000. This amount is transferred from retained earnings into the common stock and paid-in capital accounts. The common stock account is allocated $2 per share (the par value) or a total of $20,000. The paid-in capital account is allocated the remaining $480,000. The result is shown below:

Common stock ($2 par, 110,000 shares)	$ 220,000
Paid-in capital	3,480,000
Retained earnings	3,500,000
Total owners' equity	$7,200,000

The total remains constant, and only the distribution of amounts by account changes.

As a result of increasing the number of shares by 10%, the earnings per share decrease by 10%. The market price of the common stock should also decrease by 10%. However, this may not take place. Recall that market price is a function of the supply and demand for the stock. Shareholders who receive additional shares in the form of a stock dividend may not be anxious to sell their stock. Therefore, the price of the stock may stay at about the same level as before the stock dividend. *The price of the stock in the future will depend, to a great extent, on management's ability to maintain the prestock dividend level of EPS and cash dividends.*

A stock dividend may be of advantage to a shareholder even though his proportionate ownership in the firm does not change. *If the cash dividend per share is not changed, then the total cash dividend received after a stock dividend has taken place will increase.* The percentage increase in total cash dividends received will be the same as the percentage increase in the stock resulting from the stock dividend. In addition, a stock dividend can convey information. Stock dividends are usually issued by growth companies which often lack sufficient funds to increase cash dividends on a per share basis. *Many firms which issue stock dividends expect to be able to increase total after-tax profits enough to offset the dilution in earnings per share resulting from the stock dividend and thereby maintain the prestock dividend level of EPS.* Thus, the stock dividend is used as a vehicle to inform investors that the management is optimistic and expects further growth in profits.

Stock Splits

Many investors prefer to purchase stock in 100-share amounts (referred to as *round lots),* rather than in lesser amounts. One reason for this preference is that brokerage costs, per share purchased, are lower when round rather than odd size lots (less than 100 shares) are purchased. If the market price of a stock increases, many small shareholders feel reluctant to purchase it. Management can make the stock more attractive through the use of a stock split, which increases the number of shares and concurrently decreases the price. Suppose a stock were selling for $150 per share. If it were split three for one, the price would be reduced to $50, and all shareholders would receive two additional shares for each that they already owned. *When a stock is split the par value is reduced, but otherwise the capitalization is unchanged.*

Example 7:   STOCK SPLIT

Victor Industries had a capitalization shown below:

Common stock ($3 par, 200,000 shares)	$ 600,000
Paid-in capital	1,200,000
Retained earnings	3,000,000
Total owners' equity	$4,800,000

Victor split their stock three for one. Show their new capitalization.

SOLUTION

The par value is divided by 3 and the number of shares multiplied by 3, as shown below:

Common stock ($1 par, 600,000 shares)	$ 600,000
Paid-in capital	1,200,000
Retained earnings	3,000,000
Total owners' equity	$4,800,000

Usually when a stock is split, the cash dividend per share is reduced proportionately. Thus, if Victor's dividend were $1.50 before the split, it would probably be reduced to $.50 after the split.

In addition to splitting stock to increase the number of shares, a firm may also use a *reverse split* to decrease the number of shares. A firm might want to increase the price of the stock and use a reverse split to achieve the objective. With a reverse split, shareholders receive new certificates of fewer shares and the market price is automatically increased proportionately.

1. Indicate the importance of equity financing to both large and small business firms.
2. Differentiate among par, book, liquidating, and market value of common stock.
3. Why is the book value of common stock often understated?
4. Indicate the significance of the following shareholder rights: voting power, right to examine the firm's books, right to income, and preemptive rights.
5. Why might an investor prefer preferred stock over common stock?
6. Under what circumstances do preferred shareholders have the opportunity to elect members to the board of directors?
7. Why do most preferred stock issues have a call feature?
8. Preferred stock has fallen into disfavor as a means of financing most firms. Explain.
9. Explain the meaning of "deferred equity financing" in relation to convertible securities.
10. Indicate the advantage of purchasing convertible securities to an investor and to the issuing firm.
11. Why do convertible securities generally have call features?
12. Why are warrants considered to be speculative investments?
13. Explain the reason for using a privileged subscription "rights offering" rather than selling stock through an underwriter.
14. Explain the primary arguments in favor of a firm developing a stable cash dividend policy.
15. Indicate the reason a firm would issue stock dividends.
16. If stock dividends are issued, the market price of a firm's stock theoretically should fall proportionately. Frequently, however, it does not. Explain.
17. Indicate the reason for a firm splitting its stock.

This chapter introduces several new concepts involving equity financing and dividend policy. Be sure you are familiar with them.

Par Value (of Stock)
Book Value (of Stock)
Liquidating Value (of Stock)
Market Value (of Stock)

Convertible Security
Warrant
Privileged Subscription
Stock Dividends
Proxy
Preemptive Rights
Participation Feature (Preferred Stock)
Call Feature
Deferred Equity Financing
Exercise Period
Stock Rights
Cash Dividend
Stock Split

PROBLEMS

1. Ace International had the balance sheet shown below. Determine the book value of the common stock.

Ace Balance Sheet (all figures in millions)

Assets		*Liabilities and Owners' Equity*	
		Accounts payable	$ 2.0
		Accrued wages	1.0
Cash	$ 2.0	Accrued taxes	.5
Securities	1.5	Long-term debt	2.0
Accounts receivable	2.3	Common stock ($2 par, 800,000	
Inventory	4.0	shares outstanding)	1.6
Land	1.8	Paid-in capital	4.0
Fixed assets, net	5.7	Preferred stock ($50 par, 100,000	
Miscellaneous	.3	shares outstanding)	5.0
Total	$17.6	Retained earnings	1.5
		Total	$17.6

2. Referring to Problem 1, if the firm could liquidate its assets for the amounts indicated below, determine the liquidating value of the stock.

	Book Value	*Liquidating Value*
Cash	$2.0	$2.0
Securities	1.5	1.2
Accounts receivable	2.3	2.0
Inventory	4.0	2.5
Land	1.8	6.0
Fixed assets, net	5.7	6.6
Miscellaneous	.3	.2

3. Refer to the 1973 Technitrol balance sheet in Chapter 2 and determine the book value of the common stock.

4. Allied Products issued preferred stock convertible into 3.4 shares of common. If the preferred is callable at $100 per share, determine the price of common stock at which preferred shareholders would convert their stock.

5. Chemical Industries 7¾ debentures are convertible into 60 shares of common stock. The debentures are callable at 115% of their maturity value ($1,150). Suppose the price of the common stock is at $15 per share and starts to increase. At what stock price would the bondholders convert to common stock?

6. Atlas International common stock is currently selling for $12 per share. Warrants have been issued entitling the holder to purchase one share of Atlas at $16 per share. What is the theoretical value of a warrant when the common is selling at $12? If the price of the stock stock increases to $20 per share, what is the theoretical value of a warrant?

7. Referring to Problem 6, Peter Boyle purchased Atlas warrants for $3 when the stock was selling at $19 per share. If the price of the stock increases to $27 before the warrants expire, how much will Peter make on each warrant?

8. Referring to Problem 7, suppose Peter Boyle has $1,000 to invest either in common stock or the warrants described in Problem 7 (stock at $19 per share or warrants at $3 each). Indicate the profit he would have made if he had purchased the stock, and the profit he would have made if he had purchased the warrants if the price of the stock increased to $27 per share.

9. Donna Smith can buy warrants for Acorn Industries at $6 each. They permit the holders to purchase one share of common stock at $20 for each warrant held. The stock is currently selling for $22. How much above the theoretical value of the warrant did Donna pay? If the warrants expire, at what price of the common stock will Donna just break even? If the stock increases to $30 per share, how much profit will Donna make on each warrant?

10. Alexander Company has the capitalization shown. Show how the capitalization would change if they had a 5% common stock dividend when the common stock was selling for $100 per share.

Preferred stock ($40 par, 10,000 shares outstanding)	$ 400,000
Common stock ($.50 par, 300,000 shares outstanding)	150,000
Paid-in capital	2,000,000
Retained earnings	4,000,000

11. If Alexander Company (Problem 10) had split its stock three for one rather than having a stock dividend, show how the firm's capitalization would change.

The Cost of Capital

chapter 13

In Chapters 11 and 12 we dealt with the types of debt and equity financing and discussed the rationale for establishing a sound financial structure. Further, dividend policy was evaluated in order to develop a plan consistent with shareholder expectations and the firm's requirements for cash. Once a firm has established a financial structure, it may commence the process of calculating the cost of each component of its capital structure and finally determine *the cost of capital (i.e., the average cost of funds used to finance the firm).*

The average cost of funds to the firm, called the cost of capital, is extremely important since *it represents the minimum return which the firm must receive on its investments.* If a firm achieves a return on investment lower than the cost of capital, it will alternatively be unable to meet its interest obligations or be forced to reduce its dividends. Obviously, one cannot borrow funds for 8% and reinvest them at 6% and expect to remain in business very long. On the other hand, if a firm through prudent management can use funds so as to achieve a return in excess of its cost of capital, then it can look forward to increasing dividends or to expansion, with the ultimate result being an increase in shareholder wealth.

There are three sources from which a business can obtain funds: owners' investment, in the form of common and preferred stock (equity), borrowed funds (debt), and funds generated through the operations of the business. The funds generated through the operations of the business include those after-tax profits which are kept in the firm as retained earnings and cash throw-offs such as depreciation. While cash throw-offs resulting from depreciation are often an important source of funds, their cost need not be considered when calculating the firm's cost of capital. This does not mean that these funds are free but rather that they result from the use of equity, debt, and retained earnings. *Depreciation represents a return of investment.* Therefore, the cost of funds generated through depreciation is the same as the cost of capital determined by averaging the costs of equity, debt, and retained earnings in the manner described below.

The cost of capital is used as the criterion for judging the merit of proposed investments. Since it represents the minimum return which is acceptable to a firm, the cost of capital is sometimes called the *hurdle rate. The cost of capital is the weighted average of the costs of equity, debt, and retained earnings.* The cost of capital has primary significance because it represents the minimum return which a proposed investment project must return in order to be acceptable. *For large corporations, the cost of capital theoretically is the minimum return which the corporation must achieve on its investments in order to maintain the market price of the common stock at its current level.*[1]

In the capital budgeting process, the evaluation of proposed projects is gauged against the cost of capital. As a first step in determining the cost of capital, the costs of the three components, equity, debt, and retained earnings, must be calculated. Then, the costs of the three components are averaged to obtain the cost of capital.

COST OF DEBT

The cost of debt used as an input in determining the cost of capital is the after-tax interest rate on funds borrowed. Interest is deductible as an expense for determining the federal income tax liability. This is the case for all forms of business organizations. Since interest is deductible as an expense, its payment results in a smaller decrease in after-tax profits than the actual amount of the interest paid. It is the after-tax rate of interest (symbolized by k_i) which is used as an input in determining the cost of capital. The effect of interest payments on after-tax profits is shown in Example 1. Procedures for determining the after-tax rate of interest are provided following Example 1.

[1]Of course, there are many other factors, such as changing economic conditions, which greatly affect stock market prices but which cannot be controlled by the firm's management.

Example 1:   EFFECT OF INTEREST EXPENSE ON EARNINGS

The Bryan Corporation has the following income statement:

Bryan Corporation
1975 Income Statement

Sales	$ 2,000,000
Less expenses	− 1,250,000
Earnings before taxes	$ 750,000
Less taxes	− 346,500
After-tax profits	$ 403,500

If Bryan borrows $3 million at an annual interest rate of 9%, what will be the effect on after-tax profits?

SOLUTION

First, calculate the annual interest payment.

$3,000,000 × .09 = $270,000 annual interest

Second, recalculate the after-tax profits incorporating the interest expense:

Sales	$ 2,000,000
Less expenses	− 1,250,000
Less interest	− 270,000
Earnings before taxes	$ 480,000
Less taxes	− 216,900
After-tax profits	$ 263,100

Third, calculate the reduction in after-tax profits.

After-tax profits (original)	$ 403,500
After-tax profits (with interest expenses)	− 263,100
Reduction in after-tax profits	$ 140,400

Fourth, calculate the reduction in amount of federal income tax paid.

Original tax	$ 346,500
Less new tax	− 216,900
Reduction	$ 129,600

Example 1 demonstrates the fact that earnings are reduced by an amount far less than the amount of the interest paid. The fact that earnings are reduced by only a fraction of the amount of interest paid means that the after-tax rate of interest is less than the 9%. The actual dollar amount of interest paid was $270,000, but the after-tax amount, in terms of reduced earnings, was only $140,400. The difference of $129,600 represents the decrease in federal income tax liability. *The financial manager is concerned with the after-tax dollar cost of interest and the after-tax rate.*

The after-tax interest rate may be calculated using

$$k_i = \frac{\text{Interest paid} - \text{Reduction in federal income tax}}{\text{Amount borrowed}} \qquad (1)$$

Example 2: AFTER-TAX RATE OF INTEREST

Determine the after-tax rate of interest for the Bryan Corporation loan of $3 million using Eq. (1).

SOLUTION

$$\text{After-tax rate} = \frac{\$270,000 - \$129,600}{\$3,000,000} = .0468$$

The after-tax rate of interest, k_i, is 4.68%.

Another formula may be used to determine the after-tax rate of interest. Use of Eq. (2) greatly simplifies the determination of after-tax interest rates for corporations.

$$k_i = k(1 - t) \qquad (2)$$

where k_i = after-tax effective rate of interest
k = pretax effective rate of interest
t = firm's marginal tax rate (20% if the firm has a taxable income not exceeding $25,000, 22% if taxable income exceeds $25,000 up to $50,000, and 48% if the firm has a taxable income exceeding $50,000)

Example 3: AFTER-TAX RATE OF INTEREST

Determine the after-tax rate of interest for the Bryan Corporation loan of $3 million using Eq. (2). Assume Bryan has a marginal tax rate of 48%.

SOLUTION

Use Eq. (2) with a marginal tax rate of 48% and calculate the after-tax interest rate as shown:

$$k_i = .09(1 - .48) = .0468 = 4.68\%$$

Example 4:   AFTER-TAX RATE OF INTEREST

Richardson, Inc. has taxable income of $23,000. If it borrows $30,000 at a stated interest rate of 14%, determine the after-tax rate of interest.

SOLUTION

Since Richardson has taxable income of less than $25,000, it is in the 20% marginal tax bracket. The after-tax rate is determined using Eq. (2) as shown:

$$k_i = .14(1 - .20) = .112 = 11.2\%$$

It should be noted that while the formulas for calculating the after-tax interest rate have been applied to corporate examples, they are equally useful in individual cases. Normally, Eq. (1), which involves actual dollar amounts, is simpler to use to determine the after-tax interest rates on debts owed by individuals (sole proprietorships and partnerships) than Eq. (2) because the latter requires use of a marginal tax rate. The marginal tax rates for individuals change in small steps as taxable income changes. Hence, if Eq. (2) is used, more than one tax rate may be involved, adding greatly to the complexity of the calculations. Therefore, Eq. (1) is used for individuals and Eq. (2) for corporations.

In many instances, individuals or corporations may borrow from more than one source. The amounts of the loans and their interest rates often differ quite appreciably. As a result, the average interest rate must be calculated. Since the amounts of the loans differ, a weighted average must be taken. The weighted average is calculated quite easily, as shown in Example 5.

Example 5:   WEIGHTED AVERAGE INTEREST RATE

Marberger, Inc. has the following outstanding debts:

Debt	Amount	Pretax Interest Rate
Bonds, Series A	$ 2,000,000	6.0%
Mortgage	3,000,000	7.5
Bonds, Series B	2,500,000	8.3
Bonds, Series C	4,000,000	9.0
Total	$11,500,000	

Determine the weighted average *pretax* interest rate.

SOLUTION

First, determine the proportion of each type of debt. This is accomplished by dividing the amount of each debt by the total debt. In this example, the total is $11,500,000.

$$\text{Bonds, Series A:} \quad \frac{\$2,000,000}{\$11,500,000} = .174$$

$$\text{Mortgage:} \quad \frac{\$3,000,000}{\$11,500,000} = .261$$

$$\text{Bonds, Series C:} \quad \frac{\$2,500,000}{\$11,500,000} = .217$$

$$\text{Bonds, Series C:} \quad \frac{\$4,000,000}{\$11,500,000} = .348$$

$$\text{Total} \quad 1.000$$

Next, multiply the proportion of each type of debt by its interest rate (expressed in decimal form). Then add the sum to obtain the weighted average cost of debt. Performing these calculations in tabular form is desirable.

Debt	Amount	Proportion	Pretax Interest Rate (Cost)	Weighted Cost
Bonds, Series A	$ 2,000,000	.174 ×	.060 =	.01044
Mortgage	3,000,000	.261 ×	.075 =	.01958
Bonds, Series B	2,500,000	.217 ×	.083 =	.01801
Bonds, Series C	4,000,000	.348 ×	.090 =	.03132
Total	$11,500,000	1.000		.07935

The weighted average pretax cost of debt (interest rate) is 7.935%.

In determining the cost of capital for a firm, it is necessary to use the after-tax interest rate as the cost of debt. This requires that the calculation of the after-tax cost of debt (interest rate) be combined with the calculation of the weighted average cost of debt. Continuing with Marberger, Inc., the determination of the after-tax weighted average cost of debt is shown in Example 6.

Example 6:   AFTER-TAX WEIGHTED AVERAGE COST OF DEBT

Assume that Marberger, Inc. has a marginal income tax rate of 48%. Determine the after-tax weighted average cost of debt.

SOLUTION

The weighted average pretax cost of debt (interest rate) is 7.935%. Employing Eq. (2), the after-tax rate may be calculated:

$$k_i = k(1 - t)$$
$$= .07935(1 - .48)$$
$$= .04126$$

The *after-tax* weighted average cost of debt is 4.126%.

COST OF EQUITY

The cost of equity capital is the return required by the owners of the business. The return takes different forms depending on the type of organization. The types of return are listed below:

Corporations: Cash dividends on both common and preferred stock, and capital gains.

Sole proprietorships and partnerships: Business income, salaries, and capital gains. Business income is taxed as a part of ordinary income for sole proprietors and members of partnerships.

Investors are aware of the amount of return which is available to them from different types of businesses and also the risks involved. Investors purchase stock or buy businesses which meet their requirements for return on investment. For a corporation, it is the responsibility of the financial manager to make sure that the firm continues to meet investor expectations. Investors who purchase small businesses generally become directly involved with the management, and, hence, must rely on their own judgment and abilities to generate a return on their investment.

The process of determining the cost of equity capital may be simplified by considering it first for a corporation and later for a sole proprietorship and partnership. The reason for this division is that the methods of determining the cost are somewhat different.

Cost of Equity Capital for Corporations

Corporate equity consists of two parts: common stock and preferred stock. The cost of common stock equity capital will be considered first.

Investors purchasing common stock in a corporation look for return in the form of dividends and capital gains. The capital gains (or losses), of course, will not be realized until the stock is sold. Hence, in measuring the rate of return, many investors add the dividend to the average annual growth rate of the price of the stock. This sum represents the investor's projected required return. If this return meets or exceeds the investor's required return, then he will purchase the stock.

To ascertain the required rate of return by the firm's shareholders (and, hence, the cost of common stock equity capital), the financial manager can employ two procedures. The first is applicable to firms which give dividends. The second is applicable to all firms but relies more heavily on estimates than historical data.

Firms which provide dividends often employ the following formula to determine the cost of common stock equity capital:

$$k_e = \frac{D}{P} + g \tag{3}$$

where k_e = annual cost of common stock equity capital
D = annual dividend in dollar amount
P = market price of the common stock
g = annual growth rate of the dividend

The following observations apply to the application of Eq. (3).

1. The cost of common stock equity, as determined by Eq. (3), varies inversely with the price of the stock. That is, as the market price of the common stock goes up, the rate of return and the cost of common stock equity go down. Bidding the price of the stock upward means investors are so anxious to purchase the stock that they are willing to take a lower return.
2. The use of Eq. (3) rests upon the assumption that there is good correlation between the historical growth rate of the dividend [g in Eq. (3)] and the market price of the stock. The reason that the growth rate of the dividend is employed rather than the growth rate of the common stock's market price is that the former is much more constant. The market price of most stocks changes frequently, often taking very large upward and downward swings. Hence, measuring the trends in market price is often difficult. In addition, many investors are primarily interested in dividends and are much more anxious about their rate of growth than the growth rate of the common stock price.

Example 7:   COST OF COMMON STOCK EQUITY CAPITAL

The market price of Conway stock is $28 per share. If the dividend is $2 and has been growing at an average annual rate of 3%, determine the cost of common stock equity capital.

SOLUTION

Using Eq. (3), the cost is determined as follows:

$$k_e = \frac{\$2}{\$28} + .03$$

$$= .0714 + .03 = .1014$$

The cost of common stock equity capital is 10.14%.

It should be noted that *dividends on both common and preferred stock are taken from after-tax profits* (they are not deductible as expenses). Hence, it is *not* necessary to provide for any tax adjustments as was the case for determining the after-tax cost of debt.

Another approach to estimating the rate of return required by shareholders, and hence the cost of common stock equity capital, involves adding the return available from a *risk-free investment* to a pair of adjustment factors. The adjustment factors are designed to compensate for the degree of *business and financial risk* to which the investor is exposed if he purchases the stock. The method builds on the assumption that investors are risk-averters and want increasingly higher returns as their exposure to risk increases. For example, if risk-free government bonds yield 8%, investors could be expected to require a rate of return greater than 8% from any stock, because even the best "blue chip" companies will expose their shareholders to some degree of risk.

The *required rate of return method*, as it is sometimes called, may be expressed in equation form as follows:

$$k_e = i + B + \Phi \tag{4}$$

where k_e = cost of common stock equity capital
$\quad i$ = rate of return on risk-free investments
$\quad B$ = additional return to compensate for business risk
$\quad \Phi$ = additional return to compensate for financial risk

Suppose, for example, that an investor would obtain 7% by purchasing risk-free government bonds. The added amounts that he would require to compensate him for exposure to risk would depend on two factors:

1. The investor's subjective appraisal of the degree of risk to which he will be exposed.
2. The investor's subjective requirement for compensation for exposure to the risk.

For a particular stock, the investor might decide that he required 3% added return to compensate for exposure to business risk and 2% for exposure to financial risk. Thus, he would require 7% + 3% + 2% = 12%. It is this 12% that the financial manager would use as the cost of the common stock equity capital.

The second type of corporate equity financing is preferred stock. Preferred stock differs from common stock in that the dividend is, for all practical purposes, guaranteed. Also, preferred stock dividends are generally fixed. Only in those rare instances when a firm is in serious financial trouble will management ever skip a preferred stock dividend. Further, the purchasers of preferred stock do not vote and are not considered to be the owners of the firm in the same sense as common shareholders. Management is not responsible for attempting to maximize the wealth of the preferred shareholders. Unless the preferred stock is convertible to common stock, the management has little interest in the price of its preferred stock.

The cost of preferred stock equity capital is simply the annual dividend payment divided by the amount which the firm received for each share of the stock when it was originally sold. Usually the amount which the firm receives is somewhat less than the amount paid by the purchaser. This difference arises because stock is generally sold through an investment banker (stockbroker) who charges a commission for his work. The cost of preferred stock equity capital, k_p, may be determined using

$$k_p = \frac{D}{P - b} \tag{5}$$

where k_p = cost of preferred stock equity capital
D = annual dividend per share expressed in dollar amount
P = original price at which stock was purchased
b = investment banker's commission

Example 8:   COST OF PREFERRED STOCK EQUITY CAPITAL

In 1968, Carpenter Industries sold preferred stock for $50 per share. The stock pays a yearly dividend of $2.60. Carpenter received $48 for each share. Determine the cost of the 1968 issue of preferred.

SOLUTION

Since the purchase price was $50 and the amount Carpenter received was only $48, the investment banker's fee was $2. Using Eq. (5), the cost is calculated:

$$k_p = \frac{\$2.60}{\$50 - \$2} = \frac{\$2.60}{\$48.00} = .0542$$

The cost of the 1968 issue of preferred stock equity financing is 5.42%.

In some instances, a firm may have more than one issue of preferred stock. If this is the case, it is necessary to determine the cost of each issue and then take the weighted average. This weighted average is the cost of preferred stock equity capital used as an input in determining the firm's cost of capital.

Cost of Equity Capital
for Sole Proprietorships and Partnerships

The equity portion of the financing of a sole proprietorship or partnership consists of the owners' original investment plus any added funds which they put into the business. The amount of investment is likely to change appreciably as the business matures. Consider the purchase of an apartment house for $80,000 with a $60,000 mortgage. The initial equity investment is only $20,000. However, the owners pay off the mortgage and, in so doing, increase their investment. This is somewhat different from the situation for corporations, which tend to *roll over their debt* and in effect never pay it back. That is, when one bond issue is due to be paid off, corporations often issue another series of bonds and pay off the original bondholders with the proceeds from the sale of the new bonds.

The cost of equity in a small business is the return required by the owners. Individuals purchasing small businesses have widely differing financial objectives. For example, some investors purchase residential real estate expecting to operate it so that it will provide them with a tax shelter. They hope the property will increase in value and their profits will come in the form of a large capital gain when they sell it.

All investors look forward to increasing their wealth, and compare investment opportunities with a great degree of scrutiny. As an example, for an individual, the purchase of real estate as an investment could be compared with the purchase of corporate stocks and bonds. Hence, the most logical method to calculate the cost of equity capital for a sole proprietorship or partnership is to use the required rate of return method, Eq. (4). This method permits evaluation of different investments, using the return available from a risk-free investment as a basis for comparison.

COST OF RETAINED EARNINGS

When the operation of any business results in after-tax profits, the profits may be distributed to the owners or kept by the firm as retained earnings. If the earnings are distributed to the owners as dividends, the owners will have to pay federal income tax on them. Hence, the owners will have less cash in hand than the firm would have if it had kept the profits as retained earnings. For example, suppose Mr. Jones owns stock in Abbott, Inc. If Abbott declares a dividend and Mr. Jones receives $100, he will have to pay tax on it. If Mr. Jones is in the 42% marginal tax bracket (he is married and has a taxable income between $32,000 and $36,000), he will pay $42 in tax, leaving him only $58 to reinvest. (It is assumed that he already used up the dividend tax exclusion of $200.) Suppose further that Mr. Jones requires a 12% return on his investments. Investing the $58 at 12% yields $58 × .12 = $6.96. However, Mr. Jones would not be able to invest the entire $58 because he would have to pay a broker's commission. (Note that savings institutions do not pay 12%, so Mr. Jones is forced to invest in stock, bonds, or real estate. All of these involve brokers.) Assume the brokerage fee is 4%; then Mr. Jones would have $58 (1 − .04) = $55.68 actually invested. The $55.68 invested at 12% would yield $55.68 × .12 = $6.68. Based on the original $100 which Mr. Jones received, the return on his investments is only 6.68%. Mr. Jones would have been just as well off had Abbott kept the $100 and invested it to obtain $6.68. Since Jones is a shareholder in Abbott, the earnings would belong to him anyway.

Based on the fact that individuals are taxed on dividends and that they must pay brokerage fees to reinvest their funds, businesses need not obtain as great a return on retained earnings as they must obtain on equity capital. A firm must obviously do as well as the owners could do for themselves. Hence, in determining the cost of retained earnings, the firm may discount the investor's tax rate and brokerage fees. The result is Eq. (6), which provides the cost of retained earnings:

$$R = k_e \, (1 - T) \, (1 - B) \qquad (6)$$

where R = cost of retained earnings
k_e = cost of equity capital
T = owner's marginal tax rate
B = average brokerage fee

To apply Eq. (6), the financial manager of the firm must be able to estimate the owner's marginal tax rate and brokerage fees. While the owners' marginal tax rates vary among industries due to the different types of investors attracted, approximate values for T and B have been established as follows: $T = 35\%$, and $B = 4\%$.

Example 9: COST OF RETAINED EARNINGS

Smelting, Inc. has a cost of equity capital of 16%. Using the average values for the owners' marginal tax rates and brokerage fees, determine the cost of retained earnings for Smelting.

SOLUTION

Employ Eq. (6):

$$R = .16(1 - .35)(1 - .04)$$
$$= .16(.65)(.96)$$
$$= .0998.$$

The cost of retained earnings is 9.98%.

WEIGHTED AVERAGE COST OF CAPITAL

As indicated earlier, the cost of capital or hurdle rate which financial managers use as a criterion for judging investment projects is the weighted average of the costs of equity, debt, and retained earnings. The process of taking the weighted average is similar to that used in finding the weighted average cost of debt.

Example 10: WEIGHTED AVERAGE COST OF CAPITAL

Standard Products has the following funding and after-tax costs. Compute the weighted average after-tax cost of capital.

Funding	Amount	After-tax Cost
Common stock	$10,000,000	14%
Preferred stock	2,000,000	8
Debt	15,000,000	7
Retained earnings	3,000,000	9
Total	$30,000,000	

SOLUTION

First, determine the proportion of each type of financing. This is accomplished by dividing the amount of each by the total of $30 million:

$$\text{Common stock:} \quad \frac{\$10,000,000}{\$30,000,000} = .333$$

$$\text{Preferred stock:} \quad \frac{\$2,000,000}{\$30,000,000} = .067$$

$$\text{Debt:} \quad \frac{\$15,000,000}{\$30,000,000} = .5$$

$$\text{Retained earnings:} \quad \frac{\$3,000,000}{\$30,000,000} = .1$$

$$\text{Total} \quad \overline{1.000}$$

Next, multiply the proportion of each type of funding by its cost (as expressed in decimal form). Then, add the sum to obtain the weighted average cost of capital. Performing these calculations in tabular form is desirable.

Funding	Amount	Proportion		After-Tax Cost		Weighted Cost
Common	$10,000,000	.333	×	.14	=	.04662
Preferred	2,000,000	.067	×	.08	=	.00536
Debt	15,000,000	.5	×	.07	=	.03500
Retained earnings	3,000,000	.1	×	.09	=	.00900
Total	$30,000,000	1.00				.09598

Rounding gives the weighted average after-tax cost of capital as 9.6%. It should be noted that when the term *cost of capital* is used in capital budgeting decisions it is *the weighted average after-tax cost of capital.*

In Example 10, the amount of each type of funding was given. However, in many instances the amounts are not given. They must be obtained as follows:

Common stock: Multiply the number of shares of stock outstanding by the *market price* (not the book value).

Preferred stock: Use the number of shares listed on the balance sheet and multiply by the original price at which they were sold, i.e., their book value.

Debt: Use the total debt as listed on the balance sheet.

Retained earnings: Use the amount listed on the balance sheet.

Use the amounts of each source of funding, determined as indicated above, in the calculation of the cost of capital.

The firm's management may choose to alter the financing mix.

Standard Products in Example 10 had a ratio of debt to common stock of 1.5 to 1. If management were to decide to increase the use of debt in the future, then the weighted average would have to be computed using the new amounts.

Example 11:   WEIGHTED AVERAGE COST OF CAPITAL

Alexander Manufacturing has the balance sheet as shown.

Balance Sheet 1973

Assets		Liabilities and Net Worth	
Cash	$200,000	Notes payable (noninterest-bearing)	$ 50,000
Inventory	50,000	Bonds, 10%, due 1985	300,000
Fixed assets	300,000	Common stock (100,000 shares	
Other assets	50,000	authorized, 50,000 outstanding)	150,000
	$600,000	Retained earnings	100,000
		Total	$600,000

The common stock sells at $3.50 per share and pays a dividend of $.30. The dividend has grown at an average rate of 2% per year for the past five years. Alexander's taxable income in 1973 was $95,000. Its owners have a marginal tax rate of 30%. Brokerage fees average 4%. Determine Alexander's weighted average after-tax cost of capital.

SOLUTION

First, determine the cost and amount of each source of funding, keeping in mind that the after-tax cost is used.

Common stock: Use Eq. (3) to determine the cost:

$$k_e=\frac{D}{P}+g; \qquad k_e=\frac{\$.30}{\$3.50}+.02=.1057$$

The cost of the common stock is 10.57%. The amount of common stock is determined by multiplying the market price by the number of shares outstanding:

$$\$3.50 \times 50,000 = \$175,000$$

Debt: There are two types of debt. Therefore, the weighted average must be taken.

Debt	Amount	Proportion		Pretax Interest Rate		Weighted Cost
Notes	$ 50,000	.143	×	0	=	0
Bonds	300,000	.857	×	.10	=	.0857
Total	$350,000	1.000				.0857

The weighted average pretax cost of debt is 8.57%. Since Alexander has a taxable income over $50,000, they are in the 48% marginal tax bracket. Using Eq. (2), $k_i = k(1 - t)$, the after-tax cost may be obtained.

$$k_i = .0857(1 - .48) = .04456$$

Rounding gives the after-tax cost of debt as 4.5%. From the balance sheet it is seen that there is $350,000 in debt.

Retained earnings: The cost of retained earnings is obtained by using Eq. (6):

$$R = k_e(1 - T)(1 - B)$$
$$R = .1057(1 - .3)(1 - .04)$$
$$= .1057(.7)(.96)$$
$$= .071$$

The cost of retained earnings is 7.1%. The balance sheet indicates $100,000 in retained earnings.

Next, determine the weighted average after-tax cost of capital. With the cost and amount of each source of funding known, the cost of capital can be determined. Once again, performing the calculations in tabular form is desirable.

Funding	Amount	Proportion		After-tax Cost		Weighted Cost
Common stock	$175,000	.28	×	.1057	=	.0296
Debt	350,000	.56	×	.045	=	.0252
Retained earnings	100,000	.16	×	.071	=	.0114
Total	$625,000	1.00				.0662

The weighted average after-tax cost of capital for Alexander Manufacturing is 6.62%.

It should be noted that the sum of the types of financing used in the averaging process above ($625,000) differs from the total of liabilities and net worth listed on the balance sheet ($600,000). The reason for the difference results from the fact that *the amount of common stock used in the averaging process was based on the current market value, while the amount of common stock listed on the balance sheet reflects the price at which the stock was originally sold.* Evidently the shares were sold originally for $3.00 per share, while their current price is $3.50.

In capital budgeting problems, the weighted average after-tax cost of capital is commonly called just the *cost of capital*. The cost of capital is the minimum return which firms must receive from their investments. However, in many instances financial managers may require a higher return for potential investments involving greater degrees of risk. For example, a firm may divide investments into categories and apply a particular hurdle rate to each, as shown:

Type of Investment	Required Return
Profit maintaining—increasing production facilities for current product	Cost of capital
New product manufacturing facilities	Cost of capital plus 5%
Research and development	Cost of capital plus 10%

In Chapter 17 we shall discuss some of the methods used to compensate for risk in the capital budgeting process.

The cost of capital as calculated above is based on historical costs of debt and preferred stock. *In periods when interest rates are changing rapidly, it may not be advisable to use the historical values.* For example, suppose that a firm had a $1 million bond issue outstanding at an interest rate of 6% and that the issue was approaching maturity. The financial manager would have to consider the cost of new debt to replace that which would be retired. Suppose that a new bond issue would bear interest at the rate of 10%. Then this higher rate should be used as an input in calculating the cost of capital. The financial manager must always be aware of trends in interest rates and other economic factors which may affect the firm's ability to raise capital and its cost of capital.

QUESTIONS FOR DISCUSSION

1. Why is the net cash inflow the primary consideration when a firm reviews a proposed investment project?
2. Why is the after-tax cost of debt used as an input in determining the cost of capital rather than the pretax cost?
3. Explain why it is generally easier to use Eq. (1) than Eq. (2) to calculate the after-tax cost of debt for individuals.
4. Differentiate between the two methods of calculating the cost of equity capital, and explain when each might be preferable.
5. In estimating the cost of common stock equity, why is the rate of growth of dividends more frequently employed than the rate of growth of the stock's market price?
6. In calculating the cost of common stock equity, the market price of the stock is used as one input. In calculating the cost of preferred, the original price at which the preferred stock was sold is used. Why isn't the market price of the preferred used?

CONCEPTS
TO
REMEMBER
The material in this chapter draws heavily from the preceding chapters in Section II. Some new concepts are also introduced. Be sure you understand all of them.

Return *on* Investment
Return *of* Investment
Hurdle Rate
Cost of Capital

PROBLEMS

1. Knight Products has the following income statement:

Sales		$2,000,000
Cost of goods	$1,300,000	
Administrative costs	200,000	
Depreciation	100,000	
		− 1,600,000
Earnings before taxes		$ 400,000

a. Calculate their current federal income tax liability and after-tax profit.
b. Suppose they borrowed $1 million at an annual interest rate of 9%. How would this affect their federal income tax liability and after-tax profits?
c. What is the after-tax interest rate on the debt?

2. Jefferson, Inc., borrowed $10,000 at 8% for two years on a discount basis. Jefferson's marginal tax rate is 48%.
a. Determine the effective interest rate on the loan.
b. Determine the after-tax effective rate of interest.

3. Peters, Inc. has the following liabilities:

Debt	Amount	Pretax Interest Rate
Accounts payable	$ 500,000	0%
Notes payable	700,000	12
Bonds, Series A	2,000,000	8
Bonds, Series B	1,000,000	9

Their marginal tax rate is 48%.
a. Determine their weighted average after-tax cost of debt.
b. Suppose they delayed payments of some of their accounts and increased their accounts payable to $1.5 million. How would this affect the weighted average after-tax cost of debt? Assume the cost of accounts payable financing remains at zero.

4. Johnson Clothing, Inc. pays dividends of $3.00 per share. The dividend has been growing at an annual rate of 3%. If the market price of the stock is $40, what is the cost of equity?

5. Krothers, Inc. believes their cost of equity to be 16%. The price of their common stock is $35, and it pays a $3 dividend. If they are correct and the cost of equity is 16%, by how much should they increase their dividend next year? Express your answer in dollars.

6. Atlantic Industries, Inc. sold $100 preferred stock in 1967. It pays $6.30 per year dividend. The underwriting cost for issuing the stock was 2½%. Determine the cost of the preferred to Atlantic.

7. Allen Corporation has a cost of equity capital of 12%. If its average shareholder is in the 36% marginal tax bracket and the average brokerage fee is 4%, what is the cost of retained earnings to Allen Corporation?

8. Corbett Corporation has funding and after-tax costs of funds as shown. Determine its weighted average after-tax cost of capital.

Funding	Amount	After-tax Cost
Common stock	$3,000,000	12%
Preferred stock	1,000,000	8
Debt	4,000,000	7
Retained earnings	2,000,000	8

9. Concord, Inc. has the following balance sheet:

Balance Sheet, December 31, 1973

Assets		Liabilities and Net Worth	
Cash	$ 1,000,000	Accounts payable	$ 2,000,000
Accounts receivable	4,000,000	Notes payable (12%)	3,000,000
Inventories	2,000,000	Bonds, 8½%, due 1990	6,000,000
Fixed assets	10,000,000	Common stock (1 million	
Total	$17,000,000	shares authorized,	
		300,000 outstanding)	3,000,000
		Paid-in capital	1,000,000
		Retained earnings	2,000,000
		Total	$17,000,000

The common stock currently sells at $20 per share and pays a $1.50 dividend, which has been growing at an annual rate of 4%. Their average shareholder has a marginal tax rate of 36%, and brokerage fees are 4%. Concord's taxable income in 1973 was $20 million. Determine the firm's cost of capital.

10. Bob and Clara Jones have an adjusted gross income of $18,000. They have itemized deductions of $3,000 and have two children. If they borrow $7,000 at 9% annual interest, determine the after-tax dollar cost and interest rate.

11. The following information is known about the Zeron Corporation:
a. $5 million in bonds having an 8% coupon are outstanding.

b. The common stock sells for $50.00 per share and pays a $2.50 dividend. The dividend has been increasing at an annual rate of 4%. 600,000 shares of common stock are outstanding.

c. $2.4 million in preferred stock, representing 200,000 shares, is outstanding. The dividend per share is $.60. The preferred was originally sold for $12 per share with a 6% brokerage fee.

d. The firm's marginal tax rate is 48%.

Calculate the following:

a. The after-tax cost of debt.

b. The cost of common stock.

c. The cost of preferred stock.

d. The firm's cost of capital.

12. Knox Company believes its cost of retained earnings to be 10%. If its cost of common stock equity, k_e is 16% and the average brokerage fee 4%, what is the average value of the owners' marginal tax rate?

13. Referring to the "required rate of return model" for computing the cost of common stock equity, if k_e is 14%, the risk-free rate of interest 8%, and the additional return required for business risk 3%, what is the additional return required for financial risk?

14. Apple Industries, Inc. has the balance sheet shown:

Dec. 31, 197x (in millions)

Assets		*Liabilities and Owners' Equity*	
Cash	$ 6.0	Accounts payable	$ 8.0
Accounts receivable	8.0	Notes payable (8%)	2.0
Inventory	12.0	Long-term debt (9%)	14.0
Land	6.0	Preferred stock (20,000 shares,	
Fixed assets, net	14.0	par value $100)	2.0
Other	2.0	Common stock (500,000 shares	
	$48.0	outstanding, par $6)	3.0
		Paid-in capital	5.0
		Retained earnings	14.0
			$48.0

The common stock sells for $25 per share and pays a dividend of $2, which has been growing at an annual rate of 4%. The preferred stock underwriting fee was 5% of the sale price of the stock. It pays a $7 dividend. Their average shareholder has a marginal tax rate of 30%. Brokerage fees average 4%. Determine the following if Apple had profits of $8 million:

a. The cost of common stock.

b. The cost of the preferred stock.

c. The after-tax cost of debt.

d. The cost of retained earnings.

e. The firm's cost of capital.

CAPITAL BUDGETING
AND LEASING

section III

AN OVERVIEW

Capital budgeting has to do with the investment of a firm's funds in assets such as plant, facilities, vehicles, machinery, and the like. For most firms, it is the use of these assets which results in the firm's ability to make a profit. Hence, optimum allocation of funds to purchase plant and equipment is very important to management.

The procedures used to analyze and evaluate proposed capital expenditures require establishment of a bench mark criterion for return on investment. This bench mark has been established as the *firm's cost of capital.* Using the cost of capital as the minimum requirement for return on investment, proposed investments may be ranked by profitability. The procedures for evaluation and ranking are discussed in detail in this section.

The tax laws relating to methods of depreciation and investment tax credit heavily impact to the capital budgeting evaluative process. Hence, a chapter detailing the effects of accelerated depreciation and investment tax credit is included.

The sources of funding for capital investments were described in the previous section. They included equity, debt, profits, and cash throw-offs generated through depreciation. Another important source of funding for capital projects is available through the use of leases. Leasing has grown rapidly in importance during the last ten years.

219

While the study of leasing may logically be included as a part of the subject of financing the firm, the mathematical methods required to analyze leasing are presented as a part of the capital budgeting procedures. Therefore, leasing is included with the study of capital budgeting.

The same mathematical procedures used to evaluate capital investment proposals may also be applied to other areas of finance. A chapter describing such applications for small businesses, annuities, including tax deferred (Keogh plans), and bond yields to maturity is thus included in this section.

General Concepts
of
Capital Budgeting

chapter 14

Capital budgeting is that part of financial management which deals with establishing goals and criteria for the allocation of funds to capital investment projects. A central function of the capital budgeting process involves the evaluation of alternative proposals to purchase assets and the selection of those proposals which best meet the requirements of the firm. Capital investment projects include land, buildings, facilities, and capital equipment such as tools, machinery, and vehicles. The capital budgeting techniques outlined in this book may be applied to form the basis for the evaluation and selection of such assets.

THE IMPORTANCE OF CAPITAL BUDGETING

In Chapter 1, the primary financial goal of a business was indicated to be the *maximization of the owners' wealth as represented by the value of the business.* A fundamental factor in achieving this goal is the investment of the owners' money in land, buildings, and associated capital equipment. The investment in these assets and the subsequent application of labor and materials to them result in the production of the output of the firm. It is this production which results in the profit (or loss) and the cash flow. *The profits attributable to the utilization of these assets greatly exceed the profits from all other sources, both in total dollar amount and per dollar of investment, for nearly all nonfinancial firms.* Business generates profits through the use of its land, machinery, and the like. Thus, investment in these assets is of crucial importance to the financial manager.

Nearly all of the firm's other assets are maintained to support the operations of the firm's plant and equipment. That is, accounts receivable, inventory, cash balances, and other current assets are all necessary to support the use of the firm's facilities and capital equipment. Other asset accounts are also affected. Land, for example, may be purchased and held for future plant expansion. Further, the liabilities which the firm assumes, the retained earnings, and other forms of equity are all sources of funds used to support the asset structure.

Changes in the asset structure have a great impact on both the liability and equity accounts. Therefore, any capital budgeting decision must consider the effect which the investment will have on all of the other asset, liability, and owner's equity accounts. Because of the great importance of the firm's plant and equipment, management must utilize an efficient and systematic procedure for selecting investments which are most desirable within the limits of available funding. The process of developing, coordinating, and executing a program for the selection of investment projects is called *capital budgeting.*

The use of the capital budgeting process is not limited to the private sector. Every level of government is involved in making capital budgeting decisions. The goal of government agencies is to provide the highest quality of products and services at the minimum cost. To do so, they must choose among alternatives. At the federal level, the navy must choose among various forms of arms such as ships and airplanes. State governments allocate funds among new facilities for colleges, road building projects, and improved-quality penal institutions. County government and local communities choose between local versus regional sewage collection and disposal plants. Capital budgeting procedures are extremely important to both short- and long-term operations of government at every level.

THE CAPITAL BUDGETING PROCESS

Capital budgeting involves the evaluation of alternative possible investments and the selection of those which are most desirable based on some predetermined criteria. The process of budgeting for capital investment used by business can be divided into several phases, which are outlined below:

1. Determine the objectives of the owners of the firm and evaluate the firm's position within the market place so as to develop long- and short-run business plans. The business plans provide the basis for the formulation of policies.
2. Develop a criterion for assessing the worth of potential capital investment projects and a procedure for ranking them in terms of their expected benefit to the firm.
3. Evaluate possible capital projects using the criterion and rank them accordingly.
4. Implement those projects which rank highest by order of superiority within the constraint of available funds.

With the exception of phase 1, the procedures for capital budgeting used by government agencies closely coincide with those of business. The primary difference in developing both long- and short-range plans lies in the fact that government at all levels must consider the needs of its constituency as well as the laws which may require or prevent certain types of actions. For example, environmental protection laws passed at the federal level may force local governments to provide improved treatment facilities for disposal of their solid waste, even though local officials might view other projects as having higher priority.

In business, the process of capital budgeting starts when a person first considers investing his money. He may either purchase stock in a large business, buy an ongoing business *in toto,* become a partner therein, or start a new business. In the first instance, the purchase of stock really amounts to the purchase of a portion of the physical plant, management skill, etc., in an existing firm. Unless the firm is offering new stock (a primary stock offering), a prospective shareholder must purchase stock from an existing owner. While the firm does not receive any of the proceeds from this secondary sale, it is nonetheless responsible to the new shareholder, for when an investor purchases stock, he is placing trust in the firm's management to carry out an efficient and profitable capital investment program. The shareholder has invested his funds with the belief that the firm will endeavor to maximize his wealth. Therefore, the wise investment of these funds so as to maximize the owners wealth becomes a major responsibility facing the firm's management.

In deciding to purchase stock in a firm, the shareholder has, in effect, worked through a mini-capital budgeting procedure. While a *firm's managers examine various possible capital investments to determine which best meet the needs of the firm, the investor examines various firms to determine which best satisfy his financial require-*

ments. The methods of analysis may differ, but in each case the fundamental goal is the same: the maximization of the owners' wealth.

Investors constantly reassess the operation of the firm to decide if they should purchase additional stock or if they should sell the shares they already own. This underscores the importance of assuring that the firm's capital investment process is ongoing. A wise investor does not place his stock certificates in his mattress and forget about them. Similarly, the financial manager must continually evaluate the profitability of existing capital investments to determine whether they should be maintained in operation, whether they should be replaced, or if more of the same type should be purchased. Likewise, government officials evaluate the adequacy and usefulness of their investments. This feedback leads to updating equipment which is out of date, expanding roadways which receive use beyond the capacity for which they were designed, placing traffic lights at high-density intersections, and the like.

While many investors purchase stock in large enterprises, others prefer to invest in small businesses. If an investor contemplates the purchase of all or a portion of a small business, the evaluation of the business is, in essence, a capital budgeting decision. The purchaser must closely examine the physical plant both from the viewpoint of a total package and as individual assets. Then he must apply a capital budgeting criterion to determine if the purchase represents a good investment. Similarly, a person starting a new business must decide how best to allocate funds in the purchase of capital equipment, patents, processes, and the like. Hence, whether a person owns and operates his own business or is a shareholder in a large firm, the problem of allocating funds for capital investment is crucial to the operation of the firm and the welfare of the owners.

The four-phase capital budgeting process outlined at the start of this section is applicable at all levels in both the public and the private sectors. The development of long- and short-range capital investment plans and guidelines for investment is discussed in the following section.

GUIDELINES FOR CAPITAL BUDGETING

Guidelines for capital budgeting result from the formulation and implementation of both long- and short-range plans. The long-range plans generally emanate from the firm's upper level of management: the board of directors and the executives of a large firm, and the owners and managers of a small firm. In government the long-range plans are generally formulated by the heads of the various agencies, who then recommend them to the elected officials for evaluation and implementation. In business, long-range plans for capital expenditures result from a thorough analysis of the firm's objectives. Five major areas must be considered:

1. Needs and objectives of the owners.
2. Size of the market in terms of existing and proposed product lines and anticipated growth of market share.
3. Size of existing plants and plans for new plant sites and plant expansion.
4. Economic conditions which may affect the firm's operations.
5. Business and financial risk associated with the replacement of existing assets or the purchase of new assets.

The same basic areas must be considered in the development of government capital budgeting guidelines. The primary difference lies in the consideration of the group affected rather than of the owners of the business as well as the fact that most government agencies have little competition. Since many government agencies operate in a relatively noncompetitive atmosphere, their share of the market is irrelevant. However, market size, i.e., the size of the constituency, is very important. Business risk is also very important to government capital budgeting decisions since many government agencies actually are "in business." For example, the operation of a high-speed transit system is a business; indeed, it is extremely sensitive to changes in consumer preferences.

Short-term plans for capital budgeting generally represent modifications of long-range plans. Day-to-day conditions such as competitive activity, sales forecasts, wage rates, material costs, fuel shortages, and similar items provide input into the formulation of short-range modifications to long-range plans. Changes in these factors in economic conditions may have drastic effects on capital budgeting decisions. Chrysler Corporation anticipated growth in the 1960s and therefore started construction of a new assembly plant in Scranton, Pennsylvania. As sales showed a downward trend, Chrysler stopped work on the plant. Subsequently, as sales rebounded, construction was resumed. Again, as sales slumped in 1974, construction was halted. Firms may be forced to modify long-range plans or to restructure them to meet changing conditions.

The example of Chrysler underscores the necessity of considering the relative urgency of projects. *The extent to which proposed projects cannot be postponed is of critical importance.* Generally, management will assign priorities to given projects and will plan to allocate funds accordingly. However, in the short run, equipment failures, rapidly changing market conditions, rapid inflation, or fuel shortages can all result in the reordering of priorities.

In the formulation of both long- and short-range plans, it is most important to focus on the key factor in all capital investments: the value of the proposed investment to the firm or government agency depends on the future earnings and other cash inflows which will result. Earnings may be measured either in business terms of *earnings per share* or in government terms of improved service or cost reduction. Other cash inflows include those which may result from depreciation and the like.

Estimates of the benefits must be made using the best available data pertaining to wage rates, market size and preferences, price levels, etc. Without accurate data, even the application of the most sophisticated capital budgeting techniques will result in poorly formulated plans. Further, benefits expected to result from an investment should be projected over its life since they may vary in amount from year to year.

CATEGORIES OF CAPITAL INVESTMENTS

Capital investments fall into two basic categories: *profit-maintaining* and *profit-adding* when viewed from the perspective of a business, or *service-maintaining* and *service-adding* when viewed from the perspective of a government agency. The first type includes replacement and improvement of existing facilities, while the latter includes new facilities that will increase output, improve product quality, or reduce production costs. Some fall into both categories. For example, the replacement of a worn-out printing press with a new machine having twice the hourly production capacity is both profit-maintaining and profit-adding. If the new machine had the same output as its predecessor, the investment would have been profit-maintaining. Within the public domain, the widening of a two-lane highway into four lanes is an investment that both maintains and adds service.

Since there is often an overlap in the profit- or service-maintaining and adding aspects of an investment, it is more convenient to view investments as either replacement or new. These two types are further discussed below.

Replacement Investments

Several important factors should be considered when making a replacement decision. These factors represent an expansion of the underlying considerations in formulating long-range capital budgeting plans which were discussed above:

1. The annual operating costs of the existing and proposed assets.
2. The cost and effectiveness of an overhaul of the existing assets.
3. The potential alternative uses of the new assets if market conditions change.
4. The probability of new and more efficient equipment becoming available in the future.
5. The anticipated continuing demand for products or services currently being produced.

The five-part guideline is perhaps most obviously applicable to decisions regarding replacement of equipment rather than to manufacturing procedures or processes. However, with rapidly changing technology, the latter are becoming increasingly more important. *Manufacturing engineers view manufacturing processes as the primary factor in plant design (or redesign). Further, they view buildings, facilities, and equipment as a part of the process. The capital budgeting process is applicable not only to single pieces of equipment, but also to entire plants.* As a plant ages, the primary question is not whether to replace individual machines but rather whether improved manufacturing processes and technological changes warrant designing a new plant.

In the evaluation of replacement investments, it is necessary to evaluate carefully those projects which are justified on the grounds that they are needed to maintain existing profits. For example, suppose that a plant operates at an annual profit of $200,000. The steam boiler is aging, and breakdowns are anticipated. A new boiler will cost $75,000. It would appear logical to purchase a new boiler, spending $75,000 to maintain the profit. But suppose the electrical system, air conditioning, water system, etc., are also aging and in marginal condition. On an individual basis, replacement of each could be justified to maintain profit. When viewed in total, however, the real question is whether or not to replace the whole plant. The same reasoning may be applied to replacing versus repairing an older automobile.

Expansion and New Product Investment

Most of the capital investment undertaken by business is for replacement of machinery, plant, and facilities which either wear out or become obsolete. While a good deal of analysis is necessary in making replacement capital budgeting decisions, the analysis is simplified by the general availability of detailed accurate data on which a decision may be based. The management has experience using the old equipment. Wage rates, material costs, and the market demand are all known with a good degree of precision. Accurate data regarding costs, market conditions, and profitability are much more difficult to obtain for expansion and new business investments. Hence, it is much more difficult to reach decisions regarding investments in these areas.

Expansion and new business investments can generally be divided into four groups:

1. Expansion of current production to meet increased demand. The expansion may entail more complete utilization of existing facilities, such as operating three shifts instead of two. Expansion could also involve expanding existing plant size or new site location and plant construction.
2. Expansion of production into fields closely related to current operations. For example, a firm producing household furniture might expand into office furniture. This process is known as *horizontal integration.* Expansion also includes *vertical integration,* which is the purchase or development of supply and distribution lines for products currently being manufactured. For example, a company which is currently using the services of a distributor to sell its products might decide to establish retail outlets and sell to the public directly.
3. Expansion of production into new fields not associated with the current operations. Such expansion often comes about by a firm acquiring another business.
4. Research and development of new products.

For purposes of analyzing proposed capital investments with respect to their risk, the four groups may be subdivided. It is possible to categorize proposed capital expenditures into several groupings, using their degree of risk as the baseline for subdivision. The analysis of risk as a part of the capital budgeting decision is discussed in Chapter 17.

As a firm enters into areas in which it has had little experience, the capital budgeting decisions become increasingly more difficult and risky. For example, expansion of a current product line to meet existing demand involves little risk. Management has expertise in making the product and knows the demand. However, undertaking basic research and development is very risky. Although research may be directed in certain areas, there is no guarantee that the research will ever result in a profitable, marketable product. *Since management generally wants to avoid risk, it requires increasingly higher returns from investments as their degree of risk increases.* Management wants to be reimbursed for losses which are incurred on risky projects and, therefore, requires a high projected return on all risky projects.

The general guidelines for making capital budgeting decisions were outlined earlier in this chapter. However, the detailed analysis of any expansion or new investment decision goes far beyond these guidelines. As an example, suppose a firm is considering the selection of a new site for a plant location. A few of the numerous factors which must be evaluated are listed below:

1. Availability, skill, and cost of labor.
2. Accessibility to highways, railroads, and other transportation.
3. Cost of housing.
4. State and local taxes.
5. Availability of utilities, especially fuel, such as natural gas.
6. Freight costs to markets.
7. Community attitude toward plants located in the area.
8. Adequacy of law enforcement and fire protection.
9. Recreational facilities.

Management must investigate each of these factors (and many others) for a number of potential sites and weigh the relative advantages of each in order to determine which site best meets its needs.

The detailed analysis required in making expansion and new business investment decisions is complex, time-consuming, and expensive. Once the needed data are gathered, the capital budgeting analysis is undertaken, using analytical procedures such as *payback, present value,* and *internal rate of return.* These are discussed in detail in the following chapters.

COST OF INVESTMENT PROJECTS

All capital investments, whether profit-adding or -maintaining, replacement, or expansion, ultimately result in the purchase of assets such as land, facilities, buildings, equipment, patents, and processes. In addition to the funds required for these purchases, additional *working capital funds are usually required to support the operation* once it is underway. The total cost of a proposed investment is the sum of the following three parts:

1. Purchase price of the land, facilities, buildings, vehicles, and the like, less any tax credits and funds secured from the sale of assets being replaced;
2. Costs relating to the purchase, such as shipping and installation;
3. Additional working capital required to support their operation.

Each of these costs is discussed below, with special emphasis on the relevant tax laws.

Land

Funds spent for the purchase of land must be capitalized. That is, the expenditure is not reflected on the income statement but rather is shown as an addition to the fixed assets on the balance sheet. Land may not be depreciated. Any property taxes assessed on the land are, of course, tax-deductible expenses at the time they are incurred. When the land is subsequently sold, capital gains and losses may be involved.

Facilities and Equipment

Funds spent for the purchase of buildings, machinery, tools, or other equipment must be capitalized. In addition, related costs of transportation, installation, and the like must be capitalized. Once capitalized, these costs may be depreciated in accordance with applicable depreciation procedures. Investment tax credits may apply to some assets. Investment tax credit provides for the reduction of federal income tax liability by permitting part of the cost of certain assets to be deducted from the tax liability in the year the property is placed in service. Investment tax credit and its implications to the capital budgeting decision are discussed in Chapter 18.

Facilities and equipment are subject to property taxation in many locations. Property taxes and depreciation are deductible for purposes of calculating federal income tax liability. When facilities and equipment are sold, the possibility of resulting capital gains or losses and recapture of depreciation must be considered.

Patents and Production Processes

Funds spent for the purchase of patents and production processes must be capitalized. Once capitalized, patents are amortized over their legal lives. The legal life of a patent is 17 years. If, for example, an 8-year-old patent were to be purchased, it would be amortized over its remaining life of 9 years. Production processes are amortized over their estimated useful lives. When patents and processes are amortized, salvage value is assumed to be zero, and the straight-line depreciation method is used. If patents or processes are sold, capital gains or losses and recapture of amortization may be involved.

Working Funds (Working Capital)

Working capital is necessary to support the use of capital assets. *When plant capacity is increased, added funds are often needed to pay for raw, in-process, and finished goods inventories, increase accounts receivable and cash balances, and the like.* Similarly, some current liability accounts such as accounts payable may increase. It is the *difference* between the increase in current assets and current liabilities which constitutes the *change in working capital*. This change (which is almost always an increase) must be considered as a part of the capital budgeting process.

Working capital funds are recovered when the operation terminates. The use of such funds has no overall tax impact. Depreciation deductions are not allowed, and the full amount may be recovered tax free.

Total Funding Requirements

The total funding requirements for any project may be summarized as shown below:

Total fund requirements equal:

Land purchased
Equipment and facilities purchased
Patents and processes purchased
All costs relating to purchases (transportation, legal fees, installation, etc.)
Additional working capital required
Tax liability resulting from the sale of replaced assets (if any)

Less:

Funds realized from the sale of replaced assets
Tax benefits resulting from the sale of replaced assets (if any)
Investment tax credits

It is extremely important to consider all of the potential requirements for funds when making capital expenditures.

Example 1:   FUNDING REQUIREMENTS

Ajax Manufacturing, Inc. is considering the purchase of a replacement for an older-model packaging machine. Ajax is in the 48% marginal tax bracket. Costs are summarized below:

New machine purchase price	$25,000
Installation, shipping costs	2,000
Old machine sale price	1,500

The old machine will be sold at its book value of $1,500. The costs of removal and selling the old machine are negligible. Determine the total amount of funds which Ajax will require in order to undertake the project.

SOLUTION

Ajax will have to spend funds to purchase, ship, and install the new machine. However, it will realize funds from the sale of the old machine.

New machine purchase price	$ 25,000
Installation, shipping costs	2,000
	$ 27,000
Less old machine sale price	− 1,500
Total	$ 25,500

Example 2:   FUNDING REQUIREMENTS

Herman Industries, Inc. is considering the construction of a new plant site to replace its somewhat outdated furniture finishing plant. Some pertinent information relating to its current site is listed below:

	Book Value	Selling Price
Land	$100,000	$2,800,000
Buildings	275,000	(60,000)*
Machinery	500,000	75,000

*Cost to demolish old buildings.

Cost factors for the new plant are listed below:

	Purchase Price	Other Costs	
Land	$2,000,000	$200,000	real estate fees
Buildings	3,600,000		
Machinery	1,600,000	$800,000	shipping and installation

Herman is in the 48% marginal tax bracket and will not require any additional working capital to support the operations in its new plant. Determine the total out-of-pocket cost to set up the operations at the new site.

SOLUTION

First, calculate the gross amount which will be received from the sale of the old property.

	Selling Price
Land	$2,800,000
Buildings	(60,000)
Machinery	75,000
Sale Price	$2,815,000

The net amount received will be the sale price less capital gains taxes. The capital gains are determined below:

	Capital Gains (Losses)
Land:	
(Sale price − book value)	
$2,800,000 − $100,000	$2,700,000
Buildings:	
(Book value + demolition cost)	
$275,000 + $60,000	(335,000)
Machinery:	
(Book value − sale price)	
$500,000 − $75,000	(425,000)
Net Capital Gain	$1,940,000

The tax on the capital gain is $1,940,000 × .3 = $582,000.

The net amount Herman would receive is the sale price less capital gains tax:

Sale Price	$2,815,000
Less Capital Gain Tax	− 582,000
	$2,233,000

Next, calculate the total cost of the new plant.

Land	$2,200,000
Buildings	3,600,000
Machines	2,400,000
Total	$8,200,000

Last, subtract the proceeds from the sale of the old plant from the cost of the new plant.

Total cost	$8,200,000
Less proceeds from sale	− 2,233,000
Net cost	$5,967,000

Constructing a new plant to replace the existing facility will result in an out-of-pocket cost of $5,967,000.

In making capital budgeting decisions, the out-of-pocket costs are of special importance since these costs (cash outflows) represent the investment in the new assets. The cash inflows which result from the use of the assets are measured against these outflows. The cash inflows include both the return *on* investment (profit) and return *of* investment (depreciation and other cash throw-offs plus salvage value of assets when they are sold, and return of working capital).

1. Provide a detailed outline of the capital budgeting process.
2. Indicate the importance of capital budgeting to both the owner and financial manager of a firm.
3. How do profits arise from the use of capital investments? How do profits arise from the use of other assets?
4. How does the purchase of capital equipment affect the other assets and liabilities?
5. How is capital budgeting used in the public sector?
6. Differentiate between long- and short-run plans for investment in capital projects.
7. How does an investor use the process of capital budgeting as an aid in deciding which securities to purchase?
8. How are long-range capital budgeting plans developed?
9. Differentiate profit-adding from profit-maintaining projects.
10. Discuss the factors which should be considered when making a replacement decision.
11. Discuss the areas of expansion and new business investment.
12. Why does management generally require higher returns from investments that may involve greater risk?
13. Why should the estimated benefits from a capital project be projected over its entire life rather than for just the first few years?
14. Why are very accurate data extremely important as inputs to the capital budgeting decision?
15. When considering potential investment projects, what costs must be included?
16. How does the financing of government-owned projects differ from that of those projects which are privately owned?

CONCEPTS
TO
REMEMBER
This chapter introduces new concepts which form a basis for the study of capital budgeting. Be sure you understand all of them.

Profit-Maintaining Projects
Profit-Adding Projects
Replacement Investments
Capital Budgeting Process
Total Funds Required for Capital Investment

PROBLEMS

1. A factory is for sale and will cost $300,000 to purchase. Another $95,000 will be spent in renovations to prepare it for use. Working capital will be required amounting to $75,000. What is the total capital requirement for this project?

2. Reynolds Products, Inc. purchased a five-acre site several years ago for $25,000, planning to construct a new warehouse there. In the interval, its value has increased to $50,000, due primarily to inflation. Another similar site is available. This site is for sale for $50,000. It will require $5,000 less in working capital than would be necessary if the presently owned site were used. Should Reynolds keep the site they now own or sell it and use the new site? Reynolds is in the 48% marginal tax bracket.

3. United Industries Corp. is considering the replacement of its current plant with new facilities at a different location. Pertinent data relating to its current plant are listed below:

	Book Value	Selling Price
Land	$500,000	$1,500,000
Buildings*	150,000	400,000
Machinery	200,000	50,000

*The original cost of the buildings was $800,000.

Cost factors for the new plant are listed below:

	Purchase Price	Related Costs
Land	$1,000,000	$100,000 real estate fees
Buildings	3,600,000	
Machinery	2,000,000	500,000 shipping and installation costs

United is in the 48% marginal tax bracket and will require $300,000 in additional working capital to support the operation of the new plant. Determine the total out-of-pocket cost to set up operations in the new plant.

Payback
and
Present Value

chapter 15

In Chapters 15 and 16 we shall deal with the development of three criteria for assessing the worth of potential capital investment projects and for developing procedures for ranking them in terms of their expected benefit to the firm. *Management's goal is to select those capital investment projects which will provide the highest return on investment, consistent with the risk involved. Selection and implementation of investments which are expected to produce returns on investment which exceed the cost of capital should lead to increased profits.* Increased profits form the basis for increasing the firm's assets or decreasing its liabilities so that owners' equity will increase, *or* increasing cash dividends.

Several varying approaches have been used by business to evaluate and rank projects. Some projects may be *mutually exclusive*, and management will need to know which is preferable. An example of two mutually exclusive projects would be the rebuilding of an older machine versus the purchase of a new machine to replace it. In other instances, the projects being evaluated are not mutually exclusive, but management still needs to rank them in order of profitability in order to utilize limited financial resources most productively.

The two most important methods of capital budgeting fall under the general heading of discounted cash flow, and are termed present value (PV) and internal rate of return (IRR). One other approach, the *payback method,* will also be discussed. *It should be noted that capital budgeting procedures always deal in after-tax cash flows.* The general procedure, in all instances, consists of the following steps:

1. Determine the after-tax cash outflows which are estimated to be required to support the proposed capital investment. The outflows include four parts:

a. purchase price of the asset,
b. costs relating to the purchase such as shipping and installation,
c. working capital required to support the operation of the new asset, and
d. any tax liability arising from the sale of replaced assets.

2. Estimate the after-tax cash inflows which are expected to result from implementation of the project over its useful life. The inflows include seven parts:

a. funds realized from the sale of replaced assets and any tax benefits which may result from their sale,
b. investment tax credits,
c. return *on* investment (after-tax profit),
d. return *of* investment (depreciation cash throw-off),
e. projected salvage value,
f. any capital gains, losses, or recapture of depreciation which may take place and be subject to taxation when the asset is retired,
g. return of working capital required for the use of the asset.

3. Using a capital budgeting procedure, such as present value, determine whether or not the project produces sufficient cash inflows to warrant the expenditures.

It should be noted that all cash flows represent projections based on the best estimates which management can develop. Initially, for the sake of simplicity, it will be assumed that the cash flows are known with certainty. This assumption represents an oversimplification since making precise estimates of revenue and costs is very difficult, if not impossible. It is difficult enough to estimate the cost of a new machine needed six months from now, as prices change frequently. Projecting into the future even five years, to predict cash inflows which will result from the use of that machine, involves even more uncertainty. No one knows what the costs of labor and materials or the sale price of the output will be in five years. There are procedures which may be utilized to adjust for uncertainty. These are described in Chapter 17.

PAYBACK METHOD CRITERION FOR CAPITAL BUDGETING DECISIONS

The *payback criterion* for capital investment is very simple. It is based on the number of years which management anticipates will be required to get back the after-tax expenditures (cash outflows) involved in making a capital investment. *Note that all cash outflows are preceded by minus signs.*

Example 1:   PAYBACK METHOD

A certain investment project will result in an initial cash outflow of $10,000. It will result in a cash inflow of $3,000 per year for five years. Determine the payback period.

SOLUTION

Divide the cash inflow per year into the cash outflow to determine the payback period:

$$\frac{\$10,000}{\$3,000} = 3.33 \text{ years}$$

It will take $3\frac{1}{3}$ years to recover the $10,000 investment.

Example 2:   PAYBACK METHOD

A certain project has yearly after-tax cash outflows and inflows as tabulated below:

Year	Outflow	Inflow
Present	− $10,000	0
1	− 5,000	$3,000
2	0	4,000
3–6	0	5,000

Determine the payback period.

SOLUTION

The total outflow is $15,000. To determine how many years it will take to pay this back, a table such as the one shown below may be employed:

Year	Total Outflow	Total Inflow	Difference
Present	− $10,000	0	− $10,000
1	− 15,000	$ 3,000	− 12,000
2	− 15,000	7,000	− 8,000
3	− 15,000	12,000	− 3,000
4	− 15,000	17,000	+ 2,000
5	− 15,000	22,000	+ 7,000
6	− 15,000	27,000	+ 12,000

At the end of the third year, all but $3,000 will have been recovered. An additional $5,000 in cash inflows will be generated during the fourth year. Three-fifths of this $5,000 will be needed to recover the remaining $3,000. Thus, it will take three and three-fifths years (just over three years and seven months) to recover the total $15,000 outflow.

The payback method for capital budgeting is used when it is necessary to recover cash rapidly. For example, a firm which is short of cash might employ the payback method and utilize a short payback period. Also, companies in industries which have frequent model changes must plan to recover their investments in those projects subject to model changes within the model life period. Automobile manufacturers are in this category of industry.

When the method is employed, a payback period is established and is used as a bench mark against which projects are evaluated. For example, suppose a firm used 3½ years as their maximum payback period. The firm would accept those projects which would result in the recovery of their costs in 3½ years or less and reject those which require more than 3½ years. Using the 3½ year criterion the project in Example 1 would have been accepted, while the project in Example 2 would have been rejected.

A noteworthy flaw in using the payback method is that it does not look beyond the established payback period. Therefore, the use of this method as a criterion for capital budgeting decisions may result in rejection of some projects which have high cash inflows in the years following the payback period. Further, the payback method does not consider the time value of money as described below. Hence, the payback method is not generally recommended as a criterion for selection of capital investments, with the exception of the situations described above. The reason for inclusion of the payback procedure herein is that many firms still employ it. The use of the payback procedure is, however, decreasing, and most firms have changed to the discounted cash flow methods described below.

PRESENT-VALUE CRITERION FOR CAPITAL BUDGETING

The two discounted cash flow methods are based on the concept that funds (cash) to be received in the future are worth less than funds in hand today. Funds to be received in the future are worth less for three reasons:

1. There is always a degree of risk inherent in any funds to be received in the future. A chance always exists that the funds may never be received.
2. Funds in hand may be utilized for whatever purpose they are needed. Funds to be received in the future cannot be utilized today.
3. In periods of inflation the purchasing power of funds to be received in the future will be less than that of funds available for expenditure at the present time.

Based on the conclusion that funds to be received in the future are worth less than cash in hand, the two discounted cash flow methods have been developed.

The value of funds to be received at some future time is termed their present value. The primary question which must be addressed is how much more cash in hand is worth than funds expected to be received in the future. That is, what is the present value of funds to be received in the future. One approach to solving this problem involves computing how much a dollar invested today at a specified rate would yield in one year. If 8% were specified, the value would be calculated as follows:

$$S = P(1 + i) \tag{1}$$
$$S = \$1(1 + .08)$$
$$S = \$1.08$$

where S is the compound sum and P is the amount invested (in this case $1.00). Thus, at 8%, a dollar today is equivalent to $1.08 to be received a year from now. It is also possible to use Eq. (1) to solve the problem: How much would have to be invested *now* at 8% to yield a dollar in one year?

$$S = P(1 + i)$$
$$\$1 = P(1 + .08)$$
$$\$1 = 1.08P$$
$$P = \frac{\$1}{1.08} = \$.9259$$

The answer can be expressed as follows: *The present value of $1.00 to be received one year from now is $.9259 when invested at an 8% annual rate of growth.* Using the same method, it is possible to compute the present value of funds to be received for different numbers of years in the future at varying rates. A small table giving the results is shown below:

Present Values of $1 Discounted at Various Rates

Periods	2%	4%	8%	12%
1	.9804	.9615	.9259	.8929
2	.9612	.9246	.8573	.7972
3	.9423	.8890	.7938	.7118
4	.9239	.8548	.7350	.6355
5	.9057	.8219	.6806	.5674

For example, the present value of $1 to be received in four years using 12% as the rate of return is $.6355. A more complete listing of present values is included in Table III of Appendix A at the end of the book. However, even the short table may be used to solve a variety of problems.

The present-value criterion for capital budgeting involves summing the present values of the cash outflows required to support an investment project and the present value of the cash inflows resulting from the operations of the project. The inflows and outflows are discounted to present value using the appropriate discount rate corresponding to the cost of capital. The difference in the inflows and outflows is the net present value (NPV):

$$\text{Net present value} = \frac{\text{Present value of after-tax cash inflows} -}{\text{Present value of after-tax cash outflows}} \quad (2)$$

If the NPV is positive, it means that the project is expected to yield a return in excess of the cost of capital. If the NPV is zero, the yield is expected to exactly equal the cost of capital. If the NPV is negative, the yield is expected to be less than the cost of capital. Hence, only those projects having positive or zero NPVs are acceptable.

Example 3: PRESENT VALUE

Hastings International will receive $3,000 in five years. If the 12% discount rate is used, determine the present value of the amount.

SOLUTION

Multiply the discount factor corresponding to five years and 12% by the $3,000. Refer to Table III, 12% column, five-year row.

$$\$3,000 \times .5674 = \$1,702.20$$

The present value of the $3,000 to be received in five years is $1,702.20.

Another way to look at the answer to Example 3 is that if the $1,702.20 were invested at 12% for five years with interest compounded annually, it would be worth $3,000. This can be verified by referring to the compound interest table (Table I), noting that the compounding factor for five years at 12% is 1.7623. Then,

$$\$1,702.20 \times 1.7623 = \$3,000$$

Example 4:   PRESENT VALUE (New investment)

A proposed investment having an after-tax cost of $10,000 is expected to produce after-tax cash inflows as shown in the table below. If the firm's hurdle rate (cost of capital) is 8%, should the investment be made?

Time	After-tax Cash Inflows
1	$2,000
2	2,000
3	3,000
4	3,000
5	4,000

SOLUTION

This problem may be easily solved by constructing a solution table as shown. *Note: Outflows are shown as negative numbers.* The discount factors are obtained from Table III of Appendix A.

Solution Table for 8%

Time	Amount		Discount Factor		Present Value
Present	− $10,000	×	1	=	− $10,000
1	2,000	×	.9259	=	1,852
2	2,000	×	.8573	=	1,715
3	3,000	×	.7938	=	2,381
4	3,000	×	.7350	=	2,205
5	4,000	×	.6806	=	2,722
		Net present value		=	$ 875

The net present value is the algebraic sum of the present value of the cash flows. In Example 4, the PV of the outflows was $10,000, while the PV of the inflows was $10,875.00. The NPV in this problem is positive. This means that the investment is expected to yield a return *in excess of the 8% hurdle rate.* Hence, the investment should be made provided sufficient funds are available. If the NPV had been zero, it would indicate that the return is anticipated to be exactly 8%. If the NPV had been negative, it would indicate that the return is expected to be less than 8%, and therefore the investment would not be made.

Example 5:   PRESENT VALUE (Replacement investment)

An older machine was fully depreciated to its actual salvage value of $2,000 prior to 1973. The Simmons Machine Company is considering replacing it with a new machine costing $20,000. The new machine will be depreciated over its ten-year projected life using straight-line depreciation and will have a $3,000 salvage value. It is anticipated that the new machine will reduce labor costs by $3,000 per year. Simmons' income statement for 1973 is as shown. Their cost of capital is 14%, and their marginal tax rate is 48%.

Simmons Income Statement 1973

Sales		$250,000
Materials	$ 75,000	
Labor	100,000	
Administration	21,000	
Depreciation	19,000	
Total expenses		− 215,000
Earnings before taxes		$ 35,000
Federal income tax*		− 10,300
After-tax profits		$ 24,700

*Using 1973 tax rates.

If Simmons requires an after-tax return on investment of 14%, should they buy the new machine?

SOLUTION

First: Calculate the after-tax cash outflow needed to purchase the machine. It costs $20,000, but the old machine can be sold for $2,000. Therefore, the actual cash outflow will be $18,000.

Next: Calculate the increase in the after-tax cash inflows which will result from using the machine. The current yearly cash inflow, based on the 1973 income statement, is the sum of the after-tax profit plus depreciation cash throw-off:

$$\$24,700 + \$19,000 = \$43,700$$

Using a depreciable value of $20,000 − $3,000 = $17,000 for the new machine, the depreciation will be $1,700 per year for the machine's projected ten-year life. However, labor costs will be reduced by $3,000 per year. The changes are incorporated into the pro-forma income statement below:

Simmons, Inc.
Pro-forma Income Statement

Sales		$250,000
Materials	$75,000	
Labor	97,000	
Administration	21,000	
Depreciation	20,700	
Total expenses		− 213,700
Earnings before taxes		$ 36,300
Federal income tax		− 10,924
After-tax profits		$ 25,376

The yearly cash inflow is expected to be $25,376 + $20,700 = $46,076. The yearly after-tax cash inflow has been increased, to $46,076 from $43,700. This amounts to a yearly increase of $2,376. Keeping in mind that the $3,000 salvage value will be recovered in the tenth year, a solution table can be constructed. Refer to Table III, 14% column, for the discount factors.

Solution Table for 14%

Time	Amount		Discount Factor		Present Value
Present	− $18,000	×	1	=	− $18,000
1	2,376	×	.8772	=	2,084
2	2,376	×	.7695	=	1,828
3	2,376	×	.6750	=	1,604
4	2,376	×	.5921	=	1,407
5	2,376	×	.5194	=	1,234
6	2,376	×	.4556	−	1,083
7	2,376	×	.3996	=	949
8	2,376	×	.3506	=	833
9	2,376	×	.3075	=	731
10	5,376	×	.2697	=	1,450
			NPV	=	− $ 4,797

Since the NPV is negative, the machine does not yield the required 14% and should not be purchased.

The calculations in Example 5 were rather tedious. To avoid the process of having to multiply a given number ($2,376 in Example 5) so many times, Table IV (present value of an annuity of $1) has been provided in Appendix A. The use of Table IV is demonstrated below.

Example 6:   PRESENT VALUE

Refer to Example 5, and solve the problem using present value of annuity tables.

SOLUTION

Reconstruct the solution table as shown below:

Solution Table for 14%

Time	Amount		Discount Factor		Present Value
Present	− $18,000	×	1	=	− $18,000
1–9	2,376	×	4.9464	=	11,752
10	5,376	×	.2697	=	1,450
			NPV	=	− $ 4,798

The discount factor 4.9464 was obtained by using Table IV and finding the 14% column, nine-year row. *Table IV gives the present value of an annuity. That is, it gives the present value of $1 per year to be received for a given number of years.* Multiplying the value given in the table by $2,376 gives the present value of the $2,376 to be received each year for nine years, which is $11,752.

Example 7:   PRESENT VALUE (Replacement investment)

Refer to Example 5, and assume that the old machine could be sold for $6,000 and originally cost $10,000. How would this affect the profitability of the project?

SOLUTION

The sale of the machine for $6,000 would result in a recapture of depreciation of $4,000, based on a salvage value of $2,000. The $4,000 would be taxed at 48%,[1] since Simmons has taxable income exceeding $25,000. The result is $1,920 in tax. Thus, $4,080 of the original $6,000 would remain. Based on the cost of the new machine of $20,000, the actual outflow of cash required to buy it would be $20,000 − $4,080 = $15,920. The $15,920 would replace the $18,000, and the solution table would appear as follows:

[1]Note that this example refers to 1973 at which time taxable income in excess of $25,000 was taxed at a rate of 48%.

Solution Table for 14%

Time	Amount		Discount Factor		Present Value
Present	− $15,920	×	1	=	− $15,920
1–9	2,376	×	4.9464	=	11,752
10	5,376	×	.2697	=	1,450
			NPV	=	− $ 2,718

Based on the 14% cost of capital, the project would still be rejected.

Example 8: Present Value (New investment)

A firm can purchase a mechanical sweeper for $75,000. It has a projected life of ten years and negligible salvage value and will be depreciated straight-line. Its use will result in reduction of labor cost by $12,000 per year. The firm has a cost of capital of 10% and is in the 48% marginal tax bracket. Decide whether or not the firm should purchase the machine.

Solution

The firm's income statement will be changed as follows:

Reduction in labor	$12,000
Increase in depreciation	− 7,500
Net reduction in expenses*	$ 4,500
Increase in taxes	− 2,160
Increases in after-tax profit	$ 2,340

*Same as increase in earnings before taxes.

The reduction in yearly expenses by $4,500 will result in additional after-tax profit of $2,340. The total yearly increased cash inflow will, therefore, be $2,340 + 7,500 = $9,840. The $7,500 represents the depreciation cash throw-off.

The solution table is shown below:

Solution Table for 10%

Time	Amount		Discount Factor		Present Value
Present	− $75,000	×	1	=	− $75,000
1–10	9,840	×	6.1446	=	60,463
			NPV	=	− $14,537

Since the NPV is negative, the machine does not yield the required 10% return and should not be purchased.

Example 9: PRESENT VALUE (Replacement investment)

The Marx Co., Inc. owns a machine which is in current use. It was purchased for $80,000 and had a projected life of 15 years with $5,000 salvage value. It has been depreciated straight-line for 5 years to date and could be sold for $60,000. A new machine can be purchased at a total cost of $100,000. It will have a 10-year life and salvage value of $10,000 and will be depreciated straight-line. The new machine will reduce labor expenses by $7,000 per year. If the firm requires a 10% return on investment, determine whether the new machine should be purchased. The firm is in the 48% marginal tax bracket. The income statement for the firm using the current machine is shown below:

Marx Co., Inc. Income Statement, For Period Ending Dec. 31, 1975

Sales		$1,000,000
Labor	$400,000	
Materials	200,000	
Depreciation	100,000	
Total expenses		− 700,000
Earnings before taxes		$ 300,000
Federal income tax*		− 130,500
After-tax profit		$ 169,500

*Using 1975 tax rates.

Thus, the cash inflow at present is $169,500 + $100,000 = $269,500.

SOLUTION

First, determine the after-tax cash outflow required to purchase the new machine. The old machine has been depreciated straight-line for five years at $5,000 per year ($75,000 ÷ 15 years = $5,000 per year) for $25,000 accumulated depreciation. The book value is calculated as shown:

Purchase price	$ 80,000
Less accumulated depreciation	− 25,000
Book value	$ 55,000

The old machine could be sold for $60,000, resulting in a recapture of depreciation of $5,000. The recapture would be taxed at 48% for a tax of $2,400. Thus, the actual cash outflow to purchase the new machine is calculated as follows:

Total cost of new machine	$ 100,000
Less sale price of old machine	− 60,000
	$ 40,000
Additional tax on recapture of depreciation	2,400
Cash outflow required to purchase new machine	$ 42,400

Second, determine the after-tax cash inflows which will result from the use of the new machine. The new machine has a depreciable value of $90,000. Therefore, since its life is ten years, the annual depreciation is $9,000 per year. *Thus, the annual depreciation will be increased by $4,000.* Note that the depreciation on the old machine was $5,000 per year. The pro-forma income statement reflecting the cost reduction and increased depreciation is as follows:

Marx Co., Inc. Pro-forma Income Statement

Sales		$1,000,000
Labor	$393,000	
Materials	200,000	
Depreciation	104,000	
Total expenses		− 697,000
Earnings before taxes		$ 303,000
Federal income tax		− 131,940
After-tax profits		$ 171,060

Thus, the cash inflow is $171,060 + $104,000 = $275,060. The purchase of the new machine will result in an increase in cash flow for ten years of $275,060 − $269,500 = $5,560.

Third, determine the present value of the cash inflow which will take place in ten years when the new machine is sold at salvage value. The new machine has a projected salvage value of $10,000, while the old machine had a projected salvage value of $5,000. Thus, if the new machine is purchased, an additional $5,000 would be realized at the end of the tenth year.

Last, set up a solution table for the cash flows to determine whether or not the purchase will yield the required 10%.

Solution Table for 10%

Time	Amount		Discount Factor		Present Value
Present	− $42,400	×	1	=	− $42,400
1–10	5,560	×	6.1446	=	34,164
10	5,000	×	.3855	=	1,928
			NPV	=	− $ 6,308

Since the NPV is negative, the new machine is not expected to yield the required 10% and should not be purchased.

RANKING PROJECTS USING THE PROFITABILITY INDEX

In addition to indicating whether or not a proposed investment meets the required rate of return, the present-value method may be used to rank projects in order of their profitability. The ranking is accomplished through the use of the profitability index (PI):

$$\text{Profitability index} = \frac{\text{Present value of after-tax inflows}}{\text{Present value of after-tax outflows}} \qquad (3)$$

The profitability index provides a measure of the profitability of investments on a per dollar basis of their after-tax cash cost. Thus, it permits the comparison of projects requiring significantly different cash outflows. The return on a $100,000 investment could be compared with that of a much smaller investment of perhaps $10,000, since *the profitability index indicates the return per dollar of investment.*

The profitability index is based on the present value of the after-tax cash inflows and outflows as shown in Eq. (3). As indicated earlier, only projects having net present values equal to or greater than zero have expected yields equal to or greater than the required rate of return. It follows, therefore, that if a project has a profitability index equaling 1, then its net present value would be zero, and it would yield exactly the required rate of return. Similarly, if a project had a profitability index greater than 1, it would have an expected yield in excess of the required amount. The relation among net present value, profitability index, and required return is summarized in tabular form below:

Net Present Value	Profitability Index	Expected Return
Negative	Less than 1	Less than required rate
Zero	1	Exactly equal to required rate
Positive	Greater than 1	Exceeds required rate

The use of the profitability index is demonstrated below.

Example 10:   RANKING INVESTMENT PROJECTS

Three projects have been suggested to Rahway Industries, Inc. The after-tax cash flows for each are tabulated below. If Rahway's cost of capital is 12%, rank them in order of profitability.

After-Tax Cash Flows

Time	Project A	Project B	Project C
Present	− $10,000	− $30,000	− $18,000
1	2,800	6,000	6,500
2	3,000	10,000	6,500
3	4,000	12,000	6,500
4	4,000	16,000	6,500

SOLUTION

Each project must be evaluated to obtain the present value of the cash inflows and outflows.

Project A, Solution Table for 12%

Time	Amount		Discount Factor		Present Value
Present	− $10,000	×	1	=	− $10,000
1	2,800	×	.8929	=	2,500
2	3,000	×	.7972	=	2,392
3	4,000	×	.7118	=	2,847
4	4,000	×	.6355	=	2,542
			NPV	=	$ 281

For project A, the present value of the outflows is $10,000, and the present value of the inflows is

$$\$10,281 = (\$2,500 + 2,392 + 2,847 + 2,542).$$

The profitability index for project A is

$$PI_A = \frac{\$10,281}{\$10,000} = 1.0281$$

Project B, Solution Table for 12%

Time	Amount		Discount Factor		Present Value
Present	− $30,000	×	1	=	− $30,000
1	6,000	×	.8929	=	5,358
2	10,000	×	.7972	=	7,972
3	12,000	×	.7118	=	8,542
4	16,000	×	.6355	=	10,168
			NPV	=	$ 2,040

The profitability index for project B is

$$PI_B = \frac{\$32,040}{\$30,000} = 1.068$$

Project C, Solution Table for 12%

Time	Amount		Discount Factor		Present Value
Present	− $18,000	×	1	=	− $18,000
1–4	6,500	×	3.0374	=	19,743
			NPV	=	$ 1,743

The profitability index for project C is

$$PI_c = \frac{\$19,743}{\$18,000} = 1.0968$$

The projects are ranked in order of highest profitability index. Therefore, C would be first, B second, and A last. *Note that the ranking using the profitability index measures return per dollar of investment.* Thus, although project B has the highest NPV, it is not the most profitable per dollar of investment. Rather, project C is the most profitable. Note further that all of the projects have positive net present values and that, hence, all meet the 12% required rate of return. If the firm had sufficient funds, it would invest in all of them, provided, of course, that none were mutually exclusive.

Ranking projects using the profitability index provides a measure of the profitability of projects per dollar of investment. However, it has a limitation in that there is no way to convert a profitability index to a rate of return. As indicated above, a project which had a profitability index exactly equal to 1 would have a yield exactly equal to the required rate of return (cost of capital). If another project being evaluated had a profitability index equal to 1.1, it would have a higher return than the project with the index of 1. However, the return on the latter project *would not necessarily be* 1.1 times greater than the return on the first project. Management may want to rank projects by their expected rates of return (their internal rate of return). This may be accomplished by finding the rate of return for each project, as described in the following chapter.

QUESTIONS
FOR
DISCUSSION 1. Indicate why the payback method is not recommended as a good procedure to use for capital budgeting decisions. Why do some firms continue to use it?

2. Give some examples of investment projects which are mutually exclusive.
3. Why is it important to use after tax cash flows in all calculations used for capital budgeting?
4. Why are funds in hand today worth more than funds to be received in the future?
5. How is the profitability index used to rank investment projects?
6. What does it mean if an investment project has a negative net present value?
7. What is the significance of a profitability index of less than 1?

CONCEPTS TO REMEMBER

This chapter introduces several new concepts which have to do with methods of capital budgeting. It is important for you to familiarize yourself with them.

Discounted Cash Flow
Payback Method
Internal Rate of Return
Profitability Index
Present-Value Method
Net Present Value
Discount Rate

PROBLEMS

1. Johnston Corporation requires a maximum payback period of four years. A certain investment will result in after-tax cash flows as shown. Determine if it should be purchased.

Time	Amount
Present	− $10,000
1	3,000
2	2,000
3	2,000
4	4,000
5	3,000

2. Washington Manufacturing Company, Inc. will have added pre-tax income of $15,000 per year for the next four years. If they have to pay 48% tax on the income, determine the present value of the after-tax cash inflows based on a 10% discount rate.

3. A new machine will result in after-tax cash flows as shown. If the owner has a 14% cost of capital, determine the net present value and the payback period for the machine.

Time	Amount
Present	− $50,000
1	20,000
2	20,000
3	25,000
4	25,000

4. Can Company, Inc. has a policy of rejecting any investment project that will not result in recovery of the cost within three years. They are considering the three projects listed below.

After-Tax Cash Flow

Time	Project A	Project B	Project C
Present	− $10,000	− $12,000	− $3,000
1	4,000	0	500
2	4,000	0	500
3	2,000	4,000	500
4	2,000	4,000	500
5	2,000	4,000	500
6	2,000	4,000	3,000
7	2,000	4,000	3,000

Determine the payback period for each project and indicate whether or not it should be accepted based on the Can Company criteria.

5. Referring to Problem 4, determine the following for each project based on a cost of capital of 14%:
   a. The present value of the cash inflows and outflows.
   b. The net present value.
   c. The profitability index.
   Based on the profitability index, rank the projects. Are there any differences in the decision regarding acceptance or rejection of the projects using the 14% present-value criteria as opposed to the payback criteria?

6. An old machine has been fully depreciated to its actual salvage value of $5,000. A new machine, having a total cost of $30,000, is available. It would increase after-tax income by $4,000 per year, have zero salvage value, and be depreciated straight-line over a ten-year period. The firm requires a 12% return on investments. Determine the net present value of the new machine. Assume the old machine can be sold for $5,000.

7. A trash compactor will reduce labor costs by $15,000 per year for its life of ten years. If it costs $50,000, is depreciated straight-line, and has zero salvage value, should it be purchased? The owners are in the 48% marginal tax bracket, require a 10% return on investments and use a discounted cash flow capital budgeting procedure.

8. A machine purchased five years ago for $30,000 has been depreciated to a book value of $20,000. It originally had a projected life of 15 years and zero salvage value. A new machine will cost $45,000 and result in a reduced operating cost of $6,000 per year for the next ten years. The older machine could be sold for $10,000. The resulting capital loss will offset a capital gain, and hence the company, which is in the 48% marginal tax bracket, will enjoy a tax savings. The cost of capital is 12%. The new machine will be depreciated straight-line over a ten-year life with $10,000 salvage value. Determine the net present value of the new machine.

Internal Rate of Return and Capital Rationing

chapter 16

In Chapter 15 we presented the basic concepts of the time value of money and demonstrated how they could be employed in making capital budgeting decisions through use of the present-value method. The present-value method provides a systematic approach to determining whether or not proposed investment projects would provide the required rate of return. Further, through the use of the profitability index, projects can be ranked in terms of their profitability. However, the present-value method does not indicate the actual rate of return which a given project is expected to yield. The internal rate of return criterion for evaluating capital investments gives the actual after-tax rate of return. Once the internal rate of return is known, projects can be evaluated using the cost of capital as the bench mark for acceptance. Further, projects can be easily ranked: The project having the highest internal rate of return is ranked first, etc.

INTERNAL RATE OF RETURN CRITERION FOR CAPITAL BUDGETING DECISIONS

The internal rate of return for any project is the rate which exactly equates the present value of the after-tax cash inflows with the present value of the after-tax cash outflows. It is the rate of return which, when applied, will result in a net present value of zero.

Example 1: INTERNAL RATE OF RETURN

$92.59 is invested in a project. After one year, the project will yield a return of $100 after taxes. Determine the internal rate of return of the project.

SOLUTION

A solution table of the type used in present-value calculations provides a convenient way to express the problem:

Time	Amount		Discount Factor		Present Value
Present	− $ 92.59	×	1	=	− $92.59
1	100.00	×	Unknown	=	92.59
			NPV	=	$ 0.00

Recall that the internal rate of return exactly equates the present value of the after-tax cash inflows with the present value of the cash outflows. Therefore, the present value of the inflows must equal $92.59, as shown in the solution table. The discount factor is unknown but may be readily determined by recognizing that $100 multiplied by the discount factor equals $92.59. Algebraically, this may be expressed as follows:

$$\$100 \times d.f. = \$92.59$$

$$d.f. = \frac{\$92.59}{\$100.00} = .9259$$

The discount factor is .9259. Once the discount factor has been obtained, the internal rate of return may be determined by referring to Table III in Appendix A. The investment is for only one year, so look at the row corresponding to one year and search for the discount factor .9259. It is apparent that the factor is located in the 8% column. Therefore, the internal rate of return for this project is 8%.

Example 2: INTERNAL RATE OF RETURN

A new project has an after-tax cost of $10,000 and will result in after-tax cash inflows of $3,000 in year 1, $5,000 in year 2, and $6,000 in year 3. Determine the internal rate of return.

SOLUTION

First, set up a solution table:

Time	Amount		Discount Factor		Present Value
Present	− $10,000	×	1	=	− $10,000
1	3,000	×	Unknown	=	Unknown
2	5,000	×	Unknown	=	Unknown
3	6,000	×	Unknown	=	Unknown
			NPV	=	$ 0.00

Unlike Example 1, the present value of each individual cash flow is not known. We only know that the sum of the three present values (shown as "unknown" under the present value column) must total $10,000 in order that the NPV = $0. There is no direct way of obtaining the internal rate of return; it must be estimated and then checked. To make an intelligent estimate of the answer, *it is possible to reconstruct the problem using an average cash inflow each year rather than the exact amounts given*. The average of $3,000, $5,000, and $6,000 is $4,666 per year. Based on the amount of $4,666, we can reconstruct a solution table:

Time	Amount		Discount Factor		Present Value
Present	− $10,000	×	1	=	− $10,000
1–3	4,666	×	Unknown	=	10,000
			NPV	=	$ 0.00

Now there is only one unknown to work with, and this may be found as in Example 1:

$$\$4,666 \times \text{d.f.} = \$10,000$$

$$\text{d.f.} = \frac{\$10,000}{\$4,666} = 2.1431$$

The discount factor is 2.1431. To determine the corresponding internal rate of return, refer to Table IV in Appendix A. Table IV is used because it gives discount factors for annuities, and since the inflow of $4,666 is shown each year for three years, it is, in essence, an annuity. Look at the three-year row in Table IV for 2.1431. The closest factor is 2.1399, which corresponds to 19%. Thus, 19% is the estimate to be used in solving the problem. Refer back to the original solution table, and replace the unknown discount factors with the discount factors corresponding to 19% in Table III. Then multiply these by the cash inflows to determine the present values. The table is shown below:

Solution Table for 19%

Time	Amount		Discount Factor		Present Value
Present	− $10,000	×	1	=	− $10,000
1	3,000	×	.8403	=	2,521
2	5,000	×	.7062	=	3,531
3	6,000	×	.5934	=	3,560
			NPV	=	− $ 388

The NPV is negative. This means that the discount factors applied to the inflows are *too small*. Larger discount factors are obtained by using *lower* rates of return. The solution table for 17% is shown below:

Solution Table for 17%

Time	Amount		Discount Factor		Present Value
Present	− $10,000	×	1	=	− $10,000
1	3,000	×	.8547	=	2,564
2	5,000	×	.7305	=	3,652
3	6,000	×	.6244	=	3,746
			NPV	=	− $ 38

The NPV is much closer to zero but still negative. Therefore, the rate of return must be lower than 17%. The solution table for 16% is shown below:

Solution Table for 16%

Time	Amount		Discount Factor		Present Value
Present	− $10,000	×	1	=	− $10,000
1	3,000	×	.8621	=	2,586
2	5,000	×	.7432	=	3,716
3	6,000	×	.6407	=	3,844
			NPV	=	$ 146

The NPV for 16% is positive. Therefore, *we can conclude that the actual internal rate of return is between 16% and 17%.*

As demonstrated in Example 2, determining the internal rate of return often requires a series of repetitive calculations using different rates of return until the correct rate is obtained. Making a good first estimate of the internal rate of return is very helpful. However, once the initial solution table is prepared, even if the resulting NPV is much greater or much lower than zero, the direction is established. *If the NPV is less than zero, use a lower discount rate.* This was illustrated in Example 2. *If the NPV is positive, use a higher discount rate.*

In some instances, it is necessary to determine the internal rate of return more precisely than just to say that it lies between 16% and 17%, as was the case in Example 2. To determine a more precise value, linear interpolation is used, as demonstrated in Example 3.

Example 3:   LINEAR INTERPOLATION

Refer to Example 2 and find the precise answer using linear interpolation.

SOLUTION

The answer lies between 16% and 17%. The NPVs corresponding to those rates are as follows:

Rate of Return	NPV
16%	$146
17	− 38

The actual rate of return corresponds to NPV = 0. The situation is shown in Fig. 1.

FIGURE 1.

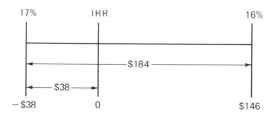

The width of the lower scale is $146.00 + $38.00 = $184.00, as shown. The zero value is

$$\frac{\$38}{\$184} = .2$$

or .2 of the way from the 17% point. The width of the upper scale is 1% (i.e., 17% − 16%). Therefore the internal rate of return is 17% − .2(1%) = 16.8%.

Once the IRR of a project has been determined, it is a simple matter to compare it with the cost of capital to decide whether or not the project is acceptable. *If the IRR equals or exceeds the cost of capital the project is acceptable.*

RANKING PROJECTS USING INTERNAL RATE OF RETURN

Ranking projects is a simple matter, using their internal rates of return. Projects are ranked according to their IRRs: The project with the highest IRR is ranked first, etc. In almost all instances, the use of either the present value or internal rate of return methods will lead to the same order of ranking of projects. Occasionally, a difference in ranking will occur. This is due to a basic difference in the underlying assumptions of the two methods. *The present-value method assumes that the cash inflows resulting from the use of an asset will be reinvested at the cost of capital. The internal rate of return method as-*

sumes that the cash inflows will be reinvested at the calculated internal rate of return. Hence, if both methods are used and a difference in ranking does occur, the financial manager will choose the appropriate ranking based on his expectations as to how much return he will receive from the cash inflows as they are received and reinvested.

CAPITAL RATIONING

Most firms have a limited amount of funds available for capital investment. This constraint forces a firm's management to ration the funds available among the proposed capital investments.

The first step in capital rationing is to evaluate all of the proposed projects using one of the capital budgeting ranking procedures (payback, present value, or internal rate of return). Those proposed projects which do not meet the required return are eliminated. For example, if the payback criterion were employed with a maximum payback period of four years, all projects having a payback period greater than four years would be eliminated. Similarly, if present-value or internal rate of return methods were used, all proposed projects having a projected return lower than the firm's cost of capital would be discarded.

Once those proposed projects which do not meet the firm's requirements are discarded, the remaining projects are ranked. The method of ranking depends on the capital budgeting method being used, as shown in the table below:

Capital Budgeting Method	Ranking of Projects
Payback	Rank projects by their payback period. *The project with the shortest payback period is ranked first.* The remaining projects are ranked with those having shorter payback periods first, followed by those with longer payback periods.
Present value	Rank projects by their profitability index. *The project having the highest profitability index is ranked first.* The remaining projects are ranked with those having higher profitability indices first, followed by those having lower profitability indices.
Internal rate of return	Rank projects by their internal rate of return. *The project having the highest internal rate of return is ranked first.* The remaining projects are ranked with those having higher internal rates of return first, followed by those having lower internal rates of return.

Example 4: Ranking Proposed Capital Investment Projects

Ace International has six proposed investment projects. Their cost of capital is 12%. The projects are listed below along with their expected internal rates of return:

Project	Internal Rate of Return
A	18%
B	11
C	14
D	19
E	7
F	12

Rank the projects in order of their internal rate of return.

SOLUTION

The projects are ranked with those having the highest internal rate of return first. Note that only those projects having an internal rate of return equal to or greater than the firm's cost of capital are included. The other projects are not considered because they are not expected to yield the required rate of return.

Project	Internal Rate of Return
D	19%
A	18
C	14
F	12

Once projects have been ranked, any projects which are mutually exclusive or contingent upon another project must be given further consideration. Suppose that in Example 4 projects D and C were mutually exclusive. That is, if project D were undertaken, then C would not be and vice versa. We would eliminate project C since D has a higher expected return. Suppose further that project A were contingent on the acceptance of project F. That is, if F were not undertaken, it would be impossible to carry out A. In this instance we would have to evaluate the two projects together as a part of the capital rationing process.

The next step in the capital rationing process consists of the actual selection of projects to implement. Basically this means selecting the most profitable projects until their cumulative costs consume the available funds. Example 5, below, demonstrates ranking of projects using the profitability index. The same procedure holds for ranking when the internal rates of return are known.

Example 5:   CAPITAL RATIONING

Gilmore, Inc. has capital budgeting funds for this year amounting to $1 million. Several projects have been proposed. They have been evaluated using the present-value method. The profitability index and cost of each are listed below:

Project	PI	Cost
A	1.20	$200,000
B	1.07	100,000
C	.86	90,000
D	1.34	180,000
E	1.56	240,000
F	1.03	130,000
G	.97	200,000
H	1.13	300,000
I	1.23	110,000
J	1.41	220,000

Determine which projects should be included in this year's capital expenditure program.

SOLUTION

List the projects in order of their profitability index, and add a column giving the cumulative cost of the projects. List only those projects with a profitability index of 1 or greater since all of the other projects are unacceptable.

Project	PI	Cost	Cumulative Cost
E	1.56	$240,000	$ 240,000
J	1.41	220,000	460,000
D	1.34	180,000	640,000
I	1.23	110,000	750,000
A	1.20	200,000	950,000
H	1.13	300,000	1,250,000
B	1.07	100,000	1,350,000
F	1.03	130,000	1,480,000

Since only $1 million are available, not all of the projects can be accepted. Only the five most profitable can be planned since their total cost is $950,000. Acceptance of the sixth, project H, would require more than the available funds.

Example 6:   CAPITAL RATIONING

Suppose in Example 5 that projects J and A were mutually exclusive. How would this affect the capital rationing decision?

SOLUTION

The projects would be ranked as they were in Example 5. Since projects J and A are mutually exclusive and project J has a higher profitability index, project A would be eliminated as shown below:

Project	PI	Cost	Cumulative Cost
E	1.56	$240,000	$ 240,000
J	1.41	220,000	460,000
D	1.34	180,000	640,000
I	1.23	110,000	750,000
H	1.13	300,000	1,050,000
B	1.07	100,000	1,150,000
F	1.03	130,000	1,280,000

Gilmore, Inc. has a choice of selections in this instance. They should definitely accept the first four projects since they have a total cost of only $750,000. If Gilmore could obtain an additional $50,000 beyond the $1 million already allocated for capital expenditures, they would invest in project H. If the additional funds are not available, then they should skip project H and go with B and F since the total cost of the first four projects plus B and F is only $980,000.

Another aspect of the capital rationing process is the evaluation of projects to determine which are the most urgently needed, or which could be postponed. It may be that a particular project is highly essential to an ongoing operation and must be implemented even though it may have a lower expected return than another project. Further, some projects may be postponable until such time that additional funds will be available for investment. Also, some projects may require expenditures over a period of time; several years may be required to plan and construct a new facility. Therefore, total cost will not be borne in any one year. All of these factors must be considered by management in developing their capital investment program. The rankings provided using payback periods, probability indices, or internal rates of return give guidelines, but management must consider other factors, such as those discussed above.

The capital rationing procedures discussed in this chapter were presented within the context of investment projects which had returns which could be accurately predicted. In many instances the expected return may not be known with complete certainty. In Chapter 17 we shall examine the problems involved with such projects. Using the procedures discussed in Chapter 17, profitability indices and internal rates of return may be developed for projects which have uncertain returns. The capital rationing procedures developed in this chapter may be used in ranking those projects in the same manner as projects were ranked in Examples 4 through 6.

QUESTIONS FOR DISCUSSION

1. Indicate how projects are ranked using the internal rate of return method.
2. Why is it necessary to estimate the internal rate of return of many proposed projects as a first step in determining the actual rate of return?
3. How is linear interpolation used as a part of the process of determining the internal rate of return of a project?
4. Why in some instances does the use of the present-value and internal rate of return methods for ranking proposed investment projects result in different rankings?
5. Indicate how projects are ranked for purposes of capital rationing using the payback, present-value, and internal rate of return methods.
6. Describe the steps in capital rationing.

CONCEPTS TO REMEMBER

This chapter discusses another method for capital budgeting and capital rationing procedures. Students should be familiar with the newly introduced concepts:

Internal Rate of Return
Linear Interpolation
Capital Rationing
Ranking Investment Projects

PROBLEMS

1. A project costs $10,000 and will result in an after-tax cash inflow of $12,000 in one year. What is the internal rate of return?
2. A project costs $25,000 and will result in after-tax cash inflows of $5,000 per year for six years. Determine the internal rate of return.
3. Gomar Industries, Inc. has evaluated the purchase of a new machine. After-tax cash flows are tabulated below:

Time	Amount
Present	− $100,000
1–20	10,000
20	20,000

Determine the internal rate of return for the project using linear interpolation.

4. A project has the after-tax cash flows shown below. Determine the internal rate of return.

Year	Outflow	Inflow
Present	− $10,000	0
1	0	$6,000
2	− 5,000	6,000
3	0	5,000
4	− 5,000	6,000

5. A new machine costs $55,000 and has a life of ten years with negligible salvage value. It can be used to reduce labor costs by $8,000 per year. If the firm is in the 48% marginal tax bracket, determine the internal rate of return of the machine. The new machine will be depreciated straight-line.

6. Four projects have been proposed to Baker Industries. Pertinent information is listed below:

	A	B	C	D
Cost	$100,000	$300,000	$300,000	$500,000
Life	5 years	5 years	10 years	20 years
After-tax profit	$ 5,000	$ 15,000	$ 27,000	$ 46,000
Depreciation cash throw-off	$ 20,000	$ 60,000	$ 30,000	$ 25,000

a. Determine the payback period for each project.
b. Determine the net present value of each using 10% as the cost of capital.
c. Determine the internal rate of return.
d. Rank the projects by profitability index and internal rate of return.
e. Discuss the differences in the ranking of projects using the three methods.

7. Systems Engineering is considering two mutually exclusive projects. Each will require an immediate cash outlay of $1,000. They will be depreciated straight-line and have no salvage value. The marginal tax rate is 48%. Project A has a four-year life, and project B, five years. They will result in pretax reductions in operating costs as shown.

Year	Project A	Project B
1	$300	$500
2	300	200
3	400	200
4	450	200
5	0	200

Determine which project has the higher internal rate of return.

8. Consolidated Products has been using a somewhat outdated manufacturing process in its shipment plant. The machinery, which originally cost $300,000, has been fully depreciated and now has a book value of $75,000. Actually, it could be sold for about $130,000. Purchase and installation of the new equipment will require funds as follows:

Purchase costs	$1,000,000
Installation	50,000
Added working capital	100,000

The new equipment will have a useful life of 20 years and a salvage value of $100,000. It will result in savings in labor costs of $170,000 per year for 20 years. Determine the internal rate of return of the new equipment using a projected 20-year life. Consolidated has a marginal tax rate of 48%.

9. Ronald Industries has a cost of capital of 13%. They have funding of $1.5 million for capital investment this year. Several projects have been suggested and evaluated. If projects A and D are mutually exclusive, determine which projects should be undertaken by Ronald.

Project	Internal Rate of Return	Cost
A	18%	$300,000
B	14	200,000
C	16	600,000
D	16	250,000
E	12	100,000
F	9	200,000
G	13	350,000
H	15	200,000
I	8	300,000
J	15	400,000
K	17	150,000

Capital Budgeting
Under Conditions of Uncertainty
chapter 17

The procedures used to analyze capital expenditures and make capital budgeting decisions already introduced assume that the amounts of cash inflows and outflows are known with certainty. This assumption seldom, if ever, holds in actual business operations. Although projections can be made as to the cost of a new project, such as replacing an older machine with a newer model, seldom is it possible to predict the exact cost of the replacement. Further, *business risk* must be considered. Unforeseen costs may be incurred. For example, a wildcat railroad strike might cause a delay in receiving parts needed for installation of the new machine, which would then sit idle and unproductive until the parts are received. Unanticipated union action might slow or halt production if the new machine requires fewer operators than the old machine. Further, in periods of rapid inflation, costs may increase by 10% or 15% from the time a project is proposed until it can be implemented—even if the time span is only a short six months. The costs of large projects, including construction of new facilities, may increase by 50% over a two- or three-year construction period. Hence, even though the financial manager attempts to secure the best possible estimates of costs, the estimates frequently differ substantially from the actual costs. The more variable the costs and returns of a project, the more risk is involved. Such risk must be considered in the capital budgeting process.

Cash inflows are based on projections of economic conditions, business and financial market trends, and consumer demands. Most large firms have departments which predict economic and business conditions in order to forecast consumer and business expenditures. Also, market research provides information relating to consumer preferences. All of the available information is integrated to estimate sales and the cash inflows which will result from the sales. Sales are difficult to predict in the short run, and when looking ahead 5 to 20 years, sales are even more difficult to project. Trends can be determined, but rapidly changing prices, especially in the costs of fuel and utilities, result in major changes in consumer purchasing power and product preferences.

All of the numerous uncertainties in costs and revenues are categorized under the general heading of *business risk*. Business risk includes all of the hazards inherent in the operations of the business. Investors, quite naturally, want to avoid risk. *Most investors are risk-averters. That is, as the riskiness of an investment increases, they demand increasingly greater returns on their investments.* Graphically, investor risk aversion is shown in Fig. 1. Note that the required rate of return increases at a faster rate than the risk. The return designated Y_1 is the rate which investors can receive on risk-free investments. Such investments include the various bonds and other securities issued by the U.S. government.

As a consequence of the uncertainties inherent in investment and the risk aversion attitude of investors, it is necessary for financial managers to consider business risk as an important aspect of the capital budgeting decision. Determining the degree of business risk associated with any proposed investment project is difficult at best. *The least risky types of investment are profit-maintaining.* For example, replacement of an old machine with a new machine to produce the same product which has enjoyed consistent sales would add little risk. In fact, operating risk might very well decrease because of reduced rate of machine breakdowns. Increasing production facilities for an estab-

FIGURE 1.

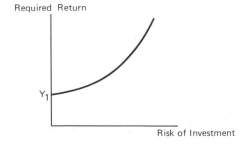

Required Return

Y_1

Risk of Investment

lished product line may or may not increase risk. On the one hand, management is already very familiar with the manufacturing processes, the sales, etc. However, if consumer preferences or economic conditions change so that sales decrease, the firm may have a lower profit than it would have had without the new facility. This is really a question of "placing all of one's eggs in one basket." Risk may be reduced through diversification into dissimilar product lines. The basis for the potential reduction in risk lies in the fact that economic fluctuations are not likely to have the same impact on sales of all goods. As a consequence, if sales in one product line decrease, sales in another may increase and thereby counterbalance each other. For this reason, many firms develop products in a variety of different lines.

While business risk may be reduced through product line diversification, the same diversification may also greatly increase business risk due to lack of managerial competence. Many firms have sought to diversify and have failed because the management lacked knowledge and expertise in the new area. Frequently, large firms purchase small profitable businesses in order to diversify only to find in two or three years that the small business is running at a loss. Management is the key element underlying the success of any operation. Good management recognizes its limitations and avoids involving itself in investments in which it has little expertise.

Probably the most risky of all investments are those in research and development. Basic research is especially hazardous since goals are often loosely defined, and a profitable product may never result from many years of research and millions of dollars of investments. However, when new products such as nylon, plastics, transistors, and the like are developed, profits may be enormous.

Since the risk inherent in any capital budgeting decision is substantial, it must be considered. Business tends to approach the problem in three ways. Some ignore risk and hope for the best. This procedure obviously has inherent limitations. Some firms try to utilize very sophisticated mathematical systems employing statistical trends and probabilistic estimates. While in theory these methods work very well and can produce quantitatively accurate results, most firms (especially smaller ones) lack the statistical information required as input to the systems. Further, many lack the skilled statisticians and computer facilities necessary to implement the procedures. Since the output is only as good as the input, the mathematical approaches are, for many firms, not feasible. A third set of procedures requires a limited degree of input. These include *discount rate adjustment* and *certainty equivalent.*

ADJUSTMENT OF DISCOUNT RATE

A very simple and easily understood method used to compensate for risk is to adjust the rate of return required for acceptance of projects. The minimum required rate of return used in making capital budgeting decisions is the firm's cost of capital. This is the minimum average return which the firm must achieve on their investments. It must be recognized that some investments will not have a return equal to the cost of capital even though they may have been expected to have a return in excess of the cost of capital. Plans do not always work out. *Based on management experience, it is logical to divide projects into groups and require different minimum expected returns from each group, depending on the anticipated amount of risk associated with the projects in each group.* The minimum expected return would be established drawing on past experience. Depending on the degree of refinement desired and the amount of past experience available, it is possible to categorize proposed capital expenditures into several groupings. Once the groupings are established, management assigns a required return for all proposed capital expenditures falling into that group. A simple and workable plan is presented in Table 1 as an example.

Once a firm has adopted a plan such as the one shown in Table 1, proposed capital investments are categorized by group. Then, using present value or internal rate of return, the projects may be evaluated and ranked. The ranking is easiest when the present-value method is used since the profitability index takes into consideration the appropriate required rate of return. Ranking profits when internal rate of return is employed is not so simple. Recall that the ranking used for IRR under conditions of certainty requires that projects be listed by their IRR. The listing is in descending order, with those having the highest IRR listed first, etc. This procedure is not satisfactory under conditions of uncertainty. *Rather, projects are ranked based on how much greater their IRR is than the required IRR for that category of project.*

Example 1:   RANKING PROJECTS BY INTERNAL RATE OF RETURN UNDER CONDITIONS OF UNCERTAINTY

Thomas, Inc. has five proposed projects. They utilize the return requirements outlined in Table 1. The projects which they are considering are

TABLE 1

Return Requirements

Investment Grouping	*Required Return*
Replacement investments—category I (new machines or equipment, vehicles, etc., which will perform essentially the same function as older equipment which is to be replaced)	Cost of capital
Replacement investments—category II (new machines or equipment which replace older equipment but are more technologically advanced, require different operator skills, require different manufacturing approaches, or the like; examples would include implementation of electronic data processing equipment to replace manual accounting and payroll systems)	Cost of capital plus 3%
Replacement investments—category III (new facilities such as buildings and warehouses which will replace older facilities; the new plants may be in the same or a different location)	Cost of capital plus 6%
New investment—category I (new facilities and associated equipment which will produce or sell the same products as already being produced)	Cost of capital plus 5%
New investment—category II (new facilities or machinery to produce or sell a product line closely related to the existing product line)	Cost of capital plus 8%
New investment—category III (new facilities or machinery or acquisition of another firm to produce or sell a product line which is unrelated to the company's primary business)	Cost of capital plus 15%
Research and development category I (research and development which is directed toward specific goals such as developing new computer circuitry with which the firm's engineers are already very familiar)	Cost of capital plus 10%
Research and development—category II (research in basic areas where goals have not been precisely defined and the outcome may be unknown)	Cost of capital plus 20%

tabulated below with expected return. Thomas' cost of capital is 10%. Rank the projects.

Project	Category	Expected Return
A	Replacement—category II	15%
B	Replacement—category III	19
C	New—category I	17
D	New—category I	18
E	New—category III	22
F	R&D—category I	21

SOLUTION

First, list each project with its required return (cost of capital plus the appropriate added return as shown in Table 1) and its expected rate of return. Then find the difference.

Project	Column 1 Required Return	Column 2 Expected Return	Column 2 − 1 Difference
A	13%	15%	2%
B	16	19	3
C	15	17	2
D	15	18	3
E	25	22	−3
F	20	21	1

Projects having a negative difference are not acceptable since the expected return is not as great as the required return.

Last, rank the projects by their differences. Projects which have the greatest difference between expected and required rates of return are ranked first.

Project	Difference
B	3%
D	3
A	2
C	2
F	1

Projects B and D exceed the required rate of return by 3% so they are ranked first. Projects A and C exceed the required rate by 2% and are ranked second, and so on. The actual acceptance of projects would now be made in accordance with capital rationing procedures.

CERTAINTY EQUIVALENT

Adjusting the discount rate allows for risk compensation by category of project but does not compensate for increased risk over the life of a project. Many financial managers feel, and with good justification, that the probability of a project achieving its expected return during the early years of its life is greater than during the later years. Since the future is so very uncertain, it is difficult to predict with accuracy what may happen five years ahead, and beyond that many managers feel that prediction is more like speculation. *The certainty-equivalent approach permits risk adjustment for time. A set of certainty-equivalent coefficients is established corresponding to time periods and multiplied by the expected cash inflow for that period.* A table of certainty equivalent coefficients is shown in Table 2 as an example.

TABLE 2

Project Life Certainty—Equivalent Coefficients

Project Life Period	*Certainty-Equivalent Coefficient*
1–4 years	1.0
5–9 years	.9
10–14 years	.7
15 years and more	.5

Example 2:   CERTAINTY-EQUIVALENT RISK ADJUSTMENT

Cash flows for a project are given below. If the certainty-equivalent coefficients in Table 2 are used, determine whether or not the project should be accepted. Use present value with a required rate of return of 10%.

Time	*Expected Cash Flow*
Present	− $10,000
1–4	1,000
5–7	2,000
8–12	3,000

To solve this problem a table is constructed, and each expected cash flow is multiplied by the *certainty-equivalent coefficient* (CEC). The product is the *certainty adjusted cash flow* (CACF). The CACF is multiplied by the appropriate discount factor.

Time	Amount		CEC		CACF		Discount Factor		Present Value
Present	− $10,000	×	1	=	− $10,000	×	1	=	− $10,000
1–4	1,000	×	1	=	1,000	×	3.1699	=	3,169
5	2,000	×	.9	=	1,800	×	.6209	=	1,118
6	2,000	×	.9	=	1,800	×	.5645	=	1,016
7	2,000	×	.9	=	1,800	×	.5132	=	924
8	3,000	×	.9	=	2,700	×	.4665	=	1,260
9	3,000	×	.9	=	2,700	×	.4241	=	1,145
10	3,000	×	.7	=	2,100	×	.3855	=	810
11	3,000	×	.7	=	2,100	×	.3505	=	736
12	3,000	×	.7	=	2,100	×	.3186	=	669
							NPV	=	$ 847

The NPV is positive. This means that the project has an expected return in excess of 10% after compensating for risk.

It is possible to combine the adjustment of discount rate with the certainty equivalent. This permits compensating for both the riskiness of the investment and the risk of time.

1. Why is business risk important as a part of the capital budgeting process?
2. Explain what is meant by *risk-averter* in terms of the relationship between the required return on investment and the investment risk.
3. Explain how product line diversification can both increase and decrease business risk.
4. Explain how the discount rate may be adjusted to compensate for risk.
5. Why is the certainty-equivalent method used? What advantage does it have as a method for risk compensation over the adjustment of discount rates?

This chapter has to do with methods used in capital budgeting under conditions of uncertainty. Some new terms are introduced. Be sure you understand them:

Business Risk
Risk Averter
Product Line Diversification
New Investments
Discount Rate Adjustment
Certainty Equivalent
Replacement Investments
Research and Development

PROBLEMS

1. A proposed investment having an after-tax cost of $10,000 will produce after-tax cash flows as tabulated below. The firm utilizes a certainty equivalent approach to compensate for risk and uses the certainty-equivalent coefficients shown in Table 2. Based on a cost-of-capital of 8%, should the investment be made?

Time	Amount
Present	− $10,000
1	2,000
2	2,000
3	3,000
4	3,000
5	4,000

2. A project costing $12,000 is expected to yield after-tax cash flows of $2,376 for nine years and $5,376 in the tenth year. The firm's cost of capital is 14%. The firm uses the certainty-equivalent method with the certainty-equivalent coefficients shown in Table 2. Decide if the investment should be made.

3. Carlos Industries, Inc. has eight projects which they are considering. They utilize the return requirements for projects having varying degrees of risk outlined in Table 1. The projects which they are considering are listed below. Carlos's required rate of return is 10%. Rank the projects.

Project	Category	Expected Return
A	New—category I	17%
B	Replacement—category II	14
C	R&D—category II	22
D	Replacement—category III	19
E	Replacement—category I	14
F	New—category II	16
G	New—category I	17
H	R&D—category I	11

Effects of Accelerated Depreciation and Investment Tax Credit on Capital Budgeting Decisions

chapter 18

All of the methods used for evaluating proposed capital investment projects involve the examination of expected cash outflows and inflows. The payback criterion requires that all cash outflows be recovered within a given period of time. Present value and internal rate of return require that cash flows be discounted back to their present values. The major portion, if not the entire cash outflow, usually takes place at the time the project is implemented. Exceptions, of course, include projects such as the construction of a nuclear power plant which may require expenditures over several years before it is built and placed into operation. The inflows occur after the project is in use and generally extend for several years.

In capital budgeting decisions it is usually desirable to have the cash inflows come in as soon as possible after the project has been implemented. Table 1 shows two projected cash inflow patterns, each totaling the same amount. Note that while total inflows are the same, project B is far superior to project A because the inflows are expected to be received earlier in the life of project B.

One method which may be employed to increase the cash flows in the earlier years of a project's life is accelerated depreciation. *Use of accelerated depreciation rather than straight-line, for purposes of calculating federal income taxes, will result in lower profits and greater cash inflows in the earlier years of a project's life.* The profits will be greater and the cash inflows lower in the latter years of the project's

TABLE 1

	Cash Inflows	
Time	Project A	Project B
1	$ 3,000	$ 5,000
2	3,000	4,000
3	3,000	3,000
4	3,000	2,000
5	3,000	1,000
Totals	$15,000	$15,000

life. *For purposes of determining earnings per share and reporting income to shareholders, most firms use straight-line depreciation, regardless of whether or not they used accelerated depreciation in computing their taxes.*

A second method which may be used to increase cash flows in the early years of a project's life is investment tax credit. *Investment tax credit provides for the reduction of federal income tax liability by permitting part of the cost of certain types of assets to be deducted from the firm's tax liability.* Use of investment tax credit thus results in a reduction of tax which is equivalent to a reduction in the cost of the capital project.

EFFECTS OF ACCELERATED DEPRECIATION ON CAPITAL BUDGETING

For the sake of simplicity, all of the capital budgeting problems demonstrated thus far have been based on the use of straight-line depreciation. However, accelerated methods are often used. Their use results in an increase in the rate of return expected to be received from capital investment. The change in return results from the increase in cash flow in the early years of the life of the project. The results of using accelerated depreciation methods are demonstrated below.

Example 1: ACCELERATED DEPRECIATION AND PAYBACK METHOD

Conway Industries is considering the purchase of a new machine having a total cost of $28,000, a life of seven years, and salvage value of $4,000. The machine will result in decreased costs of $9,000 per year over its seven-year life. Conway is in the 48% marginal tax bracket. If Conway requires a maximum payback period of four years, should they purchase the machine? Determine the payback periods using straight-line and double-declining depreciation.

SOLUTION

First, consider the problem using straight-line depreciation. The depreciable value of the machine is $24,000. The depreciation will therefore be $3,429 per year. The income statement will be affected as shown:

Income Statement

Reduction in expenses	$ 9,000
Added depreciation	− 3,429
Net reduction in expenses	$ 5,571
Increase in taxes	− 2,674
Increase in after-tax profits	$ 2,897

The yearly increase in cash inflow is the sum of the after-tax income and the depreciation cash throw-off:

$$\$2,897 + \$3,429 = \$6,326$$

At the end of the seventh year, an additional $4,000 will be realized from the sale of the machine. Dividing the $28,000 purchase price by the yearly cash inflow of $6,326 indicates a payback period of 4.43 years. This is not acceptable since Conway requires four years as the maximum pay back period.

Next, consider the problem using double-declining-balance depreciation. The depreciation is based on a seven-year life. The straight-line rate for seven years is 14.28%. Therefore, the double-declining rate is 28.56% per year. The depreciation table is provided below. Note that the salvage value is $4,000 so that the depreciation is limited to $24,000, but the basis for calculating the depreciation is the full $28,000 since declining balance is being used.

Year	Rate					Yearly Depreciation	Cumulative Depreciation
1	.2856	×	$28,000		=	$7,997	$ 7,997
2	.2856	×	($28,000	$ 7,997)	=	5,713	13,710
3	.2856	×	($28,000 −	$13,710)	=	4,081	17,791
4	.2856	×	($28,000 −	$17,791)	=	2,916	20,707
5	.2856	×	($28,000 −	$20,707)	=	2,083	22,790
6			$24,000 −	$22,790	=	1,210	24,000
7						0	24,000

With the yearly depreciation calculated, a cash flow table can be formulated:

Year	Reduction in Expenses (1)	Depreci- ation (2)	Net Reduction in Expenses (3) (3) = (1) − (2)	Increase in Taxes (4) (4) = (3) × .48	Increase in After- Tax Profit (5) (5) = (3) − (4)	Increase in Cash Flow (6) (6) = (2) + (5)
1	$9,000	$7,997	$1,003	$ 481	$ 522	$8,519
2	9,000	5,713	3,287	1,578	1,709	7,422
3	9,000	4,081	4,919	2,361	2,558	6,639
4	9,000	2,916	6,084	2,920	3,164	6,080
5	9,000	2,083	6,917	3,320	3,597	5,680
6	9,000	1,210	7,790	3,739	4,051	5,261
7	9,000	0	9,000	4,320	4,680	4,680

Using the cash flows determined above, the payback period can be determined:

Year	Total Outflow	Total Inflow	Difference
Present	− $28,000	$ 0	− $28,000
1	− 28,000	8,519	− 19,481
2	− 28,000	15,941	− 12,059
3	− 28,000	22,580	− 5,420
4	− 28,000	28,660	+ 660
5	− 28,000	34,340	+ 6,340
6	− 28,000	39,601	+ 11,601
7	− 28,000	44,281	+ 16,281

After three years, $5,420 remains unrecovered. Since $6,080 will be generated during the fourth year, it will take $\frac{\$5,420}{\$6,080} = .89$ of the fourth year to recover the entire $28,000. The payback period using double-declining-balance depreciation is therefore approximately 3.89 years. Hence, the project would be acceptable if depreciated using double-declining-balance but would not be acceptable if depreciated using straight-line.

Example 2: ACCELERATED DEPRECIATION AND PRESENT-VALUE METHOD

Solve Example 1 using the present-value method with a cost of capital (hurdle rate) of 15%.

SOLUTION

First, determine if the machine is acceptable when depreciated using straight-line. The solution table employing data generated in Example 1 is shown below:

Solution Table for 15% with Straight-Line Depreciation

Time	Amount		Discount Factor		Present Value
Present	− $28,000	×	1	=	− $28,000
1–7	6,326	×	4.1604	=	26,319
7 (salvage value)	4,000	×	.3759	=	1,504
			NPV	=	− $ 177

Since the net present value based on the 15% required rate of yield using straight-line depreciation is less than zero, the machine does not yield the required return and therefore should not be purchased.

Next, determine if the machine will yield 15% if depreciated using double-declining-balance. The solution table employing the cash flows generated in Example 1 is shown below:

Solution Table for 15% with Accelerated Depreciation

Time	Amount		Discount Factor		Present Value
Present	− $28,000	×	1	=	− $28,000
1	8,519	×	.8696	=	7,408
2	7,422	×	.7561	=	5,612
3	6,639	×	.6575	=	4,365
4	6,080	×	.5718	=	3,477
5	5,680	×	.4972	=	2,824
6	5,271	×	.4323	=	2,279
7	8,680	×	.3759	=	3,263
			NPV	=	$ 1,228

Since the net present value is positive, the machine yields more than the required 15% when depreciated using double-declining-balance and therefore should be purchased.

Examples 1 and 2 indicate the significance of the selection of the method of depreciation to be used. *Projects which may not be acceptable when depreciated straight-line are often acceptable when depreciated using an accelerated method.*

INVESTMENT TAX CREDIT

Introduction to the Law of Investment Tax Credit

Investment tax credit provides for the reduction of federal income tax liability by permitting part of the cost of certain types of assets to be deducted from the tax liability in the year the property is placed in service. For 1975 and 1976 the investment tax credit was increased to 10% of the value of purchased equipment from the previous limits of 7% for most businesses and 4% for utilities. Unless the 1975 law is extended, the investment tax credit will revert to the lower amounts commencing in 1977. *Investment credit does not affect depreciation calculations and represents a completely separate calculation.* The purpose of the tax credit is to stimulate the purchase of certain types of property meeting the following qualifications: The property must (1) be depreciable; (2) have a useful life of at least three years; (3) be tangible personal property or other tangible property (except buildings and their structural components) used as an integral part of manufacturing, production, or extraction, etc.; and (4) be placed in service in a trade or business or for the production of income during the year. Property is considered to be placed in service in the earlier of the following:

1. The tax year in which the depreciation begins, or
2. The tax year in which the property is placed in condition or state of readiness and availability for service.

Tangible personal property includes depreciable tangible property except land and land improvements such as buildings. Machinery and equipment are the principal types of property that qualify as tangible personal property. Other types of property include accessories to a business, such as grocery counters and air conditioners, automobiles used for business, and livestock.

The amount of the investment tax credit allowed for qualifying property depends on the property's useful life and whether it is new or used. Moreover, the amount of tax credit allowed in any one year is limited, but any excess may be carried back 3 years and forward 7 years in a manner similar to capital and operating losses. The process of carry back and carry forward is not discussed herein.

For purposes of computing investment tax credit, the amount qualifying is the total purchase price less the trade-in value of old property, if there is any. This applies, in general, to both the purchase of new and used property. Although the total cost of qualifying new property is eligible, *no more than $100,000 of the cost of qualifying used property* may be counted toward investment tax credit.

The useful life of an asset is determined at the time it is put in service and is the same life used in computing depreciation or amortization. Property with a useful life *of less than three years* does not qualify for the credit. Only one-third of the investment in qualifying property with a useful life of at least three years but less than five years is subject to credit. Two-thirds of the amount invested is subject to credit if the property has a useful life of at least five years but less than seven years. *The full investment is subject to the credit if the property has a useful life of at least seven years.* If property is disposed of before the end of its estimated useful life, the tax for the year of its disposal is *increased* by an amount equal to the *difference* between the credit originally allowed *and* the credit which would have been allowed if the computation had been based on the shorter useful life.

The amount of investment tax credit taken in any one year is limited to the income tax liability shown on the tax return, or $25,000 plus 50% of the tax liability in excess of $25,000, whichever is less. Unused credits may be carried back or forwarded as discussed above. Reference should be made to IRS Publication 572 for further information on this process.

Example 3:   INVESTMENT TAX CREDIT

A firm having a tax liability of $30,000 purchased a new machine during the year for a price of $50,000. The machine has a useful life of ten years. Determine the investment tax credit savings which will result from the purchase.

SOLUTION

Since the life is over seven years, the full purchase price of the machine is eligible for tax credit. Thus, the credit is $50,000 × .10 = $5,000. The tax savings would be $5,000. Rather than paying $30,000 in tax, the firm would have to pay only $25,000.

Example 4:   INVESTMENT TAX CREDIT

Babrock Mfg. Co. is considering the purchase of a new machine to replace an older model. The new machine has a cost of $20,000, while the old machine has a salvage value (trade-in value) of $3,000. The new machine has a life of six years. The firm has income tax liability of $30,000. Determine the tax savings resulting from the purchase.

SOLUTION

The basis for the tax credit is the difference in cost of the new machine and salvage of the old, that is, $17,000. Since the life is six years, only two-thirds of the basis is subject to credit. Therefore, the tax credit is $17,000 × ⅔ × .10 = $1,134. The tax savings would be $1,134.

Example 5:   INVESTMENT TAX CREDIT

During the year Delanco Co. purchased two new machines at costs of $40,000 and $60,000 and one used machine at a cost of $120,000. All the machines had lives of ten years. The firm has an income tax of $30,000 for the year. Compute the tax savings resulting from the purchases.

SOLUTION

The full cost of both new machines and $100,000 of the cost of the used machine form a basis for the tax credit. The total basis is, therefore, $40,000 + $60,000 + $100,000 = $200,000. The tax credit would be the full 10% since their useful lives all exceed seven years. The tax credit is $200,000 × .10 = $20,000.

Example 6:   INVESTMENT TAX CREDIT

Garold, Inc. purchased new equipment with a life of three years, used machinery with a life of four years, used machinery with a life of six years, and new machinery with a life of eight years. The prices paid were $10,000, $8,000, $12,000, and $16,000, respectively. The firm has a tax liability of $60,000. Determine the reduction in taxes resulting from investment tax credit.

SOLUTION

The tax credit may be calculated using the tabular method shown below:

Property	Life	Basis		Part To Be Counted		Amount Subject to Credit
New equipment	3	$10,000	×	⅓	=	$ 3,333
Used machinery	4	8,000	×	⅓	=	2,667
Used machinery	6	12,000	×	⅔	=	8,000
New machinery	8	16,000	×	1	=	16,000
		Amount of investment subject to credit			=	$30,000

The tax investment credit would be $30,000 × .10 = $3,000. Hence, Garold would save $3,000 in taxes. The new tax would be $57,000 rather than $60,000.

Effect of Investment Tax Credit on Capital Budgeting Decisions

When property is purchased which is subject to the advantages of investment tax credit, the amount of the credit is shown as a cash inflow at the time property is put into service. The process is demonstrated in the examples below.

Example 7:   INVESTMENT TAX CREDIT APPLIED TO CAPITAL BUDGETING

Ronald Industries is considering the purchase of a new machine having a life of ten years. The purchase price is $20,000. Salvage value is expected to be negligible. The machine will result in cost reductions of $5,000 per year over its life. Ronald is in the 48% marginal tax bracket. Based on straight line depreciation and *no* investment tax credit, determine the internal rate of return for the machine.

SOLUTION

First, determine the cash flow which will result from use of the machine each year. The depreciation will be $2,000 per year based on a ten-year life and $20,000 depreciable value. Ronald's income statement will be affected as shown:

Income Statement

Reduction in expenses	$ 5,000
Added depreciation	− 2,000
Net reduction in expenses	$ 3,000
Increase in taxes	− 1,440
Increase in after-tax profits	$ 1,560

The yearly increase in cash inflow is the sum of the after-tax income and the depreciation cash throw-off:

$$\$2,000 + \$1,560 = \$3,560$$

Second, construct a cash flow table showing the cash flow over the life of the machine:

Time	Amount		Discount Factor		Present Value
Present	− $20,000	×	1	=	− $20,000
1–10	3,560	×	Unknown	=	Unknown
			NPV	=	$ 0.00

The internal rate of return exactly equals the present value of the after-tax cash inflows with the after-tax cash outflows. Therefore, the present value of the inflows must be $20,000:

$$\$3,560 \times d.f. = \$20,000$$
$$d.f. = 5.618$$

Referring to Table IV in Appendix A, this corresponds roughly to 12%. The internal rate of return, based on straight-line depreciation, without using investment tax credit is, therefore, 12%.

Example 8:   INVESTMENT TAX CREDIT APPLIED TO CAPITAL BUDGETING

Rework Example 7, this time including the investment tax credit.

SOLUTION

First, determine the amount of investment tax credit. Since the machine has a life of ten years, the full purchase price qualifies:

$$\$20,000 \times .10 = \$2,000 \text{ investment tax credit}$$

Second, construct a cash flow table. Remember that the investment tax credit does not affect depreciation. Further, the amount of the investment tax credit is deducted from the federal tax liability, not from the taxable income.

Time	Amount		Discount Factor		Present Value
Present	− $20,000	×	1	=	− $20,000
Present	2,000	×	1	=	2,000
1–10	3,560	×	Unknown	=	Unknown
			NPV	=	$ 0.00

The $20,000 outflow and $2,000 inflow can be combined for a net $18,000 outflow:

$$\$3,560 \times \text{d.f.} = \$18,000$$
$$\text{d.f.} = 5.056$$

Again, referring to Table IV, the discount factor corresponds to approximately 15%. Thus, using the investment tax credit has increased the internal rate of return by about 3%.

By combining the use of investment tax credit and accelerated depreciation, it is possible to substantially improve the expected profitability of some investment projects. The timing of cash flows is extremely important and in many instances makes the difference between implementing versus rejecting a proposed project.

QUESTIONS
FOR
DISCUSSION

1. Why are accelerated depreciation and investment tax credit important to capital budgeting decisions?
2. From an economic viewpoint, what is the purpose of investment tax credit?
3. Indicate the types of property which qualify for investment tax credit.

CONCEPTS
TO
REMEMBER

Accelerated depreciation and investment tax credit are important to the capital budgeting process. Concepts dealing with these topics are listed below:

Investment Tax Credit
Tangible Personal Property

PROBLEMS 1. A firm can purchase a mechanical sweeper for $90,000. It has a pro-
jected life of ten years and negligible salvage value and may be depreciated either straight-line or double-declining-balance. It will result in
savings of labor of $16,000 per year. The firm has a 48% marginal tax
rate. Determine the net present value for the machine using straight-
line and double-declining-balance depreciation. The firm requires an
8% after-tax return on investment.

2. An old machine has been fully depreciated to its actual salvage value
of $5,000. A new machine, having a total cost of $30,000, is available.
It would result in an increase in after-tax profits of $4,000 per year,
using straight-line depreciation, have a zero salvage value and have a
ten-year life. If the firm requires a 12% after-tax return on investment,
determine whether the new machine should be purchased. Consider
both straight-line and double-declining-balance depreciation methods.
The firm has a 48% marginal tax rate.

3. A firm having a tax liability of $50,000 purchased a new machine for
$100,000. The machine has a useful life of nine years. Determine the
impact the investment tax credit will have on the firm's tax liability.
Suppose the useful life of the machine were only six years. How would
the investment tax credit change?

4. Gerold Mfg. Co. has a taxable income of $100,000. They purchased a
new machine during the year for $20,000. The machine has an esti-
mated life of eight years. Determine the impact of investment tax credit
on Gerold's tax liability.

5. Ronald Electronics is considering the purchase of replacement machinery for construction of circuit boards. The new machinery costs
$100,000. Older, fully depreciated equipment will be traded in, reduc-
ing the cash outlay to $80,000. If the new equipment has a projected
life of six years and Ronald has a 48% marginal tax rate, determine the
impact of the investment tax credit on Ronald's tax liability.

6. Suppose the new equipment in Problem 5 will be depreciated straight-
line over its six-year life and will have negligible salvage value. Further,
the new equipment will result in pretax cost reductions of $20,000 per
year. Determine the internal rate of return for the new machine based
first on not using the investment tax credit and next on using the tax
credit.

7. Continuing with Problem 5, suppose the new equipment is to be depreciated using sum-of-the-years'-digits and investment tax credit taken.
Determine the internal rate of return for the equipment.

8. A new piece of equipment costs $11,000 and has a projected salvage
value of $2,000. It will result in cost reductions of $6,000 per year

over its life of three years. The owners are in the 48% marginal tax bracket and require a 12% return on investment. Determine the NPV of the machine using straight-line and sum-of-the-years'-digits depreciation. Assume the machine will be sold for $2,000 after the end of the third year of its use.

9. An old machine has been depreciated to its salvage value of $5,000. A new machine costing $40,000 is available as a replacement. It would increase after-tax profits by $5,000 per year, have a $10,000 salvage value, and be depreciated straight-line over a ten-year life. The owners are in the 48% marginal tax bracket and require a 10% return on investment. The old machine would be traded in on the new machine and $5,000 received for the trade-in. Determine the NPV of the new machine first not considering investment tax credit and then considering the impact of investment tax credit.

Special Applications
of
Discounted Cash Flow Techniques

chapter 19

Capital Budgeting for Small Businesses

The basic methods of capital budgeting including payback, present value, and internal rate of return apply to businesses of all sizes. However, there is a major difference in how the cash flows are developed. This results from the fact that *the financing mix for big businesses tends to be relatively constant*, especially the ratio of debt to equity. Large firms which borrow funds do so primarily through long-term bonds, and, in general, as one bond issue is due for repayment, the firm issues another so that the debt is essentially perpetual. This process is known as "rolling over" the debt. Funds which are generated from the use of equipment and facilities are generally reinvested or distributed as dividends rather than used to pay off debt. On the other hand, most *small businesses must repay debt*. Small businesses usually do not sell bonds because the underwriting costs are too expensive. The form of long-term debt most commonly used by small businesses is a mortgage, which requires regular repayment of principal. Thus, a portion of funds generated by a small business must be used to repay debt. The *repayment of debt tends to constantly change the debt-to-equity ratio*. The capital budgeting process applied to a small business is demonstrated in Example 1.

Example 1:   CAPITAL BUDGETING FOR A SOLE PROPRIETORSHIP

Charles Crothers is married and has three children. He and his wife both work, and together they earn $14,000. They use a standard deduction and

291

have no other income. The Crothers are considering the purchase of a small machine shop for $75,000. An additional $10,000 will also be needed for working capital. They could invest $20,000 which they recently inherited and borrow the remaining $65,000 at 10%. Charles figures that he can work at the shop 30 hours a week as well as keep his current job. In addition, he would hire a helper. Including the helper's salary of $6.00 per hour, he anticipates the following income statement:

Crothers' Machine Shop
Pro-forma Income Statement

Sales		$50,000
Cost of goods sold	$ 6,000	
Labor	18,000	
Interest (10% × $65,000)	6,500	
Depreciation*	4,333	
Heat and utilities	3,500	
Maintenance	5,000	
Total expenses		− 43,333
EBT =		$ 6,667

*Based on depreciating $65,000, which represents the cost of the building and equipment, straight-line over 15 years, with zero salvage value. The land is valued at $10,000.

Charles will have to repay the loan principal of $65,000 over the next 10 years at $6,500 per year. Charles feels that he should be able to earn 10% after taxes on his investment. He expects to sell the business in 10 years for $50,000. Using the present-value criterion, determine whether or not Charles will earn 10% after taxes on the investment. For calculation of taxes, assume the 1975 law for standard deduction applies.

SOLUTION

First, determine the Crothers' federal income tax liability based on Charles working in the machine shop for 30 hours per week in addition to their other income.

Salaries (Current)	$ 14,000
Added salary (50 weeks)	9,000
Adjusted gross income	$ 23,000
Less standard deduction	− 2,600
	$ 20,400
Less deduction for dependents	− 3,750
Taxable income	$ 16,650
Federal income tax	$ 3,442

It should be noted that his salary is *not* considered a part of the return on the investment since it is presumed that he could work in another machine shop and earn the same amount for 30 hours' work.

Next, determine the actual cash flows involved. Initially, $20,000 will be invested; then each year an additional $6,500 will be invested as the loan is paid off. The interest will decrease each year as the principal is repaid. However, Charles anticipates increased maintenance costs as his equipment ages. Therefore, he projects the sum of interest plus maintenance to be $11,500 each year that he owns the shop. The EBT of $6,667 must be added to the Crothers' income and their tax recomputed to determine the after-tax profit from the machine shop.

Salaries	$ 14,000
Added salary (50 weeks)	9,000
Business income	6,667
Adjusted gross income	$ 29,667
Less standard deduction	− 2,600
	$ 27,067
Less deduction for dependents	− 3,750
Taxable income	$ 23,317
Federal income tax	$ 5,441

The tax increased to $5,441 from $3,442, resulting in $1,999 in added tax. Thus the machine shop would result in a cash flow as follows:

EBT	$ 6,667
Less tax	− 1,999
ATP	$ 4,668
Plus depreciation	4,333
After-tax cash inflow	$ 9,001

Third, calculate the cash inflow when the business is sold. The building, land, and equipment cost $75,000. After depreciating the building and equipment for 10 years at $4,333 per year, the total accumulated depreciation is $43,330. Thus, the book value after ten years would be $31,670. If sold for $50,000, an $18,330 recapture of depreciation would be realized. It is difficult to estimate the amount of tax to be paid on the recapture. However, based on the Crothers' projected taxable income of $23,317, the new taxable income would be $41,647. This assumes that the Crothers have the same number of deductions for dependents and use the standard deduction. Their tax liability on the $41,647 taxable income would be $12,931. This represents a difference of:

$$\$12,931 - \$5,441 = \$7,490 \text{ additional tax}$$

Thus, the cash inflow at the time of sale can be summarized as follows:

Sale price	$ 50,000
Less added tax	− 7,490
	$ 42,510
Plus return of working capital	10,000
Total	$ 52,510

The total cash inflow resulting from selling and terminating the business would be $52,510.

Last, set up a solution table:

Solution Table for 10%

Time	Outflow	Inflow	Difference		Discount Factor		Present Value
Present	− $20,000	0	− $20,000	×	1	=	− $20,000
1–10	− 6,500	$ 9,001	2,501	×	6.1446	=	15,368
10	0	52,510	52,510	×	.3855	=	20,243
					NPV	=	$15,611

Since the NPV based on the required 10% yield exceeds zero, the investment has a yield in excess of 10% and therefore should be undertaken.

Example 2: INTERNAL RATE OF RETURN

Calculate the IRR for the machine shop in Example 1.

SOLUTION

The solution table in Example 1 indicated a NPV of $15,611. This means that the actual IRR is substantially greater than 10%. 20% might be a good estimate. The solution table for 20% is shown below:

Solution Table for 20%

Time	Amount		Discount Factor		Present Value
Present	− $20,000	×	1	=	− $20,000
1–10	2,501	×	4.1925	=	10,485
10	52,510	×	.1615	=	8,480
			NPV	=	− $ 1,035

The negative NPV indicates that a lower rate should be used, perhaps 18%.

Solution Table for 18%

Time	Amount		Discount Factor		Present Value
Present	− $20,000	×	1	=	− $20,000
1–10	2,501	×	4.4941	=	11,280
10	52,510	×	.19106	=	10,033
			NPV	=	$ 1,313

The IRR is between 18 and 20%. The exact return may be determined using linear interpolation.

ANNUITIES

In the process of financial planning, it is sometimes necessary to incorporate interest and annuity calculations in conjunction with discounted cash flow computations. Such problems arise, for example, when a person plans for an income after retirement, as demonstrated below.

Example 3:   INTEREST AND ANNUITIES

Herman Jones is 40 years old and plans to work until age 65. He wants to have a pretax retirement income of $15,000 per year until age 85. At present, he can obtain 8% return on funds he invests. However, he anticipates receiving only 6% return on his funds once he retires. How much must he save each year to have an income of $15,000 per year for 20 years starting at retirement? Ignore the effects of federal income taxes.

SOLUTION

First, determine the present value of the $15,000 per year for 20 years at 6%. Employ Table IV in Appendix A.

$$\text{Present value of the annuity} = \text{Annuity factor} \times \text{yearly annuity}$$
$$S = 11.4699(\$15,000)$$
$$S = \$172,049$$

At retirement, Mr. Jones needs to have $172,049. If this is invested at 6%, he will be able to draw $15,000 from it for 20 years. At the end of 20 years, none of the $172,049 would remain.

Next, determine how much Mr. Jones must save for 25 years at 8% to acquire the $172,049. Use Table II, 8% column, 25-year row, to find the future value of an annuity.

$$\$172,049 = \text{Yearly contribution} \times 73.1059$$

$$\text{Yearly contribution} = \frac{\$172,049}{73.1059} = \$2,353$$

Mr. Jones must save $2,353 at 8% for 25 years to acquire the needed $172,049. It should be noted that Mr. Jones would have to pay federal income tax on the interest, dividends, or capital gains received on the savings, both before and after retirement. In essence, this means that he would actually have to put aside more than $2,353 per year to accumulate the needed $172,049, and he would receive less than $15,000 per year after retirement. During the years prior to retirement, he would have to save the $2,353 as well as pay the tax on the return from the savings he had accumulated in prior years unless he set up a tax-deferred annuity. Tax-deferred annuities are discussed in the following section.

The same types of calculations used in Example 3 can be employed to determine the amount of an annuity which will result from the investment of a lump sum of money.

Example 4:   INTEREST AND ANNUITIES

Mrs. Collins' husband died recently, leaving her an estate including life insurance of $45,000. Mrs. Collins is 55 years old, does not work, and cannot collect Social Security until age 60. She believes that she will require $5,000 per year to cover her living expenses and federal income taxes until age 60 and $4,000 thereafter.

She can invest the $45,000 and receive an annual yield of 8%. Based on withdrawing the amounts indicated, determine how long her estate will last.

SOLUTION

First, determine the value of her estate based on investing the $45,000 at 8% and drawing $5,000 for five years. This requires two sets of calculations. The present value of $5,000 for five years at 8% from Table IV is calculated to be $5,000 × 3.9927 = $19,964. Subtract this amount from the initial $45,000:

Initial estate	$ 45,000
Less PV of $5,000 for 5 years	− 19,964
	$ 25,036

Next, multiply the $25,036 by the compound interest factor from Table I corresponding to 8% for five years:

$$\$25,036 \times 1.4693 = \$36,785$$

At age 60, Mrs. Collins would have $36,785 remaining of the original $45,000. Last, determine how many years Mrs. Collins can continue to collect $4,000 per year until she exhausts her estate. This is accomplished by using Table IV. The appropriate discount factor is determined as follows:

$$\$36,785 = \$4,000 \times \text{d.f.}$$
$$\text{d.f.} = \frac{\$36,785}{\$4,000} = 9.196$$

Refer to the 8% column of Table IV and look for a discount factor in the range of 9.196. The discount factor corresponding to 17 years is 9.1216. Therefore, Mrs. Collins will exhaust her estate in approximately 17 years, when she is 77.

Example 5:   INTEREST AND ANNUITIES

The Smiths are 50 years old and have accumulated savings of $15,000. They will be able to save an additional $3,000 per year until retirement at age 65. They can obtain 8% return on their savings. How much will they be able to draw each year for a period of 25 years if they continue to receive 8% return on their funds?

SOLUTION

First, determine the amount they will have in 15 years. This requires the use of Tables I and II.

$15,000	×	3.1722	=	$ 47,583
3,000	×	27.1521	=	81,456
			Total	$129,039

They will have accumulated $129,039 in 15 years. Next, determine the amount they can draw each year for the next 25 years. Use Table IV to obtain the present value annuity factor.

$$\text{Annuity} \times 10.6748 = \$129,039$$
$$\text{Annuity} = \frac{\$129,039}{10.6748} = \$12,088$$

The Smiths can draw $12,088 for 25 years.

The impact of inflation was not taken into account in any of the examples given above. However, inflation, or decrease in the purchasing power of money, is a most crucial factor. If, for example, the inflation rate were 6% annually over a period of 25 years, the purchasing power of the dollar would be reduced to about 23 cents. This means that when the Smiths retired in 25 years, their income of $12,088 would be worth only about $2,780 in terms of current purchasing power.

TAX-DEFERRED ANNUITIES (KEOGH AND OTHER RETIREMENT PLANS)

Many employers have pension funds which permit employees to contribute a portion of their earnings to a retirement fund on a tax-deferred basis. That is, the contribution to the pension fund is deducted from adjusted gross income so that *the amount contributed is not taxed in the year it is earned.* Further, interest, dividends, and capital gains received on the invested funds are accumulated on a tax-deferred basis until retirement. At retirement the funds are paid out as an annuity and taxed as ordinary income at that time. Although the annuity payments are taxed as ordinary income, usually persons on retirement are in lower tax brackets and, if over age 65, enjoy two exemptions. *Thus, a tax-deferred annuity is valuable in that it permits a person to accumulate funds more rapidly than if he were subject to taxation and, second, generally results in a lower total tax paid on the funds when they are taxed during retirement.*

People who are self-employed may also set up a tax-sheltered annuity under the Keogh Act (pronounced "kee-oh"). Self-employed persons may deduct up to 15% of their earned income to a maximum of $7,500 (and a minimum of $750) each year. The funds have to be placed in a qualified retirement plan, that is, one approved by the Internal Revenue Service. Sometimes a self-employed person has employees. If so, the employer must contribute to the pension fund for employees who have worked for him three or more years. The contribution is the same percentage of the employees' salary as the employer puts in for himself. Similar tax-deferred pension funds may be established by persons who are employed but not covered by a pension plan at work.

Example 6:   TAX-DEFERRED ANNUITY

Charles Campbell is 45 years old and expects to retire at 65. He has sufficient income to contribute $2,000 a year to a tax-deferred pension fund. He can contribute to either a tax-deferred fund or put the equivalent after-tax funds in savings certificates. In either case, the before-tax yield is expected to be 7% a year. He is in the 30% marginal tax bracket. Compute the amount he would have at age 65 if he put the funds in a tax-deferred plan and in savings certificates.

SOLUTION

First, determine the amount he would have if he put the funds in a tax-deferred pension fund. The contribution would be $2,000 per year for 20 years, compounded at 7%. Using Table II, $2,000 × 40.9955 = $81,991. Charles would have $81,991 at age 65.

Next, determine the amount he would have if he put the funds in savings certificates. Since his marginal tax rate is 30%, he would have to pay tax of .30 × $2,000 = $600 each year. Thus, the amount available for investment would be $1,400 per year after taxes. Further, he would have to pay tax on the interest received each year from the savings certificates. The interest rate is 7%. Thirty percent of this 7% would go in tax. This is approximately 2%. Thus, the effective after-tax rate of interest would be only 5%. $1,400 invested at 5% each year for 20 years amounts to the following:

$$\$1,400 \times 33.0660 = \$46,292.$$

Charles would have $46,292 at age 65. This is substantially less than using the tax-deferred plan.

Example 7:   TAX-DEFERRED ANNUITY

Continue with Example 6. Charles Campbell wants to receive an annuity payment (pension) for 15 years. Determine the amount he will receive based on the two investment plans proposed in Example 6 if he retires at age 65. In addition to the annuity, he will have taxable income of $3,000 per year. He and his wife will both be over 65 years of age and use a standard deduction.

SOLUTION

First, determine the annuity based on the tax-deferred plan. Using Table IV, we have

$$\text{Annuity payment} \times 9.1079 = \$81,991$$
$$\text{Annuity payment} = \$9,002$$

He would receive $9,002. All of this is subject to tax as ordinary income. Thus, his tax liability would be calculated as follows:

Annuity income	$	9,002
Other income		3,000
Adjusted gross income	$	12,002
Less standard deduction	−	1,920
Less deduction for dependents (4 × $750)	−	3,000
Taxable income	$	7,082
Income tax liability	$	1,206

Based on the tax-deferred plan, he would have $12,002 − $1,206 = $10,796 of after-tax income.

Next, determine his income based on having funds in savings certificates. Using Table IV, we have

$$\text{Annuity payment} \times 9.1079 = \$46,292$$
$$\text{Annuity payment} = \$5,083$$

He would receive $5,083. This is not subject to tax since he already paid tax on the income. However, he would have to pay tax on the interest received each year from the savings certificates. At the start of the year he had $46,292 in certificates. While he would use some of the principal during the year, he would receive interest at the rate of 7% on approximately $46,000. This amounts to $3,220. Thus, during the first year of his retirement he would have to pay tax on about $3,220 in interest. During subsequent years the principal and tax on the interest would decrease. The tax liability is calculated as follows:

Interest income	$ 3,220
Other income	3,000
Adjusted gross income	$ 6,220
Less standard deduction	−1,990
Less deductions for dependents (4 × $750)	−3,000
Taxable income	$ 1,320
Income tax liability	$ 188

Based on savings certificates, he would have $5,083 + $3,000 − $188 = $7,895 in after-tax income.

Example 8:   TAX-DEFERRED ANNUITY

Continue with Example 7 and compare Charles' retirement income situation using the two plans.

SOLUTION

Using the tax-deferred plan, Charles would have total income of $12,002, less tax of $1,206, leaving $10,796. Using savings certificates, his total income would have been $8,083, less tax for the first year of $188, leaving $7,895. Thus, using the tax-deferred plan, Charles' after-tax income would be $2,901 greater.

DISCOUNTED CASH FLOW APPLIED TO VALUATION OF SECURITIES

The internal rate of return criterion for capital budgeting is extremely useful in evaluating the return of securities such as bonds. Bonds, almost without exception, are sold in $1,000 denominations and $1,000 is received by the owners when the bonds are redeemed at maturity. However, *since their return is fixed, the market price tends to change inversely with prevailing interest rates.* In periods of high interest rates, many bonds sell at discount. Several American Telephone and Telegraph bonds were selling at the prices shown below:

Maturity Date	Yearly Dollar Yield	Market Price
2003	$71.25	$850
1979	65.00	940
1980	27.50	770

The yield on bonds such as those listed above is expressed in three ways:

1. *Stated yield or coupon yield:* The yearly dollar interest payment divided by the maturity price ($1,000).
2. *Current yield:* The yearly dollar interest payment divided by the market price.
3. *Yield to maturity:* The yearly dollar interest payment and capital appreciation (or loss) discounted to present value.

The *current yield* is the yield listed in financial papers such as the *Wall Street Journal*. It is calculated simply as demonstrated below.

Example 9:   CURRENT YIELD

Determine the current yield of the AT&T bond due 2003.

SOLUTION

Divide the yearly dollar interest payment by the market price:

$$\frac{\$71.25}{\$850.00} = .0838$$

The current yield is 8.38%.

The yield is pretax. If, for example, a person owning the bond yielding 8.38% had a marginal tax rate of 30%, the after-tax yield would be calculated as follows:

$$k_i = k \ (1 - T) \tag{1}$$

Where k_i — after-tax interest yield

$k =$ pretax interest yield

$T =$ investor's marginal income tax rate

To calculate the after-tax yield of the AT&T bonds, the formula is applied as follows:

$$k_i = k (1 - T)$$
$$k_i = .0838 (1 - .3)$$
$$k_i = .0587$$

The after-tax current yield is 5.87%.

The *yield to maturity* represents the internal rate of return of the cash inflows and outflows resulting from investment in the security. To calculate this yield, the internal rate of return method is used as shown in example 10.

Example 10:   YIELD TO MATURITY

Calculate the pretax yield to maturity for the AT&T bond due 1980, assuming that there are five years to maturity.

SOLUTION

Express the problem in terms of cash flows. A cash outflow of $770 will result in pretax cash inflows of $27.50 for five years and $1,000 in the fifth year. A solution table may be used to express the problem. A solution table at 8% is shown:

Solution Table for 8%

Time	Amount		Discount Factor	Present Value
Present	−$ 770	×	1	−$ 770
1–5	27.50	×	3.9927	110
5	1,000	×	.6806	680
			NPV =	$ 20

Since the NPV is positive, the yield is more than 8%.

Solution Table at 9%

Time	Amount		Discount Factor	Present Value
Present	−$ 770	×	1	−$ 770
1–5	27.50	×	3.8897	107
5	1,000	×	.6499	650
			NPV =	−$ 13

The exact pretax yield to maturity of the bond is between 8 and 9% and may be determined by using linear interpolation.

The after-tax yield is much more important to an investor. *The yield actually consists of two parts: yearly after-tax interest plus the maturity value of the bond less any capital gain tax.* The yearly interest is taxed as ordinary income. However, if the bond is held for more than six months, the capital gain is long-term and hence taxed at one-half the ordinary income rate. For this reason, persons having very high taxable incomes prefer to purchase bonds having low yearly dollar interest payments and a large capital gain at maturity. For example, the yield to maturity of the AT&T 1980 bond would be much higher than the 1979 bond for a person with a high marginal tax rate.

Example 11:　　AFTER-TAX YIELD TO MATURITY

Determine the after-tax yield to maturity for a bond selling at $600, maturing in ten years, and paying $50 per year interest for a person with a marginal tax rate of 50%.

SOLUTION

First, determine the after-tax interest payments. Since the tax rate is 50% and the pretax interest is $50, the tax would be $25. This leaves $25 as the amount of after-tax interest.

Next, determine the capital gain and tax on it·

Bond redemption price	$1,000
Purchase price	− 600
Capital gain	$ 400

The tax on the capital gain, based on one-half the tax rate on ordinary income, is $100. Therefore, the person redeeming the bond at maturity would actually have an after-tax cash inflow of $900. A 7% solution table is shown below:

Solution Table at 7%

Time	Amount		Discount Factor		Present Value
Present	− $600	×	1	=	− $600
1–10	25	×	7.0236	=	176
10	900	×	.5084	=	458
				NPV =	$ 34

Since the NPV is positive, the yield exceeds 7%.

Solution Table at 8%

Time	Amount		Discount Factor		Present Value
Present	− $600	×	1	=	− $600
1–10	25	×	6.7101	=	168
10	900	×	.4632	=	417
			NPV	=	− $ 15

The actual return as determined by linear interpolation is 7.7%.

The after-tax rate of return is substantially less than the pretax and hence is much more important to the bondholder.

1. Indicate the differences in capital budgeting for a large versus a small business.
2. Indicate the importance of tax-deferred annuities.
3. Differentiate among stated, current, and yield to maturity of a bond. Which do you consider most important? Why?

The capital budgeting procedures may be used for a variety of special applications. Several new terms are introduced:

Annuity
Stated Yield
Current Yield
Yield to Maturity
Deferred-Tax Annuity
Keogh Plan

1. John Conway is considering the purchase of a small company. He is married, has three children and an adjusted gross income of $16,000, and uses a standard deduction. He is considering the purchase of a small business. It will cost $70,000 and is expected to produce *pretax income* as shown below. In addition, depreciation cash throw-off will amount to $5,000 each year.

Year	Pretax Business Income
Present	− $70,000 (purchase price)
1–10	5,500
10	45,000

All of the business income is subject to tax as ordinary income, with the exception of the $45,000 to be received in year 10. The $45,000 is the anticipated sale price of the business and includes $25,000 book value with the remainder being recapture of depreciation. John requires a 12% after-tax return on investment. Based on his current income, deductions, etc., determine the after-tax net present value of the investment.

2. Carlton Smith is planning to retire in 30 years. He wants to have an income of $10,000 per year for 20 years after retirement. If he can obtain 7% return on his savings until retirement and 5% thereafter, how much must he save each year? Do not consider the effect of federal income taxes.

3. Arlene Kline was 50 years old when her husband died suddenly. She was left with an estate of $100,000, which can be invested at an average annual return of 7%. She will need $7,000 per year to meet her expenses and pay taxes until age 60 when she will start to receive Social Security. After age 60, she will need only $6,000 per year. What will the value of her estate be at age 65? If she finds that because of inflation she will need $9,000 per year after age 65, how long will her estate last? Do not consider the effect of federal income taxes.

4. Rework Problem 3 using an 8% rate of return. Commencing at age 65, how much could Mrs. Kline draw per year without eroding her principal?

5. Cathy Douglas was widowed at age 45. She had an estate of $60,000, which she was able to invest at 6%. Although she was able to secure employment, due to the expenses of running a home and supporting her two children, she anticipated drawing $3,000 per year from the estate until age 60. She expects to retire at age 60 and receive Social Security benefits. However, she anticipates needing $6,000 per year from her estate since she will not be working. Do not consider the effect of federal income taxes. Determine the following:
   a. The amount of her estate when she is 60.
   b. The number of years her estate will last once she starts to draw the $6,000 per year at age 60. (Do not interpolate.)

6. A bond maturing in ten years yields $63 per year and is currently selling for $800. At maturity it will be worth $1,000. Determine the following:
   a. Pretax current yield.
   b. Pretax yield to maturity.
   c. After-tax yield to maturity for a person having a marginal tax rate of 40%. Assume the dividend tax exclusion has already been used.

7. A bond is selling for $680 and has a coupon yield of 8%. At maturity it will be worth $1,000. It will mature in 15 years. If the owner has a

36% marginal tax rate, determine the yield to maturity. Assume the dividend tax exclusion has already been used.

8. Suppose a person had $25,000 to invest at age 25. How much would the person have at age 65 if the $25,000 were invested at 8%? If the person wanted to draw an annuity of $12,000 per year starting at age 65, how many years would the annuity continue before the funds were depleted? Do not consider the effect of federal income taxes.

9. Joe Richardson, who is married, is considering setting up a tax-deferred annuity. He has 15 years to retirement at age 65 and can put $3,000 per year (before taxes) into the annuity. Assume he is in the 36% marginal tax bracket and will receive 7% pretax return both before and after retirement. After retirement he will have other income of $4,000 per year, will use a standard deduction, and will have four exemptions (for his wife and himself). Determine the amount of after-tax income Joe would receive using a tax-deferred plan and the amount using a non-tax-deferred plan, based on a 20-year retirement period, for the first year of his retirement.

Leasing

chapter 20

Leasing is a process whereby the user (lessee) enters into a contract with the owner (lessor) for the use of particular equipment or facilities belonging to the lessor for a specific period of time, for which the lessee will pay a certain amount to the lessor. The term *leasing* is sometimes used interchangeably with *renting*. However, the former generally implies a longer time duration. Thus, an automobile is rented for a weekend but leased for a year.

From a financial viewpoint, leasing and renting also differ. The underlying advantage for leasing is, of course, that it *may be* less expensive to lease than to purchase. One reason for the lower cost results from the fact that the lessor's cost of capital is frequently less than the lessee's. For example, a manufacturing firm might have a cost of capital of 12%, whereas a leasing company which might be a subsidiary of a national bank could have a cost of capital of 9%. There is enough difference in the two costs of capital that both lessee and lessor may profit.

The profitability in renting to both the owner and renter comes about from the *rate of utilization* of the rented item as opposed to the significant difference in the cost of capital. For example, consider a large wheelbarrow costing about $125 and having a life of five years. Such wheelbarrows may be rented for about $4 per day. From the viewpoint of the renter, who may only need the wheelbarrow two or three days a year, purchasing would be an unwarranted expense. In addition he would have to store the wheelbarrow, which would result in use of valuable storage space. From the viewpoint of the owner of the wheelbarrow, renting may be very profitable. If, for example, the wheelbarrow were rented only one day in five, the owner would gross $365 \div 5 \times \$4 = \$292$ per year. Over the five-year life, the owner would gross $1,460 on an investment of $125. Of course, the owner would have many expenses such as the cost of the leasing or owning a rental center, etc. Another example of renting is of hearses and funeral limousines. These vehicles are extremely expensive, and their ownership can be justified only if they are used very frequently. Since many smaller funeral directors have use for such vehicles only once or twice a week it is much less expensive to rent them as needed. The owner can maintain a fleet of such vehicles and rent them to many funeral directors. This ensures both *frequent use plus economy of scales in maintenance, insurance, storage, and the like*. Thus, both leasing and renting may be financially advantageous.

Basically, anything that can be sold can be rented or leased. Some general categories include real estate; transportation equipment (trucks, buses, automobiles, ships, railroad cars); equipment for special industries such as farming, oil, and textiles; computers; and miscellaneous other manufacturing equipment such as power plants and nuclear fuel. The vast majority of leases are for equipment worth $50,000 or less, but some leases run over $100 million.

Leasing provides an alternative to purchasing. Until recently, leasing represented only a small industry within the United States, and many businessmen considered it to be an expensive source of financing which should be avoided. However, with the authorization of national banks to engage in direct leasing and high interest rates, many businesses have turned to leasing as a source of financing. While it is difficult to estimate the precise amount of equipment leasing in the United States, the leasing industry has been valued at over $55 billion.

The primary consideration in deciding to lease or rent versus purchasing is, "Which will result in the greater after-tax returns?" In this chapter we shall indicate how discounted cash flow techniques may be used in the decision-making process. Aside from this financial question, there are other significant factors which must be considered when making the lease versus purchase decision. The primary considerations are discussed below.

1. Leasing provides 100% financing for the lessee. A down pay-

ment is not required. Even costs such as installation, sales taxes, delivery charges, and the like can be included in the lease. However, the first lease payment is generally payable at the beginning of the lease period. That is, the payments are made in advance.

2. The entire amount of the lease payment is deductible as an expense for the lessee. This is especially significant if land is involved in the lease. If the lessee has purchased the land, it cannot be depreciated, but lease payments on land are deductible for purposes of calculation of federal income tax liability. Further, the lessee may obtain investment tax credit on his federal income tax if the lessor waives it for himself. The investment credit would be the same amount as if the lessee had made the purchase.

3. Flexible lease payment schedules are often easily arranged to accommodate seasonal cash flows of the lessee.

4. Leasing often provides a method for firms to secure the use of capital equipment which they could not otherwise purchase because they could not borrow funds to do so. This is especially important for small companies which lack a firm equity basis to support debt.

5. Lease obligations are not shown on the balance sheet of a firm, whereas debt is shown. Hence, a firm can, in essence, borrow without the "debt" being reflected on the balance sheet. This is very important because creditors such as banks examine debt to equity relationships carefully and limit credit extension to firms which already have heavy debt burdens. But, of course, statements audited by CPAs would disclose any lease obligations in footnotes to the firm's balance sheet.

6. Leasing represents a hedge against inflation. The lease payment, like debt repayment, usually remains constant over the life of the lease. This is especially significant if the lease has a life of several years or more. Some leases, such as those on buildings, require the lessee to pay property taxes and utilities, which are likely to increase.

7. Leasing avoids the costs involved in underwriting and floating bond and stock issues as well as the public disclosure of financial information which is required when companies sell securities to the public.

8. There is no disposal problem associated with the equipment or other facilities at the end of the lease. Of course, this can work to the disadvantage of the lessee if, over the period of the lease, the facilities have increased in value. The lessor will benefit from any increase in value which is likely to occur when real estate is involved, but this increase seldom occurs with equipment.

9. A firm can try out a piece of equipment for a limited time period, such as a year, to determine its operational effectiveness and profitability without committing large amounts of funds. This is especially important when a firm is considering entering a new product line, etc. Leasing may thereby reduce business risk.

10. A firm can rent equipment only when needed. Many building contractors rent nearly all their equipment, using and paying for it only when it is needed.

The lease decision is part of both the financing and capital budgeting decisions. Discounted cash flow methods are applied in making the lease or rent versus purchase decision.

Example 1: LEASING USING PRESENT VALUE

Continental Products is considering the lease of a new machine. The lease will run for ten years and will cost $40,000 per year. It will result in added revenues of $85,000 and increased operating costs of $30,000. Continental is in the 48% marginal tax bracket. Continental requires 15% return on investment. Determine whether or not the leased machine will provide this return.

SOLUTION

Determine the cash flows for each year, noting that the *lease payments are made in advance*. The *year-end* cash inflow is shown as follows, along with the changes to the income statement:

Income Statement			Cash Inflow (year end)
Revenues	$85,000		$85,000
Lease payment	− 40,000		
Operating expense	− 30,000		− 30,000
Added EBT	$15,000		$55,000
Tax	− 7,200		− 7,200
After-tax profit	$ 7,800	Cash inflow	$47,800

Since the lease payment is made at the beginning of each year, the firm would pay $40,000 at the beginning and receive $47,800 at the end. The situation is shown in the "Solution Table for Leasing."

The table can be contracted as shown in the "Solution Table at 15%." Note that during the first nine years, the year-end cash inflow of $47,800 is received at approximately the same time as the next year's lease payment of $40,000 is paid out. Therefore the lease payment is subtracted from the year-end cash inflow, leaving $7,800 as the net cash inflow.

Solution Table for Leasing

Time	Amount	Discount Factor	Present Value
Present	− $40,000 (1st year payment)	× 1 =	− $40,000
1	47,800 (year end cash inflow)		
1	− 40,000 (2nd year payment)		
2	47,800 (year end cash inflow)		
2	− 40,000 (3rd year payment)		
3	47,800 (year end cash inflow)		
3	− 40,000 (4th year payment)		
.	.		
.	.		
.	.		
10	47,800 (year end cash inflow)		

Solution Table at 15%

Time	Amount	Discount Factor	Present Value
Present	− $40,000	× 1 =	− $40,000
1–9	7,800	× 4.7716 =	37,218
10	47,800	× .2472 =	11,816
		NPV =	$ 9,034

Since the NPV is positive, the leased machine yields more than the required 15%. *Note that a lease payment is not made at the end of the tenth year. Therefore, the firm receives the full cash inflow of $47,800 at that time.*

Example 2: LEASING USING INTERNAL RATE OF RETURN

Barton Industries is considering the leasing of special handling equipment for a period of 20 years. The lease will cost $20,000 per year, with payments in advance. As a result of using the machine, costs will be reduced by $23,000 per year. If Barton has a marginal tax rate of 48%, determine the internal rate of return of the machine.

SOLUTION

Determine the cash flows for each year, noting that the lease payments are made in advance.

	Income Statement		Cash Inflow (year end)
Reduction in cost	$23,000		$23,000
Lease payment	− 20,000		
Added EBT	$ 3,000		$23,000
Added taxes	− 1,440		− 1,440
After-tax profit	$ 1,560	Cash inflow	$21,560

Since the lease payment is made at the beginning of the year, the firm would pay $20,000 at the beginning and get $21,560 back at the end. The solution table is shown below:

Time	Amount		Discount Factor		Present Value
Present	− $20,000	×	1	=	− $20,000
1–19	1,560	×	Unknown	=	Unknown
20	21,560	×	Unknown	=	Unknown

As a first estimate of the IRR, consider only the $1,560 cash flow per year for 19 years:

$$\$1,560 \times d.f. = \$20,000$$
$$d.f. = \frac{\$20,000}{\$1,560} = 12.82$$

Referring to Table IV in Appendix A, this corresponds to approximately 5%. Since an added $21,560 will be received in the twentieth year, a good first estimate could be 7%. A solution table using 7% is shown below:

Solution Table for 7%

Time	Amount		Discount Factor		Present Value
Present	− $20,000	×	1	=	− $20,000
1–19	1,560	×	10.3356	=	16,123
20	21,560	×	.2584	=	5,571
			NPV	=	$ 1,694

Since the NPV is positive, a higher rate must be used. The solution table for 8% is shown below:

Solution Table for 8%

Time	Amount		Discount Factor		Present Value
Present	− $20,000	×	1	=	− $20,000
1–19	1,560	×	9.6036	=	14,982
20	21,560	×	.2145	=	4,624
			NPV	=	− $ 394

The actual IRR lies between 7% and 8%. Linear interpolation can be used to determine the actual values as shown in Fig. 1. Note that at the

FIGURE 1.

actual IRR the NPV $=0$. The width of the lower scale is $\$394 + \$1,694 =$ $\$2,088$, as shown. The zero value is $\dfrac{\$394}{\$2088} = .189$ of the way from 8%. Therefore, the internal rate of return is $8\% - .189\% = 7.811\%$.

Example 3:   LEASE VERSUS PURCHASE

A machine costing $\$10,000$ will result in increased operating income of $\$3,000$ per year. It will be depreciated straight-line over five years with no salvage value. The tax rate is 22%. The machine could also be leased for five years at $\$2,600$ per year. The lease payment would be paid at the beginning of each year. Determine whether it is more profitable to lease or purchase.

SOLUTION

First, consider the purchase. Determine the cash flow of the machine.

Income Statement		*Cash Flow (year end)*
Increased income	$3,000	
Depreciation	− 2,000	$2,000
EBT	$1,000	
Taxes	− 220	
After-tax profit	$ 780	$ 780
	Cash flow	$2,780

The machine will result in a cash flow of $\$2,780$ per year for five years if purchased.

Determine the IRR of the machine.

Solution Table for 10%

Time	*Amount*		*Discount Factor*		*Present Value*
Present	− $10,000	×	1	=	− $10,000
1–5	2,780	×	3.791	=	10,539
			NPV	=	$ 539

Since the NPV is positive, it can be concluded that 10% is too low, so try 12%.

Solution Table for 12%

Time	Amount		Discount Factor		Present Value
Present	− $10,000	×	1	=	− $10,000
1–5	2,780	×	3.605	=	10,022
			NPV	=	$ 22

The NPV is $22, which is very close to zero. Therefore, the actual return is just over 12%.

Next, consider the lease. Determine the cash flow of the machine.

Income Statement			Cash Inflow (year end)
Increased income	$3,000		$3,000
Lease payment	− 2,600		
EBT	$ 400		
Taxes	− 88		− 88
After-tax profit	$ 312	Cash inflow	$2,912

The lease payment of $2,600 is made at the beginning of each year. At the end of the year, the firm would get the $3,000 less taxes of $88, or $2,912. Thus, it would pay out $2,600 at the start of each year and get back $2,912 at the year's end.

Solution Table for 10%

Time	Amount		Discount Factor		Present Value
Present	− $2,600	×	1	=	− $2,600
1–4	312	×	3.170	=	989
5	2,912	×	.621	=	1,808
			NPV	=	$ 197

10% is too low. Try 12%.

Solution Table for 12%

Time	Amount		Discount Factor		Present Value
Present	− $2,600	×	1	=	− $2,600
1–4	312	×	3.037	=	948
5	2,912	×	.567	=	1,651
			NPV	=	− $ 1

The return is almost exactly 12%. Since the IRR of the lease is almost exactly 12% and the IRR of the purchase is just over 12%, the purchase is financially preferable to the lease. However, the returns are very close. Therefore, it would be wise for management to carefully consider all of the other advantages and disadvantages of leasing before making a final decision.

Example 4:   Lease Versus Purchase

A machine can be purchased for $20,000. It will be depreciated straight-line over ten years with zero salvage value. The firm could also lease the machine for $5,500 per year, with payments to be made at the beginning of each year. The firm requires a 10% return on investments and has a 48% marginal tax rate. Decide whether the firm should purchase or lease.

Solution

The cash inflows which will result from the use of the machine are not given, so the problem can only be solved to the extent of determining which method of acquiring the machine is least costly. There is no way to determine if the machine will yield the 10% rate of return whether leased or purchased.

First, determine the costs involved in purchase. The initial cost is $20,000. However, a tax savings will result from the yearly depreciation of $2,000. The tax savings will represent a cash inflow of 48% of the depreciation: $2,000 × .48 = $960. The solution table at 10% is shown below:

Solution Table at 10% for Purchase

Time	Amount		Discount Factor		Present Value
Present	− $20,000	×	1	=	− $20,000
1–10	960	×	6.1446	−	5,899
			NPV	=	− $14,101

Next, determine the cost of the lease, keeping in mind that the lease payments are tax deductible. The lease payment of $5,500 will result in a year-end tax savings of $5,500 × .48 = $2,640. Hence, during years 1–9, the cost will be $5,500 − $2,640 = $2,860.

Solution Table at 10% for Leasing

Time	Amount		Discount Factor		Present Value
Present	− $5,500	×	1	=	− $ 5,500
1–9	− 2,860	×	5.7590	=	− 16,470
10	2,640	×	.3855	=	1,018
			NPV	=	− $20,952

In this example, the NPVs of both the purchase and lease are negative. *The one which is least negative is preferred since it represents a lower outflow of funds.* Therefore, the purchase would be selected rather than the lease.

Leasing is becoming increasingly more important to businesses, as it represents a viable method for obtaining needed facilities and equipment. There are numerous advantages to leasing versus purchasing. In fact, for many firms leasing may represent the only way open to secure the use of needed assets since leasing provides for 100% financing. Leasing represents an alternative method of financing for many firms and deserves considerable attention by management whenever the acquisition of facilities or equipment is being considered.

QUESTIONS
FOR
DISCUSSION

1. Indicate why leasing has become a popular method of securing the use of equipment and property in recent years.
2. For a small business, list in order of importance those factors which should be considered in making the lease versus purchase decision.
3. Indicate some types of businesses where flexible lease payments would be especially advantageous.
4. From the point of view of a firm's creditors, what is the significance of a firm's lease obligations?
5. Provide examples of types of equipment or other assets which might provide a disposal problem for the lessor at the end of a lease.
6. Indicate types of businesses which use equipment periodically and for which it might be less costly to rent the equipment as needed rather than to purchase it or lease it.

CONCEPTS
TO
REMEMBER

Leasing is closely related to capital budgeting. New terms which you should be familiar with are listed below:

Lessee
Lessor
Leasing
Renting
Lease Payment

PROBLEMS

1. A machine can be leased for $30,000 per year for five years. Its use will result in cost reductions of $34,000 per year. If the firm has an after-tax cost of capital of 10% and lease payments are made at the beginning of each year, decide whether or not the machine should be leased. The lessee has a 48% marginal tax rate.

2. Special equipment can be leased by Conway Industries, Inc. for $60,000 per year and will result in cost reductions of $70,000 per year for ten years. If Conway has a marginal tax rate of 48% and lease payments are made at the beginning of each year, determine the internal rate of return for the special equipment.

3. Gladstone Manufacturing Company, Inc. can lease another warehouse for a period of ten years. This will result in added revenues of $150,000 per year due to increased sales, which are currently lost due to frequent "stockouts" of certain items. Concurrently, fixed costs will increase by $50,000 per year. The lease will cost $40,000 per year, and $45,000 will be required for labor costs in operating the warehouse. Gladstone has a 48% marginal tax rate and requires a 12% after-tax return on investment. If lease payments are made at the beginning of each year, decide if Gladstone should lease the warehouse.

4. Paving Co., Inc. uses asphalt paving equipment about 200 days each year. Such equipment may be rented for $350 per day. For the sake of simplification, assume the equipment is rented regularly throughout the year and that half the rental cost is paid at the start of each year and half at the end. If Paving purchased the equipment, it would cost $250,000, have a life of ten years and zero salvage value, and cost $15,000 per year for maintenance. If the paving equipment is rented, Paving will not have to pay the maintenance. Paving requires a 15% return on investment and has a 48% marginal tax rate. Decide whether Paving should buy or rent the equipment.

5. Conway Industries, Inc. is considering the leasing of a building which they could also buy. The lease payments are $170,000 per year for 20 years, payments to be made at the start of each year. The building could be purchased for $600,000; yearly property taxes on the building are $30,000. Conway would not pay the property tax if they lease the building. Conway requires 14% return on investment and is in the 48% marginal tax bracket. The building would be depreciated straight-line with a life of 20 years and a projected salvage of $200,000. However, in 20 years the building probably could be sold for at least $500,000. Conway would be responsible for all heat, maintenance, and other operating costs regardless of whether they purchase or lease the building. Decide whether they should buy or lease the building.

6. The Merkel Company, Inc. is faced with the decision whether to purchase or to lease a new forklift truck. The truck can be leased on a five-year contract for $1,800 a year, or it can be purchased for $5,000. The lease includes maintenance and service. The truck will have zero salvage value. The company uses straight-line depreciation. If the truck is owned, service and maintenance charges (a tax-deductible cost) would be $500 a year. Merkel has a 48% marginal tax rate, and their after-tax cost of capital is 10%. Lease payments are paid yearly and in advance. Decide whether the purchase or lease is preferable.

7. Alexander, Inc. is considering the lease versus purchase decision for a building. The lease payments are $180,000 per year for 20 years, payments to be made at the start of each year. The building could be purchased for $700,000. Yearly property taxes on the building are $40,000, but would be paid by the lessor if the property is leased. Alexander requires 12% return on investments and is in the 48% marginal tax bracket. The building would be depreciated straight-line with a life of 20 years and a projected salvage value of $250,000. However, in 20 years the building could probably be sold for $550,000. Alexander would be responsible for all heat, maintenance, and other operating costs regardless of whether they lease or purchase. Determine the NPV of the purchase and lease plans and indicate which is preferable.

WORKING CAPITAL

AND

PROFITABILITY MANAGEMENT

section IV

AN OVERVIEW

The management of working capital and the associated functions of cash, marketable securities, accounts receivable and payable, and inventory management require day-to-day management attention. The expeditious collection of receivables and prompt attention to payment of bills, investment of excess funds, and borrowing needed funds represent an ongoing management concern. Procedures which may be used to aid management in these tasks are included in this section.

Cash budgeting and inventory management are of special significance as a part of working capital management. A chapter is devoted to the discussion of procedures which may be used in cash and inventory management.

The final chapters of this section are devoted to profitability and business expansion and contraction. Break-even analysis is studied in terms of profitability analysis and plant operating capacity. The utilization of operating leverage as a method for measuring the relationship among profitability, and production and sales are addressed. Within the context of profitability, the subjects of *business expansion*, including internal and external business growth, and *business contraction*, including dissolution and bankruptcy, are discussed. This rounds out the study of profitability management.

319

Working Capital Management

chapter 21

Working capital encompasses current assets and current liabilities. Working capital management has to do with the management of these accounts, which include cash, marketable securities, accounts receivable, inventories, and accounts payable.

When reviewing the current assets as a whole, several general factors should be considered. First, *the return on the normal combination of fixed assets and supporting working capital is more than the return on funds invested temporarily*. Therefore, to as great an extent as possible, the amount of above-normal working capital should be minimized. Second, *cash and temporary investments are more liquid than receivables and inventory. Liquidity has two dimensions.* One is the time necessary to convert an asset into cash. The second has to do with the amount of cash which could be realized upon conversion. For example, if marketable securities were sold, management would want to know when they would receive the payment for the securities and how much would be received. Third, *the less liquid a firm, the greater the chance of insolvency*. Fourth, *different levels of cash must be maintained at various times so as to meet debts as they mature*.

Management must evaluate the four factors described above to establish a general policy for maintenance of current asset accounts. *The primary trade-off is liquidity versus profitability*. As a firm becomes more liquid with more funds kept as cash or near cash, the profitability generally decreases. The profit decreases because the excess current assets are not being fully utilized. Near cash assets include marketable securities such as Treasury Bonds. On the other hand, as a firm increases its liquidity, it is better able to meet its debt obligations as they mature and less likely to find itself in the position of insolvency if a *crisis* should occur. There are no hard-set rules regarding a firm's liquidity position. Rather, *the firm's liquidity is more a function of management's feelings toward profit making and risk aversion.*

As the size of a firm increases, the ratio of current to fixed assets generally tends to decrease. That is, for each dollar invested in fixed assets, large firms usually require lesser amounts to be invested in current assets than do small businesses. The reason for this changing relationship includes several parts. First, large firms have better access to the banking community and, as a result of established credit ratings, may borrow funds more readily if contingencies should arise. Second, large firms can afford to utilize cash management techniques which are not available to smaller firms. For example, if a large firm has excess funds available for a short period, such as a weekend, the firm can lend them out at interest. Small firms would not have the capability to make this possible. Therefore, any excess funds would be placed in a demand deposit (checking) account and would not generate interest. Third, large firms can utilize inventory warehousing techniques, including sophisticated computerized systems, to determine optimum inventory levels and central warehousing systems. Such systems are not usually within the province of smaller firms.

Within the general scope of working capital management, each of the current asset and liability accounts may be studied to determine the optimum financial policy. The study of these accounts, which is included in this and the following chapter, embraces cash, marketable securities, accounts receivable and payable, and inventory. As a conclusion to the study of working capital management, the subject of cash budgeting will be examined.

CASH MANAGEMENT

Cash is the most liquid of all assets. Further, since money is necessary to pay bills and meet obligations, cash balances are of extreme importance. *The practice of cash management involves three parts: speeding up collections and simultaneously slowing disbursements, determining how much cash a firm will need at any given time to meet its obligations, and deciding what to do with extra cash during short periods or how to secure needed cash during short periods.* The goal of the first part is to get the cash as fast as possible and keep it as long as possible. This topic is dealt with in this section. The second part is included under the heading of cash budgeting. The last part requires knowledge of both short-term investment opportunities and short-term loan opportunities. Short-term investments are generally made in marketable securities, the topic of the next section. Short-term loans were discussed in the section dealing with financing the firm, under the heading of short-term financing.

The process of speeding collections requires examination of the entire sequence of events which occurs from the time a credit sale takes place until the firm has use of the funds. The sequence is shown schematically in Fig. 1 with typical time requirements in days. In the sequence shown, the total time required from the sale until the firm has use of funds is 57 days. The 57 days is an average figure and, in this example, is based on customers paying their bills 30 days after receiving them. Thus, although the firm may have a 30-day credit extension period, the total period involved may be twice that. Each of the activities in the sequence must be examined to determine if the time required can be reduced and, if so, what cost will be incurred.

Once the sale is completed, the customer must be billed. In some instances this is accomplished at the time of sale. Usually, however, the customer is sent the bill at a later date. Some firms have particular monthly billing dates for all customers. For example, all customers may be billed at the end of the month. Other firms use a rotating billing system. Such a system can be based on the first initial of the customer's name. Thus, all customers with names starting with A and B are billed on the first working day of each month and so on. In either case the firm may require up to a full month before they bill a customer. For example, if all bills are sent on the thirtieth of the month and a customer makes a purchase on the first, the customer will enjoy 30 days' credit before the bill is even mailed to him. In many

FIGURE 1.

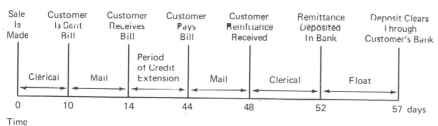

instances bills are payable upon receipt when billing is once a month.

Another billing system involves sending a bill within 1 or 2 days after the sale and sending monthly statements to remind customers of accounts due. This method assures rapid billing and can be effectively utilized by firms whose customers tend to make large but rather infrequent purchases. If a firm using this system has customers who make small frequent purchases, the firm usually holds the bill, adding each sale to it until a minimum amount is reached. When the minimum is reached, the bill is sent. This procedure tends to reduce billing costs. The minimum might be $25 for a wholesale electrical supply company.

Large firms selling at the retail level, such as major retailers and oil companies, use computerized billing systems. Customers are sent monthly statements with the minimum required payment indicated. The statement includes the purchases, previous balance, and any interest charges.

Whenever possible, a firm should endeavor to reduce the time required to prepare and send customers their bills. Small firms may be able to bill customers within 2 days of the sale or at the time of sale. Large firms often use computerized billing systems which preclude such rapid billing.

Once the question regarding the time at which customers will be sent bills has been resolved, the next step in the sequence, mailing, may be examined. Two mail periods are involved as shown in Fig. 1. Mail time can be reduced significantly by locating billing centers in close geographic proximity to customers. For example, if customers are located throughout the United States and the only billing center is in New York, 7 or 8 days may be required before mail is received from some areas. If, however, billing centers are located relatively close to customers, mail time may be reduced to 1 or 2 days, The costs involved in establishing regional collection centers are discussed under the headings of *concentration banking* and *lockbox system.*

The next phase in the sequence relates to the period of credit extension. The period of credit extension may range upwards to 90 days. Many firms use 30 days and offer a discount for early payment. Typical billings are 2/10, net 30. The "2/10" means that a customer paying within 10 days may deduct 2% from the price. Credit extension is described later in this chapter. The remaining portions of the billing-collection sequence, namely the clerical time required to process customer remittances and the float, are discussed below.

Concentration Banking

One system used to speed collections is *concentration banking*. Concentration banking involves establishing strategic collection centers in geographic locations near customers. The firm selects a local bank to act as a depository and transfer agent for collected funds. Customers are instructed to mail payments to a collection center, usually a post office box. Often preaddressed envelopes are included with the customer's bill to assure correct mailing. Clerks pick up the mail from the post office box and deliver it to the collection center. If there is a large volume of mail, it may be picked up several times a day. At the collection center, where the mail is opened, the checks are removed and taken to the selected local bank where they are deposited. The local bank collects the funds from the banks on which the firm's customers' checks have been drawn. As the funds are collected, the local bank transfers the funds to the firm's main bank. The firm's main bank is usually the bank from which the firm pays its bills. The main bank is thus referred to as the *disbursal bank*. Most of the checks drawn by the customers in a particular region will be on local banks. In fact, some of the checks may be drawn on the firm's local bank. Therefore, the time to collect funds from the customers' banks is minimized. The time required by one bank to collect funds from another is called the *float*.

The concentration banking system results in reducing both the mailing and float time. The time required for mail to reach a regional collection center is much less than the time that would be required for the same mail to reach the firm's central office. Further, the time required by the firm's local bank to collect funds from other local banks is much less than the time which the firm's disbursal bank would require to collect funds from local banks spread over the country. The two time savings are appreciable and may reduce the total period from the time a customer mails a check to the time the funds are available in the firm's disbursal bank by several days. The saving of time by reducing the float and mailing period is significant to a firm's cash management. The sooner the funds are received, the sooner they may be put to use.

Example 1:   CONCENTRATION BANKING

Alexander, Inc. has customers located throughout the United States. Currently, all bills are sent to the firm's headquarters in New York. The checks are deposited as quickly as possible in the firm's disbursal bank. Studies have shown that, on the average, the customers' remittances are in the mail for seven days. Further, it takes four days for the firm's disbursal bank to collect the funds from the customers' banks. A financial analyst has suggested that a concentration banking plan be initiated. Estimates which have been made indicate that using the concentration banking plan would reduce mailing time by three days and the float period by two days. The cost of implementing the system would be $400,000 per year. Average daily collections amount to $1.5 million, and the firm's cost of capital is 8%. Evaluate the plan to determine if it should be implemented.

SOLUTION

The total reduction in time which would result from use of the concentration banking plan is five days. Alexander would, therefore, have the use of five days' receipts which otherwise would be in the mail or in the float. The receipts for five days amount to $7.5 million (5 × $1.5 million). The value of $7.5 million at 8% is $600,000 per year. Since the concentration banking system will reduce financing costs by $600,000 while itself requiring only $400,000, it should be implemented. It is assumed in this solution that the $7.5 million would be invested in such a manner so as to return at least the firm's cost of capital, i.e., 8%.

Lockbox System

Another method used to reduce mailing and processing time in the collection of bills is the *lockbox* system. The lockbox arrangement is similar to concentration banking in that regional collection centers are established in appropriate geographical locations. *The primary difference is that with the lockbox system a bank messenger picks up customer remittances from a local post office box*, often more than once per day. The messenger takes the remittances directly to the bank where the mail is opened and the checks are deposited rapidly in the firm's account. As funds are collected, they are transferred frequently from the local bank to the firm's disbursal bank. Information regarding customer remittances (i.e., how much they paid) is mailed to the firm's central collection office. The lockbox system results in an additional time savings by eliminating the time between the receipt of customer remittances and their deposit in the bank. Further, the lockbox system results in a cost savings to the firm in that they need not have their personnel at regional centers to process collections. However, the participating banks charge for their services.

Example 2: LOCKBOX SYSTEM

Continuing with Example 1, suppose Alexander considers replacing the concentration banking system with a lockbox system. Elimination of the firm's personnel at the regional collection centers will reduce costs by $400,000. However, participating banks in the regional areas will charge $450,000 per year for the collection services required in a lockbox system. Use of the lockbox will reduce the time of mailing and processing bills by one day. Determine the action Alexander should take with respect to changing from concentration banking to lockbox.

SOLUTION

Saving one day's time will result in increasing Alexander's cash balances by $1.5 million (the average daily collection). At 8%, the $1.5 million is worth $120,000 per year. Since the banks will charge only $50,000 more than the cost of operating the regional collection centers, the lockbox will result in a savings of $70,000 per year. Therefore, the lockbox should be used.

Example 3: LOCKBOX SYSTEM

Rynex Corporation has a central billing and collection system. They serve three general geographic regions: the northeast, south, and southwest. The receipts from these three areas average about $200,000, $150,000, and $100,000, respectively. Currently all remittances are sent to Rynex's headquarters in New York.

A study has been made which shows that if collection centers were established in Atlanta to serve the south and in Phoenix to serve the southwest, substantial reductions in mailing, processing, and float period could be achieved. Specifically, the Atlanta collection center, using a lockbox system, would save 3½ days, while the Phoenix center would save 5 days. Rynex has contacted banks in these areas. A bank in Atlanta has offered to provide the lockbox service if Rynex will maintain an average demand deposit balance of $400,000 with them. A bank in Phoenix will perform the lockbox service for a monthly fee of $4,000. If Rynex's cost of capital is 8%, decide whether they should employ either of the banks.

SOLUTION

Each situation must be evaluated separately. Consider the Atlanta proposal first. The time savings is 3½ days. With collections of $150,000 per day, Rynex's cash balances would be increased by $525,000 if the lockbox were implemented in Atlanta. At 8%, the $525,000 is worth $42,000 per year. The Atlanta bank requires an average demand deposit balance of $400,000 as compensation for performing the lockbox services. Rynex will not receive interest on this account. At 8%, the equivalent cost to Rynex of maintaining the $400,000 balance is $32,000 per year. Thus, the overall savings to Rynex would be $10,000 per year. Hence, they should use the Atlanta bank as their collection agent in the South.

The southwest collections amount to $100,000 per day. A 5-day time savings would result in increased cash balances of $500,000. At 8%, this is worth $40,000 per year to Rynex. The Phoenix bank requires a monthly fee of $4,000 for their services, or $48,000 per year. Since the yearly fee exceeds the savings by $8,000, Rynex should not use the lock-box system with this particular bank in Phoenix. Rynex should continue to have its customers in the southwest send their remittances to New York.

MARKETABLE SECURITIES

Marketable securities represent an opportunity for investment of excess cash for periods ranging from overnight to several months or more. There are several types of marketable securities of which U.S. Treasury Securities, commercial paper, and certificates of deposit are very popular. There are various types of Treasury Securities, including Treasury Bills, which are issued weekly and mature in 90 days and 180 days; Treasury Notes, which mature in 1 to 7 years; and Treasury Bonds, which have a maturity greater than 7 years. *Commercial paper* consists of unsecured promissory notes with maturities of a year or less, usually 4 to 6 months.

A certificate of deposit (CD) *is a receipt for a short-term deposit made in a bank.* There are two classes of CDs: *demand and time.* The first are payable by the bank on demand, while the latter are payable on a specific date. Time CDs are similar to passbook savings deposits but have a definite maturity. Most CDs are negotiable, and thus the holder may sell a CD before it matures if the funds are needed. CDs generally bear interest and mature in periods ranging from 1 month to a year.

All of the types of securities described above are bought and sold in *money markets.* If a company has excess cash available for a short period, they might purchase a Treasury Security and resell it when funds were again needed. Even though a particular security might have a maturity of 120 days, for example, a firm could purchase it, hold it for only a short period, and then sell it.

If a firm has excess cash and plans to enter the money markets to purchase securities, it must consider several important factors. First, transaction costs are involved when securities are purchased and sold. If the securities are to be held for only a short period, the interest which will accrue may not equal the transaction costs, and hence the securities should not be purchased. Security transactions usually involve minimum fees regardless of the dollar value of the securities traded. Therefore, only firms having large cash balances can afford to buy and sell securities with only a short holding period. Small firms with small cash balances cannot turn over securities rapidly since the transaction costs are greater than the interest which would be received.

The other important factor in trading marketable securities is liquidity. Usually transactions in marketable securities are handled rapidly. That is, the markets are very active, and purchases and sales can be made quickly. However, the prices of securities fluctuate daily. Therefore, when a firm invests in securities, it subjects itself to risk of losing money if the price of the security happens to decrease. Further, there is a risk that *securities may go into default*. Normally, this risk is negligible. However, a classic example is the Penn Central commercial paper. When Penn Central went into bankruptcy it had millions of dollars of commercial paper outstanding. The holders of this paper have not been and may never be repaid by Penn Central. As a consequence of the Penn Central bankruptcy, the market for commerical paper contracted rapidly. Investors who normally purchased commercial paper became reluctant to do so. However, with the passage of time the use of commercial paper has regained broad acceptance.

Marketable securities offer a way for firms with excess cash to obtain additional income. Since larger firms are apt to have greater cash balances, their opportunities for making money by investing in marketable securities greatly exceed those of smaller firms. Larger firms can afford to employ the financial analysts and portfolio managers required to administer such an investment program. Smaller firms cannot afford this type of financial expertise.

ACCOUNTS RECEIVABLE AND PAYABLE

The management of accounts receivable has to do with the extension of credit to customers. The management of accounts payable is concerned with the payment of bills and was described as a part of the study of short-term financing. Therefore, this section is devoted to the study of credit extension to customers through the use of accounts receivable.

The extension of credit to customers involves several important aspects. Decisions must be made in the following areas:

Should a firm extend any credit?
How much credit should be extended and to whom?
How long should credit be extended?
What will be the terms of repayment?
If bills are not paid, what collection policies should be implemented?

While each of these questions is examined in detail below, it must be remembered that a firm has to meet competition in the industry. Thus, if other firms are extending credit to 60 days, a firm may be forced to do so even if it may not be the most profitable policy. If it does not extend credit, it will lose customers.

Credit Extension

Most firms must extend credit as a normal course of doing business. In dealings among businesses, very few transactions are completed with cash on delivery. Most firms are not organized to pay for materials when received. Normally, when a shipment is received, it is inspected for proper quantity and quality by a receiving clerk. If the shipment complies with the purchase specifications, the receiving department notifies the accounting department, which pays the bill in accordance with that firm's policy regarding accounts payable.

Extension of credit involves a basic trade-off. Extension of credit is expensive. The cost of extending credit includes the cost of carrying the accounts receivable (i.e., the cost of the money tied up in the accounts receivable), bad debt losses, and cost of operating the credit and collection department. The total of these costs can be considerable. To justify these costs, the firm must be able to demonstrate sufficient profit on credit sales. Credit may be extended beyond the normal practice of the firm. For example, a firm could increase its credit period from 30 to 45 days in hopes of increasing sales. Naturally, the cost of increasing the credit period must be considered. The profit from new sales must be *at least* sufficient to cover the costs of extending the credit.

Example 4:   EXTENSION OF CREDIT

Miles Company has been operating on a cash sales basis. Its sales have been slowly decreasing since its competitors offer credit to their customers whereas Miles has operated on a C.O.D. basis. Miles has made an extensive study to determine whether or not they should extend credit to their customers. Their study indicates the following: The cost of producing their products is about 80% of the sale price. The average collection period would be 30 days. On the average, comparable firms lose 3% of their credit sales as bad debts. The cost of operating a credit and collections department would be $20,000 per year. Miles' cost of capital is 10%. Miles estimates that sales could be increased by $200,000 per year if they initiated the 30-day credit plan under study. Decide whether or not Miles should initiate the credit policy.

SOLUTION

$200,000 in new sales would generate $40,000 in added pretax profit, based on the fact that the products cost Miles 80% of the sale price. The costs involved are somewhat more difficult to calculate. Three costs are involved: the bad debt expense, the cost of the credit and collection department, and the cost of the money tied up in accounts receivable. These will be examined individually.

1. Bad debt expense: The cost of the bad debt is 3% of the added sales or .03($200,000) = $6,000.
2. Cost of credit and collection department: This is given as $20,000 per year.
3. Cost of funds to support the accounts receivables: The new sales will take place throughout the year and average $16,667 per month ($200,000 ÷ 12 = $16,667). Since the average collection period is 30 days, the sales may be thought of as taking place on the first day of each month and the collection taking place on the last day. Thus, an average of $16,667 in accounts receivable will be outstanding at any given time. The actual amount of funds Miles will have tied up in accounts receivable will be $13,333, (80% of $16,667). With a cost of capital of 10%, the cost of having an average of $13,333 invested in accounts receivable is $1,333 per year.

Total costs are listed below:

Bad debt	$ 6,000
Credit & collection department	20,000
Funds to support the accounts	1,333
Total credit cost for new accounts	$27,333

Since the projected profit from the additional sales is $40,000, Miles should implement the credit policy.

Miles Company in Example 4 overlooked one very important fact: Their current customers who pay cash may also want to use any credit extension which Miles would offer to new customers.

Example 5:   EXTENSION OF CREDIT

Miles' total sales, which are all cash, amount to $2 million per year. They estimate that 70% of these cash sales would become credit sales if the credit policy under study were implemented. For their current customers, Miles estimates a bad debt loss of only 1% of credit sales. They also estimate that another $5,000 per year will be needed to operate the credit and collections department. Evaluate the new situation.

SOLUTION

The calculations are analogous to Example 4. The costs are divided into three categories, but there are no additional sales to offset the costs.

1. Bad debt expense: If 70% of Miles' $2 million current sales become credit sales and 1% of these default, the bad debt expense will amount to .7 × $2 million × .01 = $14,000.
2. Cost of credit and collection department: This is given as an additional $5,000 per year.
3. Cost of funds to support accounts receivable: If 70% of the current cash sales become credit sales, the credit sales will be $1.4 million per year or $116,667 per month. Thus, an average of $116,667 of accounts receivable will be outstanding at any time. (Note, this is in addition to the average accounts receivable resulting from the new $200,000 in sales.) The actual amount of funds Miles will have invested in this portion of its accounts receivable is $93,333 (80% of $116,667). With a cost of capital of 10%, the annual cost is $9,333. The cost of extending credit to Miles' original customers is summarized:

Bad debt	$14,000
Credit and collection department	5,000
Funds to support the accounts receivable	9,333
Total credit cost for old accounts receivable	$28,333

The total cost for new and current customers is $27,333 + $28,333 = $55,666. The increase in profit resulting from the additional $200,000 sales was projected to be $40,000. Thus, implementation of credit would result in a pretax reduction in profits of $15,666.

The actual implementation of credit by Miles depends on the aggressiveness of their management and of their competitors. If management feels further growth is dependent on credit extension and they want growth, then credit implementation is the direction to take.

Amount of Credit To Be Extended and to Whom

The dollar amount of credit to be extended depends on the needs of the customers and their credit worthiness. *In general, customers fall into two categories with respect to their purchases. Some customers purchase on a regular basis, while others make one-time purchases.* Further, some customers purchase goods which are sold throughout the year, while others may purchase seasonal products. In any event, information must be obtained regarding the credit worthiness of the applicant, the information must be analyzed, and finally a decision made. There are various sources of information which should be used. These include financial statements, credit rating by a rating agency such as Dun & Bradstreet, bank references, the firm's own experience, and exchange of information among firms.

For a small firm, personal experience with a regular customer is probably the best source of information. If the customer has paid his bills regularly in the past, there is a high probability that this trend will continue in the future. Also, exchange of information between firms is most valuable. Thus, an applicant for credit will be asked to list other firms where he has credit. Finally, a bank reference is extremely important. Banks maintain accurate records with respect to payment of debts and bank account balances. They can provide a very accurate picture of a person's or a firm's credit worthiness.

Once the information regarding an applicant has been received, a credit analysis is undertaken. Credit analysis has tended to be a somewhat subjective practice. In an attempt to provide more objective criteria, quantitative methods are being developed which examine factors such as critical financial ratios, past experience, bank recommendations, and the like. Each of these factors is weighed, and a numerical rating is provided for the applicant. The numerical rating may correspond to a projected probability of default. For example, a rating of 8 could mean there is only a 6% probability that the customer will not pay. If management is willing to take a risk of 6%, then they would extend the credit.

Period of Credit Extension

Deciding on the length of a credit period is similar to deciding whether or not to provide any credit. The trade-off is exactly the same.

Added profits resulting from new sales must be balanced against increased costs of bad debt, credit and collections department expenses, and the cost of funds tied up in receivables.

Once a firm has established a credit extension period, they should check periodically to determine whether the period is being maintained. The firm needs to know if customers are not paying their bills on time. One way to examine this question is with the use of the "average collection period" ratio:

$$\text{Average collection period} = \frac{\text{Average receivables} \times 360}{\text{Annual credit sales}} \qquad (1)$$

Example 6:   AVERAGE COLLECTION PERIOD

Ridgeway Steel has annual credit sales of $4 million. Its average receivables amount to $500,000. Determine the average collection period.

SOLUTION

Using Eq. (1),

$$\text{Average collection period} = \frac{\$500,000 \times 360}{\$4,000,000} = 45 \text{ days}$$

Terms of Repayment

At the time a firm agrees to extend credit to its customers, the terms of the billing are established. Often the terms are established so that if a customer pays before the bill is due he gets a small discount. Thus, many billings are set up whereby a customer receives a 2% discount if the bill is paid within 10 days of the billing date. Other terms may be devised to meet the particular requirements of the customer. For example, terms could be established for payment of one-third of the price at delivery, another third in 30 days, and the remainder in 90 days. Normally, all federal government agencies take discounts when they are offered.

Some firms use *seasonal dating*. Seasonal dating refers to billing a customer who purchases seasonal goods prior to the season in which they will be sold. For example, suppose a firm manufactured bathing suits, which are sold primarily in the summer. The firm's customers would want the bathing suits in early spring. With seasonal dating, instead of manufacturers constructing warehouses, storing the bathing suits as they are manufactured, and shipping them in the spring, they would ship the bathing suits throughout the year and bill the customers in the spring. There are inherent risks in seasonal dating, namely that the product may be lost or stolen from the customer. Also the customer may want special discounts for storing the goods. On the other hand, the manufacturer may save high storage costs by using seasonal dating.

Collection Procedures

A firm should monitor all of its accounts on a frequent and regular basis to determine which are overdue. The problem facing a firm is when to institute collection procedures. The longer a firm waits, the less the chance of the account being collected. However, if a firm starts collection procedures prematurely, it may annoy its customers, and, of course, the customer relationship with the marketing department must be considered. The actual collection procedure includes several steps. First, a letter is sent. This is often accomplished automatically if data processing equipment is used. If a letter fails to bring results, it is followed by a telephone inquiry from the firm's credit manager. Finally, if the bill is not paid, suit may be brought either by the firm's attorney or a collection agency.

QUESTIONS FOR DISCUSSION

1. Describe the types of work involved in the management of working capital accounts.
2. Indicate the various items which should be reviewed when determining a firm's policies on current assets.
3. Describe the two dimensions of liquidity. Apply the two dimensions to the various current asset accounts.
4. What is meant by near cash assets?
5. Why does the ratio of current to fixed assets generally decrease as the size of a firm increases?
6. Describe the three parts of cash management.
7. Differentiate between concentration banking and the lockbox system.
8. What is meant by the *float?*
9. If a firm has excess cash and is considering investing it in a money market security, what factors should be examined before an investment decision is made?
10. Indicate the primary factors which are considered in deciding to sell goods on credit.
11. Indicate sources of information which can be used to decide whether or not to give credit to a customer.
12. Why is the "average collection period" important to a financial manager?

CONCEPTS
TO
REMEMBER

The management of working capital is of utmost importance to the financial manager. Several new concepts are introduced:

Liquidity
Insolvency
Marketable Securities
Float
Certificates of Deposit
Credit Extension Policy
Bad Debt Expense
Average Collection Period
Cash Management
Concentration Banking
Lockbox System
Disbursal Bank
Treasury Bills
Treasury Notes
Credit Rating
Seasonal Dating

PROBLEMS

1. Allied Products has a central billing system. A study indicates that total mailing, processing, and float period could be reduced by four days if a concentration banking plan were adopted. Daily collections average $200,000. The cost of the system would be $50,000 per year. If Allied has an average cost of capital of 8%, should they initiate the concentration banking system?

2. Continental, Inc. is considering using a lockbox system. Its collections amount to $1 million per day. It is considering using ten regional lockbox collection centers. It would cost a total of $80,000 per year, which would be paid to the ten banks for their services. The new system would reduce mail and processing time by 1½ days. If Continental can invest additional funds at 8% per annum, should it use the new system? Indicate the exact amount of pretax profit or loss which would result from implementing the system.

3. Richardson Corporation is using a concentration banking system. A lockbox system which would further reduce processing time by one day is being considered. If the lockbox were used, the regional collection centers would be closed, thus saving Richardson $40,000 per year. Participating banks want Richardson to maintain average demand account balances of $700,000 with them as compensation for their services. Richardson's average daily collections amount to $500,000 per day, and their cost of capital is 12%. Should they change from concentration banking to lockbox?

4. To increase sales from the present level of $200,000 per year, Adrox

Corporation is considering extending its credit from 30 to 60 days. Cost of goods sold in its current output averages 60%, while for additional sales the cost of goods will drop to 50%. The sales manager believes that extending credit to 60 days will result in $12,000 per year added sales. The firm requires a 20% pretax return on investment.

a. Determine the increase in the average level of investment in accounts receivable which will take place if credit is extended to all customers to 60 days.

b. Decide whether or not Adrox should extend credit to 60 days.

5. Nylex currently extends credit for a period of 30 days. They are considering more liberal credit policies. Data relating to more liberal policies are tabulated below:

Policy	Collection Period	Sales Level	Bad Debt Expenses	Credit Department Expenses
Current	30 days	$200,000/yr	2%	$ 8,000/yr
A	45 days	250,000	3	10,000
B	60 days	280,000	4	13,000

Nylex's cost of capital is 10%. Their cost of production and sales, not including bad debt, credit department, and cost of funds to support accounts receivable, is 75% of sales. Decide which of the three credit policies is preferable.

6. Continental Products has annual sales of $75,000. Sixty percent of these are credit. Currently its receivables are $8,000. Determine the average collection period.

Inventory Management
and
Cash Budgeting

chapter 22

Continuing with the study of working capital management, in this chapter we shall deal with the topics of inventory control and cash budgeting.

INVENTORY MANAGEMENT

Inventory management is one of the most complex management problems. Depending on the type of business, there may be three basic types of inventories: raw materials, in-process goods, and finished products (including service parts and components). A summary of the types of inventories is provided in Table I. Some forms of inventory may deteriorate rapidly if held beyond a short period. Milk and other dairy products deteriorate; newspapers and Christmas trees become obsolete rapidly; this year's new car decreases in value with the introduction of new models. Numerous other items also become obsolete or decrease in value when there are model-year changes. Obsolescence not only affects finished good inventories but parts and components kept for customer service. Inventories also shrink. A prime cause of shrinkage is theft. Shrinkage is a very serious problem. *At the retail level it is not uncommon for a store to lose more from inventory shrinkage than it makes in profit.* Also, at the wholesale and production levels, shrinkage is a very serious problem.

Inventory levels can be controlled, but many factors must be considered. *First, holding inventories is expensive.* The funds invested in the inventory, warehousing, risks of obsolescence, spoilage, deterioration in storage, and shrinkage all add to a firm's costs. In periods of high interest rates *the cost of funds invested in inventories is significant.* As an example, automobile dealers have to pay for shipments of new cars when received. The dealers generally finance both their new and used cars with short-term bank loans. Short-term financing is expensive. In periods of lagging sales (and concurrent high inventory levels), the cost of funds required to finance inventories may cause normally profitable businesses to become unprofitable.

Second, running out of inventory (called a "stockout") may result in production downtime or lost sales. Production downtime is extremely expensive. Avoiding this requires close monitoring of inventory levels. If inventory levels are becoming critical, rush air shipments may be necessary; such shipments add to purchasing costs. At the retail level, stockouts can result in lost sales and customer annoyance. Customer goodwill is difficult to replace, once it is lost. Hence, stockouts are to be avoided at all levels of production and sales.

Third, maintaining excess inventories may be very costly as it can result in "price slashing" or discounting prices. For firms dealing in seasonal lines, it is not unusual for end-of-season discounts to result in sale prices at or below the price which the retailer paid for the product. That is, the business may be forced to sell their inventory *below cost* in order to dispose of it.

The "right level" of inventory is the one which strikes a balance. It must be adequate to meet reasonable expected demands but not so large as to be excessively costly. Development of an inventory management plan is important and may involve use of the techniques discussed later in this chapter. Inventory management is volatile; it is an ever-changing and ongoing process. Plans are not static but very dynamic. To provide additional insight into inventory management, a typical inventory flow for a manufacturing firm is included as Fig. 1.

Closely allied to inventory control are production planning, scheduling, and control. These topics are examined briefly since they greatly affect inventory management.

Production Planning

Production planning is essential due to the need to manage production operations in the face of customer demands and limitations such as the availability of raw materials or productive capacity. Production planning deals with the manner of production, the interaction between production and distribution, and the location and size of physical stocks. Decisions are required at every step in the process: purchasing, production of in-process materials, inventorying and shipping of finished products, and customer service.

When purchasing materials or supplies, it is important to decide how much of each type of inventory to maintain, and the quantity to buy in order to obtain quantity discounts. Further possible uncertainty in delivery times must be considered when deciding the quantity to order and keep on hand.

Production departments may need to allocate customer orders among several production facilities to avoid bottlenecks. Further, the total

TABLE 1

Typical Types of Inventories Maintained by Manufacturing Firms

Inventory	Primary Usage	Inventory Management Function
Raw materials	Production and assembly	Store all components, fittings, parts and other materials needed for production
Subassemblies and in-process manufactured items	Production and assembly	Monitor movement and store (as necessary) all in-process inventories
Finished goods and service parts	Sales	Maintain adequate quantities of the firm's product lines to supply customers; maintain supply of parts needed to service customers' products in a timely manner
Repair parts	Maintenance and service	Maintain adequate supply of repair parts to avoid costly delays in the event of equipment failure
Supplies: maintenance and production	Maintenance and production	Maintain supply of light bulbs, greases, solvents, and similar supplies
Supplies: office	Administration	Stock appropriate forms, paper, pencils, and other items for clerical, bookkeeping, etc.
Supplies: computer	Data processing	Maintain tapes, cards, repair parts for data processing equipment

FIGURE 1.   Manufacturing plant inventory flow chart.

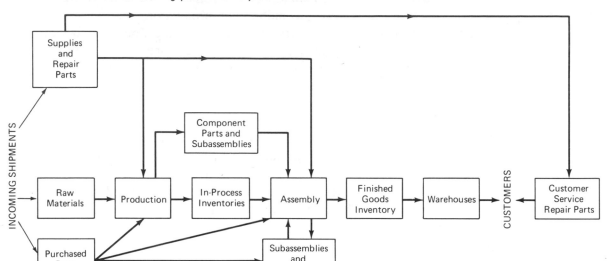

needed plant capacity must be ascertained. In *multiplant operations*, both production planning and scheduling include decisions relating to the quantity of each item to be made in each plant. This may extend to specification of the particular company warehouses to be served by individual plants. Finally, *cascaded production systems* (where the product passes from the raw material stage to the finished product stage through a series of production departments or plants, with major in-process inventories maintained among various production operations) illustrate a most complex problem of production planning, scheduling, and inventory control.

The specific steps of production planning vary by product line and production requirements. However, the essentials of a production and inventory control system can be grouped into three broad classes:

1. *Long-range planning* is required to budget capital for facilities and inventory investment. This requires development of capital requirements in view of long-range business forecasts.

2. *Intermediate policy making and planning* is required as a basis for short-term scheduling. General plans are developed for use of existing facilities in the light of sales forecasts. Then the level of stocks required to meet expected sales levels while remaining within plant capacity and keeping employment fluctuations at an acceptable level may be deter-

mined. This type of planning lays the ground rules for short-term scheduling consistent with inventory policy.

3. *Short-term scheduling* involves assignment of production to keep utilization of facilities and stocks balanced in view of the demand for output as it actually materializes. This is accomplished within the framework of policies relating to the level of production and employment to be maintained, the size of inventory investment, the service to customers, warehouse space available, and the like.

Inventory Turnover

A very important aspect of inventory control is the measurement of inventory turnover. Inventory turnover is calculated as follows:

$$\text{Inventory turnover} = \frac{\text{Cost of goods sold}}{\text{Average inventory}} \qquad (1)$$

The *average inventory* is the average of the inventory at the start and end of the year. However, for firms having seasonal production cycles, the average may be determined based on the seasonal high and low inventory levels. Inventory turnover is important since it indicates inventory level as a function of sales. Further, inventory turnover has a direct impact on working capital.

Generally, the higher the inventory turnover, the better the inventory management. However, if inventory turns over very rapidly, it may be a sign that the general level of inventory is too low. If levels of inventory are commonly maintained at low levels, stockouts may occur. These are costly since they usually result in lost sales. If, on the other hand, inventory turnover is low, it may be indicative of obsolete inventory being maintained or just excessive levels of inventory. It is useful to compare inventory turnover ratios with averages for an industry. This can be done referring to reports such as Robert Morris' *Annual Statement Studies*. A comparison with industry averages is helpful since if large differences are noted, it is a sign that an inventory management problem may exist.

Example 1:   INVENTORY TURNOVER

Refer to the balance sheet and income statements for Technitrol, Inc. in Chapter 2 and determine the inventory turnover rates for 1973.

SOLUTION

Referring to Technitrol's balance sheet, the inventories on December 31, 1972 and 1973 were $1,707,411 and $2,164,487, respectively. The average inventory for the year is, therefore,

$$\frac{\$1,707,411 + \$2,164,487}{2} = \$1,935,949$$

Referring to the 1973 income statement, the cost of goods sold was $7,855,182. The inventory turnover ratio may be determined using Eq. (1):

$$\text{Inventory turnover} = \frac{\$7,855,182}{\$1,935,949} = 4 \text{ times}$$

While the inventory turnover ratio as shown in Eq. (1) above is useful in determining the past record of inventory turnover, another similar ratio may be used to project inventory turnover. For planning purposes, Eq. (2) is very valuable:

$$\text{Projected inventory turnover} = \frac{\text{Forecasted cost of goods sold}}{\text{Current inventory}} \quad (2)$$

Equation (2) is especially important in periods of changing economic outlook. For example, suppose inflation results in rapidly increasing prices. Then the financial manager would be much more interested in the relation of forecasted cost of goods sold to inventory. Historical costs would have little importance.

Inventory Control

To implement an effective inventory control system, an analysis of customer demand must be undertaken. When analyzing customer demand, it is desirable to measure the average demand per unit of time rather than the size of individual orders. This method is generally preferred since inventory policies are dependent on time, either in the form of review periods or lead-time durations. The unit of time used may vary considerably from perhaps a year for slow-moving items such as spare parts for capital equipment to a day for fast-moving stock items.

In estimating customer demand it must be remembered that use of the previous sales data is only one source of information. Using past sales history to predict future sales will provide only general trends. However, changing economic conditions, consumer preferences, and competitive circumstances also must be considered. Further, demand in some industries tends to be cyclic. Therefore, analyses of historic data may have to be undertaken on a month-to-month basis rather than on a yearly basis.

Example 2:   AVERAGE DEMAND

Dynamo Industries' sales have been relatively consistent from year to year. However, sales do vary from month to month. The following data represent the monthly demand for a particular item which they sell. The data were taken for a 36-month period.

Demand Per Month	*Frequency of Occurrence*
1–10 units	4 months
11–20	7
21–30	6
31–40	12
41–50	7
Total	36 months

Determine the average monthly demand.

SOLUTION

Since demand varies from month to month, a weighted average must be taken. This is accomplished in tabular form below:

Demand		*Frequency*		*Probability*
1–10	×	4	=	4– 40
11–20	×	7	=	77– 140
21–30	×	6	=	126– 180
31–40	×	12	=	372– 480
41–50	×	7	=	287– 350
			Total	866–1,190

The total is divided by the number of months to give the average usage:

$$\frac{866}{36} = 24, \qquad \frac{1190}{36} = 33$$

The average use is 24 to 33 units per month.

The average monthly demand as determined in Example 2 is *not* generally useful for production planning. Rather, *the average monthly demand is useful for projecting capital requirements necessary to fund inventory.* Inventory in nearly all businesses tends to fluctuate either seasonally or in some other cyclical manner. As a consequence, production cannot be geared to average demand trends.

To predict consumer demand and set production schedules, the general manager will meet at frequent intervals with the sales, finance, and production managers. This management team, utilizing the best available estimates for sales, will decide upon the production schedule. Such meetings are generally lengthy and involve difficult decisions, especially in periods of economic uncertainty. One very important factor considered is the "days' supply" of inventory on hand. The days' supply refers to the number of days the supply is expected to last. Thus, in December 1974, the automobile industry had a 97-day supply of automobiles in inventory. After implementation of price rebate sales promotion programs, the level fell to a 79-day supply of cars in April 1975.

Once the customer demand has been projected and production planned, two important decisions can be made to develop an inventory management policy. *The first is how frequently or when to place orders for materials and the second is how much to order.*

One "reorder-level policy" often implemented is the *two-bin system.* This requires that a replenishment order be placed when the stock on hand falls below a predetermined level, usually when the first bin is empty. Stock is then withdrawn from the second bin until the replenishment order arrives. When the order arrives, both bins are refilled, and the process is repeated.

The two-bin system has some limitations in daily use. It is not a good system for items that deteriorate quickly or for stocking large items due to the space needed. To alleviate some of these limitations, a "reorder-level policy with periodic reviews" may be instituted. This policy requires that at each review period a replenishment order be placed *only* if the stock on hand is *below* or *at* the reorder level. Generally, the same quantity of materials is purchased when each order is placed.

The types of inventory reordering systems described above have primary application to businesses where sales or production tends to vary appreciably. Many firms are able to estimate with good accuracy their needs for materials and then determine the frequency of reordering based on a study of costs and other relevant factors. For example, warehouse size is a primary constraint for many firms. Often when firms use large quantities of materials, they place a "blanket" purchase order. Such an order, for example, might require delivery of a certain quantity of goods each week throughout the year.

Economic Order Quantity

One simple method for determining the optimal order size involves consideration of various costs involved in ordering and storing inventory. The economic order quantity (EOQ) model is based on the following assumptions:

1. The ordering costs per order, designated O, are constant regardless of the size of the order placed. Ordering costs include clerical costs involved in placing the order in addition to costs of receiving the goods. While the clerical costs may vary only slightly depending on the size of the order, the receiving costs do vary with order size. Hence, the assumption that ordering costs are constant is not always valid.
2. The carrying costs per unit, designated C, are constant over a given time. Carrying costs include the costs of maintaining and operating a warehouse, insuring the inventory, and the like plus the *cost of the funds required to finance the inventory*. Sometimes the carrying costs are designated in terms of warehouse space as opposed to units of inventory stored. The cost of funds used to support inventory may be very significant. This is especially true in periods of high interest rates.
3. The quantity of inventory used each period, designated S, is constant. This assumption is unrealistic for many firms. However, some firms have relatively constant production schedules, and in these cases inventory utilization can also be expected to be constant.
4. If the usage of inventory is steady over time, then the average inventory on hand is $Q/2$, where Q is the quantity to be ordered.

The cost of inventory over a period of time, such as a year, can be divided into two parts: carrying and ordering. The carrying cost is simply the average inventory kept on hand, multiplied by the carrying cost per unit or

$$C \times \frac{Q}{2} = \frac{CQ}{2}$$

The ordering cost is the number of orders placed, multiplied by the cost of placing a single order, O. If the quantity of inventory used each period is S and the quantity ordered Q, then the number of orders per period is S/Q. Hence, the ordering cost is

$$O \times \frac{S}{Q} = \frac{SO}{Q}$$

The total inventory cost, TC, is expressed as the sum of the ordering and carrying costs, as follows:

$$TC = \frac{SO}{Q} + \frac{CQ}{2} \qquad (3)$$

Example 3: INVENTORY COSTS

Peter Distributors uses an average of 1,000 bags of cement each year. They have an ordering cost per order of $60, order in quantities of 350 bags, and have carrying costs of $10 per bag per year. Determine their total inventory cost.

SOLUTION

$$TC = \frac{SO}{Q} + \frac{CQ}{2}$$

$$TC = \frac{1,000(\$60)}{350} + \frac{\$10(350)}{2}$$

$$= \$171 + \$1,750$$

$$= \$1,921$$

The total cost is $1,921 per year.

Based on the equation for total cost, it is possible using differential calculus to determine the quantity to order which will result in the minimum total cost. This quantity is designated the *economic order quantity, EOQ*:

$$EOQ = \sqrt{\frac{2SO}{C}} \qquad (4)$$

Example 4: ECONOMIC ORDER QUANTITY

Using the information provided in Example 3, determine the EOQ and the new total inventory cost based on ordering using the economic order quantity.

SOLUTION

First, determine the EOQ:

$$EOQ = \sqrt{\frac{2SO}{C}} = \sqrt{\frac{2 \times 1,000 \times \$60}{\$10}} = \sqrt{12,000} = 110$$

It is most economical to place orders in quantities of 110 bags. (Note that the square root of 12,000 is not precisely 110, but cement must be ordered in full bags.)

Second, determine the total cost based on ordering in 110-bag quantities:

$$TC = \frac{SO}{Q} + \frac{CQ}{2}$$

$$= \frac{1,000(\$60)}{110} + \frac{\$10(110)}{2}$$

$$= \$545 + \$550$$

$$= \$1,095$$

Ordering in 110-bag quantities (the EOQ) instead of 350-bag quantities results in reducing total yearly inventory cost from $1,921 to $1,095.

Example 5: ECONOMIC ORDER QUANTITY

The Contard Company sells an average of 100 cases of paint each month at a cost of $30 each. Inventory carrying costs amount to $1 per case per month and ordering costs are $200 per order.

a. Determine the economic order quantity.
b. Determine how frequently orders should be placed.
c. Determine the total inventory costs per month.

SOLUTION

Part a: The cost of the paint is irrelevant to the problem once the carrying costs are provided. It is assumed that the cost of financing the inventory is included in the carrying cost.

$$EOQ = \sqrt{\frac{2SO}{C}} = \sqrt{\frac{2 \times 100 \times \$200}{\$1}} = 200$$

Contard should order paint in 200-case lots.

Part b: Since the economic order quantity is 200 cases and only 100 are used per month, an order should be placed every other month.

Part c: Using Eq. (1),

$$TC = \frac{SO}{Q} + \frac{CQ}{2} = \frac{100(\$200)}{200} + \frac{\$1(200)}{2} = \$200 \text{ per month}$$

Note that the economic order quantity, 200 units, is used as the value of Q when calculating the total costs.

Inventory management is an important part of financial and production management. Inventory control depends on determination of the quantities required to meet production and/or customer needs, the appropriate time to reorder, and the quantity to reorder. Developing inventory policies which minimize costs aids in maintaining and increasing the profitability of the firm. Further, prudent inventory management is entirely consistent with the primary goal of the firm: maximization of the owners' wealth.

CASH BUDGETING

The cash budget is an important tool for financial management. It shows the expected amount of funds which will be utilized from day to day, week to week, etc. Such projections are essential as a tool for preventing cash shortages or temporary insolvency. The cash budget is used in conjunction with the firm's capital budget in developing a financial plan indicating when funds will be required and their amount. For example, if the firm constructs a new plant, construction costs might take place over an 18-month period. A construction loan could be arranged and timed to meet the costs. Once construction is completed a mortgage might be substituted for the construction loan.

Cash budgets are frequently projected on a yearly basis and updated so that any surplus in cash or needs for cash can be anticipated. If a firm expects to have surplus cash, it will plan to invest it. Similarly, as the firm anticipates needing added funds, it can plan for appropriate financing. The kind of financing used depends on the amount of funds which are needed and the length of time they will be needed.

The fundamental mechanics of a cash budget are very simple. The cash receipts and disbursements are projected for a given period of time. The disbursements are subtracted from the receipts. If the receipts are expected to exceed disbursements, a cash surplus is anticipated. If disbursements are expected to exceed receipts, a cash shortage will result.

While the mechanics of setting up a cash budget are relatively simple, securing the underlying data is a difficult task. *The most important factor in the development of a cash budget is the sales forecast.* An accurate sales forecast is essential since sales reflect directly on receipts and expenditures for labor, materials, and the like. Sales forecasts are best formulated using internal and external sources of information. Sales managers are asked to project sales by product line. These are then weighed by industrial and general economic information. Refer to Appendix D for sources of economic information useful in forecasting.

Once the sales forecast has been developed, cash receipts can be projected. The timing of collections depends on the amount of goods sold for cash versus credit and the average collection period involved. Many disbursements are also projected based on the sales forecast. While some costs, such as taxes, rents, and interest payments, tend to be fixed, other costs such as labor and materials tend to vary directly with output. Usually materials must be ordered in advance of production. Payment for materials will depend on the credit agreement arranged with suppliers. Labor costs also vary with production schedules. The process of developing a cash budget, given information relative to receipts and costs, is demonstrated below.

Example 6: CASH BUDGETS

The following information is given for J. P. Gamble and Co.:

a. Sales are 30% cash and 70% credit.
b. Credit sales are collected as follows: 50% during each of the two months following the sale. Bad debt losses may be ignored.
c. Sales are expected as follows:

January	$100,000	May	$160,000
February	120,000	June	200,000
March	120,000	July	200,000
April	140,000	August	150,000

d. Administrative costs are $6,000 per month.
e. Rent is $3,000 per month.
f. Cost of the goods is 60% of sales. These costs are paid in the month following the sale.
g. Labor costs (salaries) are 20% of sales and are paid in the month they occur.
h. Income tax payments are due in July. They will amount to $20,000.
i. Dividends of $5,000 are payable in June.
j. Sinking fund and interest payments of $22,000 are due in April and June.

Determine the total collections and disbursements for the period April through August.

SOLUTION

First consider the collections. A sales forecast has been provided along with the terms of the sales. The projected receipts may be determined using the tabular form shown below:

	Jan.	Feb.	Mar.	Apr.
Sales	$100,000	$120,000	$120,000	$140,000
Credit sales (70%)	70,000	84,000	84,000	98,000
Collections (1st month)		35,000	42,000	42,000
Collections (2nd month)			35,000	42,000
Cash sales (30%)	30,000	36,000	36,000	42,000
Total receipts				$126,000

	May	June	July	Aug.
Sales	$160,000	$200,000	$200,000	$150,000
Credit sales (70%)	112,000	140,000	140,000	105,000
Collections (1st month)	49,000	56,000	70,000	70,000
Collections (2nd month)	42,000	49,000	56,000	70,000
Cash sales (30%)	48,000	60,000	60,000	45,000
Total receipts	$139,000	$165,000	$186,000	$185,000

Next, consider disbursements.

	Jan.	Feb.	Mar.	Apr.
Sales	$100,000	$120,000	$120,000	$140,000
Cost of goods	60,000	72,000	72,000	84,000
Payment for cost of goods		60,000	72,000	72,000
Administrative costs	6,000	6,000	6,000	6,000
Rent	3,000	3,000	3,000	3,000
Salaries	20,000	24,000	24,000	28,000
Tax				
Dividend				
Sinking fund				22,000
Total disbursements				$131,000

	May	June	July	Aug.
Sales	$160,000	$200,000	$200,000	$150,000
Cost of goods	96,000	120,000	120,000	90,000
Payment for cost of goods	84,000	96,000	120,000	120,000
Administrative costs	6,000	6,000	6,000	6,000
Rent	3,000	3,000	3,000	3,000
Salaries	32,000	40,000	40,000	30,000
Tax			20,000	
Dividend		5,000		
Sinking fund		22,000		
Total disbursements	$125,000	$172,000	$189,000	$159,000

Example 7:   CASH BUDGETS CONTINUED

Gamble wants to maintain a month-end cash balance of $10,000. If they have a cash balance of $10,000 at the end of March, indicate the amount they will have to borrow or the excess reserves they will have for the months of April through August.

SOLUTION

The disbursements are first subtracted from the receipts.

	Apr.	*May*	*June*	*July*	*Aug.*
Receipts	$126,000	$139,000	$165,000	$186,000	$185,000
Disbursements	−131,000	−125,000	−172,000	−189,000	−159,000
Difference	($ 5,000)	$ 14,000	($ 7,000)	($ 3,000)	$ 26,000

Receipts exceed disbursements in two months, while disbursements exceed receipts in the remaining three months.

During April, Gamble will have to borrow $5,000. However, May receipts are expected to exceed disbursements by $14,000 so they will repay the $5,000 and have $9,000 excess. The $9,000 excess will cover the $7,000 outflow in June, leaving a $2,000 excess at the end of June. The $3,000 outflow in July will require Gamble to borrow $1,000. However, in August the $1,000 will be repaid, and at the end of August a surplus of $25,000 will be available.

Using a cash budget such as the one developed in Example 7, the financial manager can plan in advance to borrow funds during periods when disbursements exceed receipts. Similarly, plans can be made for investing funds as they become available.

QUESTIONS
FOR
DISCUSSION

1. Why is inventory management a complex part of the overall management of a firm?
2. Describe what is meant by a balanced inventory.
3. How is production planning related to inventory control?
4. What is meant by cascaded production systems?
5. How is customer demand related to inventory control?
6. Indicate limitations of the two-bin inventory system.
7. Review the assumptions underlying the economic order quantity model, and indicate whether or not they are valid for a particular firm of your choice.
8. Indicate the importance of measuring inventory turnover.
9. Why is cash budgeting used?

10. If a financial manager anticipated an excess of funds or a deficiency in funds, what action would be taken?

11. Why is accurate sales forecasting so important to the process of cash budgeting?

CONCEPTS
TO
REMEMBER
Inventory and cash management are important parts of working capital management. New terms which you should be familiar with are listed below:

Inventory Management
Raw Materials
In-Process Inventories
Finished Goods Inventories
Inventory Turnover Ratio
Re-Order Level
Economic Order Quantity
Sales Forecast
Inventory Shrinkage
Stockout
Price Slashing
Production Planning
"Days' Supply"
Two Bin System
Cash Budget

PROBLEMS
1. Kunkle Company has undertaken an analysis of average monthly sales for the last 48 months. The results of their survey are tabulated below:

Sales Per Month in Units	Frequency of Occurrence
400	2
500	8
550	6
600	16
650	6
700	6
750	4
	48 months

Determine the average monthly demand.

2. Fineman Brothers use an average of 31.25 tons of special steel plate each year. Their ordering cost is $80 per order, and their storage cost is $2.00 per ton per year. Determine the following: the economic order

quantity, the number of orders placed per year, and the total inventory cost.

3. Cyclops, Inc. purchases bolts for installation of cabinets aboard ships. It uses about 1.5 million of a particular size each year. Inventory carry-costs are $6 per square foot per year. A box of 1000 bolts requires a square foot of space, and the boxes may not be stacked. It costs Cyclops about $180 on the average to place an order. Determine the economic order quantity, the number of orders placed per year, and the total inventory cost.

4. A firm expects its annual sales rate to double within the next few months. Current sales are 112,500 units per year, at a sales price of $5 a unit. Ordering costs will remain at $25.00 an order. Inventory carrying costs are expected to increase from their current level of 20% of selling price to 25% of the selling price per year due to additional storage and handling requirements. If the firm wishes to minimize inventory costs, calculate the following based on the increased sales level:
   a. Optimal order size.
   b. The number of orders the firm will place per year.
   c. The dollar investment in the average inventory which the firm will keep on hand, given their cost of goods sold, is 60% of sales price.

5. The following relations for inventory purchase and storage costs have been established by analysis for the Stone Manufacturing Corporation:

   a. Orders must be placed in multiples of 100 units;
   b. Requirements for the year are 20,000 units;
   c. Carrying costs are $4.00 per unit per year;
   d. Purchasing costs per order are $16.00;
   e. Desired safety stock is 300 units (on hand initially);
   f. Two weeks are required for delivery.

   Determine the economic order quantity and total inventory costs.

6. A company has total annual sales (all credit) of $400,000. Cost of goods sold is 80% of sales. Its current assets are $80,000; current liabilities, $60,000; inventories, $30,000; and cash, $10,000. How much average inventory should be carried if management wants the inventory turnover to be 4?

7. Wright Mfg. Co., Inc. has projected sales and expenses as shown below. Develop a cash budget for the firm for the months of May through December.

   a. Sales are 20% cash and 80% credit.
   b. Credit sales are collected as follows: 60% in the month following the sale and 40% in the next month. Bad debt losses may be ignored.
   c. Sales are expected as shown:

January	$ 80,000	July	$180,000
February	80,000	August	120,000
March	90,000	September	90,000
April	110,000	October	70,000
May	140,000	November	60,000
June	160,000	December	60,000

d. Administrative expenses and rent total $5,000 per month.
e. The cost of goods sold is 65% of sales. These costs are paid in the month following the sale.
f. Salaries are 15% of sales and are paid in the month they occur.
g. Debt payments are due in March and September. They amount to $10,000.
h. Taxes are payable March, June, September, and December. They will be $2,000 per quarter.

Profitability Management

chapter 23

The profitability of any firm and its ability to generate cash depend directly on production or output. In every operation, whether it be manufacturing, wholesale distribution, or retail sales, *fixed and variable costs* are involved. *Fixed costs are those which tend to vary little with output.* Thus, rent, taxes, office supplies, telephone service, and management salaries tend to be fixed. Of course, *over long periods all costs are variable.* If, for example, a firm ceases operations and sells its assets, all costs will eventually cease to exist. Variable costs are those which do tend to vary with output. *Variable costs include such things as raw materials, labor, and energy used in production processes.* Some costs vary more with output than others. For example, at the retail level the cost of goods sold tends to vary directly with sales. Although long-term purchase commitments may result in growing inventories if sales slacken, usually management takes prompt action to reduce any excess inventories. Utilization of labor also varies with output, but generally there is a lag between changes in output and changes in labor utilization. The lag results from the fact that as output increases, labor often can pick up some slack. Similarly, if output decreases, management is often reluctant to furlough employees and, hence, may delay layoffs and plant closings as long as possible.

The basic concept of fixed and variable costs leads to the development of valuable management tools: *break-even analysis and operating leverage.*

BREAK-EVEN ANALYSIS

The development of break-even analysis rests on the use of a funda-mental economic relationship:

$$\pi = TR - TC \tag{1}$$

where π = pretax profit (earnings before taxes)
TR = total revenue
TC = total cost

Total revenue is simply the total output sold multiplied by the sales price:

$$TR = P \times Q \tag{2}$$

where P = sale price per unit of output
Q = number of units sold

Total cost is the sum of fixed costs (FC) plus variable costs (VC). For the sake of analysis it is assumed that the "fixed costs", such as rent, taxes, managerial salaries, and the like, are constant at least over short time periods. *Variable costs* represent the variable cost per unit multi-plied by the number of units produced:

$$VC = vc \times Q \tag{3}$$

where vc = variable cost per unit of output
Q = number of units produced

Note that Q has been defined in two different ways. First it was defined as the *number of units sold* and later as the *number of units produced.* To simplify the analysis, it is *assumed that the quantity produced equals the quantity sold.* In general, the output produced will approxi-mately equal the quantity sold. Any differences result in increases and decreases in inventory. If differences between output and sales persist, management either changes output or attempts to change sales. Long-term differences between output and sales cannot persist. When sales exceed output, inventories will be depleted and sales thereby forced downward—if output cannot be increased. When sales are less than output, inventories will pile up. The firm will not be able to pay for the *inputs to production* (labor, materials, etc.) and will have to de-crease production—if it cannot increase sales.

Combining the above equations provides the general equation for pretax profit:

$$\pi = P \times Q - [(vc \times Q) + FC] \tag{4}$$

At the break-even point (BEP) total revenues just equal total costs, and profits are zero. Thus, at the break-even point:

$$TR = TC \tag{5}$$

or

$$P \times Q = (vc \times Q) + FC$$

The break-even point is very important to management since it represents the minimum level of production and sales which will not result in a loss.

Example 1: PROFITABILITY

Samson Industries has fixed costs of $300,000 per year. Their per unit variable cost is $2. If they produce and sell 200,000 units at a sale price of $4 per unit, determine their pretax profit.

SOLUTION

Utilize Eq. (4):

$$
\begin{aligned}
\pi &= P \times Q - [(vc \times Q) + FC] \\
&= \$4 \times 200,000 - [(\$2 \times 200,000) + \$300,000] \\
&= \$800,000 - \$700,000 \\
&= \$100,000
\end{aligned}
$$

Samson's pretax profit is $100,000 at an output of 200,000 units.

Example 2: BREAK-EVEN ANALYSIS

Determine the output which Samson must produce and sell to just break even.

SOLUTION

Use Eq. (5). At the break-even point $TR = TC$:

$$
\begin{aligned}
TR &= TC \\
P \times Q &= (vc \times Q) + FC \\
\$4Q &= \$2Q + \$300,000 \\
\$2Q &= \$300,000 \\
Q &= 150,000 \text{ units}
\end{aligned}
$$

The break-even point (BEP) is 150,000 units.

Example 3: PROFITABILITY MANAGEMENT

Suppose Samson wants to make a profit of $300,000 per year. How much must they produce?

SOLUTION

Use Eq. (4). In this problem the desired profit is known, and the output is to be determined.

$$\pi = P \times Q - [(vc \times Q) = FC]$$
$$\$300,000 = \$4Q - (\$2Q + \$300,000)$$
$$\$300,000 = \$4Q - \$2Q - \$300,000$$
$$\$2Q = \$600,000$$
$$Q = 300,000 \text{ units}$$

Samson must produce 300,000 units in order to have a profit of $300,000.

PROFITABILITY AND PLANT CAPACITY

Profitability and plant capacity are closely interrelated. *Most plants have an optimum operating capacity which leads to maximum profitability.* From a theoretical viewpoint the relationship between profitability and plant size may be expressed in terms of the *marginal contribution of labor and capital equipment. The marginal contribution is the added output which will result from increasing labor or equipment.* For example, it is very difficult for one person to move a large refrigerator. The addition of a second person (called a unit of labor) will probably result in more than doubling the speed by which the refrigerator can be moved. Further increases in the amount of labor involved will hasten the job. However, a point will be reached when *adding more labor will decrease productivity.* Imagine 20 persons trying to carry a refrigerator. They would literally fall over one another. When the addition of another unit of labor results in decreasing output, the situation is termed *decreasing marginal contribution of labor.* The process is depicted in Fig. 1.

The concepts of marginal contribution of labor and capital equipment hold for manufacturing plants, wholesale distributors, retailers, government agencies, and all other operations. *Given a fixed plant size or store size, etc., there is an optimal capacity which will result in maximum profit.* Consider a plant operating one shift five days a week. Maintenance and janitorial functions can be handled during the evening. There are 16 hours available between shift end and restart during which maintenance or repairs can be undertaken *without interfering with production.* If a second shift is added, output may be doubled using the same amount of capital equipment. However, if breakdowns occur, they may result in more costly production delays.

FIGURE 1.

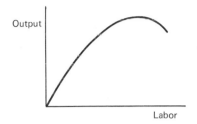

Further, labor is generally paid a shift wage differential for working second shift. Such differentials often amount to 7% of the basic hourly salary. While fixed costs tend to remain constant when utilization of labor is increased, the variable cost per unit tends to increase. Ultimately, such increases will actually result in decreasing profitability. During World War II situations in which productivity decreased due to applications of too much labor were not infrequent. The concepts of marginal contribution and the interrelationship of profitability and plant size are further examined with graphical interpretation later in this chapter.

CONTRIBUTION MARGIN

Another very useful concept relating to profitability management is the contribution margin. *The contribution margin is the difference in sale price and variable cost per unit*:

$$CM = P - vc \tag{6}$$

The contribution margin is the dollar change in pretax profit which results from each change in output. As such, the contribution margin is very important to financial analysis. The contribution margin indicates how much each unit of production contributes toward the firm's profit. The contribution margin can be expressed as an absolute dollar amount using Eq. (6) or as a percentage of sales. The contribution margin relates directly to profits as shown in

$$\Delta\pi = CM \times \Delta Q \tag{7}$$

where $\Delta\pi$ = change in pretax profit
ΔQ = change in output and sales

The symbol Δ is used to indicate a change in amount.

Example 4: CONTRIBUTION MARGIN

Determine the dollar amount of contribution margin for Samson Industries based on the information in Example 1. Then express the contribution margin as a percentage of sales price.

SOLUTION

Use Eq. (6):

$$CM = P - vc$$
$$= \$4 - \$2$$
$$= \$2$$

The pretax profit will increase by \$2 (or losses will be reduced by \$2) with every additional unit produced and sold.

Since the sales price is \$4 and the contribution margin is \$2, the contribution margin is 50% of the sales price.

Example 5: CONTRIBUTION MARGIN

Utilizing the concept of contribution margin, determine how much Samson must increase output and sales in order to increase profits by \$100,000.

SOLUTION

The contribution margin is \$2 per unit. To determine the increase in profits, Eq. (7) is employed:

$$\triangle \pi = CM \times \triangle Q$$
$$\$100,000 = \$2 \times \triangle Q$$
$$\$100,000 = \$2 \times \triangle Q$$
$$\triangle Q = 50,000 \text{ units}$$

A change in output and sales of 50,000 units will increase pretax profits by \$100,000.

The contribution margin may also be utilized to find the break-even point.

$$BEP = \frac{FC}{CM} \qquad (8)$$

Example 6: BREAK-EVEN ANALYSIS USING CONTRIBUTION MARGIN

Refer to the example for Samson and find the break-even point using Eq. (8).

SOLUTION

$$BEP = \frac{FC}{CM}$$
$$= \frac{\$300,000}{\$2}$$
$$= 150,000 \text{ units}$$

The break-even point (BEP) is 150,000 units.

OPERATING LEVERAGE

> *The operating leverage is the percentage change in pretax profits which will accompany a given percentage change in output and sales.* The concept of operating leverage is useful since management is concerned with the effect of changes in output and sales on pretax profit. The *degree of operating leverage* at a specified output is given as follows:

$$DOL = \frac{Q\,(P-vc)}{Q\,(P-vc)-FC} \tag{9}$$

Example 7: DEGREE OF OPERATING LEVERAGE

At an output of 250,000 units, determine the percentage change in pretax profits which will occur for a *one percent change* in output and sales for Samson Industries.

SOLUTION

Use Eq (9):

$$DOL = \frac{Q(P-vc)}{Q(P-vc)-FC}$$

$$= \frac{250,000(\$4-\$2)}{250,000(\$4-\$2)-\$300,000}$$

$$= \frac{\$500,000}{\$500,000-\$300,000}$$

$$= \frac{\$500,000}{\$200,000}$$

$$= 2.5$$

For an increase of 1% in output and sales when output is 250,000 units, pretax profits will increase by 2.5%. A 1% change in output at an output of 250,000 units would be 2,500 units. At an output of 250,000 units the pretax profit would be:

$$\pi = P \times Q - [(vc \times Q) + FC]$$

$$= \$4 \times 250,000 - [(\$2 \times 250,000) + \$300,000]$$

$$= \$1,000,000 - (\$500,000 + 300,000)$$

$$= \$200,000$$

A 2.5% increase in pretax profits would be $5,000. Thus, increasing sales by 1% or 2,500 units to 252,500 units will result in an increase in pretax profits of 2.5% or $5,000 to $205,000. The change in pretax profit can be verified using the contribution margin, which is $2 per unit:

$$\$2 \times 2,500 \text{ units} = \$5,000 \text{ added pretax profit}$$

GRAPHICAL ANALYSIS

To portray the relationships among the revenue and costs, it is useful to present them graphically.

Example 8:

For Samson Industries, graph the total revenue, variable costs, fixed cost, total cost, and break-even point. Show the area of profit and loss.

SOLUTION

Each of the revenue and cost curves is a straight line. To graph a straight line two points are required. The development of each line is explained below.

Total revenue: When output and sales are zero (i.e., $Q=0$), then $TR=0$. That is one point. A second point can be obtained by choosing arbitrarily a value for Q and then finding TR. If $Q=300,000$ units, $TR=$ $1.2 million ($4 \times 300,000 = 1.2 million). That is a second point.

Variable costs: When output and sales are zero (i.e., $Q=0$), then $VC=0$. That is one point. A second point can be obtained by choosing arbitrarily a value for Q and then finding VC. If $Q=300,000$ units, $VC=$ $600,000 ($2 \times 300,000 = $600,000$). That is a second point.

Fixed costs: This is given as $300,000 and is, therefore, a horizontal line at $300,000.

Total costs: This is the sum of fixed and variable costs. Graphically, the sum is obtained by graphing variable costs a second time, starting at the value of fixed costs (in this example, $300,000). See Fig. 2.

The intersection of TR and TC gives the break-even point at a value of $Q = 150,000$ units. Values of Q less than 150,000 units represent losses, while values of Q exceeding 150,000 represent profit. *The actual amount of profit or loss can be determined graphically by taking the vertical distance between the TR and TC curves.*

Figure 2 shows profit increasing with output. The total revenue and total cost curves are straight lines, and thus it would appear that output and profits could be increased indefinitely. Practical experience and

FIGURE 2.

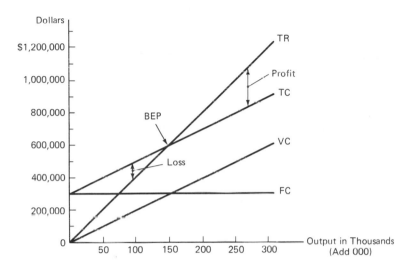

the discussion of marginal contribution of labor and capital equipment prove otherwise. First, with any given plant size, output cannot be increased indefinitely. There is a maximum output—*and generally operation at that maximum output will not result in maximum profits.* Second, unit variable costs tend to increase with expansion of output. Thus, the variable cost (and total cost) curves tend to slope upward at an *increasing rate.*

While the total cost curve slopes upward at an increasing rate, the total revenue curve usually does not. In fact, the total revenue curve generally slopes upward at a *decreasing rate.* The reason behind this change is the fact that as output increases, unit price frequently decreases. The reasons underlying changes in price are rather complex, and in some cases the reverse is true. That is, sometimes as output increases, unit price also increases. However, *it is usual for competitive market pressures to cause prices to decrease as output increases.* The situation is demonstrated graphically in Fig. 3.

When the conditions depicted in Fig. 3 exist, there are two break-even points. It is the work of the firm's management to select an operating level which will result in maximum profit. *Graphically, the maximum profit results when the total cost and total revenue curves are farthest apart.* Thus, profit is greater at output X_1 than at X_0 and decreases as output is further increased. Actually, the second break-even point may be physically unattainable. For example, it might be

FIGURE 3.

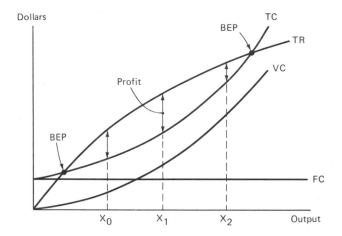

that plant output is limited by production capacity to an amount depicted by X_2. If such were the case, X_1 would still be the optimal output, but a profit would result if production amounted to X_2.

Profitability is very important to the firm and relates directly to the firm's continual existence. Further, profitability and output are primary considerations in the processes of business growth and expansion. These topics are considered in the next chapter.

QUESTIONS
FOR
DISCUSSION

1. Differentiate between fixed and variable costs, giving examples of each. Indicate why some costs may be partially fixed and partially variable (e.g., telephone).
2. Why do changes in labor costs often lag changes in production?
3. What is the purpose of break-even analysis?
4. Over long periods of time, what will happen if output and sales tend to differ? What steps can management take to rectify this situation?
5. What is the primary use of the contribution margin?
6. Explain the importance of the marginal contribution of labor. What is meant by the decreasing marginal contribution of labor?

CONCEPTS
TO
REMEMBER

Profitability is of key importance to management. Several new concepts are introduced. Be sure you are familiar with them.

Fixed Costs
Variable Costs
Break-Even Analysis

Contribution Margin
Break-Even Point
Total Revenue
Total Costs
Marginal Contribution of Labor
Operating Leverage

PROBLEMS

1. The Quinn Co., Inc. has fixed costs of $150,000 per year. It sells the only product it manufactures for $25 per unit. The variable cost per unit is $15.00.
   a. Find the break-even point.
   b. Determine the profit at an output of 18,000 units.
   c. Determine the contribution margin.
   d. Determine the operating leverage at 20,000 units of output.
   e. Graph total revenue, total cost, fixed cost, and variable cost. Show the break-even point.

2. Hilcock Mfg. Co., Inc. has fixed costs of $200,000 per year. Their variable cost per unit is $6 and the selling price is $10. To have a pretax profit of $60,000 per year, how much must they produce and sell?

3. Referring to Problem 2, at $60,000 pretax profit, determine Hilcock's degree of operating leverage.

4. Robertson Mfg. Co. has fixed costs of $800,000 per year. If their variable costs amount to $6 per unit and the sale price of their product is $10 per unit, determine the following:
   a. The break-even point.
   b. The profit at an output of 250,000 units.
   c. The contribution margin.
   d. The degree of operating leverage at an output of 250,000 units.

5. The degree of operating leverage changes for different values of output and sales. Utilize the information provided for Hilcock, and select four values of output. Determine the degree of operating leverage for each. Explain why the degree of operating leverage changes. What significance does this change have to management?

Business

Growth and Contraction

chapter 24

Businesses go through a life cycle including start-up, growth, and maturity or leveling of production. Once a firm reaches a mature or steady-state operating level, management should thoroughly examine the firm's objectives to establish plans for its future. Development of these plans may result in expansion or contraction. The processes of expansion are discussed under the headings of "business growth" and "business combinations." Contraction is discussed as a part of "capital abandonment." If a firm is not profitable, it may become bankrupt. This topic is discussed in the section "operations under conditions of insolvency and bankruptcy."

The clear definition of a firm's objectives is essential to the development of a plan for growth. While the basic goal of the firm has been defined as the maximization of the owner's wealth, this goal must be restated in terms of precise objectives. Management must examine the firm objectively to determine its strengths and weaknesses. When the firm's resources are catalogued, the need to correct deficiencies and add skills, capacity, and processes will become evident.

The process of objectively evaluating a firm's position starts with an examination of the product and marketing plan. The types of products and services which the firm provides must be viewed in terms of future market growth, consumer demand, raw material availability, and the like. Marketing objectives in terms of geographical distribution and

369

method of sales are also important factors in defining the firm's position.

Manufacturing methods must be identified. The firm may produce its product starting with basic raw materials or purchased components and subassemblies and integrate these into the final product. Consideration must also be given to the level of use of facilities (i.e., one shift, two shifts, etc.), inventory policies, warehouse capacity, and delivery schedules.

Management is the key element in the operation of every firm. Objective appraisal of a firm's management is generally obtained in terms of measuring the firm's profitability. Developing and strengthening management, especially to assure the availability of qualified personnel to fill key roles, is essential to future growth.

The objective evaluation of the firm's position is essential to the development of a positive and profitable plan for growth. Frequently, management looks to the possible acquisition of other firms or to expansion as an automatic panacea for improving profits. In some cases, such misadventures result in large outlays of cash and little or no additional profit. Business expansion, if carried out with detailed planning predicated on explicit objectives, can be profitable. However, the keystone to increasing profits is very detailed planning.

BUSINESS GROWTH

Once a firm has objectively appraised its position, it may consider the potential for growth. *Growth may be both internal and external. Internal growth can be considered from three aspects.* The first can be simply termed as "getting one's house in order." Many firms suffer from operational inefficiencies, personnel inadequacies, management weaknesses, and the like. These problem areas must certainly be attacked before the firm seriously considers growth. The second includes improvement of the existing operation by development of more efficient manufacturing or marketing systems, improvement of product quality through engineering improvements, and research and development. The third includes actual expansion of operations whether it be through greater utilization of existing plant capacity, construction of new facilities, purchase of new equipment, expansion of inventories and warehousing capacity, or similar internal growth. Such expansion has been considered under the heading of capital budgeting.

External growth is usually achieved through the processes of *merg-*

ers, acquisitions, or formation of holding companies. Such expansion may be undertaken to achieve vertical or horizontal growth objectives. *Vertical expansion* has to do with the acquisition of supplies of raw material or purchased parts, or distributors and retail outlets. *Vertical expansion involves the integration of two or more stages in the production process,* from raw materials to sales. For example, a firm might purchase a subassembly and use it as a part of its final assembly. Acquiring the facilities to produce the subassemblies would be a form of vertical growth. Similarly, a firm using manufacturers' representatives as its primary sales agents might elect to establish its own sales force. This would provide a greater degree of control over the sales efforts. *Horizontal expansion involves growth in areas closely related to the firm's current product line.* For example, a firm producing men's suits might expand into the production of winter coats. Horizontal expansion would also include the combination of manufacturers or distributors of the same or closely related product lines.

Beyond vertical and horizontal growth, many firms use external expansion as a route for *diversification.* Of course, management could achieve the same vertical or horizontal growth and diversification through internal expansion. *The advantages of external expansion are the savings in time and, most importantly, the acquisition of management talent.* Through external expansion a firm can frequently achieve its goals more efficiently, economically, and expeditiously than through internal growth.

External growth permits a firm to acquire an ongoing operation—perhaps a company which has already achieved a strong market position. Facilities which would be extremely difficult and expensive to duplicate may often be acquired at a depreciated value. However, *in the acquisition of a business the most important consideration is the existing management.* Many successful small businesses are essentially one-man operations. That is, there is one key individual who "runs the show." Frequently such a person may be older and seeking to get his money out of the business. While he may agree to stay on as manager after the takeover, the zeal and incentive he had as owner is likely to wane over time. This is an example of but one danger a firm may face when acquiring a small business. On the other hand, if it is possible to retain the top-quality management of a firm being acquired, great economies can be realized. *It is far less expensive to retain quality management than to train new personnel to take over an operation.* Every firm has peculiarities which can be learned only over time and through experience. If experienced management is available, it can prove to be the single most important asset which can be acquired.

Beyond diversification and growth there are several other reasons for external growth. Attracting capable management, as already discussed, is a key factor. Operating economies may also be achieved through elimination of duplicate manufacturing, purchasing, and other operations. Acquisition of a firm may include trademarks and brand names which elicit public confidence. Development of a reputation takes years—but may be purchased via external expansion. Some acquisitions are fostered by the tax laws pertaining to the tax loss carry backs and carry forwards. If a firm has a sizable tax loss, it may be attractive as a possible acquisition to another firm which can take advantage of the loss to offset some of its income.

BUSINESS COMBINATIONS

A merger or acquisition takes place when one firm acquires another firm. In the process, the latter firm goes out of existence and becomes an integral part of the purchasing firm. A merger may come about through one of two processes. A firm may purchase the stock *or* purchase the assets of the other business. *A consolidation differs from a merger in that it is a combination of two or more firms, all of which lose their identity and become a new corporation.* All of the original firms cease to exist. Shares of stock in the old firms are exchanged for shares in the new company. Generally, when companies are about the same size, they combine as a consolidation. When one firm is much larger than another, the smaller firm is merged into the larger.

Rather than acquiring another company through the merger process, a large firm may purchase a portion of the smaller firm's stock. Through the purchase of voting stock, the larger firm may elect members to the smaller firm's board of directors. If the larger firm is able to elect its representatives to the board, it will control the smaller firm. In this case the larger firm is called *a holding company.* The process of becoming a holding company provides a simple and flexible method to take over control of another firm. A firm may simply purchase the stock of the company it wants to control. The purchase may be rapid or gradual, open or secret, or experimental. There is no need for bargaining or negotiation or shareholder approval—all of which are required to achieve a merger or consolidation.

For a merger or consolidation to become effective, it is generally necessary for the majority of the shareholders of all the firms involved to vote for it. Shareholders voting against the combination can demand payment for their shares. If agreement as to the price cannot be reached through negotiation, the shareholder may take the case to court and request a cash settlement. The court decides the "fair market price" which the shareholder must be paid. Therefore, in setting up a combination it is important to make an offer which will not only attract a majority of shareholders but minimize the number of dissenters as well.

Assuming the shareholders approve the combination, one other obstacle can arise. The Department of Justice, Antitrust Division, may bring suit to block the combination if it feels that the combination will result in a "substantial lessening of competition." Such suits may drag on for years and, therefore, effectively preclude the combination.

CAPITAL ABANDONMENT

The topic of capital abandonment includes two parts. The first deals with the dissolution of a firm (i.e., going out of business). The second part pertains to abandonment of portions of the firm.

Dissolution of a Firm

During the life of a firm it may become evident that the firm can no longer make sufficient profits to warrant remaining as a going concern. An ongoing corporation may be dissolved by action of all the shareholders or by a corporate action taken by the board of directors and approved by a two-thirds majority of the shareholders. If the required majority of shareholders approves, then the officers take the legal action to dissolve the firm.

When dissolution occurs, the debts are paid first and any remaining funds are distributed to the shareholders (called a *liquidating dividend*). If there are not sufficient funds to pay the debts, then a receiver is appointed by the court. The court may take whatever actions are necessary to preserve the corporate assets in order to protect the creditors and shareholders. The receiver acts to collect and sell the corporate assets at which time the bills are paid, and if any funds remain, they are distributed to shareholders.

Abandonment of Projects

Management's basic function is to maintain a continuing surveillance of the asset package that represents the stockholders' invested capital so as to maximize the value of the firm. The decision to abandon a project is one which involves the use of the same analytical concepts employed in rationing of new funds—the capital budgeting decision. However, the number of projects abandoned, and the related volume of assets disposed of, is likely to be much smaller than new capital outlays, since ongoing projects or property already owned are generally more valuable in terms of actual or potential earning power than in market or salvage value. This is due to a combination of factors, including the unique properties of equipment acquired specifically for the company's purposes, the accumulated knowledge relative to risk and performance of a program already under way, and the relatively substantial costs of selling. Unfortunately, as a result of rationalization by many corporate managers, projects are sometimes maintained until technical advances or changes in demand destroy their economic value for anything but scrap.

Abandonment not only includes the decision to discontinue financing manpower and material costs of a project, but also the disposition of that capital which can not be profitably applied in another part of the firm's operation. A distinction is made between the problem of disposing of assets and that of replacement. The latter implies a decision to continue the activity, whereas disposal of an asset normally means discontinuance of the project. The question of handling product warranties and guarantees also must be addressed. If a product line is discontinued, the firm must honor its warranties and guarantees. This may require maintenance of a large inventory of parts for several years.

A plan for the discontinuance of previously started projects is an essential part of a complete capital budgeting program. Although most capital budgeting procedures concentrate on directing the flow of funds to new projects which promise highest yields, the systematic disposal of those past investments that have a lower relative yield must also be considered. Frequently, the disposal part of the capital budgeting decision is neglected as management becomes absorbed in operating existing projects. In addition, *there is a strong reluctance to recognize and realize capital losses through project abandonment due to the possible stigma of a poor decision made in the past.* However, failure to promptly discontinue a project whose true economic earnings are substandard or result in losses condones and preserves a misallocation of the stockholders' investment funds. It keeps money tied up unprofitably and prevents its reinvestment in projects which can provide superior profit return.

It is also an indication that the financial planning homework of an organization has been well prepared if the company can maintain the option of responding to unexpected cash needs. This may be accomplished through the modification of existing plans, thereby avoiding a deficit by substituting an unexpected cash requirement for a planned expenditure in the current budget. The ability to avoid a cash flow deficit by manipulating various categories of expenditures is a widely and continuously used procedure which adds a measure of mobility to the capital budgeting process.

One additional planning factor must be considered by the financial manager. The decision to abandon projects must also be based on the trend of earnings at the time of the decision. If a significant, or possibly even a continual steady increase in earnings is expected, the relatively lower risk of an ongoing project may justify its continuance.

The use of discounted cash flow selection techniques to determine which projects to continue and which to abandon is equally as useful as in the selection of new projects. Each project, whether ongoing or new, must be measured against its relative yield to the corporation. The differences which must be considered in order to equate new and ongoing projects include the following:

1. The business risk of an ongoing project resulting from past experiences is known, whereas the risk associated with a new project may be difficult to predict.
2. Additional costs may be incurred if a project is abandoned. Other costs may have to be continued even after a project is terminated.
3. The fact that an initial investment has already been made and is returnable only as a sale or salvage value must be considered from the point of view of alternative uses within the firm. The writing off of assets which are no longer profitable and cannot be otherwise used *should not* be weighed in the investment decision. The sale or salvage value *should*, of course, be considered but must be reduced by the costs of selling or termination, which may be considerable.

Once these factors have been determined and applied to ongoing projects, they may then be grouped directly with new projects in the capital rationing process. Those new projects which have yields below the required return will not be undertaken. Those ongoing projects which have yields below the cutoff should be abandoned. Utilization of net present value analysis has been instrumental in inducing alert management to the advisability of divesting themselves of assets or operations that could bring a higher value through sale or abandonment than by their continued operation or possession.

Projects should be abandoned if their yields are lower than the current cutoff rate required for new investments. Conversely, a project should be continued (and possibly increased in scope) if the yield on the current market value of the project's assets is high enough that the company would want to acquire it if it did not already own it. By considering ongoing projects together with new ones, existing projects will be required to compete for all new uses of the company's capital. Funds available for financing projects being evaluated come from the following sources:

debt
equity (common and preferred stock)
retained earnings
sale value of ongoing projects which may be terminated

More capital funds can generally be obtained for high-yield new investments by means of abandonment of existing projects having lower prospective yields.

OPERATIONS UNDER CONDITIONS OF INSOLVENCY AND BANKRUPTCY

Broadly speaking, there are two types of business failure. *Insolvency is a situation wherein a firm cannot pay its outstanding obligations.* It may be that the firm's assets exceed the liabilities but at the same time the firm is experiencing a liquidity crisis. *Bankruptcy occurs when a firm's liabilities exceed its assets.*

Business failures can be handled either through court action or voluntary settlement. There are three possible legal remedies: *reorganization, liquidation, and receivership or trusteeship.* Voluntary settlements may come about if amicable relations exist among the parties.

If a court action is sought, the court appoints a receiver to manage the insolvent firm. The receiver has several obligations, which include the following:

1. Manage the firm and keep it in operation.
2. Control creditors' claims and payment of these claims.
3. Control leases and contracts.
4. Raise funds by selling receiver's certificates.
5. Report to the court as to the progress made.

Within the scope of these broad powers, three outcomes are possible:

1. It may be possible using sound management to help the firm recover from its financial problems and reestablish it on a sound basis without financial reorganization.

2. The firm may have to be reorganized. If a reorganization plan is established, it must be approved by the court. If the reorganization plan proves to be viable, then the firm will continue as an ongoing concern.

3. The court, upon detailed review of the situation, may conclude that the firm should be liquidated. It then supervises the liquidation and payment of creditors.

1. Describe the life cycle of a business.
2. Why is the objective evaluation of a firm's position essential to the development of a plan for growth?
3. Explain horizontal and vertical growth.
4. Indicate reasons for product line diversification.
5. Contrast mergers and consolidations.
6. Describe ways in which a larger firm may take control of a smaller firm.
7. Why is capital abandonment frequently included as a part of the capital budgeting process?
8. Describe the differences between evaluating ongoing projects versus newly proposed projects.
9. Differentiate insolvency and bankruptcy.

Several new concepts are included in this chapter. Be sure you are familiar with them.

Capital Abandonment
Insolvency
Bankruptcy
Consolidation
Dissolution of a Firm
Reorganization
Internal Growth
External Growth
Merger
Acquisition
Liquidation
Voluntary Settlement

Glossary of Terms*

Accelerated depreciation—Depreciation methods used to allocate the cost of a depreciable asset over its life more rapidly than the allocation provided by straight-line depreciation. There are three generally used methods of accelerated depreciation: declining-balance, sum-of-the years'-digits, and units of production.

Accumulated depreciation—The sum of all depreciation taken for an asset to date.

Accumulated profits tax—A federal tax on accumulated corporate profits in excess of $150,000 which are held by the corporation and not distributed as dividends or needed by the firm for planned expansion or the like.

Adjusted balance system—A method of computing charge account interest based on the outstanding balance at the end of the billing period.

Adjusted gross income—Sum of the various types of income such as salaries, wages, interest, and the like which are subject to federal taxation for individuals (as opposed to corporations).

Amortization—A systematic recognition of the expense of purchasing an intangible asset in a historical framework so as to match the expense with revenues while the asset is being used. It is basically the same as depreciation of a tangible asset. Also, the repayment of debt principal according to a schedule, known as an amortization schedule.

Annuity—A series of equal payments made at given periods, usually at the end of the fiscal or calendar year.

*For further definitions in the field of finance, refer to Glenn G. Munn's *Encyclopedia of Banking and Finance,* Bankers Publishing Company, Boston, 1973.

Average daily balance system—A method of computing charge account interest based on the average balance owed for the period covering the time of purchase to the date of payment.

Balance sheet—A financial statement showing the historical value of firm's assets, liabilities, and owners' equity (or net worth) at a point in time, usually the end of the year.

Balloon repayment schedule—A schedule for loan repayment whereby most of the principal is scheduled for repayment at the end of the loan. The large final payment is called the balloon. Frequently, such loans are renewable, with the balance of the old loan becoming the amount of the new loan.

Banker's acceptance—A guarantee by a bank to pay a customer's bill. Banker's acceptances are used primarily in international trade. The bank, in effect, guarantees payment and substitutes its high credit standing for that of its customer. Naturally, the customer must pay the bank once the bank pays the customer's bill.

Best-effort selling—A method of selling new securities in which the investment banker does his best to sell the issue but makes no guarantee to sell all of the securities involved.

Bond—A long-term debt instrument usually sold in $1,000 denominations. Interest is generally paid twice yearly.

Book value of an asset—The total cost of the asset less accumulated depreciation.

Book value (of common stock)—The owner's equity, less the par value of any outstanding preferred stock, divided by the number of shares of common stock outstanding.

Break-even analysis—A procedure used to determine the output necessary to just cover all variable and fixed costs so that the firm does not have either a profit or loss.

Break-even point—The level of output which is just sufficient to cover all costs but does not result in a profit or a loss.

Business risk—All of the hazards inherent in the operation of a business such as changes in consumer preferences, labor unrest, and the like.

Call—The exercise of the right to redeem a callable bond or preferred stock by a corporation.

Call premium—The amount in excess of the maturity or par value of a security (such as a bond or preferred stock) which a company must pay if it calls the security.

Capital abandonment—The process of either dissolving a firm (going out of business) or abandoning a portion of a firm such as a product line and its accompanying production facilities.

Capital budgeting—The part of financial management which deals with establishing goals and criteria for the investment of funds in land, facilities, buildings, and other capital equipment.

Capital formation—The economic process of allocating savings to purchase capital goods (investment).

Capital gain—The profit which takes place when a firm buys and subsequently sells (at a greater price) assets or securities which are not ordinarily purchased and sold in the business of the firm.

Capitalism—An economic system wherein most of the product and distribution systems are privately owned and operated for profit.

Capital markets—Markets where intermediate- and long-term securities such as stocks and bonds are exchanged.

Capital rationing—The process of rationing funds for capital expenditures whereby proposed investment projects are ranked by profitability and the most profitable implemented within the constraint of the total amount of funds available.

Cascaded production system—A production system in which the product passes from the raw material stage to the finished product through a series of production departments or plants with major in-process inventories maintained between various production operations.

Cash budgeting—The process of projecting cash inflows and outflows over a period of time (usually a year) on a week-to-week or month-to-month basis so as to be able to accurately project needs for cash or excesses in cash balances.

Cash flow—A term used to describe the flow of a firm's receipts and expenditures.

Cashier's check—A bank's own check, and therefore a direct obligation of the bank, as opposed to someone's personal check, which is *not* a direct obligation of the bank.

Certainty equivalent (in capital budgeting)—A procedure used to compensate for the risk associated with proposed capital investments. Based on management experience, a set of certainty-equivalent coefficients is developed and multiplied by the expected cash inflows for the projects being evaluated. The higher the risk of the project's expected return, the lower the certainty-equivalent coefficient.

Certificate of deposit—A receipt for a deposit made in a bank which is generally negotiable and interest bearing. Such certificates represent a form of short-term debt and are commonly used by larger firms to invest idle funds.

Certified check—A check certified by a bank as being genuine; the bank also certifies that there are ample funds to cover the check (the funds have been set aside so that the check cannot be refused for insufficient funds).

Claim to wealth—A paper certificate representing wealth such as a bank book, stock certificate, or bond.

Collect interest loan—A loan on which interest is paid when the loan is repaid. If the loan is an installment type, then interest is paid on the outstanding balance at the time of each installment.

Commercial banking system—The banking system which includes nationally chartered banks, state-chartered banks and trust companies, trust companies, and private and industrial banks.

Commercial paper—Short-term unsecured promissory notes sold by large corporations to raise money.

Compensating balance—A demand deposit (checking account) balance required to be maintained in a bank by a customer who borrows from the bank. A compensating balance has the effect of raising the effective interest rate on the loan. Compensating balances frequently amount to 15% to 20% of the outstanding loan balance.

Concentration banking—A system used to speed collection of customer remittances whereby a firm establishes strategically located collection centers and directs customers to mail remittances to a center. An employee of the firm deposits the remittances at a local bank, which transfers the funds frequently to the firm's main bank.

Consolidation—The combination of two or more firms, all of which lose their identity to form a new corporation.

Constant payment mortgage—A mortgage established whereby the total periodic (usually monthly) payments, which consist of interest and principal, are constant over the life of the mortgage.

Contribution margin—The dollar change in pretax income which results from a change in each unit of output. The contribution margin equals the selling price per unit of the product, less the variable cost of producing the product.

Convertible securities—Preferred stocks and bonds which are convertible to common stock at a stated exchange ratio.

Cost of capital—The weighted average of a firm's costs of common stock, preferred stock, debt, and retained earnings.

Current assets—Cash, marketable securities, and other assets such as inventory and accounts receivable which are generally converted into cash within a period of a year or less.

Current yield—The bond yield obtained by dividing the annual dollar interest payment by the current market price of the bond.

Days' supply (of inventory)—The number of days the current inventory is expected to last if customer demand continues at its existing level.

Debenture—A bond secured by the general property of a firm but not by any property in particular.

Debt coverage ratios—Financial ratios used to measure the firm's ability to pay interest on outstanding debt and repay principal in a timely manner.

Demand deposits—Otherwise known as checking account deposits; they are those accounts which may be withdrawn by the depositor immediately and without notice of intention to withdraw.

Depreciable value—The difference between the total cost of an asset and its estimated salvage value.

Depreciation—A systematic recognition of the expense of purchasing an asset in a historical framework so as to match the expense with revenues while the asset is being used.

Direct placement—A method of selling new securities in which the issuer sells directly to a purchaser, usually a large insurance company.

Direct reduction mortgage—A mortgage established whereby the principal payment is equal each period. The interest payment is calculated on the outstanding principal balance and thus decreases with each payment.

Discounted cash flow (methods of capital budgeting)—Capital budgeting procedures which evaluate the present value of expected cash inflows and outflows to determine if a proposed investment will yield a required return. There are two such procedures: internal rate of return and present value.

Discount rate adjustment (in capital budgeting)—A procedure used to compensate for the risk associated with proposed capital investments. The procedure involves using a discount rate for evaluation of risky projects which exceed the firm's cost of capital. The greater the risk of the project, the higher the discount rate used.

Dividends, cash—Cash payments made to a firm's shareholders, usually at regular intervals such as four times a year.

Dividends, stock—Stock distributed to a firm's shareholders on a percentage basis so that each shareholder retains his proportionate ownership of the firm.

Earnings per share—The total after-tax profits of a firm (less preferred stock dividends, if any) divided by the number of shares of common stock outstanding.

EBIT—Abbreviation for *earnings before interest and taxes.*

Economic order quantity—The most economical size of an order, based on ordering costs, financing and other carrying costs, and rate of utilization of inventory.

EPS—Abbreviation for *earnings per share.*

EPS-EBIT analysis—A financial analytical technique used to determine the change in earnings per share (EPS) as earnings before interest and taxes (EBIT) change for a variety of financing plans. Using this analytical tool, management can project the optimum financing plan based on expected EBIT.

Equity—the owner's claim to the assets of the firm. Equity equals the value of the firm's assets, less its liabilities.

Exercise price—The price which the holder of an option such as a warrant or right must pay to purchase one share of common stock.

Explicit expense—Expenses which require payment such as labor, materials, electricity, fuels, etc.

Factoring—A method of financing accounts receivable wherein a firm sells its receivables to a factor which is a collection agency. The factor subsequently collects the receivables.

Federal funds—Funds which banks have on deposit with the FED.

Federal Reserve Banking System (FED)—The central banking system of the United States. Its primary functions include handling the banking transactions for the U.S. government, issuing currency, regulating the banking system, and regulating the money supply.

Financial analysis—The process of analyzing a firm's financial statements to ascertain the firm's financial condition.

Financial intermediary—A financial organization, such as a bank, pension fund, or the like, which accumulates savings and makes them available to individuals, businesses, and governments which require them.

Financial leverage—The use of debt as opposed to equity in order to increase the return on equity. Use of debt in this manner assumes that the cost of debt is less than the cost of equity and that the firm can maintain a rate of return greater than the interest cost of the debt.

Financial ratios—Ratios developed from a firm's financial statements used to analyze the condition of a firm over time and in comparison to other firms.

Financial risk—The risk of defaulting on debts with subsequent insolvency. Financial risk increases as a firm borrows greater sums of money.

Fixed assets—Land, machinery, plant and equipment, buildings, and natural resources used in the operation of a business.

Fixed costs—Those costs which vary little with output such as taxes, rent, and the like.

Float—The period of time during which checks are in transit and in the process of being collected and converted to cash.

Flotation costs—The costs of issuing new securities such as stock or bonds.

Goodwill—The value of a firm's intangible assets which have been purchased. The value of the goodwill equals the difference between the price paid for a going concern and the appraised value of its tangible assets.

Holding company—A parent company which owns all or the major portion of the stock in other corporations.

Horizontal growth or expansion—The process of expanding into product lines which are generally closely related to the firm's product line.

Hurdle rate (capital budgeting)—The minimum rate of return which a project must be expected to yield in order to be acceptable as an investment. The hurdle rate is usually set as the firm's cost of capital plus an additional return required to compensate for risk, if any is involved with the investment.

Implicit expenses—Expenses which do not require expenditure of cash, such as depreciation and amortization.

Indenture—The formal agreement between a corporation or government agency issuing a bond and the bondholder. The requirements of the indenture are monitored and enforced by the bond trustee.

Inflation—An economic condition during which price increases are not accompanied by increases in the production of goods and services. The net result is a decrease in the purchasing power of money.

Insolvency—A condition in which a firm is unable to pay its debts in a timely manner, even though its assets may exceed its liabilities.

Insolvency in bankruptcy—A condition which exists when a firm's liabilities exceed its assets.

Intermediate-term loan—A loan having duration of one to five years.

Internal rate of return (capital budgeting)—The rate of return which exactly equates the present value of the after-tax inflows with the present value of the after-tax cash outflows. Also, a method of capital budgeting used to determine the rate of return on a project.

Inventory turnover—The rate at which inventory is sold (or discarded if obsolete, etc.) and replaced by new inventory.

Investment—In the economic sense, the utilization of savings to purchase capital equipment. The term investment is also applied to the process of purchasing stocks, bonds, and other securities.

Investment banker—Financial intermediaries which act as middlemen between the issuers of securities (business, government, etc.) and the individuals and institutions which purchase the securities.

Investment tax credit—A tax credit allowed by the federal government when certain types of assets used in business are purchased.

Keogh Plan—A tax-deferred pension plan available to persons who are self-employed.

Lease payment—Payment made by the lessee to the lessor for the use of the lessor's equipment or facilities.

Leasing—A process whereby the user (lessee) enters into a long-term contract with the owner (lessor) for the use of particular equipment or facilities belonging to the lessor.

Leverage ratios—Financial ratios used to measure operating and financial leverage.

Line of credit—An informal (and not legally enforceable) agreement between a bank and a customer providing that the bank will lend to the customer up to a stated amount of money for a given period of time.

Liquidating value (of common stock)—The sale price of a firm's assets, less creditors' claims and the par value of preferred stock, all divided by the number of shares of common stock outstanding.

Liquidity—A term referring to a firm's cash position and its ability to meet its obligations in a timely manner.

Liquidity ratios—Financial ratios used to measure a firm's liquidity, i.e., its ability to pay its bills.

Lockbox system—A system used to speed collection of customer remittances whereby a firm establishes strategically located collection centers and directs customers to mail remittances to a center. The remittances are deposited in a local bank by a bank employee and then transferred to the firm's main bank.

Margin—In the purchase of securities, buying on margin means buying on credit.

Marginal contribution (of labor)—The amount of additional output which will result from adding one more unit of labor (employee).

Merger—The process whereby one firm acquires another firm and the latter firm goes out of existence and becomes an integral part of the purchasing firm.

Money markets—Markets where short-term funds such as commercial paper are traded.

Mortgage—Pledge of property as security for a loan.

Net cash flow—The difference between the firm's cash inflows and out-flows over a period of time.

Open market operations—The process of buying and selling U.S. Government Securities by the FED. The result of open market operations is to increase or decrease the money supply and interest rates.

Operating leverage—The percentage change in pretax profits which will accompany a one percent change in output and sales, at a specified level of output and sales.

Ordinary income—Income derived from the normal operations of a firm. Income derived from the sale of the firm's assets is not included as a part of ordinary income.

Paid-in capital—A balance sheet owners' equity account, equaling the number of shares of common stock outstanding, multiplied by the dollar amount *in excess of the par value* at which the shares were originally sold.

Payback (method of capital budgeting)—A capital budgeting procedure which provides for the determination of the number of years required for a proposed investment to recover its cost. If the payback period is sufficiently short, then the investment is accepted.

Preemptive right—The right of a shareholder to retain his proportionate ownership in a firm when additional shares of stock are being issued.

Preferred stock—Corporate stock which has preference over common stock in the event of liquidation.

Present value—The value of funds to be received in the future. The value is determined by discounting amounts to be received by an appropriate discount rate.

Present value (method of capital budgeting)—A procedure for evaluating proposed investment projects, based on discounting the expected cash inflows to their present value, then summing the present value of the in-flows and comparing the sum with the present value of the outflows required to purchase the project.

Prime interest rate—The rate of interest charged by banks to their best (prime) customers.

Profitability index (capital budgeting)—The ratio of the after-tax present value of cash inflows to outflows for a proposed investment project. The profitability index provides a measure of the profitability of investments on a per dollar basis of their after-tax cost.

Profitability ratios—Financial ratios used to measure the profitability of a firm. They usually measure profit in terms of sales or assets.

Proxy statement—A statement given by a shareholder designating another person (the proxy) to vote for him in a corporate meeting.

Reorder level policy (of inventory)—A policy for reordering inventory based on replenishing inventory when it falls to a predetermined level.

Retained earnings—That portion of the after-tax profits retained by the firm. Retained earnings are normally invested in assets and should not be thought of in terms of cash on hand.

Revolving credit—A formal agreement between a bank and a customer providing that the bank will lend the customer up to a stated amount of money for a given period of time.

Right—A short-term option to purchase a given number of shares of common stock at a stated price.

Rolling over debt—The process of securing new debt to repay existing debt as it matures. In essence, substituting one debt for another.

Salvage value—The amount which is estimated to be realizable from the sale of an asset when it is no longer useful to the firm and is retired from service.

Savings—In the economic sense, the act of giving up consumption of goods or services at a point in time so that they may be consumed by someone else or at a later date. Generally, households save, while government and businesses secure the use of saved funds for investment.

Seasonal dating—A method of billing customers for goods which are sold on a seasonal basis. The goods are shipped as they are manufactured, but the bills are not due for payment until the time of year that the goods will be sold.

Short-term debt—A debt which matures in a period of one year or less.

Sinking fund—A fund established to retire a security (generally a bond). Usually payments are made to the fund each year for a given period so that at the end of the period the needed money will be available to retire the issue.

Solvency—The ability of a firm to pay its bills as they become due. When a firm is unable to meet its obligations it is said to be insolvent.

Stated yield—The bond yield determined by dividing the yearly dollar interest payment by the price at which the bond was originally sold (usually $1,000).

Stock dividend—A dividend paid in shares of stock rather than in cash.

Stockout (of inventory)—A situation wherein a firm is out of stock and cannot replenish it rapidly enough to meet customer demand. The result generally is the loss of sales and customer goodwill.

Stock split—A procedure whereby the number of outstanding shares of a firm's stock is increased. For example, a three-for-one split would provide for each shareholder having three shares for each share originally owned.

Subchapter S Corporation—A corporation having ten or fewer share-holders wherein the shareholders declare any corporate profit as a part of their personal income.

Syndicate—Group of investment bankers (brokerage houses) which work together to sell a new security.

Taxable income—The portion of total income subject to federal tax. Taxable income equals adjusted gross income less deductions.

Tender offer—An offer by a firm to purchase the stock of another firm from the shareholders of the latter firm.

Trade credit—The extension of credit by a seller to a purchaser for a period of time. The extension of credit comes about by not requiring payment at the time goods or services are purchased.

Transaction loan—A short-term loan used to finance a particular transaction such as a purchase.

Treasury Bills—U.S. government obligations which are sold weekly and mature in three to six months. They do not pay interest but rather are sold at a price lower than their redemption price, i.e., sold at a discount.

Trust companies—Organizations established primarily to accept and carry out trusts. They act as trustees for wills, administer estates, register bonds and stocks, and may also engage in banking business.

Underwriting—The process of issuing a new security by investment bankers wherein the investment bankers are obligated to purchase any securities which are not sold to investors. This, in effect, provides for price stability of the issue during its sale and guarantees the sale of the securities.

Unit of account—The unit used to measure prices. In the United States it is the dollar, in England the pound sterling, etc.

Variable costs—Those costs which tend to vary directly with output such as labor and materials.

Vertical growth or expansion—The process whereby a firm acquires facilities to supply its raw materials or expands its control of selling by acquiring wholesale and/or retail distribution facilities.

Warrant—A long-term option to purchase a given number of shares of common stock at a stated price.

Working capital—The difference between current assets and current liabilities.

Yield to maturity—The bond yield determined by discounting the future interest payments and bond maturity value to the present and comparing it with the cost of the bond.

Tables

appendix A

TABLE I

Compound Interest of $1

Year	1%	2%	3%	4%	5%	6%	7%	8%	9%	10%	11%	12%	13%
1	1.0100	1.0200	1.0300	1.0400	1.0500	1.0600	1.0700	1.0800	1.0900	1.1000	1.1100	1.1200	1.1300
2	1.0201	1.0404	1.0609	1.0816	1.1025	1.1236	1.1449	1.1664	1.1881	1.2100	1.2321	1.2544	1.2769
3	1.0303	1.0612	1.0927	1.1249	1.1576	1.1910	1.2250	1.2597	1.2950	1.3310	1.3676	1.4049	1.4429
4	1.0406	1.0824	1.1255	1.1699	1.2155	1.2625	1.3108	1.3605	1.4116	1.4641	1.5181	1.5735	1.6305
5	1.0510	1.1041	1.1593	1.2167	1.2763	1.3382	1.4026	1.4693	1.5386	1.6105	1.6851	1.7623	1.8424
6	1.0615	1.1262	1.1941	1.2653	1.3401	1.4185	1.5007	1.5869	1.6771	1.7716	1.8704	1.9738	2.0820
7	1.0721	1.1487	1.2299	1.3159	1.4071	1.5036	1.6058	1.7138	1.8280	1.9487	2.0762	2.2107	2.3526
8	1.0829	1.1717	1.2668	1.3686	1.4775	1.5938	1.7182	1.8509	1.9926	2.1436	2.3045	2.4760	2.6584
9	1.0937	1.1951	1.3048	1.4233	1.5513	1.6895	1.8385	1.9990	2.1719	2.3579	2.5580	2.7731	3.0040
10	1.1046	1.2190	1.3439	1.4802	1.6289	1.7908	1.9671	2.1589	2.3674	2.5937	2.8394	3.1059	3.3946
11	1.1157	1.2434	1.3842	1.5395	1.7103	1.8983	2.1049	2.3316	2.5804	2.8531	3.1518	3.4786	3.8359
12	1.1268	1.2682	1.4258	1.6010	1.7959	2.0122	2.2522	2.5182	2.8127	3.1384	3.4984	3.8960	4.3345
13	1.1381	1.2936	1.4685	1.6651	1.8856	2.1329	2.4098	2.7196	3.0658	3.4523	3.8833	4.3635	4.8980
14	1.1495	1.3195	1.5126	1.7317	1.9799	2.2609	2.5785	2.9372	3.3417	3.7975	4.3104	4.8871	5.5348
15	1.1610	1.3459	1.5580	1.8009	2.0789	2.3966	2.7590	3.1722	3.6425	4.1772	4.7846	5.4736	6.2543
16	1.1726	1.3728	1.6047	1.8730	2.1829	2.5403	2.9522	3.4259	3.9703	4.5950	5.3109	6.1304	7.0673
17	1.1843	1.4002	1.6528	1.9479	2.2920	2.6928	3.1588	3.7000	4.3276	5.0545	5.8951	6.8661	7.9861
18	1.1961	1.4282	1.7024	2.0258	2.4066	2.8543	3.3799	3.9960	4.7171	5.5599	6.5435	7.6900	9.0243
19	1.2081	1.4568	1.7535	2.1068	2.5269	3.0256	3.6165	4.3157	5.1417	6.1159	7.2633	8.6128	10.1974
20	1.2202	1.4859	1.8061	2.1911	2.6533	3.2071	3.8697	4.6609	5.6044	6.7275	8.0623	9.6463	11.5231
21	1.2324	1.5157	1.8603	2.2788	2.7860	3.3996	4.1406	5.0338	6.1088	7.4002	8.9491	10.8039	13.0211
22	1.2447	1.5460	1.9161	2.3699	2.9253	3.6035	4.4304	5.4365	6.6586	8.1403	9.9336	12.1003	14.7139
23	1.2572	1.5769	1.9736	2.4647	3.0715	3.8197	4.7405	5.8714	7.2579	8.9543	11.0262	13.5524	16.6267
24	1.2697	1.6084	2.0328	2.5633	3.2251	4.0489	5.0724	6.3412	7.9111	9.8497	12.2391	15.1787	18.7881
25	1.2824	1.6406	2.0938	2.665	3.3864	4.2919	5.4274	6.8485	8.6231	10.8347	13.5854	17.0001	21.2306
26	1.2953	1.6734	2.1566	2.7725	3.5557	4.5494	5.8073	7.3963	9.3991	11.9181	15.0798	19.0401	23.9906
27	1.3082	1.7069	2.2213	2.8834	3.7335	4.8223	6.2139	7.9880	10.2451	13.1100	16.7386	21.3249	27.1094
28	1.3213	1.7410	2.2879	2.9987	3.9201	5.1117	6.6488	8.6271	11.1671	14.4210	18.5798	23.8839	30.6336
29	1.3345	1.7758	2.3566	3.1186	4.1161	5.4184	7.1142	9.3172	12.1722	15.8631	20.6236	26.7500	34.6159
30	1.3478	1.8114	2.4273	3.2434	4.3219	5.7435	7.6122	10.0626	13.2677	17.4494	22.8922	29.9600	39.1160
31	1.3613	1.8476	2.5001	3.3731	4.5380	6.0881	8.1451	10.8676	14.4617	19.1943	25.4104	33.5552	44.2011
32	1.3749	1.8845	2.5751	3.5081	4.7649	6.4534	8.7152	11.7370	15.7633	21.1137	28.2055	37.5818	49.9473
33	1.3887	1.9222	2.6523	3.6484	5.0032	6.8406	9.3253	12.6760	17.1820	23.2251	31.3081	42.0917	56.4404
34	1.4026	1.9607	2.7319	3.7943	5.2533	7.2510	9.9781	13.6901	18.7284	25.5476	34.7520	47.1427	63.7777
35	1.4166	1.9999	2.8139	3.9461	5.5160	7.6861	10.6765	14.7853	20.4139	28.1023	38.5747	52.7998	72.0688
36	1.4308	2.0399	2.8983	4.1039	5.7918	8.1472	11.4239	15.9681	22.2512	30.9126	42.8179	59.1358	81.4377
37	1.4451	2.0807	2.9852	4.2681	6.0814	8.6361	12.2236	17.2456	24.2538	34.0038	47.5279	66.2321	92.0246
38	1.4595	2.1223	3.0748	4.4388	6.3855	9.1542	13.0792	18.6252	26.4366	37.4042	52.7560	74.1799	103.9880
39	1.4741	2.1647	3.1670	4.6164	6.7047	9.7035	13.9948	20.1152	28.8159	41.1446	58.5591	83.0815	117.5060
40	1.4889	2.2080	3.2620	4.8010	7.0400	10.2857	14.9744	21.7244	31.4094	45.2591	65.0006	93.0513	132.7820
41	1.5038	2.2522	3.3599	4.9931	7.3920	10.9028	16.0226	23.4624	34.2362	49.7850	72.1507	104.2170	150.0440
42	1.5188	2.2972	3.4607	5.1928	7.7616	11.5570	17.1442	25.3394	37.3175	54.7635	80.0872	116.7240	169.5490
43	1.5340	2.3432	3.5645	5.4005	8.1497	12.2504	18.3443	27.3665	40.6760	60.2398	88.8968	130.7300	191.5910
44	1.5493	2.3901	3.6715	5.6165	8.5571	12.9854	19.6284	29.5558	44.3369	66.2638	98.6754	146.4180	216.4980
45	1.5648	2.4379	3.7816	5.8412	8.9850	13.7646	21.0024	31.9203	48.3272	72.8902	109.5300	163.9880	244.6420
46	1.5805	2.4866	3.8950	6.0748	9.4342	14.5904	22.4725	34.4739	52.6766	80.1792	121.5780	183.6670	276.4460
47	1.5963	2.5363	4.0119	6.3178	9.9060	15.4658	24.0456	37.2318	57.4175	88.1971	134.9520	205.7070	312.3840
48	1.6122	2.5871	4.1323	6.5705	10.4013	16.3938	25.7288	40.2104	62.5851	97.0168	149.7960	230.3920	352.9940
49	1.6283	2.6388	4.2562	6.8333	10.9213	17.3774	27.5298	43.4272	68.2177	106.7190	166.2740	258.0390	398.8830
50	1.6446	2.6916	4.3839	7.1067	11.4674	18.4201	29.4569	46.9014	74.3573	117.3900	184.5640	289.0030	450.7380

Compound Interest of $1 (cont.)

Year	14%	15%	16%	17%	18%	19%	20%	21%	22%	23%	24%	25%
1	1.1400	1.1500	1.1600	1.1700	1.1800	1.1900	1.2000	1.2100	1.2200	1.2300	1.2400	1.2500
2	1.2996	1.3225	1.3456	1.3689	1.3924	1.4161	1.4400	1.4641	1.4884	1.5129	1.5376	1.5625
3	1.4815	1.5209	1.5609	1.6016	1.6430	1.6852	1.7280	1.7716	1.8158	1.8609	1.9066	1.9531
4	1.6890	1.7490	1.8106	1.8739	1.9388	2.0053	2.0736	2.1436	2.2153	2.2889	2.3642	2.4414
5	1.9254	2.0114	2.1003	2.1924	2.2878	2.3864	2.4883	2.5937	2.7027	2.8153	2.9316	3.0518
6	2.1950	2.3131	2.4364	2.5652	2.6996	2.8398	2.9860	3.1384	3.2973	3.4628	3.6352	3.8147
7	2.5023	2.6600	2.8262	3.0012	3.1855	3.3793	3.5832	3.7975	4.0227	4.2593	4.5077	4.7684
8	2.8526	3.0590	3.2784	3.5115	3.7589	4.0214	4.2998	4.5950	4.9077	5.2389	5.5895	5.9605
9	3.2520	3.5179	3.8030	4.1084	4.4355	4.7854	5.1598	5.5599	5.9874	6.4439	6.9310	7.4506
10	3.7072	4.0456	4.4114	4.8068	5.2338	5.6947	6.1917	6.7275	7.3046	7.9259	8.5944	9.3132
11	4.2262	4.6524	5.1173	5.6240	6.1759	6.7767	7.4301	8.1403	8.9117	9.7489	10.6571	11.6415
12	4.8179	5.3503	5.9360	6.5801	7.2876	8.0642	8.9161	9.8497	10.8722	11.9912	13.2148	14.5519
13	5.4924	6.1528	6.8858	7.6987	8.5994	9.5964	10.6993	11.9182	13.2641	14.7491	16.3863	18.1899
14	6.2611	7.0757	7.9875	9.0075	10.1473	11.4198	12.8392	14.4210	16.1822	18.1414	20.3191	22.7374
15	7.1379	8.1371	9.2655	10.5387	11.9738	13.5895	15.4070	17.4494	19.7423	22.3140	25.1956	28.4217
16	8.1373	9.3576	10.7480	12.3303	14.1290	16.1715	18.4884	21.1138	24.0856	27.4462	31.2426	35.5271
17	9.2765	10.7613	12.4677	14.4265	16.6723	19.2441	22.1861	25.5477	29.3844	33.7588	38.7400	44.4089
18	10.5752	12.3755	14.4625	16.8790	19.6733	22.9005	26.6233	30.9127	35.8490	41.5233	48.0386	55.5112
19	12.0557	14.2318	16.7765	19.7484	23.2145	27.2516	31.9480	37.4044	43.7358	51.0737	59.5679	69.3890
20	13.7435	16.3666	19.4608	23.1056	27.3931	32.4294	38.3376	45.2593	53.3576	62.8206	73.8642	86.7362
21	15.6676	18.8216	22.5745	27.0336	32.3238	38.5910	46.0052	54.7637	65.0963	77.2694	91.5916	108.4200
22	17.8611	21.6448	26.1864	31.6293	38.1421	45.9233	55.2062	66.2641	79.4175	95.0413	113.5740	135.5250
23	20.3616	24.8915	30.3762	37.0062	45.0077	54.6487	66.2474	80.1796	96.8893	116.9010	140.8310	169.4070
24	23.2122	28.6252	35.2364	43.2973	53.1091	65.0320	79.4969	97.0173	118.2050	143.7880	174.6310	211.7580
25	26.4620	32.9190	40.8743	50.6579	62.6688	77.3881	95.3963	117.3910	144.2100	176.8590	216.5420	264.6980
26	30.1666	37.8569	47.4142	59.2697	73.9491	92.0918	114.4760	142.0430	175.9360	217.5370	268.5120	330.8720
27	34.3900	43.5354	55.0004	69.3455	87.2600	109.5890	137.3710	171.8720	214.6420	267.5700	332.9550	413.5900
28	39.2046	50.0657	63.8005	81.1343	102.9670	130.4110	164.8450	207.9650	261.8640	329.1120	412.8640	516.9880
29	44.6932	57.5756	74.0086	94.9271	121.5010	155.1890	197.8140	251.6380	319.4740	404.8070	511.9520	646.2350
30	50.9503	66.2119	85.8500	111.0650	143.3710	184.6750	237.3760	304.4820	389.7580	497.9130	634.8200	807.7940
31	58.0833	76.1437	99.5860	129.9460	169.1780	219.7640	284.8520	368.4230	475.5040	612.4330	787.1770	1009.7400
32	66.2150	87.5653	115.5200	152.0360	199.6300	261.5190	341.8220	445.7920	580.1150	753.2930	976.0990	1262.1800
33	75.4851	100.7000	134.0030	177.8830	235.5630	311.2073	410.1870	539.4080	707.7410	926.5500	1210.3600	1577.7200
34	86.0530	115.8050	155.4430	208.1230	277.9650	370.3370	492.2240	652.6840	863.4430	1139.6600	1500.8500	1972.1500
35	98.1004	133.1760	180.3140	243.5040	327.9980	440.7010	590.6690	789.7470	1053.4000	1401.7800	1861.0500	2465.1900
36	111.8350	153.1520	209.1640	284.8990	387.0380	524.4340	708.8030	955.5940	1285.1500	1724.1900	2307.7100	3081.4900
37	127.4910	176.1250	242.6310	333.3320	456.7050	624.0760	850.5630	1156.2700	1567.8800	2120.7500	2861.5600	3851.8600
38	145.3400	202.5440	281.4520	389.9990	538.9120	742.6510	1020.6800	1399.0900	1912.8200	2608.5200	3548.3300	4814.8300
39	165.6880	232.9260	326.4840	456.2980	635.9160	883.7540	1224.8100	1692.8900	2333.6400	3208.4800	4399.9300	6018.5300
40	188.8840	267.8650	378.7220	533.8690	750.3810	1051.6700	1469.7700	2048.4000	2847.0300	3946.4300	5455.9100	7523.1700
41	215.3280	308.0440	439.3170	624.6270	885.4490	1251.4800	1763.7300	2478.5700	3473.3800	4854.1100	6765.3300	9403.9600
42	245.4740	354.2510	509.6080	730.8130	1044.8300	1489.2700	2116.4700	2999.0600	4237.5300	5970.5600	8389.0200	11754.9000
43	279.8400	407.3880	591.1450	855.0520	1232.9000	1772.2300	2539.7700	3628.8700	5169.7800	7343.7800	10402.4000	14693.7000
44	319.0180	468.4970	685.7280	1000.4100	1454.8200	2108.9500	3047.7200	4390.9300	6307.1300	9032.8600	12898.9000	18367.1000
45	363.6800	538.7710	795.4450	1170.4800	1760.6900	2509.6500	3657.2700	5313.0300	7694.7000	11110.4000	15994.7000	22958.9000
46	414.5950	619.5870	922.7160	1369.4600	2025.6900	2986.4800	4388.7200	6428.7600	9387.5400	13665.8000	19833.4000	28698.6000
47	472.6390	712.5250	1070.3500	1602.2700	2390.3200	3853.9700	5266.4600	7778.8000	11452.8000	16800.9000	24593.4000	35873.2000
48	538.8080	819.4040	1241.6100	1874.6600	2820.5800	4229.1600	6319.7600	9412.3500	13972.4000	20675.0000	30495.9000	44841.6000
49	614.2410	942.3150	1440.2600	2193.3500	3328.2800	5032.7000	7583.7100	11388.9000	17046.3000	25430.2000	37814.9000	56051.9000
50	700.2350	1083.6600	1670.7100	2566.2200	3927.3700	5988.9100	9100.4500	13780.6000	20796.5000	31279.2000	46890.5000	70064.9000

TABLE II

Future Value of an Annuity of $1

Year	1%	2%	3%	4%	5%	6%	7%	8%	9%	10%	11%	12%	13%
1	1.0000	1.0000	1.0000	1.0000	1.0000	1.0000	1.0000	1.0000	1.0000	1.0000	1.0000	1.0000	1.0000
2	2.0100	2.0200	2.0300	2.0400	2.0500	2.0600	2.0700	2.0800	2.0900	2.1000	2.1100	2.1200	2.1300
3	3.0301	3.0604	3.0909	3.1216	3.1525	3.1836	3.2149	3.2464	3.2781	3.3100	3.3421	3.3744	3.4069
4	4.0604	4.1216	4.1836	4.2465	4.3101	4.3746	4.4399	4.5061	4.5731	4.6410	4.7097	4.7793	4.8498
5	5.1010	5.2040	5.3091	5.4163	5.5256	5.6371	5.7507	5.8666	5.9847	6.1051	6.2278	6.3528	6.4803
6	6.1520	6.3081	6.4684	6.6330	6.8019	6.9753	7.1533	7.3359	7.5233	7.7156	7.9129	8.1152	8.3227
7	7.2135	7.4343	7.6625	7.8983	8.1420	8.3938	8.6540	8.9228	9.2004	9.4872	9.7833	10.0890	10.4047
8	8.2857	8.5830	8.8923	9.2142	9.5491	9.8975	10.2598	10.6366	11.0285	11.4359	11.8594	12.2997	12.7573
9	9.3685	9.7546	10.1591	10.5828	11.0266	11.4913	11.9780	12.4876	13.0210	13.5795	14.1640	14.7757	15.4157
10	10.4622	10.9497	11.4639	12.0061	12.5779	13.1808	13.8164	14.4866	15.1929	15.9374	16.7220	17.5487	18.4197
11	11.5668	12.1687	12.8078	13.4864	14.2068	14.9716	15.7836	16.6455	17.5603	18.5312	19.5614	20.6546	21.8143
12	12.6825	13.4121	14.1920	15.0258	15.9171	16.8699	17.8885	18.9771	20.1407	21.3843	22.7132	24.1331	25.6502
13	13.8093	14.6803	15.6178	16.6268	17.7130	18.8821	20.1406	21.4953	22.9534	24.5227	26.2116	28.0291	29.9847
14	14.9474	15.9739	17.0863	18.2919	19.5986	21.0151	22.5505	24.2149	26.0192	27.9750	30.0949	32.3926	34.8827
15	16.0969	17.2934	18.5989	20.0236	21.5786	23.2760	25.1290	27.1521	29.3609	31.7725	34.4054	37.2797	40.4175
16	17.2579	18.6393	20.1569	21.8245	23.6575	25.6725	27.8881	30.3243	33.0034	35.9497	39.1899	42.7533	46.6717
17	18.4304	20.0121	21.7616	23.6975	25.8404	28.2129	30.8402	33.7502	36.9737	40.5447	44.5008	48.8837	53.7391
18	19.6147	21.4123	23.4144	25.6454	28.1324	30.9057	33.9990	37.4502	41.3013	45.5992	50.3959	55.7497	61.7251
19	20.8109	22.8406	25.1169	27.6712	30.5390	33.7600	37.3790	41.4463	46.0185	51.1591	56.9395	63.4397	70.7494
20	22.0190	24.2974	26.8704	29.7781	33.0660	36.7856	40.9955	45.7620	51.1601	57.2750	64.2028	72.0524	80.9468
21	23.2392	25.7833	28.6765	31.9692	35.7193	39.9927	44.8652	50.4229	56.7645	64.0025	72.2651	81.6987	92.4699
22	24.4716	27.2990	30.5368	34.2480	38.5052	43.3923	49.0057	55.4568	62.8733	71.4027	81.2143	92.5026	105.4910
23	25.7163	28.8450	32.4529	36.6179	41.4305	46.9958	53.4361	60.8933	69.5319	79.5430	91.1479	104.6029	120.2048
24	26.9735	30.4219	34.4265	39.0826	44.5020	50.8156	58.1767	66.7648	76.7898	88.4973	102.1742	118.1552	136.8315
25	28.2432	32.0303	36.4593	41.6459	47.7271	54.8645	63.2490	73.1059	84.7009	98.3471	114.4133	133.3339	155.6196
26	29.5256	33.6709	38.5530	44.3117	51.1135	59.1564	68.6765	79.9544	93.3240	109.1818	127.9988	150.3339	176.8501
27	30.8209	35.3443	40.7096	47.0842	54.6691	63.7058	74.4838	87.3508	102.7231	121.0999	143.0786	169.3740	200.8406
28	32.1291	37.0512	42.9309	49.9676	58.4026	68.5281	80.6977	95.3388	112.9682	134.2099	159.8173	190.6989	227.9499
29	33.4504	38.7922	45.2189	52.9663	62.3227	73.6398	87.3465	103.9659	124.1354	148.6309	178.3972	214.5828	258.5834
30	34.7849	40.5681	47.5754	56.0849	66.4388	79.0582	94.4608	113.2832	136.3075	164.4940	199.0209	241.3327	293.1992
31	36.1327	42.3794	50.0027	59.3283	70.7608	84.8017	102.0730	123.3459	149.5752	181.9434	221.9132	271.2926	332.3151
32	37.4941	44.2270	52.5028	62.7015	75.2988	90.8898	110.2182	134.2135	164.0370	201.1378	247.3236	304.8477	376.5161
33	38.8690	46.1116	55.0778	66.2095	80.0638	97.3432	118.9334	145.9506	179.8003	222.2515	275.5292	342.4294	426.4632
34	40.2577	48.0338	57.7302	69.8579	85.0670	104.1838	128.2588	158.6267	196.9823	245.4767	306.8374	384.5210	482.9034
35	41.6603	49.9945	60.4621	73.6522	90.3203	111.4348	138.2369	172.3168	215.7108	271.0244	341.5896	431.6635	546.6808
36	43.0769	51.9944	63.2759	77.5983	95.8363	119.1209	148.9135	187.1021	236.1247	299.1268	380.1644	484.4631	618.7493
37	44.5076	54.0343	66.1742	81.7022	101.6281	127.2681	160.3374	203.0703	258.3759	330.0395	422.9825	543.5987	700.1868
38	45.9527	56.1149	69.1594	85.9703	107.7095	135.9042	172.5610	220.3159	282.6298	364.0434	470.5106	609.8305	792.2110
39	47.4123	58.2372	72.2342	90.4092	114.0950	145.0585	185.6403	238.9412	309.0665	401.4478	523.2667	684.0102	896.1985
40	48.8864	60.4020	75.4013	95.0255	120.7998	154.7620	199.6351	259.0565	337.8824	442.5926	581.8261	767.0914	1013.7043
41	50.3752	62.6100	78.6633	99.8265	127.8398	165.0477	214.6096	280.7810	369.2919	487.8518	646.8269	860.1424	1146.4858
42	51.8790	64.8622	82.0232	104.8196	135.2318	175.9505	230.6322	304.2435	403.5281	537.6370	718.9779	964.3595	1296.5290
43	53.3978	67.1595	85.4839	110.0124	142.9933	187.5076	247.7765	329.5830	440.8457	592.4007	799.0655	1081.0826	1466.0777
44	54.9318	69.5027	89.0484	115.4129	151.1430	199.7580	266.1209	356.9496	481.5218	652.6408	887.9627	1211.8125	1657.6679
45	56.4811	71.8927	92.7199	121.0294	159.7002	212.7435	285.7493	386.5056	525.8587	718.9048	986.6386	1358.2300	1874.1647
46	58.0459	74.3306	96.5015	126.8706	168.6852	226.5081	306.7518	418.4261	574.1860	791.7953	1096.1688	1522.2176	2118.8061
47	59.6263	76.8172	100.3965	132.9454	178.1194	241.0986	329.2244	452.9002	626.8628	871.9748	1217.7474	1705.8838	2395.2509
48	61.2226	79.3535	104.4084	139.2632	188.0254	256.5645	353.2701	490.1322	684.2804	960.1723	1352.6996	1911.5898	2707.6335
49	62.8348	81.9406	108.5406	145.8337	198.4267	272.9584	378.9990	530.3427	746.8656	1057.1896	1502.4966	2141.9806	3060.6259
50	64.4632	84.5794	112.7969	152.6671	209.3480	290.3359	406.5289	573.7702	815.0835	1163.9085	1668.7712	2400.0182	3459.5072

Future Value of an Annuity of $1 (cont.)

Year	14%	15%	16%	17%	18%	19%	20%	21%	22%	23%	24%	25%
1	1.0000	1.0000	1.0000	1.0000	1.0000	1.0000	1.0000	1.0000	1.0000	1.0000	1.0000	1.0000
2	2.1400	2.1500	2.1600	2.1700	2.1800	2.1900	2.2000	2.2100	2.2200	2.2300	2.2400	2.2500
3	3.4396	3.4725	3.5056	3.5389	3.5724	3.6061	3.6400	3.6741	3.7084	3.7429	3.7776	3.8125
4	4.9211	4.9934	5.0665	5.1405	5.2154	5.2913	5.3680	5.4457	5.5242	5.6038	5.6842	5.7656
5	6.6101	6.7424	6.8771	7.0144	7.1542	7.2966	7.4416	7.5892	7.7396	7.8926	8.0484	8.2070
6	8.5355	8.7537	8.9775	9.2068	9.4420	9.6830	9.9299	10.1830	10.4423	10.7079	10.9801	11.2588
7	10.7305	11.0668	11.4139	11.7720	12.1415	12.5227	12.9159	13.3214	13.7396	14.1708	14.6153	15.0735
8	13.2328	13.7268	14.2401	14.7733	15.3270	15.9020	16.4991	17.1189	17.7623	18.4300	19.1229	19.8419
9	16.0853	16.7858	17.5185	18.2847	19.0859	19.9234	20.7989	21.7139	22.6700	23.6690	24.7125	25.8023
10	19.3373	20.3037	21.3215	22.3931	23.5213	24.7089	25.9587	27.2738	28.6574	30.1128	31.6434	33.2529
11	23.0445	24.3493	25.7329	27.1999	28.7551	30.4035	32.1504	34.0013	35.9620	38.0388	40.2379	42.5661
12	27.2707	29.0017	30.8502	32.8239	34.9311	37.1802	39.5805	42.1416	44.8737	47.7877	50.8950	54.2077
13	32.0887	34.3519	36.7862	39.4040	42.2187	45.2445	48.4966	51.9913	55.7459	59.7788	64.1097	68.7596
14	37.5811	40.5047	43.6720	47.1027	50.8180	54.8409	59.1959	63.9095	69.0100	74.5280	80.4961	86.9495
15	43.8424	47.5804	51.6595	56.1101	60.9653	66.2607	72.0351	78.3305	85.1922	92.6694	100.8151	109.6868
16	50.9804	55.7175	60.9250	66.6488	72.9390	79.8502	87.4421	95.7799	104.9345	114.0934	126.0108	138.1085
17	59.1176	65.0751	71.6730	78.9792	87.0680	96.0218	105.9306	116.8937	129.0201	142.4295	157.2534	173.6357
18	68.3941	75.8364	84.1407	93.4056	103.7403	115.2659	128.1167	142.4413	158.4045	176.1883	195.9942	218.0446
19	78.9692	88.2118	98.6032	110.2846	123.4135	138.1664	154.7400	173.3540	194.2535	217.7116	244.0328	273.5558
20	91.0249	102.4436	115.3797	130.0329	146.6280	165.4180	186.6880	210.7584	237.9893	268.7853	303.6006	342.9447
21	104.7684	118.8101	134.8405	153.1385	174.0210	197.8474	225.0256	256.0176	291.3469	331.6059	377.4648	429.6809
22	120.4360	137.6316	157.4150	180.1721	206.3448	236.4385	271.0307	310.7813	356.4432	408.8753	469.0563	538.1011
23	138.2970	159.2764	183.6014	211.8013	244.4868	282.3618	326.2369	377.0454	435.8607	503.9166	582.6298	673.6264
24	158.6586	184.1678	213.9776	248.8076	289.4945	337.0105	392.4842	457.2249	532.7501	620.8174	723.4610	843.0329
25	181.8708	212.7930	249.2140	292.1049	342.6035	402.0425	471.9811	554.2422	650.9551	764.6055	898.0916	1054.7912
26	208.3327	245.7120	290.0883	342.7627	405.2721	479.4306	567.3773	671.6330	795.1653	941.4647	1114.6336	1319.4890
27	238.4993	283.5688	337.5024	402.0323	479.2211	571.5224	681.8528	813.6760	971.1016	1159.0016	1383.1457	1650.3612
28	272.8892	327.1041	392.5028	471.3778	566.4809	681.1116	819.2233	985.5479	1185.7440	1426.5720	1716.1007	2063.9515
29	312.0937	377.1697	456.3032	552.5121	669.4474	811.5228	984.0680	1193.5130	1447.6077	1755.6835	2128.9648	2580.9394
30	356.7868	434.7451	530.3117	647.4391	790.9480	966.7122	1181.8815	1445.1507	1767.0814	2160.4907	2640.9164	3227.1743
31	407.7370	500.9569	616.1616	758.5038	934.3186	1151.3875	1419.2579	1749.6323	2156.8393	2658.4036	3275.7363	4034.9678
32	465.8202	577.1005	715.7475	888.4494	1103.4960	1371.1511	1704.1094	2118.0551	2632.3439	3270.8364	4062.9131	5044.7098
33	532.0350	664.6655	831.2671	1040.4858	1303.1252	1632.6698	2045.9313	2563.8467	3212.4596	4024.1288	5039.0122	6306.8873
34	607.5199	765.3654	965.2698	1218.3684	1538.6878	1943.8771	2456.1176	3103.2545	3920.2007	4950.6784	6249.3751	7884.6091
35	693.5727	881.1702	1120.7130	1426.4910	1816.6516	2314.2137	2948.3411	3755.9380	4783.6448	6090.3344	7750.2252	9856.7614
36	791.6729	1014.3457	1301.0270	1669.9945	2144.6489	2754.9143	3539.0093	4545.6849	5837.0467	7492.1113	9611.2792	12321.9517
37	903.5071	1167.4975	1510.1914	1954.8936	2531.6857	3279.3480	4247.8112	5501.2788	7122.1970	9216.2970	11918.9862	15403.4396
38	1030.9981	1343.6222	1752.8220	2288.2255	2988.3891	3903.4241	5098.3734	6657.5474	8690.0803	11337.0453	14780.5428	19255.2996
39	1176.3378	1546.1655	2034.2735	2678.2238	3527.2991	4646.0747	6119.0481	8056.6323	10602.8979	13945.5657	18328.8733	24070.1243
40	1342.0251	1779.0903	2360.7573	3134.5218	4163.2130	5529.8289	7343.8577	9749.5250	12936.5355	17154.0459	22728.8027	30088.6553
41	1530.9086	2046.9539	2739.4784	3668.3905	4913.5913	6581.4964	8813.6293	11797.9253	15783.5734	21100.4763	28184.7153	37611.8193
42	1746.2359	2354.9969	3178.7950	4293.0169	5799.0378	7832.9807	10577.3551	14276.4897	19256.9595	25954.5859	34950.0469	47015.7739
43	1991.7089	2709.2465	3688.4022	5023.8298	6843.8646	9322.2471	12693.8260	17275.5525	23494.4905	31925.1406	43339.0586	58770.7178
44	2271.5481	3116.6335	4279.5465	5878.8809	8076.7602	11094.4740	15233.5913	20904.4187	28664.2786	39268.9229	53741.4326	73464.3965
45	2590.5648	3585.1285	4965.2739	6879.2906	9531.5770	13203.4240	18281.3096	25295.3464	34971.4199	48301.7754	66640.3760	91831.4961
46	2954.2439	4123.8978	5760.7178	8049.7700	11248.2609	15713.0746	21938.5713	30608.3694	42666.1373	59412.1836	82635.0664	114790.3701
47	3368.0381	4743.4824	6683.4326	9419.2310	13273.9479	18699.5586	26327.2856	37037.1270	52053.6812	73077.9863	102468.4874	143488.9629
48	3841.4754	5456.0048	7753.7818	11021.5007	15664.2584	22253.4749	31593.7427	44815.9233	63506.4912	89886.9229	127061.9180	179362.2031
49	4380.2820	6275.4055	8995.3870	12896.1553	18484.8250	26482.6800	37913.4912	54228.2676	77478.9189	110561.9150	157557.7793	224203.7539
50	4994.5215	7217.7164	10435.6488	15089.5016	21813.0935	31515.3357	45497.1895	65617.2041	94515.7612	135997.1562	195372.6465	280255.6914

TABLE III

Present Value of $1

Year	1%	2%	3%	4%	5%	6%	7%	8%	9%	10%	11%	12%	13%	14%	15%
1	.9901	.9804	.9709	.9615	.9524	.9434	.9346	.9259	.9174	.9091	.9009	.8929	.8850	.8772	.8696
2	.9803	.9612	.9426	.9246	.9070	.8900	.8734	.8573	.8417	.8264	.8116	.7972	.7831	.7695	.7561
3	.9706	.9423	.9151	.8890	.8638	.8396	.8163	.7938	.7722	.7513	.7312	.7118	.6931	.6750	.6575
4	.9610	.9239	.8885	.8548	.8227	.7921	.7629	.7350	.7084	.6830	.6587	.6355	.6133	.5921	.5718
5	.9515	.9057	.8626	.8219	.7835	.7473	.7130	.6806	.6499	.6209	.5934	.5674	.5428	.5194	.4972
6	.9420	.8880	.8375	.7903	.7462	.7050	.6663	.6302	.5963	.5645	.5346	.5066	.4803	.4556	.4323
7	.9327	.8706	.8131	.7599	.7107	.6651	.6228	.5835	.5470	.5132	.4817	.4524	.4251	.3996	.3759
8	.9235	.8535	.7894	.7307	.6768	.6274	.5820	.5403	.5019	.4665	.4339	.4039	.3762	.3506	.3269
9	.9143	.8368	.7664	.7026	.6446	.5919	.5439	.5002	.4604	.4241	.3909	.3606	.3329	.3075	.2843
10	.9053	.8204	.7441	.6756	.6139	.5584	.5084	.4632	.4224	.3855	.3522	.3220	.2946	.2697	.2472
11	.8963	.8043	.7224	.6496	.5847	.5268	.4751	.4289	.3875	.3505	.3173	.2875	.2607	.2366	.2149
12	.8874	.7885	.7014	.6246	.5568	.4970	.4440	.3971	.3555	.3186	.2858	.2567	.2307	.2076	.1869
13	.8787	.7730	.6810	.6006	.5303	.4688	.4150	.3677	.3262	.2897	.2575	.2292	.2042	.1821	.1625
14	.8700	.7579	.6611	.5775	.5051	.4423	.3878	.3405	.2993	.2633	.2320	.2046	.1807	.1597	.1413
15	.8614	.7430	.6419	.5553	.4810	.4173	.3625	.3152	.2745	.2394	.2090	.1827	.1599	.1401	.1229
16	.8528	.7284	.6232	.5339	.4581	.3936	.3387	.2919	.2519	.2176	.1883	.1631	.1415	.1229	.1069
17	.8444	.7142	.6050	.5134	.4363	.3714	.3166	.2703	.2311	.1978	.1696	.1456	.1252	.1078	.0929
18	.8360	.7002	.5874	.4936	.4155	.3503	.2959	.2502	.2120	.1799	.1528	.1300	.1108	.0946	.0808
19	.8277	.6864	.5703	.4746	.3957	.3305	.2765	.2317	.1945	.1635	.1377	.1161	.0981	.0829	.0703
20	.8195	.6730	.5537	.4564	.3769	.3118	.2584	.2145	.1784	.1486	.1240	.1037	.0868	.0728	.0611
21	.8114	.6598	.5375	.4388	.3589	.2942	.2415	.1987	.1637	.1351	.1117	.0926	.0768	.0638	.0531
22	.8034	.6468	.5219	.4220	.3418	.2775	.2257	.1839	.1502	.1229	.1007	.0826	.0680	.0560	.0462
23	.7954	.6342	.5067	.4057	.3256	.2618	.2109	.1703	.1378	.1117	.0907	.0738	.0601	.0491	.0402
24	.7876	.6217	.4919	.3901	.3101	.2470	.1971	.1577	.1264	.1015	.0817	.0659	.0532	.0431	.0349
25	.7798	.6095	.4776	.3751	.2953	.2330	.1842	.1460	.1160	.0923	.0736	.0588	.0471	.0378	.0304
26	.7721	.5976	.4637	.3607	.2812	.2198	.1722	.1352	.1064	.0839	.0663	.0525	.0417	.0332	.0264
27	.7644	.5859	.4502	.3468	.2678	.2074	.1609	.1252	.0976	.0763	.0597	.0469	.0369	.0291	.0230
28	.7568	.5744	.4371	.3335	.2551	.1956	.1504	.1159	.0896	.0693	.0538	.0419	.0326	.0255	.0200
29	.7493	.5631	.4244	.3206	.2429	.1846	.1406	.1073	.0821	.0630	.0485	.0374	.0289	.0224	.0174
30	.7419	.5521	.4120	.3083	.2314	.1741	.1314	.0994	.0754	.0573	.0437	.0334	.0256	.0196	.0151
31	.7346	.5412	.4000	.2965	.2204	.1643	.1228	.0920	.0692	.0521	.0394	.0298	.0226	.0172	.0131
32	.7273	.5306	.3883	.2851	.2099	.1550	.1147	.0852	.0634	.0474	.0354	.0266	.0200	.0151	.0114
33	.7201	.5202	.3770	.2741	.2099	.1462	.1072	.0789	.0582	.0431	.0319	.0238	.0177	.0133	.0099
34	.7130	.5100	.3660	.2635	.1903	.1379	.1002	.0731	.0534	.0391	.0288	.0212	.0157	.0116	.0086
35	.7059	.5000	.3554	.2534	.1813	.1301	.0937	.0676	.0490	.0356	.0259	.0189	.0139	.0102	.0075
36	.6989	.4902	.3450	.2437	.1727	.1227	.0875	.0626	.0449	.0324	.0234	.0169	.0123	.0089	.0065
37	.6920	.4806	.3350	.2343	.1644	.1158	.0818	.0580	.0412	.0294	.0210	.0151	.0109	.0078	.0057
38	.6852	.4712	.3252	.2253	.1566	.1092	.0765	.0537	.0378	.0267	.0190	.0135	.0096	.0069	.0049
39	.6784	.4620	.3158	.2166	.1492	.1031	.0715	.0497	.0347	.0243	.0171	.0120	.0085	.0060	.0043
40	.6717	.4529	.3066	.2083	.1420	.0972	.0668	.0460	.0318	.0221	.0154	.0107	.0075	.0053	.0037
41	.6650	.4440	.2976	.2003	.1353	.0917	.0624	.0426	.0292	.0201	.0139	.0096	.0067	.0046	.0033
42	.6584	.4353	.2890	.1926	.1288	.0865	.0583	.0395	.0268	.0183	.0125	.0086	.0059	.0041	.0028
43	.6519	.4268	.2805	.1852	.1227	.0816	.0545	.0365	.0246	.0166	.0113	.0077	.0052	.0036	.0025
44	.6454	.4184	.2724	.1781	.1169	.0770	.0509	.0338	.0226	.0151	.0101	.0068	.0046	.0031	.0021
45	.6391	.4102	.2644	.1712	.1113	.0727	.0476	.0313	.0207	.0137	.0091	.0061	.0041	.0027	.0019
46	.6327	.4021	.2567	.1646	.1060	.0685	.0445	.0290	.0190	.0125	.0082	.0054	.0036	.0024	.0016
47	.6265	.3943	.2493	.1583	.1010	.0647	.0416	.0269	.0174	.0113	.0074	.0049	.0032	.0021	.0014
48	.6203	.3865	.2420	.1522	.0961	.0610	.0389	.0249	.0160	.0103	.0067	.0043	.0028	.0019	.0012
49	.6141	.3790	.2350	.1463	.0916	.0575	.0363	.0230	.0147	.0094	.0060	.0039	.0025	.0016	.0011
50	.6080	.3715	.2281	.1407	.0872	.0543	.0340	.0213	.0135	.0085	.0054	.0035	.0022	.0014	.0009

Present Value of $1 (cont.)

Year	16%	17%	18%	19%	20%	21%	22%	23%	24%	25%	30%	35%	40%	45%	50%
1	.8621	.8547	.8475	.8403	.8333	.8264	.8197	.8130	.8065	.8000	.7692	.7407	.7143	.6897	.6667
2	.7432	.7305	.7182	.7062	.6944	.6830	.6719	.6610	.6504	.6400	.5917	.5487	.5102	.4756	.4444
3	.6407	.6244	.6086	.5934	.5787	.5645	.5507	.5374	.5245	.5120	.4552	.4064	.3644	.3280	.2963
4	.5523	.5337	.5158	.4987	.4822	.4665	.4514	.4369	.4230	.4096	.3501	.3011	.2603	.2262	.1975
5	.4761	.4561	.4371	.4190	.4019	.3855	.3700	.3552	.3411	.3277	.2693	.2230	.1859	.1560	.1317
6	.4104	.3898	.3704	.3521	.3349	.3186	.3033	.2888	.2751	.2621	.2072	.1652	.1328	.1076	.0878
7	.3538	.3332	.3139	.2959	.2791	.2633	.2486	.2348	.2218	.2097	.1594	.1224	.0949	.0742	.0585
8	.3050	.2848	.2660	.2487	.2326	.2176	.2038	.1909	.1789	.1678	.1226	.0906	.0678	.0512	.0390
9	.2630	.2434	.2255	.2090	.1938	.1799	.1670	.1552	.1443	.1342	.0943	.0671	.0484	.0353	.0260
10	.2267	.2080	.1911	.1756	.1615	.1486	.1369	.1262	.1163	.1074	.0725	.0497	.0346	.0243	.0173
11	.1954	.1778	.1619	.1476	.1346	.1229	.1122	.1026	.0938	.0859	.0558	.0368	.0247	.0168	.0116
12	.1685	.1520	.1372	.1240	.1122	.1015	.0920	.0834	.0757	.0687	.0429	.0273	.0176	.0116	.0077
13	.1452	.1299	.1163	.1042	.0935	.0839	.0754	.0678	.0610	.0550	.0330	.0202	.0126	.0080	.0051
14	.1252	.1110	.0906	.0876	.0779	.0693	.0618	.0551	.0492	.0440	.0254	.0150	.0090	.0055	.0034
15	.1079	.0949	.0835	.0736	.0649	.0573	.0507	.0448	.0397	.0352	.0195	.0111	.0064	.0038	.0023
16	.0930	.0811	.0708	.0618	.0541	.0474	.0415	.0364	.0320	.0281	.0150	.0082	.0046	.0026	.0015
17	.0802	.0693	.0600	.0520	.0451	.0391	.0340	.0296	.0258	.0225	.0116	.0061	.0033	.0018	.0010
18	.0691	.0592	.0508	.0437	.0376	.0324	.0279	.0241	.0208	.0180	.0089	.0045	.0023	.0012	.0007
19	.0596	.0506	.0431	.0367	.0313	.0267	.0229	.0196	.0168	.0144	.0068	.0033	.0017	.0009	.0004
20	.0514	.0433	.0365	.0308	.0261	.0221	.0187	.0159	.0135	.0115	.0053	.0025	.0012	.0006	.0003
21	.0443	.0370	.0309	.0259	.0217	.0183	.0154	.0129	.0109	.0092	.0040	.0018	.0008	.0004	.0002
22	.0382	.0316	.0262	.0218	.0181	.0151	.0126	.0105	.0088	.0074	.0031	.0014	.0006	.0003	.0001
23	.0329	.0270	.0222	.0183	.0151	.0125	.0103	.0085	.0071	.0059	.0024	.0010	.0004	.0002	.0001
24	.0284	.0231	.0188	.0154	.0126	.0103	.0085	.0070	.0057	.0047	.0018	.0007	.0003	.0001	.0001
25	.0245	.0197	.0160	.0129	.0105	.0085	.0069	.0056	.0046	.0038	.0014	.0005	.0002	.0001	.0000
26	.0211	.0169	.0135	.0109	.0087	.0070	.0057	.0046	.0037	.0030	.0011	.0004	.0002	.0001	.0000
27	.0182	.0144	.0115	.0091	.0073	.0058	.0047	.0037	.0030	.0024	.0008	.0003	.0001	.0000	.0000
28	.0157	.0123	.0097	.0077	.0061	.0048	.0038	.0030	.0024	.0019	.0006	.0002	.0001	.0000	.0000
29	.0135	.0105	.0082	.0064	.0051	.0040	.0031	.0025	.0019	.0015	.0005	.0002	.0001	.0000	.0000
30	.0116	.0090	.0070	.0054	.0042	.0033	.0026	.0020	.0016	.0012	.0004	.0001	.0000	.0000	.0000
31	.0100	.0077	.0059	.0045	.0035	.0027	.0021	.0016	.0013	.0010	.0003	.0001	.0000	.0000	.0000
32	.0087	.0066	.0050	.0038	.0029	.0022	.0017	.0013	.0010	.0008	.0002	.0001	.0000	.0000	.0000
33	.0075	.0056	.0043	.0032	.0024	.0018	.0014	.0011	.0008	.0006	.0002	.0001	.0000	.0000	.0000
34	.0064	.0048	.0036	.0027	.0020	.0015	.0012	.0009	.0007	.0005	.0001	.0000	.0000	.0000	.0000
35	.0055	.0041	.0030	.0023	.0017	.0013	.0010	.0007	.0005	.0004	.0001	.0000	.0000	.0000	.0000
36	.0048	.0035	.0026	.0019	.0014	.0011	.0008	.0006	.0004	.0003	.0001	.0000	.0000	.0000	.0000
37	.0041	.0030	.0022	.0016	.0012	.0009	.0006	.0005	.0003	.0003	.0001	.0000	.0000	.0000	.0000
38	.0036	.0026	.0019	.0014	.0010	.0007	.0005	.0004	.0003	.0002	.0001	.0000	.0000	.0000	.0000
39	.0031	.0022	.0016	.0011	.0008	.0006	.0004	.0003	.0002	.0002	.0000	.0000	.0000	.0000	.0000
40	.0026	.0019	.0013	.0010	.0007	.0005	.0003	.0002	.0002	.0001	.0000	.0000	.0000	.0000	.0000
41	.0023	.0016	.0011	.0008	.0006	.0004	.0003	.0002	.0002	.0001	.0000	.0000	.0000	.0000	.0000
42	.0020	.0014	.0010	.0007	.0005	.0003	.0002	.0002	.0001	.0001	.0000	.0000	.0000	.0000	.0000
43	.0017	.0012	.0008	.0006	.0004	.0003	.0002	.0001	.0001	.0001	.0000	.0000	.0000	.0000	.0000
44	.0015	.0010	.0007	.0005	.0003	.0002	.0002	.0001	.0001	.0001	.0000	.0000	.0000	.0000	.0000
45	.0013	.0008	.0006	.0004	.0003	.0002	.0001	.0001	.0001	.0000	.0000	.0000	.0000	.0000	.0000
46	.0011	.0007	.0005	.0003	.0002	.0002	.0001	.0001	.0001	.0000	.0000	.0000	.0000	.0000	.0000
47	.0009	.0006	.0004	.0003	.0002	.0001	.0001	.0001	.0000	.0000	.0000	.0000	.0000	.0000	.0000
48	.0008	.0005	.0003	.0002	.0002	.0001	.0001	.0001	.0000	.0000	.0000	.0000	.0000	.0000	.0000
49	.0007	.0005	.0003	.0002	.0001	.0001	.0001	.0000	.0000	.0000	.0000	.0000	.0000	.0000	.0000
50	.0006	.0004	.0002	.0002	.0001	.0001	.0001	.0000	.0000	.0000	.0000	.0000	.0000	.0000	.0000

TABLE IV

Present Value of an Annuity of $1

Year	1%	2%	3%	4%	5%	6%	7%	8%	9%	10%	11%	12%	13%	14%	15%
1	.9901	.9804	.9709	.9615	.9524	.9434	.9346	.9259	.9174	.9091	.9009	.8929	.8850	.8772	.8696
2	1.9704	1.9416	1.9135	1.8861	1.8594	1.8334	1.8080	1.7833	1.7591	1.7355	1.7125	1.6901	1.6681	1.6467	1.6257
3	2.9410	2.8839	2.8286	2.7751	2.7232	2.6730	2.6243	2.5771	2.5313	2.4869	2.4437	2.4018	2.3612	2.3216	2.2832
4	3.9020	3.8077	3.7171	3.6299	3.5459	3.4651	3.3872	3.3121	3.2397	3.1699	3.1024	3.0374	2.9745	2.9137	2.8550
5	4.8534	4.7135	4.5797	4.4518	4.3295	4.2124	4.1002	3.9927	3.8897	3.7908	3.6959	3.6048	3.5172	3.4331	3.3522
6	5.7955	5.6014	5.4172	5.2421	5.0757	4.9173	4.7666	4.6229	4.4859	4.3553	4.2305	4.1114	3.9976	3.8887	3.7845
7	6.7282	6.4720	6.2303	6.0021	5.7864	5.5824	5.3893	5.2064	5.0330	4.8684	4.7122	4.5638	4.4226	4.2883	4.1604
8	7.6517	7.3255	7.0197	6.7328	6.4632	6.2098	5.9713	5.7466	5.5348	5.3349	5.1461	4.9676	4.7988	4.6389	4.4873
9	8.5660	8.1622	7.7861	7.4353	7.1078	6.8017	6.5152	6.2469	5.9953	5.7590	5.5371	5.3282	5.1317	4.9464	4.7716
10	9.4713	8.9826	8.5302	8.1109	7.7217	7.3601	7.0236	6.7101	6.4177	6.1446	5.8892	5.6502	5.4262	5.2161	5.0188
11	10.3676	9.7868	9.2526	8.7605	8.3064	7.8869	7.4987	7.1390	6.8052	6.4951	6.2065	5.9377	5.6869	5.4527	5.2337
12	11.2551	10.5753	9.9540	9.3851	8.8633	8.3839	7.9427	7.5361	7.1607	6.8137	6.4924	6.1944	5.9177	5.6603	5.4206
13	12.1338	11.3484	10.6349	9.9857	9.3936	8.8527	8.3577	7.9038	7.4869	7.1034	6.7499	6.4235	6.1218	5.8424	5.5832
14	13.0037	12.1062	11.2961	10.5631	9.8986	9.2950	8.7455	8.2442	7.7862	7.3667	6.9819	6.6282	6.3025	6.0021	5.7245
15	13.8651	12.8492	11.9379	11.1184	10.3797	9.7123	9.1079	8.5595	8.0607	7.6061	7.1909	6.8109	6.4624	6.1422	5.8474
16	14.7179	13.5777	12.5611	11.6523	10.8378	10.1059	9.4467	8.8514	8.3126	7.8237	7.3792	6.9740	6.6039	6.2651	5.9542
17	15.5623	14.2919	13.1661	12.1657	11.2741	10.4773	9.7632	9.1216	8.5436	8.0216	7.5488	7.1196	6.7291	6.3729	6.0472
18	16.3983	14.9920	13.7535	12.6593	11.6896	10.8276	10.0591	9.3719	8.7556	8.2014	7.7016	7.2497	6.8399	6.4674	6.1280
19	17.2260	15.6785	14.3238	13.1339	12.0853	11.1581	10.3356	9.6036	8.9501	8.3649	7.8393	7.3658	6.9380	6.5504	6.1982
20	18.0456	16.3514	14.8775	13.5903	12.4622	11.4699	10.5940	9.8181	9.1285	8.5136	7.9633	7.4694	7.0248	6.6231	6.2593
21	18.8570	17.0112	15.4150	14.0292	12.8212	11.7641	10.8355	10.0168	9.2922	8.6487	8.0751	7.5620	7.1016	6.6870	6.3125
22	19.6604	17.6580	15.9369	14.4511	13.1630	12.0416	11.0612	10.2007	9.4424	8.7715	8.1757	7.6446	7.1695	6.7430	6.3587
23	20.4558	18.2922	16.4436	14.8569	13.4886	12.3034	11.2722	10.3711	9.5802	8.8832	8.2664	7.7184	7.2297	6.7921	6.3988
24	21.2434	18.9139	16.9355	15.2470	13.7987	12.5504	11.4693	10.5288	9.7066	8.9847	8.3481	7.7843	7.2829	6.8352	6.4338
25	22.0232	19.5234	17.4132	15.6221	14.0940	12.7834	11.6536	10.6748	9.8226	9.0770	8.4217	7.8431	7.3300	6.8729	6.4641
26	22.7952	20.1210	17.8768	15.9828	14.3752	13.0032	11.8258	10.8100	9.9290	9.1610	8.4880	7.8956	7.3717	6.9061	6.4906
27	23.5596	20.7069	18.3270	16.3296	14.6430	13.2106	11.9867	10.9352	10.0266	9.2372	8.5478	7.9425	7.4086	6.9352	6.5135
28	24.3165	21.2813	18.7641	16.6631	14.8981	13.4062	12.1371	11.0511	10.1161	9.3066	8.6016	7.9844	7.4412	6.9607	6.5335
29	25.0658	21.8444	19.1885	16.9837	15.1411	13.5908	12.2777	11.1584	10.1983	9.3696	8.6501	8.0218	7.4701	6.9831	6.5509
30	25.8077	22.3964	19.6005	17.2920	15.3725	13.7649	12.4091	11.2578	10.2737	9.4269	8.6938	8.0552	7.4957	7.0027	6.5660
31	26.5423	22.9377	20.0005	17.5885	15.5928	13.9291	12.5318	11.3498	10.3428	9.4790	8.7331	8.0850	7.5183	7.0199	6.5791
32	27.2696	23.4683	20.3888	17.8736	15.8027	14.0841	12.6466	11.4350	10.4062	9.5264	8.7686	8.1116	7.5383	7.0350	6.5905
33	27.9897	23.9885	20.7658	18.1477	16.0026	14.2303	12.7538	11.5139	10.4644	9.5694	8.8005	8.1353	7.5560	7.0483	6.6005
34	28.7027	24.4986	21.1319	18.4112	16.1929	14.3682	12.8540	11.5870	10.5178	9.6086	8.8293	8.1565	7.5717	7.0599	6.6091
35	29.4086	24.9986	21.4872	18.6646	16.3742	14.4983	12.9477	11.6546	10.5668	9.6442	8.8552	8.1755	7.5856	7.0701	6.6166
36	30.1075	25.4888	21.8323	18.9083	16.5469	14.6211	13.0352	11.7172	10.6118	9.6765	8.8786	8.1924	7.5979	7.0790	6.6231
37	30.7995	25.9694	22.1673	19.1426	16.7113	14.7368	13.1170	11.7752	10.6530	9.7059	8.8996	8.2075	7.6087	7.0868	6.6288
38	31.4847	26.4406	22.4925	19.3679	16.8679	14.8461	13.1935	11.8289	10.6908	9.7327	8.9186	8.2210	7.6183	7.0937	6.6338
39	32.1631	26.9026	22.8082	19.5845	17.0171	14.9491	13.2650	11.8786	10.7255	9.7570	8.9356	8.2330	7.6269	7.0998	6.6380
40	32.8347	27.3555	23.1148	19.7928	17.1591	15.0464	13.3317	11.9246	10.7574	9.7791	8.9510	8.2438	7.6344	7.1051	6.6418
41	33.4997	27.7995	23.4124	19.9931	17.2944	15.1381	13.3941	11.9672	10.7866	9.7991	8.9649	8.2534	7.6410	7.1097	6.6450
42	34.1581	28.2348	23.7014	20.1857	17.4232	15.2246	13.4525	12.0067	10.8134	9.8174	8.9774	8.2619	7.6469	7.1138	6.6478
43	34.8100	28.6615	23.9819	20.3708	17.5459	15.3062	13.5070	12.0432	10.8380	9.8340	8.9886	8.2696	7.6522	7.1173	6.6503
44	35.4555	29.0799	24.2543	20.5489	17.6628	15.3833	13.5579	12.0771	10.8605	9.8491	8.9988	8.2764	7.6568	7.1205	6.6524
45	36.0945	29.4901	24.5187	20.7201	17.7741	15.4559	13.6055	12.1084	10.8812	9.8628	9.0079	8.2825	7.6609	7.1232	6.6543
46	36.7273	29.8923	24.7755	20.8847	17.8801	15.5244	13.6500	12.1374	10.9002	9.8753	9.0161	8.2880	7.6645	7.1256	6.6559
47	37.3537	30.2866	25.0247	21.0430	17.9810	15.5891	13.6916	12.1643	10.9176	9.8866	9.0235	8.2928	7.6677	7.1277	6.6573
48	37.9740	30.6731	25.2667	21.1952	18.0772	15.6501	13.7305	12.1891	10.9336	9.8969	9.0302	8.2972	7.6705	7.1296	6.6585
49	38.5881	31.0521	25.5017	21.3415	18.1687	15.7077	13.7668	12.2122	10.9482	9.9063	9.0362	8.3010	7.6730	7.1312	6.6596
50	39.1961	31.4236	25.7298	21.4822	18.2559	15.7619	13.8008	12.2335	10.9617	9.9148	9.0416	8.3045	7.6753	7.1327	6.6605

Present Value ot an Annuity of $1 (cont.)

Year	16%	17%	18%	19%	20%	21%	22%	23%	24%	25%	30%	35%	40%	45%	50%
1	.8621	.8547	.8475	.8403	.8333	.8264	.8197	.8130	.8065	.8000	.7692	.7407	.7143	.6897	.6667
2	1.6052	1.5852	1.5656	1.5465	1.5278	1.5095	1.4915	1.4740	1.4568	1.4400	1.3609	1.2894	1.2245	1.1653	1.1111
3	2.2459	2.2096	2.1743	2.1399	2.1065	2.0739	2.0422	2.0114	1.9813	1.9520	1.8161	1.6959	1.5889	1.4933	1.4074
4	2.7982	2.7432	2.6901	2.6386	2.5887	2.5404	2.4936	2.4483	2.4043	2.3616	2.1662	1.9969	1.8492	1.7195	1.6049
5	3.2743	3.1993	3.1272	3.0576	2.9906	2.9260	2.8636	2.8035	2.7454	2.6893	2.4356	2.2200	2.0352	1.8755	1.7366
6	3.6847	3.5892	3.4976	3.4098	3.3255	3.2446	3.1669	3.0923	3.0205	2.9514	2.6428	2.3852	2.1680	1.9831	1.8244
7	4.0386	3.9224	3.8115	3.7057	3.6046	3.5079	3.4155	3.3270	3.2423	3.1611	2.8021	2.5075	2.2628	2.0573	1.8830
8	4.3436	4.2072	4.0776	3.9544	3.8372	3.7256	3.6193	3.5179	3.4212	3.3289	2.9247	2.5982	2.3306	2.1085	1.9220
9	4.6065	4.4506	4.3030	4.1633	4.0310	3.9054	3.7863	3.6731	3.5655	3.4631	3.0190	2.6653	2.3790	2.1438	1.9480
10	4.8332	4.6586	4.4941	4.3389	4.1925	4.0541	3.9232	3.7993	3.6819	3.5705	3.0916	2.7150	2.4136	2.1681	1.9653
11	5.0286	4.8364	4.6560	4.4865	4.3271	4.1769	4.0354	3.9019	3.7757	3.6564	3.1474	2.7519	2.4383	2.1849	1.9769
12	5.1971	4.9884	4.7932	4.6105	4.4392	4.2785	4.1274	3.9852	3.8514	3.7251	3.1903	2.7792	2.4559	2.1965	1.9846
13	5.3423	5.1183	4.9095	4.7147	4.5327	4.3624	4.2028	4.0530	3.9124	3.7801	3.2233	2.7994	2.4685	2.2045	1.9897
14	5.4675	5.2293	5.0001	4.8023	4.6106	4.4317	4.2646	4.1082	3.9616	3.8241	3.2487	2.8143	2.4775	2.2100	1.9932
15	5.5755	5.3242	5.0916	4.8759	4.6755	4.4890	4.3152	4.1530	4.0013	3.8593	3.2682	2.8254	2.4839	2.2138	1.9954
16	5.6685	5.4053	5.1624	4.9377	4.7296	4.5364	4.3567	4.1894	4.0333	3.8874	3.2833	2.8337	2.4885	2.2164	1.9970
17	5.7487	5.4746	5.2223	4.9897	4.7746	4.5755	4.3908	4.2190	4.0591	3.9099	3.2948	2.8397	2.4918	2.2182	1.9900
18	5.8179	5.5338	5.2732	5.0333	4.8122	4.6079	4.4187	4.2431	4.0799	3.9279	3.3037	2.8443	2.4941	2.2195	1.9986
19	5.8775	5.5845	5.3163	5.0701	4.8435	4.6346	4.4415	4.2627	4.0967	3.9424	3.3106	2.8476	2.4958	2.2203	1.9991
20	5.9289	5.6278	5.3528	5.1009	4.8696	4.6567	4.4603	4.2786	4.1103	3.9539	3.3158	2.8501	2.4970	2.2209	1.9994
21	5.9732	5.6648	5.3837	5.1268	4.8913	4.6749	4.4756	4.2915	4.1212	3.9631	3.3199	2.8519	2.4979	2.2213	1.9996
22	6.0113	5.6964	5.4099	5.1486	4.9094	4.6900	4.4882	4.3021	4.1300	3.9705	3.3230	2.8533	2.4985	2.2216	1.9997
23	6.0443	5.7234	5.4321	5.1669	4.9245	4.7025	4.4985	4.3106	4.1371	3.9764	3.3254	2.8543	2.4989	2.2218	1.9998
24	6.0726	5.7465	5.4510	5.1823	4.9371	4.7128	4.5070	4.3176	4.1428	3.9811	3.3272	2.8550	2.4992	2.2219	1.9999
25	6.0971	5.7662	5.4669	5.1952	4.9476	4.7213	4.5139	4.3232	4.1474	3.9849	3.3286	2.8556	2.4994	2.2220	1.9999
26	6.1182	5.7831	5.4805	5.2060	4.9563	4.7284	4.5196	4.3278	4.1511	3.9879	3.3297	2.8560	2.4996	2.2221	1.9999
27	6.1364	5.7975	5.4919	5.2152	4.9636	4.7342	4.5243	4.3316	4.1541	3.9903	3.3306	2.8563	2.4997	2.2221	2.0000
28	6.1521	5.8099	5.5016	5.2228	4.9697	4.7390	4.5281	4.3346	4.1566	3.9923	3.3312	2.8565	2.4998	2.2221	2.0000
29	6.1656	5.8204	5.5099	5.2293	4.9747	4.7430	4.5312	4.3371	4.1585	3.9938	3.3317	2.8567	2.4998	2.2222	2.0000
30	6.1772	5.8294	5.5168	5.2347	4.9789	4.7463	4.5338	4.3391	4.1601	3.9950	3.3321	2.8568	2.4999	2.2222	2.0000
31	6.1873	5.8371	5.5227	5.2392	4.9825	4.7490	4.5359	4.3407	4.1614	3.9960	3.3324	2.8569	2.4999	2.2222	2.0000
32	6.1959	5.8437	5.5277	5.2431	4.9854	4.7512	4.5376	4.3420	4.1624	3.9968	3.3326	2.8569	2.4999	2.2222	2.0000
33	6.2034	5.8493	5.5320	5.2463	4.9878	4.7531	4.5390	4.3431	4.1632	3.9975	3.3328	2.8570	2.5000	2.2222	2.0000
34	6.2098	5.8541	5.5356	5.2490	4.9899	4.7546	4.5402	4.3440	4.1639	3.9980	3.3329	2.8570	2.5000	2.2222	2.0000
35	6.2154	5.8582	5.5386	5.2512	4.9915	4.7559	4.5411	4.3447	4.1644	3.9984	3.3330	2.8571	2.5000	2.2222	2.0000
36	6.2201	5.8617	5.5412	5.2531	4.9930	4.7569	4.5419	4.3453	4.1649	3.9987	3.3331	2.8571	2.5000	2.2222	2.0000
37	6.2243	5.8647	5.5434	5.2547	4.9941	4.7578	4.5425	4.3458	4.1652	3.9990	3.3332	2.8571	2.5000	2.2222	2.0000
38	6.2278	5.8673	5.5453	5.2561	4.9951	4.7585	4.5431	4.3461	4.1655	3.9992	3.3332	2.8571	2.5000	2.2222	2.0000
39	6.2309	5.8695	5.5468	5.2572	4.9959	4.7591	4.5435	4.3464	4.1657	3.9993	3.3332	2.8571	2.5000	2.2222	2.0000
40	6.2335	5.8713	5.5482	5.2582	4.9966	4.7596	4.5438	4.3467	4.1659	3.9995	3.3333	2.8571	2.5000	2.2222	2.0000
41	6.2358	5.8729	5.5493	5.2590	4.9972	4.7600	4.5441	4.3469	4.1660	3.9996	3.3333	2.8571	2.5000	2.2222	2.0000
42	6.2377	5.8743	5.5503	5.2596	4.9977	4.7603	4.5444	4.3471	4.1662	3.9997	3.3333	2.8571	2.5000	2.2222	2.0000
43	6.2394	5.8755	5.5511	5.2602	4.9980	4.7606	4.5446	4.3472	4.1663	3.9997	3.3333	2.8571	2.5000	2.2222	2.0000
44	6.2409	5.8765	5.5518	5.2607	4.9984	4.7608	4.5447	4.3473	4.1663	3.9998	3.3333	2.8571	2.5000	2.2222	2.0000
45	6.2422	5.8773	5.5523	5.2611	4.9986	4.7610	4.5448	4.3474	4.1664	3.9998	3.3333	2.8571	2.5000	2.2222	2.0000
46	6.2432	5.8781	5.5528	5.2614	4.9989	4.7611	4.5450	4.3475	4.1665	3.9999	3.3334	2.8571	2.5000	2.2222	2.0000
47	6.2442	5.8787	5.5533	5.2617	4.9991	4.7613	4.5450	4.3475	4.1665	3.9999	3.3334	2.8571	2.5000	2.2222	2.0000
48	6.2450	5.8792	5.5536	5.2619	4.9992	4.7614	4.5451	4.3476	4.1665	3.9999	3.3334	2.8571	2.5000	2.2222	2.0000
49	6.2457	5.8797	5.5539	5.2621	4.9994	4.7615	4.5452	4.3476	4.1666	3.9999	3.3334	2.8571	2.5000	2.2222	2.0000
50	6.2463	5.8801	5.5542	5.2623	4.9995	4.7615	4.5452	4.3477	4.1666	3.9999	3.3334	2.8571	2.5000	2.2222	2.0000

TABLE V

TABLE VI

Tax Rates for Single Taxpayers

Not over $500....**14% of the amount on line 5 of the Tax Computation worksheet.**

Taxable Income		*Tax*	
Over—	But not over—		of the amount over—
$500	$1,000	$70+15%	$500
$1,000	$1,500	$145+16%	$1,000
$1,500	$2,000	$225+17%	$1,500
$2,000	$4,000	$310+19%	$2,000
$4,000	$6,000	$690+21%	$4,000
$6,000	$8,000	$1,110+24%	$6,000
$8,000	$10,000	$1,590+25%	$8,000
$10,000	$12,000	$2,090+27%	$10,000
$12,000	$14,000	$2,630+29%	$12,000
$14,000	$16,000	$3,210+31%	$14,000
$16,000	$18,000	$3,830+34%	$16,000
$18,000	$20,000	$4,510+36%	$18,000
$20,000	$22,000	$5,230+38%	$20,000
$22,000	$26,000	$5,990+40%	$22,000
$26,000	$32,000	$7,590+45%	$26,000
$32,000	$38,000	$10,290+50%	$32,000
$38,000	$44,000	$13,290+55%	$38,000
$44,000	$50,000	$16,590+60%	$44,000
$50,000	$60,000	$20,190+62%	$50,000
$60,000	$70,000	$26,390+64%	$60,000
$70,000	$80,000	$32,790+66%	$70,000
$80,000	$90,000	$39,390+68%	$80,000
$90,000	$100,000	$46,190+69%	$90,000
$100,000	....	$53,090+70%	$100,000

Tax Rates for Married Taxpayers

Not over $1,000..**14% of the amount on line 5 of the Tax Computation worksheet.**

Taxable Income		*Tax*	
Over—	But not over—		of the amount over—
$1,000	$2,000	$140+15%	$1,000
$2,000	$3,000	$290+16%	$2,000
$3,000	$4,000	$450+17%	$3,000
$4,000	$8,000	$620+19%	$4,000
$8,000	$12,000	$1,380+22%	$8,000
$12,000	$16,000	$2,260+25%	$12,000
$16,000	$20,000	$3,260+28%	$16,000
$20,000	$24,000	$4,380+32%	$20,000
$24,000	$28,000	$5,660+36%	$24,000
$28,000	$32,000	$7,100+39%	$28,000
$32,000	$36,000	$8,660+42%	$32,000
$36,000	$40,000	$10,340+45%	$36,000
$40,000	$44,000	$12,140+48%	$40,000
$44,000	$52,000	$14,060+50%	$44,000
$52,000	$64,000	$18,060+53%	$52,000
$64,000	$76,000	$24,420+55%	$64,000
$76,000	$88,000	$31,020+58%	$76,000
$88,000	$100,000	$37,980+60%	$88,000
$100,000	$120,000	$45,180+62%	$100,000
$120,000	$140,000	$57,580+64%	$120,000
$140,000	$160,000	$70,380+66%	$140,000
$160,000	$180,000	$83,580+68%	$160,000
$180,000	$200,000	$97,180+69%	$180,000
$200,000	....	$110,980+70%	$200,000

Answers to Problems

appendix B

CHAPTER 2

1. 5 million shares
2. Current: 2.45
   Quick: 1.45
   Interest coverage: 2.45 times
   Profit margin: 17½%
   Return on assets: 5.3%
3. Profit margin: 5.8%
   Return on assets: 1.5%
4. Interest coverage 1973: 24.6 times
   Interest coverage 1972: No interest coverage
5. Working capital: $3,691,742
   Fixed assets and investments: $1,337,945
   Long term debt: $40,875
   Owners' equity: $4,988,812

CHAPTER 3

1. Cash inflow from operations: $80,700
2. Cash inflow from operations: $11,160
3. Cash inflow from operations: $9,600. Cash inflow after loan repayment: $5,600

4. Total sources and uses: $41 million
5. Working capital increases by $5 million
6. Working capital increases by $9 million
7. Total sources and uses: $9 million

CHAPTER 4

1. a. Depreciable value: $6,000
   b. Yearly depreciation using straight-line: $1,000 per year
   c. Book value after three years: $5,000
   d. Cumulative depreciation after 4 years: $4,000

2.

Year	Depreciation	Cumulative Depreciation
1	$400	$ 400
2	300	700
3	200	900
4	100	1,000

3.

Year	Depreciation	Cumulative Depreciation
1	$600	$ 600
2	300	900
3	100	1,000
4	0	1,000

4. Straight-line depreciation is $28,000 per year. Double-declining-balance depreciation is as shown.

Year	Depreciation	Year	Depreciation
1	$72,000	6	$47,454
2	66,240	7	43,658
3	60,940	8	40,165
4	56,065	9	36,952
5	51,580	10	33,996

5.

Year	Depreciation
1	$2,061
2	1,855
3	1,649
4	1,443
5	1,237

6.

Year	Depreciation
1	$3,333
2	2,667
3	2,000
4	1,333
5	667

7. Sixth or seventh year
8. Cumulative depreciation after 7 years is $19,151.46
9. Depreciation using straight-line: $1,667 per year. Depreciation using 1¼ declining-balance:

Year	Depreciation
1	$1,875
2	1,758
3	1,648
4	1,545
5	1,448

10. Amortization: $125,000 per year

CHAPTER 5

1. Tax: $46,500
2. Average for 1975 using 1975 rates: 37.2%
   Average for 1975 if pre-1975 rates were used: 42.8%
3. Refunds would be requested as follows:

Year	Refund Amount
1972	$89,500
1973	89,500
1974	24,000

4. 1976 tax: $58,500
5. Additional tax: $174,000
6. Total tax: $38,100
7. Total tax: $16,500
8. Additional tax: $12,600
9. Section 1231 applies; tax would be reduced by $2,400 provided the firm did not have any capital gains
10. Sold same year—tax savings: $4,800
    Sold different years—tax savings: $13,800
11. Total tax: $123,300
12. Tax paid by year:

Year	Tax
1971	$ 92,500
1972	84,400
1973	95,500
1974	112,000 (includes capital loss carry back of $5,000)
1975	124,500 (includes capital loss carry back of $20,000)

13. Total tax: $20,645
14. Request refund from 1972: $89,500
    Request refund from 1973: $48,000
    Total: $137,500
15. Cash flow: $137,500

CHAPTER 6

1.

Income	Tax			
$ 8,300	Single:	$ 1,665	Married:	$ 1,446
14,500	Single:	3,365	Married:	2,885
43,000	Single:	16,040	Married:	13,580

2. Federal income tax: $1,996

3. Federal income tax: $2,659

4. a. Federal tax: $2,738
   b. Social Security tax: $1,170
   c. Total taxes: $5,882.50

5. a. Federal tax: $6,578
   b. Social Security: $1,772.55 based on 1976 rates
   c. Federal tax: $7,861

6. About $8,000

7. Federal income tax if single: $1,506 each
   Federal income tax if married: $3,235 total

8. Federal income tax: $5,734.52

9. Social Security tax: $1,714.05

CHAPTER 7

1. a. Corporate: $5,612
   b., c. Subchapter S and sole proprietorship: $5,516

2. Corporate: $36,295
   Sole proprietorship: $51,690

3. If $20,000 of salaries were taken as a dividend, total tax would increase by $6,890 to $43,185.

4 A loss of $1,635 would be sustained before taxes
   Cash flow from operations is $1,274
   Cash flow (after principal repayment) would be reduced by $606

5. Sole proprietorship and Subchapter S: $9,374
   Corporate: $8,520

CHAPTER 10

1.

Year	Payment
1	$2,500
2	2,300
3	1,100

2.

Month	Installment Payment	Principal Payment
1	$40.00	$500
2	36.67	500
3	33.33	500
4	30.00	500
5	26.67	500
6	23.33	500
7	20.00	500
8	16.67	500
9	13.33	500
10	10.00	500
11	6.67	500
12	3.33	500

3. $33.65
4. AT&T: 9¼%
   Chrysler: 11.34%
   Philadelphia Electric: 11%
   Sears: 9½%
5. Usable principal: $3,420
   Effective interest rate: 10½%
6. Approximate interest rate: 12%
7. Auto dealer: 12.8%
   Bank: 16.3%
8. Effective interest rate: 10½%
9. Effective interest rate: 12½%
10. $106.09
11. $6,864 after four years
12. $43,319 after ten years
13. $79,058 after 30 years
14. Needs to save $2,171 each year
15. $41,583 after ten years
16. $11,049 annual sinking fund payment
17. $193,332 annual sinking fund payment
18. Effective interest rate: 5.09%
19. $1,183

CHAPTER 11

1. All common stock: EPS = $2.67
   50% debt financing: EPS = $3.33

2. 70% stock, 30% debt: EPS = $1.76
   50% stock, 50% debt: EPS = $1.60
3. All common stock: EPS = $3.90
   70% stock, 30% debt: EPS = $3.93
   40% stock, 60% debt: EPS = $3.51
4. All common stock: EPS = $4.16
   $100,000 debt financing: EPS = $4.52
   $300,000 debt financing: EPS = $4.82
5. Effective interest rate: 16%
6. Effective interest rate: 10.6%
7. Effective interest rate: 11.6%
8. Effective interest rate: 9.7%
9. a. Initial loan: $235,294
   b.

Year	Interest Payment	Principal Payment
1	$28,235	$47,058
2	22,588	47,058
3	16,941	47,058
4	11,294	47,058
5	5,647	47,058

   c. Effective interest rate: 14.1%
10. a. Initial loan, $1,111,111
    b.

Payment	Interest	Principal Repayment
1	$55,555	$277,778
2	41,667	277,778
3	27,778	277,778
4	13,889	277,778

11. Cost using long-term debt: $46,000
    Cost using short-term debt: $43,333
12. Trade credit: 12.2%
    Bank loan: 14.7%
    Factoring receivables: 34%
13. Maximum amount of loan: $90,000
    Annual dollar cost: $10,800
    Service charge: $9,000
    Effective interest rate: 22%

CHAPTER 12

1. Book value per share: $8.88
2. Liquidating value per share: $12.50
3. Book value per share: $3.66
4. Conversion price: $29.41
5. Conversion price: $19.17
6. Theoretical value of warrant: nothing
7. Profit per warrant: $8
8. Profit from warrants: $2,664
   Profit from stock: $424.00
9. Donna paid $4 in excess of theoretical value. Donna will break even if common sells at $26 per share. If the common sells at $30, she will make a profit of $4 per warrant.
10.

Preferred stock ($40 par, 10,000 shares outstanding)	$ 400,000
Common stock ($.50 par, 300,000 shares outstanding)	157,500
Paid-in capital	3,492,500
Retained earnings	2,500,000
Total	$6,550,000

11.

Preferred stock ($40 par, 10,000 shares outstanding)	$ 400,000
Common stock ($.17 par, 900,000 shares outstanding)	150,000
Paid-in capital	2,000,000
Retained earnings	4,000,000
Total	$6,550,000

CHAPTER 13

1. a. Federal tax: $178,500; after-tax profit: $221,500
   b. Federal tax: $135,300; after-tax profit: $174,700
   c. After-tax interest rate: 4.68%
2. Effective interest rate: 9.5%
   Effective after-tax interest rate: 4.95%
3. a. Weighted average after-tax cost of interest: 4.1%
   b. Weighted average after-tax cost of interest: 3.3%

4. Cost of equity capital: 10½%
5. Increase in dividend: $.22
6. Cost of preferred capital: 6.46%
7. Cost of retained earnings: 7.4%
8. Weighted average after-tax cost of capital: 8.8%
9. Weighted average after-tax cost of capital: 6.8%
10. After-tax dollar cost: $491; after-tax rate: 7%
11. a. Cost of debt: 4.16%
    b. Cost of common stock: 9%
    c. Cost of preferred stock: 5.3%
    d. Weighted average cost of capital: 8.1%
12. Owners' marginal tax rate: approximately 35%
13. Additional return for financial risk: 3%
14. a. Cost of common stock: 12%
    b. Cost of preferred stock: 7.4%
    c. After-tax cost of debt: 3%
    d. Cost of retained earnings: 8%
    e. Weighted average after-tax cost of capital: 6.7%

CHAPTER 14

1. Total capital requirement: $470,000
2. They should stay; if they sell, they will incur a tax of $7,500 while only saving $5,000 in working capital
3. Net cost: $5,925,000

CHAPTER 15

1. After four years the entire $10,000 investment would be recovered; therefore, the investment should be made
2. PV of inflows: $24,725
3. NPV: $14,611
   Payback period: 2.4 years
4.

Project	Payback Period
A	3 years
B	5
C	5⅙

5.

Project	PV of Inflows	NPV	PI	Rank
A	$11,869	$1,869	1.187	Second
B	10,567	− 1,433	.881	Not acceptable
C	4,282	1,282	1.427	First

6. NPV of new machine: $14,551
7. NPV of trash compactor: $12,675
8. NPV of new machine: −$7,084

CHAPTER 16

1. IRR: 20%
2. IRR: between 5% and 6%
3. IRR: 8.3%
4. IRR: 14%
5. IRR: approximately 4%
6.

Project	Payback Period	NPV	IRR	(PI)	Rank (IRR)	Rank (PI)
A	4 years	− $ 5,230	8%	.9477	—	—
B	4	− 15,690	8	.9477	—	—
C	5.26	50,242	14	1.16	First	Second
D	7.04	104,465	13	1.209	Second	First

7. IRR A: about 9%
   IRR B: 5.58%
8. IRR: 9.1%
9. Projects A, K, C, H, and B would be accepted using $1,450,000.

CHAPTER 17

1. NPV: $603
2. NPV: $283

3.

Project Ranking

E
D
G ⎱ Same
A ⎰
B

CHAPTER 18

1. NPV straight-line: − $5,184
   NPV double-declining-balance: − $2,507
2. NPV straight-line: $14,555
   NPV double-declining-balance: $15,671
3. Reduce tax liability by $10,000 with life of 9 years
   Reduce tax liability by $6,667 with life of 6 years
4. Reduce tax liability by $2,000
5. Reduce tax liability by $5,333
6. Without investment tax credit IRR: about 10%
   With investment tax credit: about 12½%
7. NPV: about 14%
8. NPV: straight-line $1,376; NPV: SYD $1,507
9. NPV without ITC $18,014; with ITC $21,514

CHAPTER 19

1. NPV: − $6,457
2. Save: $1,319.30 each year
3. Value at age 65: $105,755
   The estate will last about 25 years with $9,000 drawn per year.
4. Value at age 65: $133,015
   The estate will last indefinitely with $9,000 drawn per year.
   She can draw $10,641 per year without depleting the principal.
5. a. Value of estate at age 60: $73,966
   b. Years she can draw $6,000: approximately 23
6. a. Pretax current yield: 7.9%
   b. Pretax yield to maturity: 9.5%
   c. After tax yield to maturity: 6.25%
7. Yield to maturity: about 9%

8. Value at age 65: $543,110
    It will last indefinitely with $12,000 drawn per year.
9. Tax sheltered: $10,075 after-tax income.
    Not tax sheltered: $7,496 after-tax income the first year of retirement.

CHAPTER 20

1. Yield is less than 10%
2. IRR: about 8⅔%
3. The IRR exceeds 12%
4. NPV Purchase: −$228,921; NPV Rental: −$209,032
5. Purchasing is better
6. Purchasing is better
7. NPV purchase: −$732,592
    NPV lease: −$860,479

CHAPTER 21

1. Concentration banking will result in increasing EBT by $14,000 per year.
2. The lockbox system will result in increasing EBT by $40,000 per year.
3. The lockbox system will result in increasing EBT by $16,000 per year.
4. a. Average level of investments in accounts receivable will increase by $11,000.
    b. They should extend credit to 60 days.
5. Plan A is superior.
6. Average collection period: 64 days.

CHAPTER 22

1. Average monthly demand: 600 units
2. EOQ: 50 units per order
    They should reorder every 1.6 years
    Total inventory cost: $100 per year
3. EOQ: 300 boxes per order
    They should place orders five times per year
    Total inventory cost: $1,800 per year
4. a. EOQ: 3,000 units per order
    b. Number of orders to place per year: 75
    c. Dollar investment in inventory: $4,500

5. EOQ: 400 units per order
   Total inventory cost: $1,600 per year
6. Average inventory level: $80,000
7.

Month	M	J	J	A	S	O	N	D
Inflow (000)	$109.6	134.4	157.6	161.6	133.2	95.6	74.4	63.2
Outflow (000)	97.5	122.0	136.0	140.0	108.5	74.0	59.5	55.0

CHAPTER 23

1. a. BEP: 15,000 units
   b. Profit: $30,000
   c. *CM:* $10
   d. DOL: 4
2. Output: 65,000 units
3. DOL: 4.33
4. BEP: 200,000 units
   Profit: $200,000
   CM: $4
   DOL at 250,000 units: 5
5. DOL at 40,000 units: -4
   DOL at 50,000 units: indeterminate
   DOL at 65,000 units: 4.33
   DOL at 80,000 units: 2.66

Financial Formulas

appendix C

I. GENERAL FORMULAS

$$\text{Earnings per share} = \frac{\text{After-tax profits} - \text{Preferred stock dividends}}{\text{Shares of common stock outstanding}}$$

Cash flow = After-tax profits + Implicit cost cash throw-offs
   where implicit costs include depreciation, amortization, and other non-cash expenses

Working capital = Current assets − Current liabilities

Depreciable value = Total cost of an asset − Estimated salvage value

Salvage value = Estimated sale price − (Selling costs + Costs to remove asset)

Book value (of an asset) = Total cost − Accumulated depreciation

Taxable income = Adjusted gross income − Deductions

$$\text{Current yield} = \frac{\text{Yearly interest payment in dollars}}{\text{Market price of bond}}$$

$$\text{Effective interest rate on loan} = \frac{\text{Yearly interest payment in dollars}}{\text{Amount of principal received}}$$

Compound interest (one year) $S = P(1+i)$
 where $S =$ compound sum
  $P =$ principal (original deposit)
  $i =$ interest rate

Compound interest (several years) $S = P(1+i)^n$
 where n is the number of periods (years)

$$\text{Book value of common stock} = \frac{\text{Owner's equity} - \text{Par value of preferred stock outstanding}}{\text{Shares of common stock outstanding}}$$

Liquidating value of common stock =
$$\frac{\text{Sale price of assets} - \text{Creditors' claims} - \text{Par value of preferred stock}}{\text{Shares of common stock outstanding}}$$

II. COST OF CAPITAL

A. After-tax cost of interest (k_i)

$$k_i = \frac{\text{Interest paid} - \text{Reduction in federal income tax}}{\text{Amount borrowed}}$$

Also

$$k_i = k(1-t)$$

where $k_i =$ effective after-tax rate of interest
  $k =$ effective pretax rate of interest
  $t =$ firm's marginal tax rate

B. Cost of common stock

Dividend growth model

$$k_e = \frac{D}{P} + g$$

where $k_e =$ annual cost of the common stock equity capital
  $D =$ annual dividend in dollar amount
  $P =$ market price of the common stock
  $g =$ annual growth rate of the dividend

Required rate of return model

$$k_e = i + B + \Phi$$

where $k_e =$ annual cost of the common stock equity capital
  $i =$ current risk-free rate of return available to investors
  $B =$ additional return to compensate for business risk
  $\Phi =$ additional return to compensate for financial risk

C. Cost of preferred stock

$$k_p = \frac{D}{P-b}$$

where k_p = cost of preferred stock equity capital
D = annual dividend per share expressed in dollars
P = original price at which the stock was purchased
b = investment banker's commission

D. Cost of retained earnings

$$R = k_e(1-T)(1-B)$$

where R = cost of retained earnings
k_e = cost of common stock equity capital
T = owner's marginal tax rate
B = average brokerage fee

III. CAPITAL BUDGETING CALCULATIONS

Net present value = Present value of after-tax cash inflows − Present value of after-tax cash outflows

$$\text{Profitability index} = \frac{\text{Present value of after-tax cash inflows}}{\text{Present value of after-tax outflows}}$$

IV. INVENTORY COST CALCULATIONS

Economic order quantity

$$EOQ = \sqrt{\frac{2SO}{C}}$$

where EOQ = economic order quantity
O = ordering cost per order
S = usage per unit time (year, month)
C = carrying cost per unit of inventory per unit time

Total inventory cost

$$TC = \frac{SO}{Q} + \frac{CQ}{2}$$

where TC = total inventory cost
S = usage per unit time
O = ordering cost per order
Q = quantity ordered in each order

V. PROFIT CALCULATIONS

Profit

$$\pi = TR - TC$$

where π = profit
   TR = total revenue
   TC = total costs

Total revenue

$$TR = P \times Q$$

where P = sale price per unit
   Q = quantity produced and sold

Total costs

$$TC = FC + VC$$

where FC = total fixed costs
   VC = total variable costs

Total variable costs

$$VC = vc \times Q$$

where VC = total variable costs
   vc = variable cost per unit produced
   Q = quantity produced and sold

Contribution margin

$$CM = P - vc$$

where CM = contribution margin
   P = sale price per unit
   vc = variable cost per unit

VI. FINANCIAL RATIOS

A. Liquidity ratios

$$\text{Current ratio} = \frac{\text{Current assets}}{\text{Current liabilities}}$$

$$\text{Quick or acid test ratio} = \frac{\text{Current assets} - \text{Inventory}}{\text{Current liabilities}}$$

$$\text{Average collection period} = \frac{\text{Average receivables} \times 360}{\text{Annual credit sales}}$$

$$\text{Inventory turnover} = \frac{\text{Cost of goods sold}}{\text{Average inventory}}$$

B. Leverage ratios

$$\text{Debt to net worth} = \frac{\text{Total debt}}{\text{Net worth}}$$

$$\text{Degree of operating leverage} = \frac{Q(P-vc)}{Q(P-vc)-FC}$$

where Q = quantity produced and sold
$\quad P$ = sale price per unit
$\quad vc$ = variable cost per unit
$\quad FC$ = total fixed costs

C. Profitability ratios

$$\text{Profit margin} = \frac{\text{Earnings before taxes}}{\text{Sales}}$$

$$\text{Return on assets} = \frac{\text{Earnings before taxes}}{\text{Average total assets}}$$

D. Debt coverage ratios

$$\text{Interest coverage ratio} = \frac{\text{Earnings before interest and taxes (EBIT)}}{\text{Interest for period}}$$

Sources

of

Economic and Financial Information

from The Conference Board†

appendix D

This annotated bibliography of well-known sources of economic data is limited to basic references. It should not be construed as a comprehensive listing of available material on economic information.

For the convenience of the user, the bibliography has been divided into several broad categories. All, except one devoted to international economic statistics, relate to the U.S. economy. Entries in the bibliography are listed by title, publisher, and frequency of issue.

Because economists generally depend to a great extent on official statistics, most of these entries are government publications. The bibliography includes, however, a selected sample of sources published by The Conference Board and other organizations.

Publications of the federal government, unless otherwise noted, can be obtained from The Superintendent of Documents, U.S. Government Printing Office, Washington, D.C. 20402. Entries published by The Conference Board are denoted by an asterisk (*). To order them, or to inquire about further details of their contents, please contact Information Service Division, The Conference Board, 845 Third Avenue, New York, N.Y. 10022.

†The Conference Board, Inc., founded in 1916, is an independent, nonprofit institution for business and economic research. Its purpose is to promote broader understanding of business and the economy for the enlightenment both of those who manage business enterprises and of the society which shapes the business system. It pursues this by encouraging exchange of experience and opinion, by objective analyses of significant business and economic developments, and by widespread distribution of facts developed through these activities. The board is a fact-finding agency; it takes no positions on public policy issues nor does it act as a consulting organization. Its work is supported by more than 4,000 associates (members).

419

GENERAL REFERENCES

Survey of Current Business   *Monthly*

U.S. Department of Commerce, Bureau of Economic Analysis

Each issue contains over 2,000 statistical series relating to Gross National Product (GNP), prices and employment, plus a wide variety of industrial data and other business indicators. July issue contains annual revisions of national income and product accounts.

Business Statistics   *Biennial*

U.S. Department of Commerce, Office of Business Economics

A supplement to the *Survey of Current Business*. Presents historical data for the statistical series covered in that publication; also gives explanatory notes to their sources of data.

Business Conditions Digest   *Monthly*

U.S. Department of Commerce, Bureau of Economic Analysis

A compilation of numerous economic statistical series, including charts, arranged for convenient analysis of business cycles.

Federal Reserve Bulletin   *Monthly*

Board of Governors of the Federal Reserve System

Ordering address: Division of Administrative Services
Board of Governors of the Federal Reserve System
Washington, D.C. 20551

A compendium of financial, industrial and commercial statistics for the United States. Also includes data on the U.S. balance of payments and international exchange rates.

The Economic Report of the President and the Council of Economic Advisers   *Annual*

Executive Office of the President

The President's economic program and an elaboration of the goals of the U.S. economy by the Council of Economic Advisers. The analysis is supplemented by statistics on GNP, industrial production, personal income, employment, prices, profits and other aspects of the economy.

Statistical Abstract of the United States   *Annual*

U.S. Department of Commerce

A basic reference source summarizing statistics on industrial, social, political and economic organizations of the United States; includes statistics obtained from both government and private sources.

Economic Indicators   *Monthly*

U.S. Congress, Joint Economic Committee

Basic series on prices, wages, industrial production, consumer purchasing power, money supply, and receipts and expenditures of the Federal Government.

(*) The Conference Board Statistical Bulletin *Monthly*

Gives GNP forecasts and information on various statistical series, including leading business indicators, help-wanted advertising indexes, diffusion indexes, capital appropriations, profit margins, discretionary spending and automobile sales.

(*) Current Economic Trends   *Quarterly*

Presents current and historical statistics on major economic indicators in chart analysis form.

AGGREGATE MEASURES OF INCOME, DEMAND AND PRODUCTION

A. GROSS NATIONAL PRODUCT AND INCOME
Survey of Current Business   *Monthly*

U.S. Department of Commerce, Bureau of Economic Analysis

See annotation under General References.

B. CONSUMER SPENDING

(*) The Conference Board RECORD   *Monthly*

Each issue includes a section on "Consumer Markets," which reports on various facets of consumer spending.

(*) Consumer Attitudes and Buying Plans   *Bimonthly*

Statistics measuring consumer attitudes toward current and future economic conditions; also interprets consumers' intentions to purchase durable goods.

(*) **Consumer Market Indicators** *Monthly*

Statistics on consumption expenditures, consumer price index, consumer confidence index, and other market indicators.

Current Retail Trade Reports *Weekly and Monthly*

U.S. Department of Commerce, Bureau of the Census

Data on estimated weekly and monthly retail sales, by lines of business, for the United States and for selected metropolitan statistical areas (SMSA's).

(*) **A Guide to Consumer Markets** *Annual*

A statistical handbook. Contains data on employment, consumer income and expenditures, and the production and distribution of purchased goods and services.

Survey of Buying Power *Annual*

Sales Management
630 Third Avenue
New York, New York 10017
Each edition includes data related to total retail sales and consumer buying indexes for the 50 states, their counties, and selected SMSA's.

Surveys of Consumers *Annual*

Institute of Social Research
University of Michigan
Ann Arbor, Michigan 48106
National survey data on family incomes, household assets and liabilities, and consumer expenditures for durable goods. Also includes an outlook on consumer demand.

Survey of Consumer Expenditures *Irregular*

U.S. Department of Labor, Bureau of Labor Statistics

Data show expenditure patterns according to various family characteristics.

C. BUSINESS SPENDING

Survey of Current Business *Monthly*

U.S. Department of Commerce, Bureau of Economic Analysis
See annotation under General References.

Annual McGraw-Hill Survey of Business Plans for New Plants and Equipment *Annual*

McGraw-Hill Publications Co.
Economics Department
1221 Avenue of the Americas
New York, New York 10020
Statistical data on planned capital investment, broken down by industry groups and regional areas.

Census of Manufactures *Every five years in years ending in 2 and 7*

U.S. Department of Commerce, Bureau of the Census

Statistical data on size of establishments, employment and expenditures by industry, and inventories by industry for regions of the United States.

Annual Survey of Manufacturers *Annual*

U.S. Department of Commerce, Bureau of the Census

Survey of manufacturing industries published in the years between the five-year Census of Manufactures.

(*) **Quarterly Survey of Capital Appropriations** *Quarterly*

Statistics on business investment in plant and equipment based on a survey of the nation's 1,000 largest manufacturers.

(*) **Capital Investment Conditions** *Semiannually*

Data on capacity utilization and factors affecting financing of capital spending based on a survey of the nation's 1,000 largest manufacturers.

D. CONSTRUCTION

Construction Reports *See entries below*

U.S. Department of Commerce, Bureau of the Census

Housing and construction statistics under the following categories:

C20. Housing Starts *Monthly*

Statistics on new housing starts by ownership, location and type of structure.

C22. Housing Completions   *Monthly*

Data on number of new units completed and currently under construction.

C25. New One-Family Sold and for Sale
Monthly and Annually

Corresponding data on sales and number of unsold new one-family dwellings.

C30. Value of New Construction Put in Place
Monthly

Current estimates of private and public construction, by aggregate value of these classifications.

C40. Housing Authorized by Building Permits and Public Contracts   *Monthly and Annually*

Statistics on the number of new housing units authorized in the United States under private building permits and public contracts.

C50. Residential Alterations and Repairs
Quarterly and Annually

Figures on quarterly and annual expenditures, according to type of work and size of property, for geographical regions of the United States.

Construction Review   *Monthly*

U.S. Department of Commerce, Bureau of Domestic Commerce
Contains timely, in-depth articles, as well as current data on expenditures, building starts, and employment levels in the construction industry.

Dodge Construction Potentials   *Monthly*

McGraw-Hill Information Systems Co.
F.W. Dodge Division
1221 Avenue of the Americas
New York, New York 10020
Statistical summary of construction contracts for new and major alteration projects; data are broken down by types of projects and by regions of the United States.

E. GOVERNMENT SPENDING
1. Federal Government
The Budget of the U.S. Government   *Annual*

U.S. Office of Management and Budget
Contains the official text of the President's budget message, a description of the budget system, data on budget receipts and expenditures, and line-item details of the budget as a whole.

The Budget of the U.S. Government: Appendix   *Annual*

U.S. Office of Management and Budget
Detailed information on the legislative authority for the budget; also data on programs in the budget, requests for supplemental appropriations and new program proposals.

The U.S. Budget in Brief   *Annual*

U.S. Office of Management and Budget
The President's budget message and a condensed overview of the budget. Includes major summary tables.

(*)The Federal Budget: Its Impact on the Economy
Annual

Analysis of the federal budget as a whole, special analysis of some of its programs, and background information on major expenditure patterns in relation to the national economy.

Treasury Bulletin   *Monthly*

U.S. Department of the Treasury, Office of the Secretary
A monthly summary of the Treasury's activities as related to federal fiscal operations. Includes international financial statistics and data on capital transfers between the United States and foreign countries.

Monthly Statement of Receipts and Outlays of the U.S. Government   *Monthly*

U.S. Department of the Treasury, Bureau of Accounts
Details on receipts and expenditures for the U.S. budget and trust accounts.

Annual Report of the Secretary of the Treasury with Statistical Appendix   *Annual*

U.S. Department of the Treasury, Bureau of Accounts

Statistical tables include summary of the Treasury's receipts and expenditures; also data on federal aid to states and other activities of the Treasury Department.

Facts and Figures on Government Finance

Biennial

Tax Foundation, Inc.
50 Rockefeller Plaza
New York, New York 10020

Information about taxes, expenditures and debts for federal, state and local governments.

2. **State and Local Governments**
    Governmental Finances   *Annual*

U.S. Department of Commerce, Bureau of the Census

A series of reports that give fiscal data for the Federal Government, the 50 states, numerous cities, and selected SMSA's.

Census of Governments   *Every five years in years ending in 2 and 7*

U.S. Department of Commerce, Bureau of the Census

Various series of fiscal data for state and local governments of the United States.

F. **EXPORTS**
    U.S. Commodity Exports and Imports as Related to Output   *Annual*

U.S. Department of Commerce, Bureau of the Census

Statistical data on relationship between domestic output and foreign trade in commodities.

Commodity Yearbook   *Annual*

Commodity Research Bureau
140 Broadway
New York, New York 10005

Latest trends in the supply and demand of numerous commodities. Price data are illustrated by charts.

LABOR AND PRODUCTIVITY

A. **GENERAL SOURCES**
    Handbook of Labor Statistics   *Annual*

U.S. Department of Labor, Bureau of Labor Statistics

A statistical compendium of all phases of labor economics.

Manpower Report of the President   *Annual*

Executive Office of the President

Documents current and historical trends in population, labor force, employment and unemployment, productivity and occupational data.

B. **EMPLOYMENT**
    Employment and Earnings   *Monthly*

U.S. Department of Labor, Bureau of Labor Statistics

Statistics on employment, work hours, earnings, and labor turnover.

Labor Turnover   *Monthly*

U.S. Department of Labor, Bureau of Labor Statistics

Summarizes factory labor-turnover rates for major industry groups.

Monthly Labor Review   *Monthly*

U.S. Department of Labor, Bureau of Labor Statistics

Articles on employment, wages, prices, productivity and labor developments abroad. Also includes current statistics for most of these areas.

C. **PRODUCTIVITY**
    Indexes of Output per Man-Hour for Selected Industries   *Annual*

U.S. Department of Labor, Bureau of Labor Statistics

Updates indexes of output per man-hour and output per employee for industries currently included in the Federal Government's productivity measurement program.

DEMOGRAPHIC DATA

A. GENERAL SOURCES

Manpower Report of the President   *Annual*

>   Executive Office of the President
>   See annotation under Labor and Productivity (General Sources).

(*) **A Guide to Consumer Markets**   *Annual*

>   See annotation under Aggregate Measures of Income, Demand and Production (Consumer Spending).

B. POPULATION

Census of Population   *Every 10 years when the last digit is 0*

>   U.S. Department of Commerce, Bureau of the Census
>   A compendium of statistics related to the population of the United States and the social and economic living patterns of the American people. Gives statistics for U.S. territories, the 50 states and their counties, the District of Columbia, and the country's major SMSA's.

Current Population Reports   *Irregular*

>   U.S. Department of Commerce, Bureau of the Census
>   Up-to-date statistics on population, economic and social characteristics, and other demographic trends of the American people. Statistics are published in eight separate series of reports:

P-20 Population Characteristics   *Irregular*

Current national data on school enrollment, mobility and household characteristics.

P-23 Special Studies   *Irregular*

Infrequent reports containing specialized demographic data.

P-25 Population Estimates and Projections   *Irregular*

Monthly estimates of the total population of the United States, broken down by geographic area and other classifications. Includes projections on the future population of the entire United States — the 50 states, the District of Columbia, and the territories.

P-26 Federal-State Cooperative Program for Population Estimates   *Irregular*

Population estimates for counties in selected states where figures are prepared by state agencies as part of the Federal-State Cooperative Program for Local Population Estimates.

P-27 Farm Population   *Irregular*

Data on size and other selected characteristics of the U.S. farm population. Issued jointly with the Economic Research Service, U.S. Department of Agriculture.

P-28 Special Censuses   *Irregular*

Results of population censuses requested and funded by city or county governments. Reports show population changes in each locality since the last general census.

P-60 Consumer Income   *Irregular*

Information on the number of families and employed individuals at various income levels.

P-65 Consumer Buying Indicators   *Annual*

Information on home ownership and purchases of automobiles and major household appliances. Statistics are broken down by income, age of family head, residence, and other characteristics.

Vital Statistics of the United States   *Annual*

>   U.S. Department of Health, Education and Welfare, National Center for Health Statistics
>   A source of data on births, deaths, marriages and divorces. Regional information is classified by cities, counties and SMSA's.

C. EDUCATION

Digest of Educational Statistics   *Annual*

>   U.S. Department of Health, Education and Welfare, Office of Education
>   An abstract of statistical information on American education. Contains data compiled from both government and private sources on number of schools, enrollments and graduates.

Fall Enrollment in Higher Education   *Annual*

>   U.S. Department of Health, Education and Welfare, Office of Education
>   Enrollment data broken down by state, regional area, and individual institution.

Projections of Educational Statistics   *Annual*

U.S. Department of Health, Education and Welfare, Office of Education

Ten-year projections for enrollments, number of graduates and teachers, institutional budgets, and related matters.

WAGES AND PRICES

A. GENERAL SOURCES

Business Conditions Digest   *Monthly*

U.S. Department of Commerce, Bureau of Economic Analysis

See annotation under General References.

Economic Indicators   *Monthly*

U.S. Congress, Joint Economic Committee

See annotation under General References.

B. WAGE RATES

Employment and Earnings   *Monthly*

U.S. Department of Labor, Bureau of Labor Statistics

See annotation under Labor and Productivity (Employment).

Handbook of Labor Statistics   *Annual*

U.S. Department of Labor, Bureau of Labor Statistics

See annotation under Labor and Productivity (General Sources).

Manpower Report of the President   *Annual*

Executive Office of the President

See annotation under Labor and Productivity (General Sources).

C. CONSUMER PRICES

The Consumer Price Index   *Monthly*

U.S. Department of Labor, Bureau of Labor Statistics

Statistical measures of the average changes in prices of goods and services (about 400 items) purchased by urban wage earners and clerical workers living in 56 urban areas across the country.

(*) A Guide to Consumer Markets   *Annual*

See annotation under Aggregate Measures of Income, Demand and Production (Consumer Spending).

D. WHOLESALE PRICES

Wholesale Prices and Price Indexes   *Monthly*

U.S. Department of Labor, Bureau of Labor Statistics

A basic reference on wholesale price movements; includes statistical tables and technical notes.

INDUSTRY STATISTICS

A. GENERAL SOURCES

Survey of Current Business   *Monthly*

U.S. Department of Commerce, Bureau of Economic Analysis

See annotation under General References.

Federal Reserve Bulletin   *Monthly*

Board of Governors of the Federal Reserve System

See annotation under General References.

Industrial Production   *Monthly*

Board of Governors of the Federal Reserve System

Ordering address: Division of Administrative Services
Board of Governors of the Federal Reserve System
Washington, D.C. 20551

Preliminary statistics for the total FRB Index; also carries revisions of the previous month's figures.

Moody's Industrial Manual   *Biweekly and Annual*

Moody's Investors Service
99 Church Street
New York, New York 10007

Various statistics on U.S. industrial corporations; includes separate section on classification of companies by industries and products.

Predicasts   *Quarterly*

Predicasts, Inc.
11001 Cedar Avenue
Cleveland, Ohio 44106
Abstracts published forecasts for general economic indicators, industries, products and services.

Standard & Poor's Industry Survey

Quarterly and Annual

Standard & Poor's Corporation
345 Hudson Street
New York, New York 10014
More than 40 basic surveys, each devoted to a major industry group; provides both financial statistics and detailed industry data.

Industry Profiles   *Annual*

U.S. Department of Commerce, Bureau of the Census
Published as part of *Annual Survey of Manufacturers*; gives basic data series for past decade for selected major industry groups.

U.S. Industrial Outlook   *Annual*

U.S. Department of Commerce, Domestic and International Business Administration
Detailed analysis and projections for more than 200 individual manufacturing and nonmanufacturing industries.

B. SECTORS

1. Manufacturing

Current Industrial Reports   *Monthly, Quarterly and Annual*

U.S. Department of Commerce, Bureau of the Census
Information on production, shipments and inventories for 5,000 manufactured items.

Annual Survey of Manufacturers   *Annual*

U.S. Department of Commerce, Bureau of the Census
See annotation under Aggregate Measures of Income, Demand and Production (Business Spending).

Census of Manufactures   *Every five years in years ending in 2 and 7*

U.S. Department of Commerce, Bureau of the Census
See annotation under Aggregate Measures of Income, Demand and Production (Business Spending).

2. Mining and Energy

Mineral Industry Surveys   *Weekly, Monthly and Quarterly*

U.S. Department of the Interior, Bureau of Mines
Periodic reports update information published in the *Mineral Yearbook* (see below).

Mineral Yearbook   *Annual*

U.S. Department of the Interior, Bureau of Mines
A statistical handbook on U.S. production of all metallic, nonmetallic and mineral fuel commodities; also gives similar statistics for more than 100 countries.

Census of Mineral Industries   *Every five years in years ending in 2 and 7*

U.S. Department of Commerce, Bureau of the Census
Statistical data for each of 42 extractive industries on quantity and value of products shipped, quantity and cost of fuels, and electrical energy purchased.

3. Utilities

Electric Power Statistics   *Monthly*

U.S. Federal Power Commission
Summaries of statistics on production of electric power, capacities of power plants, and sales of electricity.

Statistics of Communications Common Carriers   *Annual*

U.S. Federal Power Commission
Financial and operating data for 42 major telephone and telegraph companies operating in the United States.

Statistics of Publicly Owned Electric Utilities in the U.S. *Annual*

U.S. Federal Power Commission
Financial and operating data for publicly owned utilities operating in the United States.

Statistics of Privately Owned Electric Utilities in the U.S. *Annual*

U.S. Federal Power Commission
Financial and operating data for privately owned utilities operating in the United States.

4. **Financial**

See section below on Financial Markets.

5. **Trade and Services**

Current Retail Trade Reports *Weekly and Monthly*

U.S. Department of Commerce, Bureau of the Census
See annotation under Aggregate Measures of Income, Demand and Production (Consumer Spending).

Monthly Selected Service Receipts *Monthly*

U.S. Department of Commerce, Bureau of the Census
Estimated monthly revenues for a number of service fields — including the hotel and motel trades, various personnel and office services, automobile and appliance repairs, and leisure-time industries.

Monthly Wholesale Trade: Sales and Inventories *Monthly*

U.S. Department of Commerce, Bureau of the Census
Data on sales and inventory trends of merchant wholesalers in over 70 lines of business.

Census of Business *Every five years in years ending in 2 and 7*

U.S. Department of Commerce, Bureau of the Census
National and regional statistics on retail and wholesale industries, as well as on selected service trades.

6. **Agriculture**

Agricultural Prices *Monthly*

U.S. Department of Agriculture, Crop Reporting Board
Prices received and paid by farmers compared to parity prices for all groups of agricultural products; data include state and regional analyses.

Agricultural Statistics *Annual*

U.S. Department of Agriculture
Compendium of principal statistical series on agricultural production and consumption; includes historical data for the most recent ten years.

Commodity Yearbook *Annual*

Commodity Research Bureau
140 Broadway
New York, New York 10005
See annotation under Aggregate Measures of Income, Demand and Production (Exports).

7. **Transportation**

Transport Economics *Monthly*

U.S. Interstate Commerce Commission
Ordering address: Bureau of Economics
Interstate Commerce Commission
Washington, D.C. 20423
Current statistics on the operating income and working capital of Class I railroads and Class A freight forwarders.

Transport Statistics in the United States *Annual*

U.S. Interstate Commerce Commission
Statistics on rail, motor and water carriers; also includes statistics on oil pipelines.

Handbook of Airline Statistics *Annual*

Civil Aeronautics Board
Data on finances and traffic of major U.S. trunk carriers; also similar data on local service and helicopter carriers. Includes glossary of air-transport terms.

Census of Transportation   *Every five years in years ending in 2 and 7*

U.S. Department of Commerce, Bureau of the Census
Data on uses and modes of transportation in the United States.

FINANCIAL MARKETS

A. GENERAL SOURCES
Federal Reserve Bulletin   *Monthly*

Board of Governors of the Federal Reserve System[1]
See annotation under General References.

B. THE FEDERAL RESERVE SYSTEM AND MONETARY POLICY
Annual Report of the Board of Governors of the Federal Reserve System   *Annual*

Board of Governors of the Federal Reserve System
Information about the operations and conditions of the Federal Reserve Banks for the most recent calendar year.

Deposits, Reserves and Borrowings of Member Banks   *Weekly*

Board of Governors of the Federal Reserve System
Deposits, reserves and borrowings of reserve city banks and other member banks, by district.

Factors Affecting Bank Reserves and Conditions Statement of Federal Reserve Banks   *Weekly*

Board of Governors of the Federal Reserve System
Weekly averages of daily figures on factors affecting bank reserves, along with changes from week-ago and year-ago figures.

C. COMMERCIAL BANKS
Annual Report of the Federal Deposit Insurance Corporation   *Annual*

Federal Deposit Insurance Corporation[2]
Data on both insured and noninsured banks in the United States; also discusses the structure of the nation's banking system and gives aggregate statistics on its assets and liabilities.

Assets and Liabilities — Commercial and Mutual Savings Banks   *Semiannual*

Federal Deposit Insurance Corporation
Assets and liabilities of both insured banks and all operating banks by class of bank and by state.

Assets and Liabilities of all Commercial Banks in the United States   *Weekly*

Board of Governors of the Federal Reserve System
Weekly statistics on the principal assets and liabilities of all U.S. commercial banks.

Summary of Accounts and Deposits in All Commercial Banks   *Annual*

Federal Deposit Insurance Corporation
Summarizes accounts and deposits for all commercial banks by FDIC region, state and SMSA's.

Weekly Condition Report of Large Commercial Banks and Domestic Subsidiaries   *Weekly*

Board of Governors of the Federal Reserve System
Weekly breakdowns of assets and liabilities of reporting member banks in New York, Chicago and other leading cities, with separate figures by Federal Reserve district.

D. FINANCIAL INTERMEDIARIES
Annual Report of the Federal Deposit Insurance Corporation   *Annual*

Federal Deposit Insurance Corporation
See annotation under Commercial Banks.

Assets and Liabilities — Commercial and Mutual Savings Banks   *Semiannual*

Federal Deposit Insurance Corporation
See annotation under Commercial Banks.

Federal Home Loan Bank Board Journal   *Monthly*

Federal Home Loan Bank Board
Statistical series on housing industry; includes articles on thrift institutions.

Life Insurance Fact Bank *Annual*

Institute of Life Insurance
277 Park Avenue
New York, New York 10017

Statistical tables and charts for all U.S. life insurance companies; also includes interpretive text.

National Fact Book of Mutual Savings Banking
Annual

National Association of Mutual Savings Banks
200 Park Avenue
New York, New York 10017
Basic data on all aspects of savings banking.

Savings and Home Financing Source Book *Annual*

Federal Home Loan Bank Board
Statistics on Federal Home Loan Banks, including selected balance-sheet data, flow of savings, and mortgage-lending activity.

Savings and Loan Fact Book *Annual*

United States Savings and Loan League
221 North La Salle Street
Chicago, Illinois 60601
A comprehensive reference source on savings and loan associations, giving statistics on savings, home ownership, and financing of residential construction.

Statistical Bulletin *Monthly*

U.S. Securities and Exchange Commission
Data on new securities, securities sales, common stock prices and transactions; periodically shows the asset composition of all private noninsured pension funds.

Summary of Accounts and Deposits in All Mutual Savings Banks *Annual*

Federal Deposit Insurance Corporation
Summarizes accounts and deposits for all mutual savings banks by state, county and SMSA's.

E. MONEY MARKETS

Monthly Chart Book *Monthly*

Board of Governors of the Federal Reserve System
A variety of leading financial and economic statistical series in chart form; updated monthly.

Moody's Bank and Finance Manual
Biweekly and Annual

Moody's Investors Service, Inc.
99 Church Street
New York, New York 10007
A source of comprehensive financial information on banks, insurance companies, investment companies, and miscellaneous financial enterprises.

Open Market Money Rates and Bond Prices
Monthly

Board of Governors of the Federal Reserve System
Weekly data on yields of U.S. Treasury issues, Federal Funds, and commercial paper.

Reserve Positions of Major Reserve City Banks
Weekly

Board of Governors of the Federal Reserve System
Weekly reports on the Federal Funds market and related transactions of major reserve city banks.

Weekly Condition Report of Large Commercial Banks and Domestic Subsidiaries *Weekly*

Board of Governors of the Federal Reserve System
See annotation under Commercial Banks.

F. CAPITAL MARKETS

Bond Outlook *Weekly*

Standard & Poor's Corporation
345 Hudson Street
New York, New York 10014
Analyzes all phases of current bond markets.

Census of Shareowners *Irregular*

The New York Stock Exchange
11 Wall Street
New York, New York 10005
Data on the number of shareowners of public corporations by state, region, and personal income.

Fact Book *Annual*

The New York Stock Exchange
11 Wall Street
New York, New York 10005
Summarizes various statistical series issued by the Exchange.

FHA Homes: Data for States and Selected Areas
Annual

U.S. Department of Housing and Urban Development, Federal Housing Administration
Data on mortgages, represented property values, and other FHA classifications for states and selected housing areas.

FHA Trends of Home Mortgage Characteristics
Quarterly

U.S. Department of Housing and Urban Development, Federal Housing Administration
Data on insured FHA mortgages for existing and proposed family homes.

The Money Manager
Weekly

The Bond Buyer
77 Water Street
New York, New York 10005
Daily quotations for U.S. Treasury issues and federal agency securities; also includes a weekly index of municipal and corporate bond yields.

Moody's Bank and Finance Manual
Biweekly & Annual

Moody's Investors Service
99 Church Street
New York, New York 10007
See annotation under Money Markets

Moody's Municipal and Government Manual
Biweekly & Annual

Moody's Investors Service
99 Church Street
New York, New York 10007
Financial statistics on state governments and municipalities; also rates municipal and corporate bonds for quality.

Standard Corporation Records   *Daily & Bimonthly*

Standard & Poor's Corporation
345 Hudson Street
New York, New York 10014
Factual information on corporations and their securities — for example, description and history of the company, abstracts of financial statements, and related data. Updated by daily news bulletins.

Statistical Bulletin
Monthly

U.S. Securities and Exchange Commission
See annotation under Financial Intermediaries.

Value Line Investment Survey
Weekly

Arnold Bernhard & Co.
5 East 44th Street
New York, New York 10017
Continuous review and analysis of 1,000 leading corporate stocks.

INTERNATIONAL ECONOMIC STATISTICS

A. GENERAL SOURCES

Federal Reserve Bulletin
Monthly

See annotation under General References.

General Statistics
Monthly

Statistical Office of the European Communities
P.O. Box 1003
Luxembourg
Gives key economic statistics for the European Community.

International Economic Report of the President
Annual

Executive Office of the President
Discusses international economic goals of the United States and related issues. Statistical appendix on U.S. foreign trade, balance of payments, overseas investment, and economic aid.

International Financial Statistics
Monthly

International Monetary Fund
19th and H Streets, N.W.
Washington, D.C. 20431
Statistics, by country, on exports and imports, exchange rates, and monetary reserves.

Main Economic Indicators
Monthly

Organization for Economic Cooperation and Development, Paris, France
Ordering address: OECD Publications Center
1750 Pennsylvania Avenue, N.W.
Washington, D.C. 20006
A basic source of international statistics; particularly useful for data on foreign trade.

Monthly Bulletin of Statistics   *Monthly*

United Nations
Sales Section
United Nations Plaza
New York, New York 10017
Statistics on trade, national accounts, and financial markets of over 100 countries.

Statistical Yearbook   *Annual*

United Nations
Sales Section
United Nations Plaza
New York, New York 10017
A comprehensive compilation of data on balance of payments, wages and prices, and national accounts of member countries.

B. FOREIGN ECONOMICS

Foreign Economic Trends and Their Implications for the United States   *Irregular*

U.S. Department of Commerce, Bureau of International Commerce
Each issue is devoted to a particular trading partner of the United States, and summarizes that country's key economic indicators and their trends.

OECD Financial Statistics   *Semiannual with bi-monthly supplements*

Organization for Economic Cooperation and Development, Paris, France
Ordering address: OECD Publications Center
1750 Pennsylvania Avenue, N.W.
Washington, D.C. 20006
Detailed financial statistics and descriptions of OECD countries' exchange-control regulations. Reports also discuss the institutional aspects and functioning of each country's financial system.

Overseas Business Reports   *Irregular*

U.S. Department of Commerce, Bureau of International Commerce
Individual reports give basic market and investment information on various foreign countries; include statistics related to trade, regulations governing trade, and foreign market indicators.

Yearbook of National Accounts Statistics   *Annual*

United Nations
Sales Section
United Nations Plaza
New York, New York 10017
Data on national income, disposable income, and per capita gross domestic product for over 100 countries.

C. FOREIGN TRADE

Direction of Trade   *Annual and monthly*

International Monetary Fund
19th and H Streets, N.W.
Washington, D.C. 20431
Data on foreign trade, by country, for over 100 countries.

Foreign Trade Reports   *Monthly*

U.S. Department of Commerce, Bureau of the Census
U.S. foreign trade as listed below:

FT135. U.S. Imports for Consumption and General Imports, Commodity by Country.

U.S. imports by commodities.

FT410. U.S. Exports of Domestic and Foreign Merchandise, Commodity by Country of Destination.

Quantity and value of exports of individual commodities, plus various consolidations of these items according to destination.

FT800. U.S. Trade with Puerto Rico and with U.S. Possessions

Quantity, value and tonnage of individual commodities shipped between the United States and its territories and possessions.

FT990. Highlights of U.S. Export and Import Trade

Interrelated statistical tables summarizing significant trade movements by commodity, country, U.S. Customs District, and shipping method.

Yearbook of International Trade Statistics   *Annual*

United Nations
Sales Section
United Nations Plaza
New York, New York 10017
Detailed data for individual countries, with summary tables on trade in principal commodities, and their value in foreign currencies and U.S. dollars.

D. BALANCE OF PAYMENTS

Balance of Payments Yearbook   *Monthly*

International Monetary Fund
19th and H Streets, N.W.
Washington, D.C. 20431
Balance-of-payments data for about 100 countries, presented in various formats.

E. EXCHANGE RATES

Foreign Exchange Rates   *Weekly*

Board of Governors of the Federal Reserve System
Ordering address: Division of Administrative Services
Board of Governors of the Federal Reserve System
Washington, D.C. 20551
Statistical release gives current exchange rates for various countries.

---

[1] Ordering address: Division of Administrative Services
Board of Governors of the Federal Reserve System
Washington, D.C. 20551

[2] Ordering address: Information Office
Federal Deposit Insurance Corporation
550 17th Street
Washington, D.C. 20429

Index